William Evans Darby

INTERNATIONAL TRIBUNALS

A Collection of the various Schemes which have been propounded; and of Instances since 1815

Elibron Classics
www.elibron.com

Elibron Classics series.

ISBN 1-4212-4906-5 (paperback)
ISBN 1-4212-4905-7 (hardcover)

This Elibron Classics Replica Edition is an unabridged facsimile of the edition published in 1899 by J. M. Dent & Co., London.

HIS IMPERIAL MAJESTY NICOLAS II.

International Arbitration.

INTERNATIONAL TRIBUNALS.

A Collection of the various Schemes which have been propounded; and of Instances since 1815.

THIRD EDITION, CONSIDERABLY ENLARGED.

BY

W. EVANS DARBY, LL.D.

Secretary of the Peace Society.

LONDON:

J. M. DENT & CO., 29 & 30, BEDFORD STREET, W.C.

1899.

LONDON:
PRINTED BY WERTHEIMER, LEA & CO.,
CIRCUS PLACE, LONDON WALL.

TO

HIS IMPERIAL MAJESTY NICOLAS II.,

EMPEROR OF ALL THE RUSSIAS,

This Book

IS

BY HIS MAJESTY'S GRACIOUS PERMISSION

MOST RESPECTFULLY DEDICATED.

PREFACE.

THE present work was compiled, in the first instance, at the request of a Special Committee of the International Law Association, which was appointed, at the Brussels Conference, October 1st, 1895, to study the question of an International Court of Arbitration, and to report at the next Conference. When the Committee met to fulfil its commission, the Convener was requested to examine and report upon the various published schemes for the composition of a Court of Arbitration; such report to be printed and circulated among its members. This first draft was submitted to the Committee, and an edition of a thousand copies was printed by the Association and issued jointly with the Peace Society. Copies, suitably bound, were presented to the various Rulers of the civilised world, by most of whom an acknowledgment was sent, and appreciation expressed. It was followed by an appendix containing additional matter.

In anticipation of the meeting of the Peace Conference at the Hague these two publications were combined and issued as a second edition by the Peace Society. Copies were distributed, through the courtesy of M. de Staal, among the delegates to the Hague Conference, who spontaneously and generously testified to its usefulness.

This third edition has been considerably enlarged, and no pains have been spared to secure its completeness and accuracy.

It is commended to the acceptance of the general public in the hope that the subject of which it treats may become still more a topic of popular study and discussion, and that the compilation may be increasingly useful. Should this hope be realised, it will be largely due to the generous initiative of the magnanimous young ruler who sits on the Russian throne, and to the new impetus given by the labours of the Conference which assembled at the Hague under his auspices, which, whatever the critics may say, have lifted the question into fresh altitudes, and have marked the beginning of a new era, in which the deliberations of reason and the reign of law shall be substituted for the arbitrament of the sword (falsely so called), and the *lex talionis.*

The portrait of His Imperial Majesty is, by permission, from a photograph by Messrs. W. & D. Downey, of Ebury Street, S.W.

CONTENTS.

	PAGE
The Amphictyonic Council	1
The Grand Design of Henry IV.	10
William Penn's Scheme	16
Abbé de St. Pierre's Scheme	20
Grotius on Arbitrators...	48
Pufendorf on deciding Controversies	56
Vattel on Arbitration	68
Bentham on an International Tribunal	72
Kant on a Permanent Congress	76
Kant zum Ewigen Frieden	82
Kant's Perpetual Peace	84
Mill, John Stuart; A Federal Supreme Court	90
Seeley's Possible Means of Preventing War	92
Bluntschli's Arbitration Proceedings	96
Bluntschli's Organisation of a European Federation ...	102
Field, David Dudley; A High Tribunal of Arbitration ..	122
Leone Levi's Draft Project	124
Sir Edmund Hornby's Notes on a Permanent Tribunal ...	132
Treaty of Washington	148
Traité de Washington	165
Memorial of the New York Bar Association	167
Convention between France and the United States	172
Convention between France and Chili	182
Swiss-American Arbitration Treaty	192
Plan of the Pan-American Conference	194
The Anglo-American Arbitration Treaty	204

	PAGE
ITALO-ARGENTINE TREATY, 1898...	214
,, ,, ,, ,, TESTO UFFICIALE ...	220
A CONGRESS AND COURT OF NATIONS ...	223
SPRAGUE'S HIGH TRIBUNAL OF PUBLIC INTERNATIONAL JUDICATURE	228
PEACE CONGRESS.—"CODE OF INTERNATIONAL ARBITRATION" ...	234
LEMONNIER'S (CHARLES) FORM OF INTERNATIONAL TREATY ...	252
ARNAUD'S (EMILE) MODEL OF A TREATY ...	262
A CHINESE SCHEME FOR UNIVERSAL PEACE ...	266
SKETCH OF PROPOSED TREATY AND TRIBUNAL ...	267
RULES OF THE INSTITUTE OF INTERNATIONAL LAW ...	270
PROPOSED RULES OF AMERICAN JURISTS ...	282
SCHEME OF THE INTER-PARLIAMENTARY CONFERENCE ...	290
RULES BY PROFESSOR CORSI ...	296
THE ARBITRATION TRIBUNAL, BY PROFESSOR FIORE...	322
DARBY, W. E., LL.D., ARBITRATION TRIBUNALS ...	350
BRUSSELS RULES OF THE INTERNATIONAL LAW ASSOCIATION ...	364
BUFFALO ,, ,, ,, ,, ,, ...	368
CONVENTION OF THE HAGUE PEACE CONFERENCE ...	380
HISTORY ,, ,, ,, ,, ...	410
RESULTS ,, ,, ,, ,, ...	463
THE PROVED PRACTICABILITY OF INTERNATIONAL ARBITRATION ...	486

INTERNATIONAL TRIBUNALS.

THE AMPHICTYONIC COUNCIL.

As this is the first institution of the kind known to history, and as it has been generally referred to as a model of what is desirable, some account of it is necessary.

1.—The Association.

The Council was the deliberative assembly of an Association formed among independent neighbouring tribes of Greece, for the regulation of their mutual intercourse. There were many such associations in ancient Greece. There was one, however, which gradually expanded into so comprehensive a character, and acquired so marked a predominance over the rest as to be called The Amphictyonic Assembly or League.

2.—Its Origin.

This Association had its origin in a gathering of tribes, which met at Anthela, a little town in the famous Pass of Thermopylæ, to worship Demeter (Ceres), but at a very early time the temple of Delphi and the worship of Apollo were connected with it.

3.—Its Members.

The Association was composed of those tribes which, at any rate after the invasion of Thessaly by the Thesprotians, dwelt in the immediate neighbourhood of the Pass. These originally numbered twelve, each of which might include several independent States, for the tribes are variously enumerated by different authors.

4.—Its Antiquity.

"Such festival-associations or amphictyonies," says Curtius, "are coeval with Greek history, or may even be said to constitute the first expressions of a common national history."

The League was supposed to be very ancient, as old even as the name of Hellēnes, for its founder was said to be Amphictyōn, the son of Deucalion and brother of Hellēn, the common ancestor of all Greeks. Its origin is, therefore, obscure.

5.—Its Name.

The name denotes a body referred to a local centre of union. The Greek word Amphictyones meant literally "dwellers around," but in a special sense was applied to populations which, at stated times, met at the same sanctuary to keep a festival in common, and to transact common business.

6.—Its Extent.

The Association consisted of twelve sub-races out of the number which made up entire Hellas. At first it comprehended most of the Greek States north of the Isthmus, although in the 14th century B.C., Acrisius, King of Argos, was, according to Strabo, said to have brought the Confederacy into order, and fixed the number of its members, the distribution of the votes in the Council, and the nature of the Causes which were to be subject to its jurisdiction. The Dorian conquest, which was subsequent to this event, greatly extended the salutary influence of the Amphictyonic League. For the Dorians, being constituent members, continued to attend its meetings after they had settled beyond the mountainous isthmus of Corinth. All the provinces which they conquered, gradually assumed the same privilege. The League thus became representative of the whole Grecian name, consisting not only of the three original tribes of Ionians, Dorians and Æolians, but of the several sub-divisions of these tribes, and of the various communities formed from their promiscuous combination.

7.—Its Object.

Primarily the League is said to have been a confederacy entered into by the petty princes of the provinces of the northern districts of Thessaly, which were peculiarly exposed to the dangerous fury of invaders, for their mutual defence (Marm. Oxon, E.S.). But this institution, which had been originally intended to prevent foreign invasion, was found equally useful in promoting domestic concord (Dr. Gillie's "History of Ancient Greece," I., 14). Grote, however, describes the Council as "an ancient institution, one amongst many instances of the primitive habit of religious fraternisations, but wider and more comprehensive than the rest—at first purely religious, then religious and political at once, lastly more the latter than the former." (*Grote*, II. 253.)

8.—The Council.

The affairs of the whole Amphictyonic body were transacted by a Congress, or "Council," composed of deputies sent by the several States, according to rules established from time immemorial.

9.—Annual Assemblies.

Two meetings of this Council were regularly convened every year, one in the spring, at Delphi, the other in the autumn, near Anthela, where it was held at a temple of Demeter. At each meeting the deputies visited both centres.

Here, says Freeman ("Hist. of Fed. Gov.," p. 101), "a body of Greeks, including members from nearly all parts of Greece, habitually met to debate on matters interesting to the whole Greek nation, and to put forth decrees which, within their proper sphere, the whole Greek nation respected."

10.—Popular Assembly.

Besides the Council, which held its sessions either in the temple or in some adjacent building, there was an Amphictyonic Assembly (ἐκκλησία τῶν Ἀμφικτυονῶν), described by Æschines (*Ctes.* § 1247), which met in the open air, and was composed of persons residing in the place where the Congress was held, and of the numerous strangers who were visiting it from curiosity, business, devotion, or other reason.

It would seem, however, that this Assembly was called together only in extraordinary cases, as when its aid was required for carrying into execution the measures decreed, or, when it was thought necessary, to appoint an extraordinary Convention in the interval between two regular times of meeting.

11.—Right of Representation.

The order in which the right to send Representatives to the Council, was exercised in the various States composing one Amphictyonic tribe (which as a unit was entitled to representation), was, perhaps, regulated by private arrangement; but unless one State usurped the whole right of its tribe, it is manifest that a petty tribe, forming but one community, had greatly the advantage over States in the same tribe, such as Sparta or Argos, which could only be represented in their turn, and but rarely in proportion to the importance of the tribe to which they belonged. This right would have been of still less value if it had been shared among all the colonies of an Amphictyonic tribe; and this was the case with the Ionians, but the Æolian and Dorian colonies seem not to have claimed the same privilege. (*Thirlwall.*)

12.—Members of the Council.

These consisted of delegates from each of the twelve races (or if the Hellenes be treated as a race, they must be called subraces), who were known as Hieromnemones (*i.e.*, wardens of holy things) and Pylagoræ.

At Athens three Pylagoræ were annually elected, and one Hieromnemon was appointed by lot; the practice of other States is not known.

13.—THEIR FUNCTIONS.

The duties of these deputies are very difficult to determine. According to one author, who gives as his authority Suidas (Ad Voc.), these were respectively entrusted with the religious and civil concerns of their constituents. Thirlwall says that the latter (the Pylagoræ) was the body entrusted with the power of voting, while the office of the former (the Hieromnemones) consisted in preparing and directing their deliberations, and carrying their decrees into effect. Grote says that the twelve members of the League sent sacred deputies, including a chief, called the Hieromnemon, and subordinates called the Pylagoræ (II. 248). Dr. Abbott ("A History of Greece," p. 28) says: "The deputies were themselves of two classes, the Hieromnemones and the Pylagori. The first were chosen by lot, twenty-four in number; one for each of the twenty-four votes, which they alone were competent to give. The Pylagori, on the other hand, whose number was not fixed, were orators elected for the especial purpose of supporting the interests of their States by their eloquence or skill in debate. The Hieromnemones formed the Assembly in the stricter sense, but they could call the Pylagori before them, and occasionally they summoned a universal Assembly of all the members of the tribes present at the time. But neither the Pylagori nor the Assembly could reverse the decision of the Hieromnemones." Dr. Oscar Seyffert says that, "besides protecting and preserving their two common sanctuaries, and celebrating, from the year 586 B.C. onwards, the Pythian Games, the League was bound to maintain certain principles of international right," and that, when violations of the sanctuaries or of popular right took place, the Assembly could inflict fines or even expulsion, and that a State that would not submit to the punishment had a "holy war" declared against it.

14.—THE OATH.

The original objects, or at least, the character of the institution, seems to be faithfully expressed in the terms of the oath preserved by Æschines, which bound the Members of the League not to destroy any Amphictyonic town, not to cut off any

Amphictyonic town from running water, but to punish to the utmost of their power those who committed such outrages; and if any one should plunder the property of the god, or should be cognizant thereof, or should take treacherous counsel against the things in the temple, to punish him with foot and hand and voice and by every means in their power.

"Je jure," disait chaque député, "de ne jamais détruire aucune des villes du corps des Amphictyons, de ne pas détourner le lit des fleuves, et de ne pas empêcher l'usage de leurs eaux courantes ni en temps de paix ni en temps de guerre. Et si quelque peuple enfreint cette loi, je lui déclarerai la guerre et je détruirai ses villes. Que si quelqu'un pille les richesses du dieu, ou se rend complice en quelque manière de ceux qui toucheront aux choses sacrées, ou les aide de ses conseils, je m'emploierai à en tirer vengeance de mes pieds, de mes mains, de ma voix et de toutes mes forces." (*Calvo*, 3rd Ed., I. 622.)

15.—VOTING.

The constitution of the Council rested on the theory of a perfect equality among the tribes represented by it. Each tribe had two votes in the deliberations of the Congress. Each had originally only one, but with the growth of the Ionians and Dorians, and the division of Locris into two sections, it became necessary to make a change. The original vote was therefore doubled (or split) so that each tribe which remained solid had two votes, but in the case of those which were divided, one vote was assigned to each of the two sections.

16.—DECISIONS.

The decisions of the Council, says Lempriere ("Class. Dict."), "were held sacred and inviolable, and even arms were taken up to enforce them." When violations of the sanctuaries, or of popular right, took place, the Assembly could inflict fines, or even expulsion, and a State that would not submit to the punishment had a "holy war" declared against it. Such a war was dreaded even in Athens: "You are bringing war into Attica, Æschines," was the taunt of Demosthenes, "an Amphictyonic war." The

Council had no organised means of enforcing its decrees; still it always had partisans, who undertook the duty.

17.—Later History.

By such a war, for instance, the Phocians were expelled (B.C. 346), and their two votes given to the Macedonians; but the expulsion of the former was withdrawn because of the glorious part they took in defending the Delphian temple when threatened by the Gauls in 279 B.C., and at the same time the Ætolian community which had already made itself master of the sanctuary was acknowledged as a new member of the League. The decree against Phocis was carried out by Philip of Macedon. That the institution by this time had lost its original character and become a political instrument is shown by the fact that a Council summoned by Philip, numbering 200, ratified all his transactions and declared the kingdom of Macedon the principal member of the Hellenic body.

Two years later (344 B.C.) Philip procured a decree of the Amphictyonic Council, requiring him to check the insolence of Sparta and to protect the defenceless communities which had so often been the victims of her tyranny and cruelty; and in 339 B.C. Philip was appointed general of the Amphictyonic forces.

In 191 B.C. the number of members amounted to seventeen, who, nevertheless, had only twenty-four votes, seven having two votes each, the rest only one.

Under the Roman rule the League continued to exist, but its action was now limited to the care of the Delphian temple. It was reorganised by Augustus, who incorporated the Malians, Magnetians, Ænianes and Pythians with the Thessalians, and substituted for the extinct Dolopes the city of Nicopolis in Acarnania, which he had founded after the battle of Actium.

The last notice we find of the League is in the 2nd century A.D.

18.—Council not a National Assembly.

The Amphictyonic Council, says Abbott (Part II., 29), was not a national assembly; it neither conducted the policy of Greece, nor had it power to settle disputes between great cities.

Nor was the Association national in the sense that it included the whole of Greece. Freeman says that the Amphictyonic Council represented Greece as an Ecclesiastical Synod represented Western Christendom, not as a Swiss Diet or an American Congress represents the Federation of which it is the common legislature (Hist. of Fed. Gov., p. 98), but he is careful to add (p. 102), "The Amphictyons were a religious body, but they were not a clerical body"; that is, they were not officially a religious body. There is nothing to indicate that it in any sense corresponded to what is known as a Tribunal of Arbitration, or that the principle of Arbitration was applied or even recognised by it.

19.—But a Peace Organisation.

The Association, says Abbott, was as powerless as any other to prevent strife and bloodshed among the members, some of whom, such as the Phocians and Thessalians, were deadly enemies. But a number of adjacent tribes could not meet together twice a year to share in a common sacrifice, and, it might be added, to discuss common interests, without feeling that they were united by a peculiar tie. This feeling was shown in the oath. And the oath was not wholly without effect; it marked a departure from the savage warfare depicted in the Homeric poems, and it supplied the Greeks with an ideal, which was present to their minds, even when they failed to act up to it. The political philosophers of the fourth century, when regulating the practice of war among the Greeks, proceeded on the lines laid down in the Amphictyonic oath. The Hellenes were to quarrel "as those who intend some day to be reconciled"; they were to "use friendly correction," and "not to devastate Hellas, or burn houses, or think that the whole population of a city, men, women and children, were equally their enemies, and therefore to be destroyed." (*Abbott*, Part II., p. 20.)

20.—And an Effective One.

Historians deplore the fact that the Amphictyonic Council seldom had the ability to execute its sentences, and therefore pronounce it "almost powerless for good" and even mischievous. But Professor Curtius gives expression to a juster estimate of its influence, which even others cannot wholly overlook. "The terms of the Amphictyonic oath," he says, "are first attempts at procuring admission for the principles of humanity in a land filled with border feuds. There is as yet no question of putting an end to the state of war, still less of combining for united action; an attempt is merely made to induce a group of States to regard themselves as belonging together, and on the ground of this feeling to recognise mutual obligations, and in the case of inevitable feuds at all events, mutually to refrain from extreme measures of force."

But the action of the Council as a factor in Greek life, existing as it did from the earliest ages to the second century A.D., was even more influential.

"In case of dispute between the Amphictyones, a judicial authority was wanted to preserve the common peace, or punish its violation in the name of the god. But the insignificant beginning of common annual festivals gradually came to transform the whole of public life; the constant carrying of arms was given up, intercourse was rendered safe, and the sanctity of temples and altars recognised. And the most important result of all was, that the members of the Amphictyony learnt to regard themselves as one united body against those standing outside it; out of a number of tribes arose a nation which required a common name to distinguish it and its political and religious system from all other tribes. And the federal name fixed upon by common consent was that of Hellenes, which, in the place of the earlier appellation of Graeci, continued to extend its significance with every step by which the federation advanced. The connection of this new national name with the Amphictyon is manifest from the circumstance that the Greeks conceived Hellen and Amphictyon, the mythical representatives of their nationality and fraternal union of race, as nearly related to and connected with one another." (*Curtius*, "History of Greece," Vol. I., 116, 117.)

THE GRAND DESIGN OF HENRY IV. 1603.

(*Translated from Sully's Memoirs, new ed.*, 1822, *Vol. VI., pp.* 129 *et seq.*)

I.—The Object.

The object of the New Plan was to divide proportionately the whole of Europe between a certain number of Powers, which would have had nothing to envy one another for on the ground of equality, and nothing to fear on the ground of the Balance of Power.

II.—The Number of States.

Their number was reduced to fifteen, and they were of three kinds, viz.:—Six great hereditary monarchical Powers; five elective monarchies, and four sovereign republics. The six hereditary monarchies were France, Spain, Great Britain, Denmark, Sweden, and Lombardy. The five elective monarchies, the Empire, the Papacy, Poland, Hungary, and Bohemia. The four republics; the Republic of Venice (seigniorial), the Republic of Italy (which in the same way may be called ducal, because of its dukes), the Swiss Republic (Helvetian or Confederated), and the Belgian Republic (provincial).

III.—The Laws and Statutes.

The laws and statutes calculated to cement the union of all these members, and to maintain amongst them the order once established; the reciprocal oaths and pledges as regards religion and politics; the mutual assurances for the liberty of commerce; the measures for making all these divisions with equity, to the general contentment of the parties; all these can be understood without any enlarging further on Henry's precautions. Only small difficulties of detail could arise which would be easily met in the General Council representing the States of all Europe, whose establishment was undoubtedly the happiest possible idea for the introduction of reforms, such as time renders needful in the wisest and most useful institutions.

IV.—The General Council.

The model of this General Council of Europe had been founded on that of the ancient Amphictyons of Greece, with the modifica-

GRAND DESSEIN DE HENRI IV. 1603.

(*Mémoires du Duc de Sully, VI.*, 129 *et seq.*: *mot pour mot.*)

I.—L'Objet

L'objet du nouveau plan était de partager avec proportion toute l'Europe, entre un certain nombre de puissances, qui n'eussent eu rien à envier les unes aux autres du côté de l'égalité, ni rien à craindre du côté de l'équilibre.

II.—Le Nombre des Etats

Le nombre en était réduit à quinze, et elles étaient de trois espèces, savoir : six grandes dominations monarchiques héréditaires, cinq monarchiques électives, et quatre républiques souveraines. Les six monarchiques héréditaires étaient la France, l'Espagne, l'Angleterre ou Grande-Bretagne, le Danemark, la Suède et la Lombardie ; les cinq monarchiques électives, l'Empire, la Papauté ou le Pontificat, la Pologne, la Hongrie, et la Bohême ; les quatre républiques, la république de Venise, (ou seigneuriale), la république d'Italie, qu'on peut de même nommer ducale, à cause de ses ducs, la république suisse, helvétique ou confédérée, et la république belgique (autrement provinciale).

III.—Les Lois et les Statuts

Les lois et les statuts propres à cimenter l'union de tous ces membres entre eux, et à y maintenir l'ordre une fois établi ; les sermens et engagemens réciproques, tant sur la religion, que sur la politique ; les assurances mutuelles pour la liberté du commerce ; les mesures pour faire tous ces partages avec équité, au contentement général des parties ; tout cela se sous-entend de soi-même, sans qu'il soit besoin que je m'étende beaucoup sur les précautions qu'avait prises Henri, à tous ces égards. Il ne pouvait survenir au plus que quelques petites difficultés de détail, qui auraient été aisément levées dans le conseil général représentant comme les états de toute l'Europe, dont l'établissement était sans doute l'idée la plus heureuse qu'on pût former, pour prévenir les changemens que le temps apporte souvent aux règlemens les plus sages et les plus utiles.

IV.—Le Conseil Général

Le modèle de ce conseil général de l'Europe, avait été pris sur celui des anciens Amphictyons de la Grèce, avec les modifications

tions suitable to our usages, climate, and the end of our policy. It consisted of a certain number of commissioners, ministers, or plenipotentiaries from all the Powers of the Christian Republic, continually assembled as a Senate to deliberate on affairs as they arose, to occupy themselves with discussing different interests, to pacify quarrels, to throw light upon and oversee the civil, political, and religious affairs of Europe, whether internal or foreign. The form and procedure of this Senate would have been more particularly determined by the votes of the Senate itself. The advice of Henry was that it should be composed, *e.g.*, of four commissioners for each of the following Powers: The Emperor, the Pope, the Kings of France, Spain, England, Denmark, Sweden, Lombardy, Poland, the Venetian Republic, and of two only for the other republics and lesser Powers, which would have made a Senate of about seventy persons, whose election might have been renewed every three years.

V.—The Place of Meeting.

As to the place, it would have to be decided whether it was more suitable for the Council to be permanent or movable, divided into three parts or united. If it were divided into parts, of twenty-two magistrates each, their residence might be in three places, which would be like so many convenient centres, such as Paris or Bourges for one, Trent or Cracow, or their environs, for the two others. If it were judged more expedient not to divide them, the place of meeting, whether fixed or movable, should be pretty near the centre of Europe, and consequently be fixed in one of the fourteen following towns: Metz, Luxembourg, Nancy, Cologne, Mayence, Trèves, Frankfort, Wirtzbourg, Heidelberg, Spire, Worms, Strasbourg, Bâle, Besançon.

VI.—Minor Councils.

I think that besides this General Council it would still have been suitable to form a certain number of smaller ones, for the special convenience of different cantons. By making six, one would have had them placed, *e.g.*, at Dantzic, Nuremburg, convenables à nos usages, à notre climat, et au but de notre politique. Il consistait en un certain nombre de commissaires, ministres ou plénipotentiaires, de toutes les dominations de la république chrétienne, continuellement assemblés en corps de sénat pour délibérer sur les affaires survenantes, s'occuper à discuter les différens intérêts, pacifier les querelles, éclaircir et vider toutes les affaires civiles, politiques et religieuses de l'Europe, soit avec elle-même, soit avec l'étranger. La forme et les procédures de ce sénat, auraient été plus particulièrement déterminées par les suffrages de ce sénat lui-même. L'avis de Henri était qu'il fût composé, par exemple, de quatre commissaires, pour chacun des potentats suivans, l'empereur, le pape, les rois de France, d'Espagne, d'Angleterre, de Danemark, de Suède, de Lombardie, de Pologne, la république vénitienne ; et de deux seulement, pour les autres républiques et moindres puissances, ce qui aurait fait un sénat d'environ soixante-dix personnes, dont le choix aurait pu se renouveler de trois ans en trois ans.

V.—Le Lieu

A l'égard du lieu, on déciderait s'il était plus à propos que ce conseil fût permanent, qu'ambulatoire, divisé en trois, que réuni. Si on le partageait par portions de vingt-deux magistrats chacune, leur séjour devait être dans trois endroits qui fussent comme autant de centres commodes, tels que Paris ou Bourges, pour l'une ; Trente ou Cracovie, ou leurs environs, pour les deux autres. Si on jugeait plus expédient de ne point le diviser, le lieu d'assemblée, soit qu'il fût fixe ou ambulatoire, devait être à peu près le cœur de l'Europe, et être par conséquent fixé dans quelqu'une des quatorze villes suivantes : Metz, Luxembourg, Nancy, Cologne, Mayence, Trèves, Francfort, Wirtzbourg, Heidelberg, Spire, Worms, Strasbourg, Bâle, Besançon.

VI.—Des Conseils moindres

Je crois qu'outre ce conseil général, il eût encore convenu d'en former un certain nombre de moindres, pour la commodité particulière de différens cantons. En en créant six, on les aurait placés, par exemple, à Dantzick, à Nuremberg, à Vienne en

Vienna, in Germany; at Bologna, in Italy; at Constance; and the last in the place most convenient for the kingdoms of France, Spain, and England, and the Belgian Republic, which it more particularly concerned.

VII.—Appeal to the General Council.

But, whatever were the number and the form of these special Councils, it was of the utmost utility that they should have recourse by appeal to the Great General Council, whose decisions should have the force of irrevocable and unchangeable decrees, as being considered to emanate from the united authority of all the Sovereigns, pronouncing as freely as absolutely.

VIII.—Political Objects.

The political part of the Plan . . . . was to despoil the House of Austria of all its possessions in Germany, Italy, and the Netherlands—in a word, to confine it to the kingdom of Spain, bounded by the Atlantic, the Mediterranean and the Pyrenees, leaving to it, for equality with the other Powers, Sardinia, Majorca, Minorca (and other islands on these coasts), Canary Isles, the Azores, Cape Verde Island, with its possessions in Africa; Mexico, with the American islands which belong to it; countries which would of themselves suffice to found great kingdoms; and finally, the Philippines, Goa, the Moluccas, and its other Asiatic possessions.

IX.—Conquered Countries.

One precaution to take in relation to all conquered countries would be to form out of them new kingdoms, which would be declared joined to the Christian Republic, and which would be apportioned to different Princes, carefully excluding those who already held rank among the Sovereigns of Europe.

X.—Expenses.

It only remains that the Powers should tax themselves for the maintenance of armed forces, and for all the other things necessary to make the plan succeed, until the General Council should specify all these amounts.

Allemagne, à Bologne en Italie, à Constance, et le dernier dans l'endroit jugé le plus commode pour les royaumes de France, d'Espagne et d'Angleterre, et la république belgique, qu'il regardait plus particulièrement.

VII.—Appel au Conseil Général

Mais quels que fussent le nombre et la forme de ces conseils particuliers, il était de toute utilité qu'ils ressortissent par appel au grand conseil général, dont les arrêts auraient été autant de décrets irrévocables et irréformables, comme étant censés émaner de l'autorité réunie de tous les souverains, prononçant aussi librement qu'absolument.

VIII.—La Partie du Dessein Politique

La partie du dessein purement politique . . . . c'était de dépouiller la maison d'Autriche de l'empire de tout ce qu'elle possède en Allemagne, en Italie, et dans les Pays-Bas ; en un mot, de la réduire au seul royaume d'Espagne renfermé entre l'Océan, la Méditerranée et les Pyrénées, auquel on aurait laissé seulement, pour le rendre égal aux autres grandes dominations monarchiques de l'Europe, la Sardaigne, Majorque, Minorque et autres îles sur ces côtes ; les Canaries, les Açores et le Cap-Vert, avec ce qu'il possède en Afrique ; le Mexique, avec les îles de l'Amérique qui lui appartiennent ; pays qui suffiraient seuls à fonder de grands royaumes ; enfin, les Philippines, Coa, les Moluques, et ses autres possessions en Asie.

IX.—Les Pays conquis

Une précaution unique à prendre, par rapport à tous les pays conquis, eût été d'y fonder de nouveaux royaumes, qu'on déclarerait unis à la république chrétienne, et qu'on distribuerait à différens princes, en excluant soigneusement ceux qui tiendraient déjà rang parmi les souverains de l'Europe.

X.—Des Frais

Il n'est question que d'engager chacun d'eux à se taxer lui-même pour l'entretien des gens de guerre, et pour toutes les autres choses nécessaires à la faire réussir, en attendant que le conseil général eût spécifié toutes ces valeurs.

WILLIAM PENN'S EUROPEAN DIET, PARLIAMENT, OR ESTATES, 1693—94.

This is not a reproduction of Henry IV.'s grand design. Penn may have owed to it the formal suggestion of his plan, but that is all.

That plan was the creation of a permanent Sovereign Tribunal—an International Parliament or Congress, which should exercise judicial functions as well as deliberative, and also act as a Committee of Safety.

The judicial function was the chief feature of this proposed permanent Diet. Penn's proposals were :—

1. That the Sovereign Princes of Europe should, for the love of Peace and Order, agree to meet, by their appointed Deputies, in a General Diet, Estates, or Parliament, and there establish Rules of Justice for their mutual observance.

2. That this body should meet yearly, or once in two or three years at furthest, or as they should see cause.

3. That it should be styled the Sovereign, or Imperial, Diet, Parliament, or States of Europe.

4. That before this Sovereign Assembly should be brought all differences depending between one Sovereign and another that cannot be adjusted by diplomatic means, before its sessions begin.

5. That if any of the Sovereignties constituting this Imperial Diet should refuse to submit their claims or pretensions to the

Diet, or to accept its judgment, and should seek their remedy by arms, or delay compliance beyond the time specified, all the other Sovereignties, uniting their forces, should compel submission to, and performance of, the sentence and payment of all costs and damages.

6. The composition of this Imperial Diet should be by proportionate representation.

7. The determination of the number of persons or votes for every Sovereignty would not be impracticable if it depended on an estimate of the yearly value of their respective countries.

8. This estimate was to be reached "by considering the revenues of lands, the exports and entries at the Custom Houses, the books of rates, and surveys, that are in all Governments, to proportion taxes for their support."

9. It is not absolutely necessary that there should be as many Delegates as votes; for the votes may be given by one Delegate as well as by ten or twelve.

10. Though the fuller, that is, the *larger*, the assembly is, the more solemn, effectual, and free, the debates will be, and its resolutions will carry greater authority.

11. The place of the first session should be central, as much as is possible; afterwards as the Assembly itself shall determine.

12. To avoid quarrel for precedency the room may be round, and have several doors to come in and go out at.

13. The Assembly may be divided into sections, containing each ten members, each section to elect one of its number to preside over the Assembly in turn.

14. All speeches should be addressed to the President, who should collect the sense of the debates and state the question before the vote is taken.

15. The voting should be by ballot, after the prudent and commendable method of the Venetians.

16. Nothing should pass except by a three-quarters vote, or at least by a majority of seven.

17. All complaints should be delivered in writing—in the form of *Memorials* and *Journals*, kept by a proper person, in a *trunk* or *chest*, which should have as many different locks as there are sections in the Assembly ("tens in the States").

18. There should be a secretary for each section ("a clerk for each ten"), and a desk or table for these secretaries in the Assembly.

19. At the end of every session, one [member] out of each section ("ten") appointed for the purpose should examine and compare the records of those secretaries ("journals of those clerks"), and then lock them up in the common *trunk* or *chest*.

20. Each Sovereignty, if they please, as is but very fit, may have an *exemplification*, or *copy*, of the said *Memorials*, and the *Journals of Proceedings* upon them.

21. Rules and regulations of debate will not fail to be adopted by the Assembly, which will be composed of the wisest and noblest of each Sovereignty, for its own honour and safety.

22. If any difference arise among the Delegates from the same Sovereignty, one of the members forming the majority should take their votes on the question.

23. It is extremely necessary that every Sovereignty should be represented at the Diet under great penalties, and that none leave the session without permission till all the business be finished; and also that no neutrality in debate should be allowed; "for any such latitude will quickly open a way to unfair proceedings, and be followed by a train both of seen and unseen inconveniences."

24. The language spoken in the session of the Sovereign Estates must be either *Latin* or *French*. "The first would be very well for civilians, but the latter more easy for men of quality."

HENRY IV.'S SCHEME,

ELABORATED BY THE ABBÉ SAINT-PIERRE.

The ABBÉ DE ST. PIERRE *was born* 1658, *died* 1743.

I.—FUNDAMENTAL ARTICLES.

The present Sovereigns, by their undersigned Deputies, have agreed to the following Articles:—

1. There shall be from this day forward a Society, a permanent and perpetual Union between the undersigned Sovereigns, and, if possible, among all Christian Sovereigns, to preserve unbroken peace in Europe. The Sovereigns shall be perpetually represented by their Deputies in a perpetual Congress or Senate in a free city.

2. The European Society shall not at all interfere with the Government of any State, except to preserve its constitution, and to render prompt and adequate assistance to rulers and chief magistrates against seditious persons and rebels.

3. The Union shall employ its whole strength and care in order, during regencies, minorities, or feeble reigns, to prevent injury to the Sovereign, either in his person or prerogatives, or to the Sovereign House, and in case of such shall send Commissioners to inquire into the facts, and troops to punish the guilty.

4. Each Sovereign shall be contented, he and his successors, with the Territory he actually possesses, or which he is to possess by the accompanying Treaty. No Sovereign, nor member of a Sovereign Family, can be Sovereign of any State besides that or those which are actually in the possession of his family. The

EXTRAIT DU PROJET DE PAIX PERPÉTUELLE DE M. L'ABBÉ DE SAINT PIERRE. (*Mot pour mot.*)

CHARLES IRÉNÉE CASTEL DE ST. PIERRE, 1658-1743.

1.—ARTICLES FONDAMENTAUX.

Les souverains presens par leurs Députez soussignez sont convenus des articles suivans :

1. Il y aura de ce jour à l'avenir une Société, une Union permanente et perpetuelle entre les Souverains soussignez, et s'il est possible, entre tous les Souverains Chrétiens, dans le dessein de rendre la Paix inaltérable en Europe.

Les Souverains seront perpetuellement representez par leurs Deputez dans un Congrez ou Senat perpetuel dans une Ville libre.

2. La Société Européenne ne se mêlera point du Gouvernement de chaque Etat, si ce n'est pour en conserver la forme fondamentale, et pour donner un prompt et suffisant secours aux Princes dans les Monarchies, et aux Magistrats dans les Republiques, contre les Séditieux et les Rebelles.

3. L'Union employera toutes ses forces et tous ses soins pour empêcher que pendant les Regences, les Minoritez, les Regnes foibles de chaque Etat, il ne soit fait aucun préjudice au Souverain, ni en sa personne, ni en ses droits, soit par ses Sujets, soit par des Estrangers ; et s'il arrivoit quelque Sédition, Révolte, Conspiration, soupçon de poison, ou autre violence contre le Prince ou contre la Maison Souveraine, l'Union, comme sa Tutrice et comme sa Protectrice née, envoyera dans cet Etat des Commissaires exprès pour estre par eux informez de la verité des faits, et en même temps des Troupes pour punir les coupables.

4. Chaque Souverain se contentera pour luy et pour ses Successeurs du Territoire qu'il possede actuellement, ou qu'il doit posseder par le Traité cy-joint.

Aucun Souverain, ni aucun Membre de Maison Souveraine ne pourra estre Souverain d'aucun Etat, que de celuy, ou de ceux qui sont actuellement dans sa maison.

annuities which the Sovereigns owe to the private persons of another State shall be paid as heretofore. No Sovereign shall assume the title of Lord of any Country of which he is not in possession, and the Sovereigns shall not make an exchange of Territory or sign any Treaty among themselves except by a majority of the four-and-twenty votes of the Union, which shall remain guarantee for the execution of reciprocal promises.

5. No Sovereign shall henceforth possess two Sovereignties, either hereditary or elective, except that the Electors of the Empire may be elected Emperors, so long as there shall be Emperors. If by right of succession there should fall to a Sovereign a State more considerable than that which he possesses, he may leave that which he possesses, and settle himself on that which is fallen to him.

6. The Kingdom of Spain shall not go out of the House of Bourbon, &c.

* * * * * *

7. The Deputies shall incessantly labour to codify all the Articles of Commerce in general, and between different nations in particular; but in such a manner that the laws may be equal and reciprocal towards all nations, and founded upon Equity. The Articles which shall have been passed by a majority of the votes of the original Deputies, shall be executed provisionally according to their Form and Tenour, till they be amended and improved by three-fourths of the votes, when a greater number of members shall have signed the Union.

The Union shall establish in different towns Chambers of Commerce, consisting of Deputies authorised to reconcile, and to judge strictly and without Appeal, the disputes that shall arise either in relation to Commerce or other matters, between the subjects of different Sovereigns, in value above ten thousand pounds; the other suits, of less consequence, shall be decided, as usual, by the judges of the place where the defendant lives. Each Sovereign shall lend his hand to the execution of the

Les rentes que doivent les Souverains aux particuliers d'un autre Etat, seront payées, comme par le passé.

Aucun Souverain ne prendra le titre de Seigneur d'aucun Péïs, dont il ne sera point en actuelle possession, ou dont la possession ne luy sera point promise par le Traité cy-joint.

Les Souverains ne pourront entr'eux faire d'échange d'aucun Territoire, ny signer aucun autre Traité entr'eux que du consentement, et sous la garantie de l'Union aux trois quarts des vingt-quatre voix, et l'Union demeurera garante de l'execution des promesses reciproques.

5. Nul Souverain ne pourra desormais posseder deux Souverainetez, soit héreditaires, soit électives; cependant les Electeurs de l'Empire pourront être élûs Empereurs, tant qu'il y aura des Empereurs.

Si par droit de succession il arrivoit à un Souverain un Etat plus considerable que celuy qu'il possede, il pourra laisser celuy qu'il possede, pour s'établir dans celuy qui luy est échû.

6. Le Royaume d'Espagne ne sortira point de la maison de Bourbon, etc.

* * * * * *

7. Les Députez travailleront continuellement à rediger tous les Articles du Commerce en general, et des differens Commerces entre les Nations particulieres, de sorte cependant que les Loix soient égales et reciproques pour toutes les Nations, et fondées sur l'équitè.

Les Articles qui auront passé à la pluralité des voix des Députez presens, seront executez par provision selon leur forme et teneur, jusqu'à ce qu'ils soient reformez aux trois quarts des voix, lors qu'un plus grand nombre de Membres auront signé l'Union.

L'Union établira en differentes Villes des Chambres pour le maintien du Commerce, composées de Députez autorisez à concilier, et à juger à la rigueur, et en dernier ressort les procez qui naîtront pour violence, ou sur le Commerce, ou autres matieres entre les Sujets de divers Souverains, au-dessus de dix mille livres; les autres procez de moindre consequence seront decidez à l'ordinaire par les Juges du lieu où demeure le Défendeur: chaque judgments of the Chambers of Commerce, as if they were his own judgments.

Each Sovereign shall, at his own charge, exterminate his inland robbers and banditti, and the pirates on his coasts, upon pain of making reparation; and if he has need of help, the Union shall assist him.

8. No Sovereign shall take up arms, or commit any hostility, but against him who shall be declared an enemy to the European Society. But if he has any cause to complain of any of the Members, or any demand to make upon them, he shall order his Deputy to present a memorial to the Senate in the City of Peace, and the Senate shall take care to reconcile the difference by its mediating Commissioners; or, if they cannot be reconciled, the Senate shall judge them by arbitral judgment, by majority of votes provisionally, and by three-fourths of the votes definitely. This judgment shall not be given until each Senator shall have received the instructions and orders of his master upon that point, and until he shall have communicated them to the Senate.

The Sovereign who shall take up arms before the Union has declared war, or who shall refuse to execute a regulation of the Society, or a judgment of the Senate, shall be declared an enemy to the Society, and it shall make war upon him, until he be disarmed, and until its judgment and regulations be executed, and he shall even pay the charges of the war, and the country that shall be conquered from him at the close of hostilities shall be for ever separated from his dominions.

If, after the Society is formed to the number of fourteen votes, a Sovereign should refuse to enter thereinto, it shall declare him an enemy to the repose of Europe, and shall make war upon him until he enter into it, or until he be entirely despoiled.

9. There shall be in the Senate of *Europe* four-and-twenty Senators or Deputies of the United Sovereigns, neither more nor less, namely :—*France*, *Spain*, *England*, *Holland*, *Savoy*, *Portugal*,

Souverain prêtera la main à l'execution des Jugemens des Chambres du Commerce, comme si c'étoient ses propres Jugemens.

Chaque Souverain exterminera à ses frais les Voleurs et les Bandits sur ses Terres, et les Pirates sur ses Côtes, sous peine de dédommagement, et s'il a besoin de secours, l'Union y contribuera.

8. Nul Souverain ne prendra les armes et ne fera aucune hostilité que contre celuy qui aura esté declaré ennemi de la Societé Européenne : mais s'il y a quelque sujet de se plaindre de quelqu'un de ses Membres, ou quelque demande à luy faire, il fera donner par son Député son memoire au Senat dans la Ville de Paix, et le Senat prendra soin de concilier les differens par ses Commissaires Mediateurs, ou s'ils ne peuvent estre conciliez, le Senat les jugera par Jugement Arbitral à la pluralité des voix pour la provision et aux trois quarts pour la definitive. Ce jugement ne se donnera qu'après que chaque Senateur aura reçû sur ce fait les instructions et les ordres de son Maistre, et qu'il les aura communiquez au Senat.

Le Souverain qui prendra les armes avant la declaration de Guerre de l'Union, ou qui refusera d'executer un Reglement de la Societé, ou un Jugement du Senat, sera declaré ennemi de la Societé, et elle luy fera la guerre, jusqu'à ce qu'il soit desarmé, et jusqu'à l'execution du Jugement et des Reglemens ; il payera même les frais de la Guerre, et le péïs qui sera conquis sur luy lors de la suspension d'armes, demeurera pour toûjours séparé de son Etat.

Si après la Societé formée au nombre de quatorze voix, un Souverain refusoit d'y entrer, elle le declarera ennemi du repos de l'Europe, et lui fera la Guerre jusqu'à ce qu'il y soit entré, ou jusqu'à ce qu'il soit entièrement dépossedé.

9. Il y aura dans le Senat d'Europe vingt quatre Senateurs ou Députez des Souverains unis, ni plus, ni moins ; scavoir, France, Espagne, Angleterre, Hollande, Savoye, Portugal, Baviere et Associez, Suisse et Associez, Lorraine et Associez, Suede, Dane-

Bavaria and Associates, *Venice*, *Genoa* and Associates, *Florence* and Associates, *Switzerland* and Associates, *Lorrain* and Associates, *Sweden*, *Denmark*, *Poland*, the Pope, *Muscovy*, *Austria*, *Courland* and Associates, *Prussia*, *Saxony*, *Palatine* and Associates, *Hanover* and Associates, Ecclesiastical Electors and Associates. Each Deputy shall have but one vote.

10. The Members and Associates of the Union shall contribute to the expenses of the Society, and to the subsidies for its security, each in proportion to his revenues, and to the riches of his people, and everyone's quota shall at first be regulated provisionally by a majority, and afterwards by three-fourths of the votes, when the Commissioners of the Union shall have taken, in each State, what instructions and information shall be necessary thereupon; and if anyone is found to have paid too much provisionally, it shall afterwards be made up to him, both in principal and interest, by those who shall have paid too little. The less powerful Sovereigns and Associates in forming one vote, shall alternately nominate their Deputy in proportion to their quotas.

11. When the Senate shall deliberate upon anything pressing and imperative for the security of the Society, either to prevent or quell sedition, the question may be decided by a majority of votes provisionally, and, before it is deliberated upon, they shall begin by deciding, by majority, whether the matter is imperative.

12. None of the eleven fundamental Articles above-named shall be in any point altered, without the *unanimous* consent of all the members; but as for the other Articles, the Society may always, by three-fourths of the votes, add or diminish, for the common good, whatever it shall think fit.

II.—Important Articles.

1. The Senate shall be composed of one of the Deputies of each of the Voting Sovereigns who shall have signed the Treaty of the twelve Articles mentioned, and afterwards their number shall be augmented by one Deputy from each of the other

mark, Pologne, Pape, Moscovie, Autriche, Curlande et Associez, Hanovre et Associez, Archevêques Electeurs et Associez.

Chacun Deputé n'aura qu'une voix.

10. Les Membres et les Associez de l'Union contribueront aux frais de la Societé, et aux subsides pour la sûreté a proportion chacun de leur revenus et des richesses de leurs Peuples, et les contingens de chacun sera reglez d'abord par provision à la pluralité, et ensuite aux trois quarts des voix, après que les Commissaires de l'Union auront pris sur cela dans chaque Etat les instructions et les éclaircissemens necessaires, et si quelqu'un se trouvoit avoir trop payé par provision, il luy en sera fait raison dans la suite en principal et interest par ceux qui auroient trop peu payé. Les Souverains moins puissans et Associez pour former une voix, alterneront pour la nomination de leur Deputé à proportion de leurs contingens.

11. Quand le Senat deliberera sur quelque chose de pressant et de provisoire pour la sureté de la Societé, ou pour prévenir, ou appraiser quelque Sédition, la question pourra se décider à la pluralité des voix pour la provision, et avant que de déliberer on commencera par decider à la pluralité, si la matiere est provisoire.

12. On ne changera jamais rien aux onze Articles fondamentaux cy-dessus exprimez, sans le consentement *unanime* de tous les Membres ; mais à l'égard des autres Articles, la Societé pourra toûjours aux trois quarts des voix y ajoûter, ou y retrancher pour l'utilité commune ce qu'elle jugera à propos.

2.—Articles Importans.

1. Le Senat demeurera composé d'un des Députez de chacun des Souverains votans qui auront signé le Traité des douze Articles cy-dessus, et dans la suite leur nombre sera augmenté d'un Député de chacun des autres Souverains ; à mesure qu'ils

Sovereigns, in the order in which they shall sign it; and the assembly of the Senate shall provisionally be held at Utrecht.

2. The Senate, in order to keep up a continual correspondence with the members of the Society, and to free them from all cause of fear and distrust one of another, shall always maintain, not only an Ambassador with each of them, but also a Resident in each great province of two millions of subjects.

The Residents shall dwell in the capital cities of those provinces, that they may be perpetual and irreproachable witnesses to the other Sovereigns, that the Prince in whose dominions they reside, has no thought of disturbing the peace and tranquillity.

These Ambassadors and Residents shall all be chosen from among the native inhabitants of the territory of the City of Peace, or those naturalised in that territory.

Each Sovereign shall, as much as lies in his power, facilitate all inquiry concerning things that may be included in the instructions of the Residents, and shall order his Ministers, and his other officers, to give them all the information they shall desire for the public security and tranquillity, to the intent they may every month give an account of things to the Senate, and to the Ambassador of the Senate.

The Residents shall be of the number of those Commissioners whom the Senate shall send to verify the account of the revenues and charges of the Sovereign and of his State, in order to give the definitive regulation of his *Quota.*

3. When the Union shall employ troops against an enemy, there shall be no greater number of soldiers of one nation than of another; but to make the levying and maintaining a great number of troops easy to the less powerful, the Union shall furnish them with what money is necessary, and that money shall be furnished to the Treasurer of the Union by the most powerful Sovereigns, who shall pay, in money, the *surplus* of their extraordinary *quota.*

le signeront, et l'Assemblée du Senat se tiendra par provision à Utrecht.

2. Le Senat pour entretenir une correspondance perpetuelle avec tous les Membres de la Societé, et pour les delivrer de tout sujet de crainte et de défiance les uns des autres, entretiendra toujours non seulement un Ambassadeur chez chacun d'eux, mais encore un Resident par chaque grande Province de deux millions de sujets.

Les Residens demeureront dans les Villes Capitales de ces Provinces, pour estre témoins perpetuels et irréprochables à l'égard des autres souverains, que le Prince dans l'Etat duquel ils résident, ne pense qu'à conserver la Paix et la tranquilité.

Ces Ambassadeurs et ces Residens seront pris d'entre les Habitans naturels du Territoire de la Ville de Paix, ou naturalisez dans ce même Territoire.

Chaque Souverain facilitera, autant qu'il sera en son pouvoir, toutes les informations des choses qui seront dans les instructions des Residens, et il ordonnera ses Ministres, et à ses autres Officiers de leur donner sur toutes leurs demandes tous les éclaircissemens qu'ils desireront pour la sûreté et la tranquilité publique, afin qu'ils puissent en rendre compte tous les mois au Senat, et à l'Ambassadeur du Senat.

Les Residens seront du nombre des Commissaires que le Senat enverra pour verifier le Memoire des revenus et des charges du Souverain et de son Etat, afin de regler son Contingent pour la définitive.

3. Quand l'Union employera des Troupes contre son ennemi, il n'y aura point un plus grand nombre de Soldats d'une Nation que d'une autre : mais pour faciliter aux Souverains moins puissans la levée et l'entretien d'un grand nombre de Troupes, l'Union leur fournira les deniers necessaires, et ces deniers seront fournis au Tresorier de l'Union par les Souverains plus puissans qui fourniront en argent le surplus de leur contingent extra ordinaire.

If any Member of the Union should omit to pay duly his extraordinary *quota* in troops or money, the Union shall borrow, make advances, and cause itself to be reimbursed with the interest of the loan by the Sovereign that shall be in default.

In time of Peace, after all the Sovereigns have signed, the most powerful shall keep up no more troops of his own nation than the less powerful, which shall be limited for the latter, who has a full vote, to six thousand men. But a very powerful Sovereign may, with the consent of the Union, borrow and maintain at his own charge in his dominions, other troops for his garrisons, so as to prevent seditions, provided they are all foreign soldiers and officers, and neither those officers nor those soldiers shall, upon pain of being disbanded, invest in any government security, purchase any estate, or marry anywhere but in the country of their nativity.

4. After the united Princes shall have declared war against any Sovereign, if one of his provinces revolt in favour of the Union, that province shall remain divided from its kingdom, and be governed like a Republic, or given as a Sovereignty to that one of the Princes of the Blood whom the province shall have chosen for its head, or to the General of the Union.

Any minister, general, or other officer of the enemy, who shall retire either to a Sovereign who is a Member of the Union, or into the territory of the Union, shall be there protected by the Senate, which, during the war, shall give him a revenue equal to that which he possessed in his own country; and the Union shall not make Peace until it be repaid what it has given him, and until the enemy, when reconciled, has given the Union the value of what the refugee possesses in his own country, that he may choose his habitation elsewhere.

Two hundred of the principal ministers or officers of the enemy who shall have omitted to retire into foreign countries at the beginning of such war, shall be delivered to the Union, and punished with death or imprisonment for life, as disturbers of the Peace of the common country.

Si quelque Membre de l'Union ne fournissoit pas à temps son contingent extraordinaire en Troupes ou en argent, l'Union empruntera, fera les avances, et se fera rembourser avec les interests de l'emprunt ou du prest par le Souverain qui seroit en défaut.

En temps de Paix, après que tous les Souverains auront signé, le plus puissant n'entretiendra pas plus de Troupes de sa Nation que le moins puissant, ce qui sera reglé pour le moins puissant qui a suffrage entier à six mille hommes: mais un Souverain fort puissant pourra du consentement de l'Union emprunter et entretenir à ses frais dans son Etat d'autres Troupes pour ses Garnisons, et pour prevenir les Séditions, pourvû que ce soient tous Soldats et Officiers étrangers, et ni ces Officiers ni ces Soldats ne pourront, sur peine d'estre cassez, acquerir aucune rente, aucun fond, se marier ailleurs que dans le Péïs de leur naissance.

4. Apres que les Princes unis auront declaré la Guerre à un Souverain, si une de ses Provinces se revolte en faveur de l'Union, cette Province demeurera démembrée, et elle sera gouvernée en forme de Republique, ou donnée en Souveraineté à celuy des Princes du Sang que cette Province aura choisi pour son Chef ou au General de l'Union.

Le Ministre, le General ou autre Officier de l'Ennemi qui se retirera ou chez un Souverain Membre de l'Union, ou dans le Territoire de l'Union, y sera protegé par le Senat qui luy fournira pendant la Guerre un revenu pareil à celuy qu'il possedoit dans son Péïs, et la Paix ne se fera point que l'Union ne soit remboursée de ce qu'elle luy aura fourni, et jusqu'à ce que l'Ennemi reconcilié ait fourni à l'Union la valeur des biens que le Refugié a dans son Péïs, afin qu'il puisse choisir ailleurs son habitation.

Deux cens des principaux Ministres ou Officiers de l'ennemi qui ne se seront pas retirez en Péïs étranger au commencement de la Guerre, seront livrez à l'Union, et punis de mort ou de prison perpetuelle, comme Perturbateurs de la Paix de la commune Patrie.

5. The Union shall give useful and honourable rewards to him who shall discover anything of a conspiracy against its interests, and that reward shall be ten times greater than any the discoverer could have expected had he remained in the conspiracy.

6. In order to increase the security of the Union, the Sovereigns, the Princes of the Blood, and fifty of the principal officers and ministers of their State, shall every year, on the same day, renew in their capital city, in the presence of the Ambassador and Residents of the Union, and of all the people, their Oaths, in the form agreed on, and shall swear to contribute as much as they are able, to maintain the General Union, and punctually to cause its regulations to be executed, in order to keep the Peace undisturbed.

7. As there are several lands in America and elsewhere which are inhabited only by savages, and as the Sovereigns of Europe, who have settlements there, ought to have certain, visible, and immutable bounds to their territory, for avoiding occasions of war, the Union shall appoint Commissioners, who shall, on the spot, get information about those limits, and on their report it shall give decision by three-fourths of the votes.

8. When in any one of the States of the Union there shall remain no person capable to succeed the reigning Sovereign, the Union, to prevent disturbances in that State, shall settle, and that, too, if it can, in concert with the then Sovereign, the person who shall succeed him; but this shall be always in the event of his leaving no children; and as he may die suddenly, the Union shall, immediately upon his death, either nominate the successor, or turn the Government into a Republic, in case the Sovereign is against having a successor.

III.—Useful Articles.

1. Security and Privileges of the City of Peace.

The City of Peace shall be fortified with a new inclosure and citadels shall be placed round that new inclosure. There

5. L'Union donnera des recompenses utiles et honnorables à celuy qui découvrira quelque chose d'une conspiration contre ses interests, et cette recompense sera dix fois plus forte que celle que le Dénonciateur auroit pû esperer en demeurant dans la conspiration.

6. Pour augmenter la sûreté de l'Union, les Souverains, les Princes du Sang et cinquante des principaux Officiers et Ministres de leur Etat renouvelleront tous les ans au même jour dans leur Capitale en presence de l'Ambassadeur et des Residens de l'Union et de tout le Peuple, leurs sermens, selon les Formules dont on conviendra, et jureront de contribuer de tout leur pouvoir à maintenir l'Union generale, et à faire executer ponctuellement ses Reglemens, pour rendre la Paix inalterable.

7. Comme il y a beaucoup de Terres en Amérique et ailleurs qui ne sont habitées que de Sauvages, et qu'il est à propos que les Souverains de l'Europe qui y ont des Etablissemens ayent dans ce Péïs-là des bornes certaines, évidentes et immuables de leur Territoire, pour éviter les sujets de la Guerre, l'Union nommera des Commissaires qui travailleront sur les lieux à l'éclaircissement de ces limites, et sur leur rapport, elle en fera la décision aux trois quarts des voix.

8. Lorsque dans un Etat Membre de l'Union, il ne restera plus personne habile à succeder au Souverain Regnant, l'Union pour prévenir les troubles de cet Etat, reglera, et s'il se peut, de concert avec le Souverain quel doit estre son Successeur, mais toûjours sous la condition qu'il ne laisse point d'enfans ; et comme il peut mourir de mort subite, l'Union ne perdra point de temps ou à designer le Successeur, ou à regler le Gouvernement en Republique, en cas que le Souverain ne veüille point de Successeur.

III.—Articles Utiles.

1. Sûreté & Privileges de la Ville de Paix.

La Ville de Paix sera fortifiée d'une nouvelle Enceinte, et on placera des Citadelles au tour de cette nouvelle Enceinte ; il y shall be in it magazines of provisions, of ammunitions, and of all things necessary for sustaining a long siege or blockade. The Ambassadors of the Union, the Residents, the five Deputies of each Frontier Chamber, and especially the Officers of the garrisons of the city, shall be all as nearly as possible natives or inhabitants, and married in the city and territory of the Union; the soldiers of the garrison shall be enlisted in the same territory, if possible, and the others shall not be enlisted anywhere but amongst the subjects of the Commonwealths of Europe.

The Union by the lessèning of the quota will indemnify the States-General of the United Provinces for what they usually draw as subsidies from the Lordship of Utrecht. So, instead of a larger sum, they will pay only 900,000 livres as their quota; and, in order to compensate Individuals of that Lordship for any loss they might suffer through the incorporation of the Sovereignty in the Union, while securing the inhabitants in their Laws, Property, Religion, and Employments, the Union will, in addition, furnish these persons with more profitable and honourable posts, as Ambassadors, Residents, Judges of the Chambers, Consuls, Treasurers, etc., and as to the ordinary taxes due from subjects, they will be diminished by one-half.

2. Generalissimo of the Union.

If the Union enter upon a war against any Sovereign it shall name a *Generalissimo* by a majority of votes; he shall not be of a Sovereign family; he shall be revocable at pleasure; he shall have command over the Generals of the troops of the united Sovereigns; he shall dispose of no employments among those troops; but if any of those Generals, or other General officers, should disobey or fail in their duty, he may have them brought before a Council of War.

The Union, in case there be no prince of the Sovereign family which it shall have conquered, may resolve to give all or part of what it may conquer from the enemy to be erected into a principality for the Generalissimo.

aura des Magasins de vivres et de munitions, et tout ce qui peut être necessaire pour soûtenir un long siége et un long blocus.

Les Ambassadeurs de l'Union, les Résidens, les cinq députez de chaque Chambre Frontiere, et surtout les Officiers des Garnisons de la Ville seront autant qu'il sera possible Natifs ou Habitans et mariés dans la Ville et Territoire de l'Union, les soldats de la garnison seront pris du même Territoire s'il est possible; et le reste ne pourra être pris que parmi les Sujets des Républiques de l'Europe.

L'Union par la diminution du contingent dedomagera les Etats Generaux des Provinces unies de ce qu'ils tirent ordinairement de subsides de la Seigneurie d'Utrecht; ainsi au lieu d'une plus grande somme, ils ne payeront que neuf cens mille livres de contingent, et pour dédommager les Particuliers de la même Seigneurie du préjudice qu'ils pourroient souffrir de ce que leur Souveraineté sera incorporée à l'Union, les Habitans seront non seulement conservés dans leurs Loix, dans leurs biens, dans leur Religion, et dans leurs emplois, mais l'Union leur fournira encore des postes plus profitables et plus honorables, comme Ambassadeurs, Résidens, Juges des Chambres, Consuls, Tresoriers et autres, et à l'égard des subsides ordinaires des Sujets, ils seront diminués de moitié.

2. Generalissime de l'Union.

Si l'Union entre en Guerre contre quelque Souverain, elle nommera un Generalissime à la pluralité des voix, il ne sera point de Maison Souveraine, il pourra être révoqué toutes fois et quantes, il commandera aux Generaux des Troupes des Souverains unis, il ne disposera d'aucuns emplois parmi ces Troupes; mais si quelqu'un de ces Generaux ou autres Officiers Generaux déobéïssoit ou manquoit à son devoir, il pourra le mettre au Conseil de Guerre.

L'Union en cas qu'il n'y eût point de Prince de la Maison Souveraine vaincûë, pourra se déterminer à donner en Principauté au Generalissime, tout ou partie de ce qu'il pourra conquerir sur le Souverain ennemi.

3. Deputies, Vice-Deputies and Agents.

Every Prince, every State, shall keep in the City of Peace for the whole year round one Deputy, of at least forty years old, and two Vice-Deputies of the same age, to fill up his place in case of absence or sickness; and two Agents to fill up the place of the Vice-Deputies.

The Vice-Deputies shall in their credentials be distinguished as first and second, in order that the first, in case of illness and absence, may succeed by full right to the rank and office of the absent Deputy; the Agents shall be likewise distinguished as first and second, in order that the first Agent may perform the duty of the absent Vice-Deputy.

The Princes who shall appoint them, shall in their choice have regard to superiority of parts, capacity in business, knowledge of Public Law and of commerce; likewise to their character, whether they be moderate, patient, zealous for the preservation of Peace; as also to their knowledge of the language of the Senate, and especially to their industry and application to labour. Each Prince may recall them, and substitute others, when he shall think fit, and shall not be allowed to employ the same Deputy for above four years together, in that function.

If a Senator is found to be of a temper opposite to peace and tranquillity, the Senate may by two-thirds of its votes declare him incapable to exercise the functions of Senator, and order that his Prince be desired by the Union to nominate another; and from that day he shall be excluded the Assemblies.

After the first appointment, no one shall be appointed Deputy, but one who has been for two years a Vice-Deputy; and no one shall be Vice-Deputy who has not been two years Agent in the City of Peace.

Similarly, no one shall be nominated Judge of a Frontier Chamber who has not dwelt two years together in the City of Peace.

4. Functions of the Deputies.

Each of the Senators or Deputies shall, in his turn, week by week, be Prince of the Senate, Governor or Director of the City

3. Qualités des Deputez, des Vice-Deputez et des Agens.

Chaque Prince, chaque Etat tiendra dans la Ville de Paix pendant toute l'année un Deputé, au moins de 40 ans, et deux Vice-Députez de même âge pour le remplacer en cas d'absence, ou de maladie; et deux Agens pour remplacer les Vice Députez.

Les Vices-Deputez seront nommez dans les lettres de leur Souverain par premier et second; afin que le premier en cas de maladie et d'absence succede de plein droit au rang, et à la fonction du Député absent; les Agens seront de même nommez par premier et second afin que le premier Agent puisse faire la fonction du Vice-Deputé absent.

Les Princes qui les nommeront, auront égard dans leur choix à la supériorité d'esprit, à la capacité dans les affaires, à la connaissance du Droit public et des diverses sortes de commerce, au caractère moderé, patient, zelé pour la conservation de la Paix, à la connaissance de la langue du Senat; et surtout à l'application au travail: chaque Prince pourra les revoquer, et en substituer d'autres, quand il le jugera à propos, et il ne pourra employer le même Deputé plus de quatre ans de suite dans cette fonction.

Si un Senateur par son caractere d'esprit se trouvoit opposé à la Paix, et à la tranquilité, le Senat pourra aux deux tiers des voix le déclarer incapable d'en faire les fonctions, et ordonner que le Prince sera prié par l'Union d'en nommer un autre, et de ce jour-là il sera exclû des Assemblées.

Nul ne pourra dans la suite être nommé Deputé, qu'il n'ait été deux ans Vice-Deputé; nul ne pourra être Vice-Deputé qu'il n'ait été deux ans Agent dans la Ville de Paix.

Nul ne pourra dans la suite être nommé Juge d'une Chambre Frontiere, qu'il n'ait demeuré deux ans de suite à cette Ville de Paix.

4. Fonctions des Deputés.

Chacun des Senateurs ou Deputez sera tour à tour, et par semaine Prince du Senat, Gouverneur ou Directeur de la Ville de of Peace; he shall preside in the General Assemblies, and in the Council of Five.

There shall be a Council of five Senators appointed to govern the daily affairs that are pressing and important, and that regard the safety of the Senators and of the City of Peace, such as the watchword, orders to seize anyone, etc. The President may not give the watchword, but in their presence, nor shall he give any order without their consent in writing, by a majority of votes.

The Deputy of the Sovereign who shall first have signed the Treaty, shall be the first President of the Senate, and the other Senators shall arrange themselves in the Senate Chamber according to the order of the signatures on the Treaty; so that he who shall be found upon the seat at the right side of the chair of the President shall succeed him in that dignity, on the day that his enjoyment of it comes to an end; and the one who retires from that function shall place himself on the left hand of his successor, and shall not be President again till all the members of the Assembly have presided in their turn.

When any Sovereign shall enter into the Union after it is already formed, his Deputy shall not be qualified to be President of the Senate until two months after he has taken his place; to the intent that he may have time in the Assembly to learn its customs, and the duties of the post he has to fill.

The sitting of Senators in private committees, and in public assemblies, shall be regulated every week by their sitting in the Senate; so that they who are nearest the Presidency shall have the precedence in the weeks; but in private visits every one shall be *incognito*, and without any distinction.

5. Form of Deliberations, etc.

The Assembly shall not deliberate upon any statement of the case till it be signed by three Senators, who shall certify that it is desirable to examine it. All deliberations shall be conducted in regard to printed statements only, which shall be distributed by the Secretary to all the members. Eight days after the distribution, the Assembly shall decide by a majority of votes, whether

Paix, il présidera aux Assemblées generales, et au Conseil des cinq.

Il y aura un Conseil de cinq Senateurs destiné à gouverner les affaires journalieres, pressantes et importantes, qui regarderont la Sureté des Senateurs, et de la Ville de Paix, le mot du guet, les ordres pour arrêter quelqu'un, etc. Le Prince ne pourra donner le mot qu'en leur presence, n'y rien ordonner que de leur consentement par écrit, à la pluralité des voix.

La Deputé du Souverain qui aura signé le premier le Traité d'Union, commencera par être Prince du Senat, et chacun des autres Senateurs se rangeront dans la Chambre du Senat, par rapport au rang qu'ils auront tenu en signant, en sorte que celui qui se trouvera sur le banc à la droite du Fauteüil du Prince, luy succedera à cette Dignité, le jour que finira l'exercice du premier, et celui qui sortira de fonction se mettra à la gauche de son successeur, et ne redeviendra Président, qu'après que tous les membres de l'Assemblée auront présidé tour à tour.

Lorsque quelque Souverain entrera dans l'Union déja formée, son Deputé ne pourra être Prince du Sénat que deux mois après la Séance prise ; afin que dans l'Assemblée il ait le loisir d'apprendre l'usage de cette Compagnie, et les fonctions de cet emploi.

La Séance des Senateurs dans les Bureaux particuliers, dans les Assemblées publiques, se reglera, chaque semaine, sur la Séance qu'ils prennent dans le Sénat, en sorte que les plus proches de la Principauté auront le pas et la Préséance dans les semaines, où ils en seront plus proches ; mais dans les visites particulieres, chacun sera 'incognito', et sans rang marqué.

5. Forme des Déliberations, etc.

L'Assemblée ne déliberera sur aucun memoire, qu'il n'ait été signé de trois Sénateurs qui certifieront qu'il est à propos de l'examiner, toutes les déliberations se feront sur memoires imprimés, ils seront distribués par le Secretaire à tous les Deputez ; huit jours après la Distribution on déliberera dans l'Assemblée à la pluralité, s'il est à propos de faire examiner ce memoire, si la it is necessary to have the statement examined. If it be resolved to have it examined, the Secretary shall give it to the Chairman of the Committee, whose business it is to take cognisance of the subject matter of the statement. When a statement has been sent to a committee, it shall be examined there according to the procedure agreed upon; the Chairman of the Committee shall give to the Secretary of the Senate the opinion of the Committee, with the grounds thereof; the Secretary shall get copies printed, which he shall distribute to all the Senators. A day shall be appointed by the President of the Senate by a majority of votes, when everyone may give his vote according to the importance of the affair. When the day appointed is come, each Senator shall write down and sign his opinion at the foot of the statement of the case, and shall return it to the Secretary.

On the day of the Assembly, the Secretary shall read *seriatim*, all the opinions of either side in turn, and shall count them. The President shall then, with an audible voice, declare which set of opinions prevail, and the judgment shall be entered at the bottom of the printed statement, which shall be carried into the Secretary's Office by the Chairman of that Committee which had examined the affair. The judgment, or decision, of the Assembly shall be signed by the President, by the members of the Council of Five, and by the Secretary. All these decisions shall be recorded in various registers; whereof a printed copy shall be every year given to each Senator. Care shall be taken to avoid, as much as possible, the mentioning by name, in any judgment, of the Sovereign against whom the award is given; but the Senate shall make a general law upon the particular fact, which is under decision, without naming anyone; and the Sovereign, after that law, shall of himself execute what is decreed in it.

In the first Committee shall be examined the letters of the Ambassadors and Residents of the Union, and the replies to them, after they shall have been approved by the General Assembly; that Committee shall also choose persons to fill up the places of Ambassadors, Residents, Officers of the Frontier Chambers, Councils of the Senate, etc.

résolution passe à l'examen, le Secretaire le donnera au Président du Bureau, qui a la connaissance de la matiere du memoire.

Le memoire renvoyé à un Bureau, y sera examiné suivant les formes dont on conviendra, le Président du Bureau donnera au Secretaire du Senat l'avis du Bureau avec les motifs, le Secretaire en fera faire des copies imprimées, qu'il distribuera à tous les Senateurs, le jour sera marqué par le Prince du Senat à la pluralité des voix, afin que chacun y puisse apporter son souffrage, selon l'importance de l'affaire; le jour marqué arrivé, chaque Senateur écrira, et signera son avis au pied du memoire, et le renvoyera au Secretaire.

Au jour de l'Assemblée le Secretaire lira de suite tous les avis semblables l'un après l'autre, et les comptera; et le Prince dira tout haut à quel avis la chose passe, et le Jugement sera mis au pied du memoire, apporté à la Secretairerie par le Président du Bureau, où l'affaire avoit esté examinée; le Jugement, ou décision de l'Assemblée sera signé par le Prince, par les Membres du Conseil des cinq, et par le Secretaire; toutes ces décisions se mettront en divers Registres, dont on donnera tous les ans une copie imprimée à chaque Sénateur, on fera en sorte autant qu'il sera possible d'éviter de condamner nommément un Souverain par aucun Jugement; mais le Sénat fera une Loy generale sur le fait particulier, qui est à décider, sans nommer aucune partie, afin que le Souverain après cette Loy passe de luy-même ce qu'elle ordonne.

Dans le premier Bureau on examinera les lettres des Ambassadeurs et des Résidens de l'Union, et on y fera les réponses après qu'elles auront esté approuvées de l'Assemblée generale, on y choisira les Sujets pour remplacer les Ambassadeurs, les Résidens, les Officiers des Chambres Frontieres, les Conseils du Senat, etc.

In the second shall be chosen the Officers of the Garrison, and the affairs of War, if there be any, enquired into; the choice of a General of the Union shall be there made, and whatever else concerns the troops of the frontiers of Europe.

In the third shall be examined all affairs of Finance, the accounts, and the selection of the officers of Finance.

In the fourth shall be examined the memorials about such regulations as may concern either the Union in general or the City of Peace, and its territory, or the laws of the Frontier Chambers.

Besides these four Standing Committees, there shall be other temporary Committees, formed expressly to reconcile differences between Sovereign and Sovereign. These Committees of Conciliation shall consist of members nominated by letters patent of the Senate by a majority of votes; the Commissioners of the Committee shall be thanked, and shall receive an acknowledgment in the event of their effecting the conciliation of the parties, and getting them to sign an agreement; and if they cannot succeed, the Chairman shall give the opinion of the Committee to the General Secretary, who shall distribute printed copies thereof to all the Senators; so that, being well informed, they may give their opinion, in writing, in full Assembly to the Secretary, and if after the law is made by the Senate for all such cases, the Sovereign who is in the wrong will not submit to the law, then the President of the Senate shall pronounce a judgment by name against the Sovereign whose claim or defence has not approved itself to the other Sovereigns.

This arbitral judgment shall be pronounced by a majority of votes provisionally, and six months afterwards definitively, on a second judgment by three-fourths of the votes; thus there will be always two judgments upon every dispute.

A time shall be appointed for the votes to be given, and such a time as will admit of the plenipotentiaries of the most distant States receiving the instructions of their Sovereigns. If one or more have not received an answer within the time appointed, the Senate may, by a majority of votes, give further time; and when

Dans le second on choisira les Officiers de la Garnison, on y examinera les affaires de la Guerre, s'il y en a ; le choix d'un General de l'Union et tout ce qui regardera les Troupes des Frontieres de l'Europe.

Dans le troisième on examinera les affaires de Finances, les comptes, les choix des Officiers de Finances.

Dans le quatrième on examinera les memoires sur les Règlemens, qui peuvent regarder, ou l'Union generale, ou la Ville de Paix et son Territoire, ou les Lois des Chambres Frontières.

Outre ces quatre Bureaux perpetuels, il y aura des Bureaux passagers, formés exprès pour concilier les differents entre Souverain et Souverain : ces Bureaux de conciliation seront composés de membres nommés par lettres du Sénat à la pluralité des voix, les Commissaires de ce Bureau seront remerciés, et auront une gratification, en cas qu'ils parviennent à la conciliation des Parties, et à leur faire signer un accord ; et en cas qu'ils n'y réussissent pas, le Président donnera l'avis du Bureau au Secretaire General, qui en distribuera des copies imprimées à tous les Sénateurs, afin qu'étant informés, ils puissent donner leur avis par écrit en pleine Assemblée au Secretaire, et si après la Loy faite par le Sénat pour tous les cas pareils, il arrivoit que le Souverain qui a tort ne voulût pas deferer à la Loy, alors le Prince du Sénat prononcera un Jugement nommément contre le Souverain, dont la demande, ou la deffense n'aura pas parû juste aux autres Souverains.

Ce Jugement arbitral sera prononcé à la pluralité des voix pour la provision, et six mois après par un second Jugement aux trois quarts des voix, pour la définitive ; ainsi il y aura toûjours sur chaque different deux Jugements

Il sera marqué un tems pour donner les suffrages, et un tems tel que les Plenipotentiaires des Etats les plus éloignés, puissent avoir les instructions de leurs Souverains. Si quelqu'un ou quelques uns n'avoient pas reçû réponse dans le délai prescrit, le Sénat pourra à la pluralité des voix, donner un nouveau délai, après that has expired it shall proceed to judgment, whether the plenipotentiary that refuses to give his vote be absent or not.

All the Committees shall assemble within the bounds of the President's Palace, unless the health of the Chairman of Committee requires to it to meet at his house.

The Senate, by a three-fourths majority, shall appoint the Chairman and members of the Committees, which shall consist of five Deputies and of ten Vice-Deputies; the Secretary of the Committee shall be a subject of the Union, either by birth or by naturalisation.

The Deputies of the Republics of Holland, Venice, the Swiss, and the Genoese, shall be always of the Council of Five; when a Deputy of one of these Republics shall be President of the Senate, the place that shall be vacant in the Council shall be filled by turns, beginning with the Deputy who shall have last presided in the General Assembly.

The language of the Senate, in which the deliberations shall be made and the printed statements given, shall be the language most in use, and the most common in Europe of all the living languages.

Every Deputy shall have, for the free exercise of his religion, a chapel in his palace, with whatever ministers are necessary; those who are of his religion, whether they be of his nation or of any other, shall there enjoy the same liberty. The Senate shall make very express prohibition, upon pain of imprisonment and greater punishments, according to the circumstances, against any disturbance there, or against turning anything publicly into ridicule, or writing or printing anything against any particular religion in the territory of the Republic. And the turning into ridicule shall be considered public if done in the presence of any person belonging to the religion attacked.

The Union shall endeavour to agree upon the standard and weight of coins, upon the same weights and measures, and upon the same astronomical calculations throughout all Europe; and especially upon the beginning of the year.

lequel il sera procédé au Jugement, soit que le Plenipotentiaire, qui refuse de donner son suffrage, soit present ou absent.

Tous ces Bureaux s'assembleront dans l'Enceinte du Palais du Prince, a moins que la santé du Président d'un Bureau ne demandât que l'on s'assemblât chez lui.

Le Sénat aux trois quarts des voix nommera les Présidents, et les membres des Bureaux qui seront composés de cinq Deputez, et de dix Vice-Deputez; le Secretaire du Bureau sera Sujet de l'Union, soit par naissance, soit par lettres.

Les Deputez des Républiques de Hollande, de Venise, des Suisses et de Genues seront toujours du Conseil des cinq, quand un Député d'une de ces Républiques sera Prince du Sénat, la place qui vaquera dans ce Conseil sera remplie tour à tour, à commencer par le Député du Prince qui aura présidé le dernier à l'Assemblée generale.

La langue du Sénat dans laquelle ces déliberations seront faites, les memoires donnez, sera la langue qui se trouve le plus en usage, et la plus commune en Europe, entre les langues vivantes.

Chaque Député aura libre exercice de sa Religion, un Temple dans son Palais, avec les Ministres convenables; ceux qui seront de sa Religion, soit de sa Nation, soit d'autre Nation, y auront la même liberté : le Sénat fera très expresses deffenses, sous peine de prison, et de plus grandes peines, selon les cas, d'y apporter aucun trouble, d'en tourner quelque chose en raillerie publiquement, et de rien écrire, ou imprimer contre elle dans le Territoire de la République, et ce sera une raillerie censée, publique, quand elle sera faite en presence de quelqu'un de la Religion attaquée.

L'Union tâchera de convenir du titre, et du poids des monnoyes, d'une même livre, d'un même pied, du même calcul astronomique par toute l'Europe; et surtout au commencement de chaque année.

6. Security of the Frontiers of Europe.

Not of modern interest.

7. Quotas or Ordinary Revenues of the Union.

The Revenue of the Union shall consist of the ordinary quotas payable by each Sovereign; this quota shall be settled provisionally, at the rate of three hundred thousand pounds yearly, which shall be paid by the least powerful Sovereign, who shall have but one vote; the others shall pay in proportion to their revenues; the quota shall afterwards be lessened according to the diminution of the requirements of the Union, which would then have finished its buildings, fortifications, magazines, &c. The quota for the Frontiers of Europe, and the quota in case of war, shall be settled, in proportion, by the Senate.

The quota shall be paid by the General Treasurer of each State in equal parts, the first of each month, to the order of the General Treasurer of the Union, and upon the receipt of his clerk, who shall be residing in the capital city of the State. The clerk shall every month pay the salaries of the Ambassador, of the Residents, and of the Judges of the Frontier Chambers in that State.

The Union shall every month calculate the interest of the sums which shall not have been paid regularly to the Clerk of the Treasurer, in order to repay those who shall have made advances to him.

8. Asiatic Union.

The European Union shall endeavour to procure in Asia a Permanent Society, like that of Europe, that peace may be maintained there also; and especially that it may have no cause to fear any Asiatic Sovereign, either as to its tranquillity, or its commerce in Asia.

6. Sûreté des Frontières de l'Europe.

. . . .

7. Contingens, ou Revenus ordinaires de l'Union.

Le Revenu de l'Union sera composé du contingent ordinaire que payera chaque Souverain, le contingent sera réglé par provision, à raison de trois cents mille livres par un monnoye presente de France, ou valeur en autre monnoye que payera le Souverain le moins puissant, qui aura seul une voix, les autres payeront à proportion de leurs revenus ; ce contingent sera diminué dans la suite eû égard à la diminution des besoins de l'Union, qui aura alors fait ses bâtimens, ses fortifications, ses magasins, etc. Le contingent pour les Frontières d'Europe, et le contingent en cas de Guerre, seront reglez à proportion par le Sénat.

Le contingent se payera par le Tresorier General de cet Etat, par parties égales, le premier de chaque mois, sur la procuration du Tresorier General de l'Union, et sur la quittance de son Commis, qui résidera dans la Ville Capitale de cet Etat. Ce Commis payera par mois les appointmens de l'Ambassadeur, des Résidens et des Juges des Chambres Frontières.

L'Union reglera par mois les interêts des sommes, qui ne seront pas payées régulièrement au Commis du Trésorier, pour rembourser ceux qui en auront fait les avances.

8. Union Asiatique.

L'Union Européenne tâchera de procurer en Asie une Societé permanente semblable à celle d'Europe, pour y entretenir la Paix ; et surtout pour n'avoir rien à craindre d'aucun Souverain Asiatique, soit pour sa propre tranquilité, soit pour son Commerce en Asie.

GROTIUS ON ARBITRATORS.

HUGO GROTIUS, *or De Groot, was born* 1583, *died* 1645.

I.—FOR PREVENTING WAR.

There are three ways in which controversies may be prevented from breaking out into war. The first is, Conference; the third way is by Lot.

Book II. Chap. xxiii. § viii—1. Another way, between parties who have no common judge, is, by reference to Arbitration. As Thucydides says, "*It is wicked to proceed against him as a wrong-doer, who is ready to refer the question to an Arbitrator.*" So, as narrated by Diodorus, Adrastus and Amphiarus referred the question concerning the kingdom of Argos to the judgment of Eriphyle. To decide the question concerning Salamis, between the Athenians and the Megareans, five Lacedæmonian Judges were chosen. In Thucydides, just quoted, the Corcyreans notify to the Corinthians that they are ready to refer the matters in controversy between them to such cities of Peloponnesus as they should agree upon. And Aristides praises Pericles, because, to avoid war, he was willing "*to accept Arbitrators.*" And Isocrates (Aeschines) in his oration against Ctesiphon, praises Philip of Macedon, because he was ready "*to refer his controversies with the Athenians to any impartial State.*"

2. So the Ardeates and the Aricinians in old time, and the Neapolitans and the Nolans later, referred their controversies to the Roman people. And the Samnites in controversy with the Romans referred to common friends. Cyrus makes an Indian King the arbitrator between himself and Assyria. The

HUGO GROTIUS DE ARBITRIS.

Natus 1583—*Moritus* 1645.

I.—Ad Vitandum Bellum.

Tres autem sunt modi, quibus vitare potest, ne controversiae in bellum erumpant. Primum est, colloquium ; tertia ratio est per sortem.

Liber II. Caput xxiii. § viii.—1. Alterum est inter eos, qui communem judicem nullum habent, compromissum : ἐπὶ τὸν δίκας διδόντα οὐ νόμιμον ὡς ἐς ἀδικοῦντα ἴεναι, ait Thucydides : *in eum, arbitrium accipere paratus est, nefas ut in injuriosum ire.* Sic de regno Argivo Adrastus et Amphiatus Eriphylae judicium, permiserunt, narrante Diodoro. De Salamine inter Athenienses et Megarenses lecti judices Lacedaemonii quinque. Apud dictum modo Thucydidem Corcyrenses Corinthiis significant, paratos se disceptare controversias apud Peloponnesi civitates de quibus inter ipsos convenisset. Et Periclem laudat Aristides, quod, ut bellum vitaretur, voluerit δίκῃ διαλύεσθαι περὶ τῶν διαφόρων, *de controversiis arbitros sumere.* Et Isocrates oratione adversus Ctesiphontem laudat Philippum Macedonem, quod quas habebat cum Atheniensibus controversias, de iis paratus esset ἐπιτρέπειν πόλει τινὶ ἴσῃ καὶ ὁμοίᾳ, *arbitrium permittere alicui civitati aequae utrique parti.*

2. Sic olim Ardeates et Aricini, postea Neapolitani et Nolani, contraversias suas arbitrio populi Romani permiserunt. Et Samnites in controversia cum Romanis ad communes amicos provocant. Cyrus sibi et Assyrio arbitrum fert regem Indorum.

Carthaginians, in their controversies with Masinissa, appeal to an arbitral judgment, in order to avoid war. The Romans themselves in their differences with the Samnites, according to Livy, refer to their common allies. Philip of Macedon, in his disputes with the Greeks, says that he will take the judgment of peoples who are at Peace with both. At the request of the Parthians and Armenians, Pompey appointed Arbitrators to settle their boundaries. Plutarch says that the main office of the Roman Feciales was this, "*not to allow an appeal to arms till all hope of a peaceable settlement was lost.*" And Strabo says of the Druids of the Gauls, that "*formerly they were Arbitrators between hostile parties, and often separated without fighting those who were drawn up in warlike array against each other.*" The same writer testifies that the priests in Spain performed the same office.

3. But especially are Christian Kings and States bound to try this way of avoiding War. For, if in order to avoid being subject to the judgments of persons who were not of the true religion, certain arbiters were appointed both by Jews and by Christians, and that course was commanded by Paul, how much more ought it to be done in order to avoid a much greater inconvenience, namely, War. So Tertullian argues somewhere that a Christian may not serve as a soldier, since he may not even go to law; which, however, according to what we have said elsewhere, must be understood with a certain qualification.

4. And both for this reason and for others, it would be useful, and indeed it is almost necessary, that Congresses of Christian Powers should be held, in which the controversies which arise among some of them may be decided by others who are not interested, and in which measures may be taken to compel the parties to accept Peace on equitable terms. This indeed was the office of the Druids of old among the Gauls, as related by Diodorus and Strabo. We read, too, that the Frankish Kings referred to their nobles the judgment of questions concerning the division of the Kingdom.

Poeni in controversiis cum Masinissa, ut bellum vitent, ad judicia provocant. Romani ipsi de controversia cum Samnitibus apud Livium ad communes socios. Et Philippus Macedo in controversia cum Graecis ait se arbitrio usurum populorum, cum quibus pax utrisque fuisset. Parthis et Armeniis postulantibus Pompeius finibus regendis arbitros dedit. Fecialium Romanorum hoc praecipuum ait officium fuisse Plutarchus; οὐκ ἐᾷν στρατεύειν πρότερον ἢ πᾶσαν ἐλπίδα δίκης ἀποκοπῆναι· ne *sinerent prius ad bellum veniri, quam spes omnis judicii obtinendi periisset.* De Gallorum Druidibus Strabo; ὥστε καὶ πολέμους διῄτων πρότερον καὶ παρατάττεσθαι μέλλοντας ἔπαυον· *olim et inter bellantes erant arbitri, ac saepe jam acie congressuros diremerunt.* Eodem officio functos in Iberia sacerdotes idem testis est.

3. Maxime autem Christiani reges et civitates tenentur hanc inire viam ad arma vitanda. Nam si, ut judicia alienorum a vera religione judicum vitarentur, et a Judaeis et a Christianis arbitri quidam sunt constituti, et id a Paulo praeceptum, quanto magis id faciendum est, ut majus multo vitetur incommodum, id est, bellum? Sic alicubi Tertullianus augmentatur, non militandum Christiano, ut cui ne litigare quidem liceat: quod tamen, secundum ea, quae alibi diximus, cum temperamento quodum est intelligendum.

4. Et tum ob hanc, tum ob alias causas utile esset, imo quodammodo factu necessarium, conventus quosdam haberi Christianarum potestatum, ubi per eos, quorum res non interest, aliorum controversiae definiantur; imo et rationes ineantur cogendi partes, ut aequis legibus pacem accipiant: quem et ipsum olim apud Gallos Druidum fuisse usum Diodoro ac Straboni proditum. Etiam proceribus suis de regni divisione judicium permisisse Francos reges legimus.

II.—For Terminating War.

Book III. Chap. xx. § xlvi.—1. Of Arbitrations there are two kinds, as Proculus teaches us: one, in which, whether the decision is just or unjust, we must submit to it; which is the rule, he says, whenever there is a reference by formal agreement o an Arbitrator; another, in which the decision is accepted only as the judgment of a fair and just man. Of this we have an example in the opinion of Celsus. "If a freedman," he says, "*has sworn to give as many days' work as his master shall decide, the master's decision is not valid except he judge fairly.*" But this mode of interpreting an oath, though it may be introduced by the Roman laws, is not in agreement with the simple meaning of the words. Still it is true that an Arbitrator may be taken in two different ways, either as a mediator only, as we read that the Athenians were between the Rhodians and Demetrius, or as one whose decision must be absolutely obeyed. And this is the kind of which we are here treating, and of which we have already said somewhat, when we were speaking of the means of preventing War.

2. Although, even with regard to those Arbitrators to whom reference is made by formal agreement, the Civil Law may provide, and in some places has done so, that it shall be lawful to appeal from their decision, and to make complaint of their injustice; yet this cannot have place between kings and peoples. For in their case, there is no superior power which can either bar or break the binding character of the promise. And therefore the sentence must stand, whether it be just or unjust; so that the saying of Pliny may be rightly applied here: "*Every man makes the supreme judge of his case him whom he chooses as umpire.*" For it is one thing to discuss the office of an Arbitrator, and another the obligation resting on those who form the agreement to arbitrate.

§ xlvii.—1. In regard to the office of an Arbitrator, we must consider whether he be elected in the capacity of a Judge or

II.—Ad Finem Belli Faciendam.

Liber III. Caput xx. § xlvi.—1. Arbitriorum Proculus nos docet duo esse genera: unum ejusmodi, ut sive aequum, sive iniquum, parere debeamus, quod observatur, ait, cum ex compromisso ad arbitrum itum est: alterum ejusmodi, ut ad boni viri arbitrium redigi debeat, cujus generis exemplum habemus in Celsi responso: *si libertus*, iniquit, *ita juraverit dare se quot operas patronus arbitratus sit, non aliter ratum fore arbitrium patroni quam si aequum arbitratus sit.* Sed haec jurisjurandi interpretatio, ut Romanis legibus induci potuit, ita verborum simplicitati per se spectatae non convenit. Illud tamen verum manet, utrovis modo arbitrum sumi posse, aut ut conciliatorum tantum, quales Athenienses inter Rhodios et Demetrium fuisse legimus, aut ut cujus dicto parendum omnino sit. Et hoc est genus de quo nos hic agimus, et de quo nonnulla supra diximus cum ne cavendi belli rationibus loqueremur.

2. Quanquam vero etiam de talibus arbitris, in quos compromissum est, lex civilis statuere possit, et alicubi statuerit, ut ab iis provocare et de injuria queri liceat; id tamen inter reges ac populos locum habere non potest. Nulla enim hic est potestas superior, quae promissi vinculum aut impediat, aut solvat. Standum ergo omnino, sive aequum, sive iniquum pronuntiaverint, ita ut Plinii illud huc recte aptes: *summum quisque causae suae judicem facit, quemcunque eligit.* Aliud enim est de arbitri officio, aliud de compromittentium obligatione quaerere.

§ xlvii. — 1. In arbitri officio spectandum, an electus sit in vicem judicis, an cum laxiore quadam potestate, quam arbitri with some more elastic power such as Seneca deems to be that appropriate to an Arbitrator, when he says "*A good cause had better be referred to a Judge than an Arbitrator, because the former is limited by rules of law which he may not infringe, the latter, being left unrestricted, except by the dictates of his conscience, may diminish or add something, and pronounce his award not as directed by law and justice, but as moved by humanity and mercy.*" Aristotle also says that a just and reasonable man "*will rather have recourse to an Arbitrator than a Judge, because the Arbitrator looks to what is equitable, the Judge to law; the Arbitrator is therefore chosen that equity may prevail.*"

2. In this place *equity* does not mean, as elsewhere, that part of justice which interprets the general terms of the law strictly according to the mind of its author (for this is committed to the Judge also), but it means everything that is better done than not done, even though it may be outside the rules of justice properly so called. But although such Arbiters are frequent in cases between private persons and citizens of the same empire, and are especially recommended to Christians by the Apostle Paul, I. Cor. vi., yet in a doubtful case so much power is not understood to be assigned to them. For in doubtful cases, we are to follow that which is least. And this especially holds between parties who possess supreme power: for these, since they have no common Judge, must be considered to have bound the Arbitrator by the rules by which the office of a Judge is commonly bound.

§ xlviii. — This, however, is to be noted, that Arbitrators chosen by peoples or Sovereign Powers ought to decide concerning the merits of the case, and not concerning possession; for judgments concerning possession belong to Civil Law. By the Law of Nations the right of possession follows ownership. Therefore, while the case is undergoing investigation, no innovation is to be made, both to avoid prejudice, and because recovery is difficult. Livy in his history of the Arbitration between the Carthaginians and Masinissa, says, "*The commissioners did not change the right of possession.*"

quasi propriam vult Seneca, cum dicit: *Melior videtur conditio causae bonae, si ad judicem, quam si ad arbitrum mittitur; quia illum formula includit, et certos, quos non excedat, terminos ponit; hujus libera et nullis adstricta vinculis religio et detrahere aliquid potest et adjicere, et sententiam suam, non prout lex aut justitia suadet, sed prout humanitas et misericordia impulit, regere."* Aristoteles quoque ἐπιεικοῦς, id est, aequi et commodi hominis esse ait, *εἰς δίαιταν κᾶλλον ἢ εἰς δίκην βούλεσθαι ἰέναι, malle ire ad arbitrum quam in jus*, rationem adjiciens, *ὁ γὰρ διαιτητὴς τὸ ἐπιεικὲς ὁρᾷ. ὁ δὲ δικαστὴς τ.ν νόμον. καὶ τούτου ἕνεκα διαιτητης εὑρέθη ὅπως τὸ ἐπιεικὲς ἰσχύῃ· nam arbiter id quod aequum est respicit, judex legem: imo arbiter ejus rei causa repertus est, ut valeret aequitas.*

2. Quo in loco aequitas non proprie significat, ut alibi partem illam justitiae, quae legis sonum generalem ex mente auctoris adductius interpretatur (nam hac et judici commissa est) sed omne id, quod rectius fit quam non fit, etiam extra justitiae proprie dictae regulas. Sed tales arbitri sicut inter privatos et ejusdem imperii cives frequentes sunt, et specialiter Christianis commendantur ab Apostolo Paulo, I. Cor. vi., ita in dubio non debet tanta potestas concessa intelligi: in dubiis enim, quod mimimum est, sequimur; praecipue vero id locum habet inter summam potestatem obtinentes, qui cum judicem communem non habeant, arbitrum censendi sunt adstrinxisse iis regulis, quibus judicis officium adstringe solet.

§ xlviii. — Illud tamen observandum est, arbitros lectos a populis aut summis potestatibus de principali negotio pronuntiare debere, non de possessione: nam possessoria judicia juris civilis sunt: jure gentium possidendi jus dominium sequitur. Ideo, dum causa cognoscitur, nihil est innovandum, tum ne praejudicium fiat, tum quia difficilis est recuperatio. Livius in historia disceptatorum inter populum Carthaginiensem et Masinissam, *legati*, inquit, *jus possessionis non mutarunt.*

PUFENDORF
ON THE WAY OF DECIDING CONTROVERSIES IN THE LIBERTY OF NATURE.

SAMUEL, BARON VON PUFENDORF, *born* 1631, *died* 1694.

I.—WHAT IS DUE TO OTHERS IS WILLINGLY TO BE PERFORMED.

By the Law of Nature men are required voluntarily to fulfil, and mutually to render, those things, which for any reason whatsoever are due to others.

It is inhuman and brutish indeed, not to be satisfied with anything less than the blood of an offender, and when a misunderstanding has once arisen to cherish it for ever.

II.—IN A STATE OF NATURE THERE IS NO JUDGE.

But all men are not so benevolently disposed as to be willing of their own accord to perform their duty; and, besides, controversies may arise about the certitude and amount of a debt, the valuation of a given damage, the competency to exercise certain rights, the determination of boundaries, the interpretation of agreements, and other contentious matters. In such matters, among those who live in the liberty of nature, there is provided no judge, who, by virtue of his authority, may determine and adjust the disputes that arise. For the rest though every man in that state, may either neglect or defend his own right, may put aside or follow up an injury, yet he cannot in his own affair give sentence so as to oblige him, with whom he has the controversy, to abide by it. For although he may desire to the utmost, and even protest upon oath, that he will give judgment according to

PUFENDORFIUS
DE MODO LITIGANDI IN LIBERTATE NATURALI.

I.—Quae aliis debentur ultro sunt implenda.

Id equidem lex naturalis requirit, ut homines ultro praestent, et exhibeant invicem ea, quae quocunque nomine aliis debent. Inhumanum quippe et belluinum est, non nisi reposito laedenti dolore velle adquiescere, et susceptas semel inimicitias in aeternum alere.

II.—In statu naturali judex non datur.

Enimvero praeterquam quod non omnibus mortalibus ea est ingenii bonitas, ut officium ultro velint explere, aliquando etiam super certitudine ac quantitate debiti, taxatione damni dati, competentia, et exercitis certorum jurium, super regundis finibus, interpretatione pactorum, aliisque praetensionibus controversiae oriuntur. Heic igitur inter eos, qui in naturali libertate vivunt, judex non datur, qui lites exortas pro imperio definiat et componat.

De cætero licet in illo statu penes quemque sit, negligere, an tueri suum jus, necessitare an exsequi injuriam velit: non tamen de suo negotio sententiam ferre potest, qua stare teneatur is, qui cum ipsi controversia intercedit. Nam si vel maxime cupiat, idque vel juratus protestetur, se pronunciaturum, quod sibi justum what seems to him right, yet since the other may have an equal respect for his own opinion, if they happen to disagree, nothing can be done on account of their equality, which is incidental to a state of nature.

III.—Controversies, which cannot be decided by Conference, are to be referred to Arbitrators.

The Law of Nature by no means allows any one to assert by arms the right he has determined by his own judgment, and to make the sword the arbiter of his own controversies before milder methods have been attempted.

Therefore the parties ought first to endeavour by some friendly discussion, at a meeting between themselves or their agents, to compose the difference. Very often, indeed, after arms have been taken up, and the inflexibility of temper has been broken by the evils of war, the difference is, according to the usual custom, adjusted by discussion and agreement.

But if neither a discussion between the parties can put an end to the controversy, nor either is disposed to entrust to a decision by lot what he thinks is based on valid reasons, the only thing to be done is to refer to an Arbitrator, to whose award both parties mutually bind themselves by agreement to adhere.

IV.—No Covenant can exist Between an Arbitrator and the Contending Parties.

The Arbitrator, it is evident, is chosen because every man's judgment, by reason of that natural affection which each bears to himself, is suspected to be partial to his own cause.

He must, therefore, before everything else, take care not to show more favour to one than the other, except so far as arises from the merits of the case.

Therefore it is manifest that no one can with propriety be chosen arbitrator in any case wherein there may seem to be more hope of personal advantage or credit through the success fuerit visum: cum tamen alter pari dignatione suam sententiam aestimare queat, ubi eas contingat discrepare, propter æqualitatem, status naturalis comitem, nihil agetur.

III.—Controversia, quae colloquio inter partes expediri nequeunt, ad arbitros sunt deferenda.

Haut quidquam tamen lege naturali concessum est quod quisque suo ex judicio definivit, jus statim armis asserere controversiarumque suarum arbitrum Martem sumere antequam molliora media fuerint tentata. Inde primo omnium conandum, an per amicam disceptationem, congressis inter se partibus, aut earundem mandatariis, controversia componi queat.

Quanquam et saepissime, postquam armis fuit certatum, animorumque rigor belli malus est fractus, controversia per tractatus et transactionem componi soleat.

Enimvero ubi nec partium disceptatio exitum controversiae invenire potest, neque sorti committere placet, quod solidis rationibus subnixum existimatu, proximum est, ut ad arbitrum eatur, cujus sententia quod utique stare velint, partes sese pacto invicem adstringant.

IV.—Inter arbitrum et partes non intercedit pactum.

Scilicet sumitur iste, quia cujuslibet de sua causa judicium suspectum habetur propter insitum illum amorem, quo quis in se suaque regulariter propendet. Igitur id cum primis observabit arbitrer, ut ne plus favoris adversus unum quam alterum ostentet, nisi quantum ex meritis causae oritur.

Sed et ob id ipsum patet, nenimem recte posse capi arbitrum in ea causa, cui commodi vel gloriae peculiaris spes major adparet ex victoria unius partis, quam alterius, seu cujus peculiariter of one party rather than the other, or in which it is specially to his interest that one should, by any means, gain the case. Otherwise he cannot so strictly observe the impartiality and neutrality which are necessary.

Hence it follows that no agreement or promise should exist between the Arbitrator and the Parties whereby he may be prejudiced in favour of either of them; nor ought he to have any other reward for his sentence than the satisfaction of having judged well.

The reason of this is not so much that the law of nature. which can acquire no obligation by any such agreement, enjoins upon the Arbitrator the duty of judging according to justice, as that, by such a course, the object of having recourse to an arbitrator would be frustrated, and there would be no finality.

It follows further from this, that the agreement to arbitrate ought to be framed absolutely that the parties are willing to abide by the award pronounced by the Arbitrator; and not on the condition that he pronounces a just award. Else should either of the contending parties raise a doubt as to the equity of the award, the question would have to be submitted to another Arbitrator, who would investigate that issue; and if again doubt were raised, another Arbitrator would have to be appointed and so on without end.

It is also manifest that there cannot be any appeal from Arbitrators, because there is no superior Judge who can revise their award. This principle prevails in States, where parties have voluntarily agreed to refer to an Arbitrator, provided the case be such as it does not interest the Government to have settled. If, however, it is anywhere permissible to make such an appeal it is by reason of some positive law.

But when it is said that the parties ought to abide by the award of the Arbitrator, whether he has given it justly or not, that must be accepted with some reservation. For though we cannot recede from an agreement to arbitrate because the award is given against us, whatever hopes we had cherished, yet the award of the Arbitrator will surely not be binding if it manifestly appears that interest, unum quocunque modo causam obtinere. Alias enim indifferentiam illam, et velut medietatem ita accurate observare non poterit.

Ex quo etiam consequitur, nullum pactum aut promissum debere intercedere intea arbitrum, et partes, cujus vi iste teneatur praeter merita causae pronunciare in gratiam partis alterutrius.

Nec aliud sententiae ipsius pretium esse debet, quam bene judicasse.

Cujus rei ratio non tam haec est, quod alias per legem naturæ sit injunctum arbitro pronunciare, quod justum sibi visum fuerit; cujus legis obligationi nihil queat ex pacto accedere; quam quod hoc modo finis arbitri sumti reddatur irritus, ac fiat progressus in infinitum.

Ex quo itidem patet, pactum quo partes in arbitrum compromittunt, pure conceptum esse debere, quod velint stare ea sententia, quam arbiter pronunciaverit; non autem sub hac conditione, siquidem aequam iste sententiam pronunciaverit. Nam hoc modo, ubi super aequitate sententiae alteruter litigantium dubium moveret, ad alium foret arbitrum eundum, qui super ista cognosceret. De cujus aequitate si iterum ambigeretur, alius esset constituendus arbiter; et sic in infinitum.

Ceterum id manifestum est, ab arbitris non posse provocari; cum nullus sit superior judex, qui sententiam eorum corrigere queat. Id quod etiam in civitatibus obtinet, ubi partes ultro in arbitrum compromiserint; siquidem disceptetur super causa, quam quocunque modo componi rectorum civitatis nihil intersit. Quod si tamen alicubi ab hisce quoque licet provocare; id ex jure positivo est.

Quod autem dicitur, standum esse sententia arbitri, sive aequum, sive iniquum pronunciaverit, id cum grano salis est accipiendum. Nam uti ideo quidem a compromisso resilire non licet, quod contra nos fuerit pronunciatum, utut ipsi largius de nostra causa sperabamus; ita tunc sane arbitri sententia nos non stringet, si manifeste adpareat, ipsum cum altera parte he was in collusion with the other party, or was corrupted by a bribe from him, or entered into an agreement for our detriment.

For he who openly attaches himself to either side cannot any longer sustain the character of an Arbitrator.

But this also is clear, if more Arbitrators than one are chosen, it is better to have an uneven number, for if on giving sentence there should be an equality of votes, the case could not be concluded.

V.—Arbitrators in a Case of Doubt are bound to judge by Law.

The paragraph of Grotius (pp. 52-54.) on this point is considered, and it is added :—

If it be doubtful under which of these two qualifications (whether as a judge or with wider powers) the Arbitrator be chosen, it is presumed that he will be subject to those rules which have to be followed by a judge, since it is for want of a judge and judicature that he is chosen ; and in a case of doubt we must follow that which is least. Besides, it is easier for either party to suffer injury at the hands of an Arbitrator who has wider powers than of one who has been entrusted with more limited functions.

For the rest it is manifest, that as he who passes judgment between fellow citizens, judges, as a matter of course, according to the civil law, to which the litigants are subject, so he who is about to pronounce judgment between those who do not acknowledge the same Civil laws will have as his rule the law of nature; unless the parties themselves subject their case to the positive Laws of a particular State.

VI.—Arbitrators are not to decide in regard to Possession.

See Grotius, p. 54.

colludere, aut ab eadem donis corruptum, aut pactum in fraudem nostram inivisse. Nam qui aperte ad alterutram sese partem adplicat, arbitri personam gerere amplius nequit. Sed et hoc patet, si plures uno arbitri sumantur, praestare, ut sint numero impari, ne si ipsis dissentionibus pares sint sententiae, res non possit invenire exitum.

V.—Arbitri in dubio intelliguntur adstricti jure.

In dubio (*i.e.* in vicem judicis, an vero cum laxiore aliqua potestate) tamen praesumitur arbitrum ad regulas judici sequendas obligatum, quippe cum ob defectum fori et indicis ille sumtus sit; et in dubio id, quod minimum est, sequamur. Facilius autem est, ut quis laedatur, si arbitro laxo, quam strictior facultas sit concessa. Caeterum illud manifestum est, uti qui inter cives jus dicit, regulariter sequitur leges civiles, quibus litigantes sunt subjecti, ita qui pronunciaturus est inter eos, qui communes leges civiles, non agnoscunt, jus naturale pro norma habebit. Nisi ipsae partes actum suum ad certae civitatis leges positivas attemperarint.

VI.—Arbitris non sufficit pronunciasse super possessione,

(*Vide* Grotium *in loco.*)

VII.—Concerning Mediators.

Mediators, as they are termed, who of their own accord interpose between contending parties and nations, either preparing for, or already waging war, and who endeavour by their authority, their arguments and their entreaties, to bring them to a peaceful settlement and a prudent application to law, are not strictly speaking Arbitrators.

These cannot be peremptorily rejected without the greatest inhumanity, seeing they have such a sacred purpose, even though they should appear to be intimately allied to either party. For in any case, it is in my power to accept or refuse what is offered to me by others; and it is the especial function of friends when they cannot take part in the dispute, to endeavour to bring it to an amicable composition.

VIII.—What if Documents be lost?

The form and procedure of conducting the pleadings carried on before Arbitrators will be best determined by common sense, according to the particular circumstances of the case. For it would be impertinent to lay down prescriptions how each party should open his case; how to state the question; how, after the arguments on both sides have been weighed, the sentence ought to be pronounced. This only needs to be said, that if the contention on the part of either side cannot be sustained in any other way than by documents, and they are lost, nothing remains but for the Arbitrator, with the consent of the other party, to administer an oath. I say, *with the consent of the other party;* for in the liberty of nature, no one is obliged to make the issue of his cause depend upon the conscience of his opponent.

IX.—Of Witnesses.

Arbitrators have this in common with judges, that in regard to matters of fact they ought to treat alike the bare and unattested

VII.—De mediatoribus pacis.

Arbitri tamen proprie dicti non sunt mediatores, quos vocant qui litigantibus, bellumque parantibus aut jam gerentibus ultro sese interponunt, eosque autoritate, rationibus, precibus ad pacifice transigendum, litesque sapiendas permovere nituntur. Hos cum tam sanctum propositem prae se ferant, praefracte rejicere summa inhumanitas foret; ne quidem ex eo solum praetextu, quod cum altera parte ipsis peculiaris quaedam conjunctio videatur intercedere. Nam penes me utique est, quantum ea, quae ab istis offeruntur, velim admittere: et amicorum solet hoc praecipuum esse munus, ut ubi ipsi mecum in litem descendere nolunt, ad amicam compositionem eandem deducere laborent.

VIII.—Quod si instrumenta fuerint amissa?

Formam et processum disceptationum coram arbitris institutarum ipsa communis ratio satis designat, perspecta cujusque negotii indole. Sic ut putidum foret multis praescribere, quo modo partes intentionem suam debeant proponere, quomodo status controversiae formandus, quomodo post expensa utriusque partis argmenta sententia demum sit concipienda. Illud duntaxat monendum, ubi intentio alterutrius alia ratione, quam per instrumenta probari nequeat, et vero illa sint amissa, arbitro nihil superesse quam ut uni partium cum consensu alterius juramentum deferat. *Cum consensu alterius*, dico. Nam in libertate naturali alias nemo videtur teneri, ut ex adversæ partis conscientia causam suam suspendat.

IX.—De testibus.

Illud arbitri cum judicibus habent commune, quod circa quæstiones facti adversus nudam et injuratam assertionem partium assertions of both parties, *i.e.*, when they firmly adhere to contradictory statements, to believe neither. But when autographs, accounts, and genuine documents cannot be produced in evidence, judgment will then have to be given according to the testimony of witnesses.

The witnesses again ought, therefore, not to be favourably disposed towards either party, so that it shall not seem likely that either favour or hatred and a desire of revenge should have more weight with them than their conscience.

Therefore as my adversary may take exception to my relatives as witnesses, so may I to my avowed enemies. Indeed, sometimes, near relations are excused from giving evidence in a case, upon a principle of humanity, lest they should be forced to offer violence either to their affections or to their conscience.

Lastly, it is thoroughly in accordance with reason that no case whatsoever should be decided on the testimony of any one single witness.

X.—Of the Execution of the Sentence.

With regard to the execution of the award there is not much that we may add; for in a state of nature, if any one does not of his own accord fulfil what is due to another, the latter may by all the forces and arms that he has himself, or that his friends may supply him with, procure the execution. How far such proceeding may be carried will be shown more fully later, when we treat of war. Here it may be merely observed, that in such an execution, I not only become the owner of the thing adjudged to me, when by any method whatsoever I have taken possession of it, but even if I cannot get possession of the thing itself, I may, when the execution is made, seize upon anything else I can which amounts to the same in value (the estimated charges of the execution itself being included), so as to become its owner.

æquales sese debeant præbere, *i.e.*, cum contradictoria simul vera asseverent, neutri credere. Sed ubi signa rationesque et incorrupta instrumenta in cognitionem veritatis haut perducunt, secundum effata testium sententia erit ferenda.

Testes porro ergo alterutram partem non oportet ita esse affectos, ut probabile videri queat, gratiam ipsos aut odium, vindictæque libidinem, ante conscientiam habere.

Igitur uti adversarius meos necessarios, sic et ego professos meos inimicos recte possum rejicere. Quanquam interdum per humanitatem a testimonis in causa necessarii sui excluduntur propinqui, ne vel affectus suos, vel conscientiam lædere cogantur.

Denique et id rationi optime congruit, ne unius testimonium ad causæ cujuslibet decisionem valeat.

X.—De executione rei judicatæ.

Circa exsecutionem rei judicatæ non est quod multa addamus, cum in statu naturali, ubi ab altero non expletur ultro, quod debetur, sibi quisque suis, sociorumque viribus et armis exsecutionem faciat; quæ quousque progredi possit, inferius, ubi de bello agemus, latius ostendetur. Illud duntaxat heic monendum, in ejusmodi exsecutione me non solum fieri dominum rei mihi adjudicatæ, postquam ejusdem possessionem quocunque modo adprehendi; sed etiam, si ista potiri nequeain, me aliam rem posse, quæ tantundem valet, arripere (computatis simul impensis in ipsam exsecutionem factis) cum hoc effectu, ut ejus rei fiam dominus.

VATTEL ON ARBITRATION.

EMMERICH VATTEL, *born* 1714, *died* 1767.

In Book II. Chap. xviii. § 329, of his work "The Law of Nations," Monsieur de Vattel says:—

When Sovereigns cannot agree about their pretensions, and are nevertheless desirous of preserving or restoring peace, they sometimes submit the decision of their disputes to Arbitrators chosen by common agreement.

When once the contending parties have entered into an Arbitration Agreement, they are bound to abide by the sentence of the Arbitrators; they have engaged to do this, and the faith of treaties should be religiously observed.

If, however, the Arbitrators, by pronouncing a sentence evidently unjust and unreasonable, should forfeit the character with which they were invested, their judgment would deserve no attention; the parties had appealed to it only with a view to the decision of doubtful questions. Suppose a board of Arbitrators should, by way of reparation for some offence, condemn a sovereign State to become subject to the State she has offended, will any man of sense assert that she is bound to submit to such decision? If the injustice is of small consequence, it should be borne for the sake of Peace; and if it is not absolutely evident, we ought to endure it, as an evil to which we have voluntarily exposed ourselves. For if it were necessary that we should be convinced of the justice of a sentence before we would submit thereto it would be of very little use to appoint Arbitrators.

There is no reason to apprehend that, by allowing the parties a liberty of refusing to submit to a manifestly unjust and unreasonable sentence, we should render Arbitration useless; and this

DE L'ARBITRAGE, PAR M. DE VATTEL.

1714.—1767.

Dans Livre II., Chap xviii., § 329, Monsieur de Vattel dit :—

Quand les souverains ne peuvent convenir sur leurs prétentions et qu'ils désirent cependant de maintenir, ou de rétablir la paix, ils confient quelquefois la décision de leurs différens à des arbitres choisis d'un commun accord.

Dès que le compromis est lié, les parties doivent se soumettre à la sentence des arbitres : elles s'y sont engagées ; et la foi des traités doit être gardée.

Cependant, si par une sentence manifestement injuste, contraire à la raison, les arbitres s'étoient eux-mêmes dépouillés de leur qualité, leur jugement ne meriteroit aucune attention ; on ne s'y est soumis que pour des questions douteuses. Supposez que des arbitres, pour réparation de quelque offense, condamnent un Etat souverain à se rendre sujet de l'offense ; aucun homme sensé dira-t-il que cet Etat doit se soumettre? Si l'injustice est de petite conséquence, il faut la souffrir pour le bien de la paix ; et si elle n'est pas absolument évidente, ou doit la supporter comme un mal auquel on a bien voulu s'exposer. Car s'il falloit être convaineu de la justice d'une sentence pour s'y soumettre, il seroit fort inutile de prendre des arbitres.

On ne doit pas craindre qu'en accordant aux parties la liberté de ne pas se soumettre à une sentence manifestement injuste et déraisonnable, nous ne rendions l'arbitrage inutile ; et cette decision is by no means contrary to the nature of the submission or of the Arbitration agreement. There can be no difficulty in the affair, except in the case of a vague and unlimited agreement in which they have not precisely specified the subject of the dispute or marked the limits of their conflicting pretensions. It may then happen, as in the example just alleged, that the Arbitrators will exceed their power, and pronounce on what has not been really submitted to their decision. Being called in to determine what satisfaction a State ought to make for an offence, they may condemn her to become subject to the State she has offended. But she certainly never gave them a power so extensive, and their absurd sentence is not binding. In order to obviate all difficulty and cut off every pretext of which fraud might take advantage, it is necessary that the Arbitration agreement should precisely specify the subject in dispute, the respective and opposite pretensions of the parties, the demands of the one and the objections of the other.

These are what are submitted to the decision of the Arbitrators, and it is upon these points alone that the parties promise to abide by their judgment. If, then, their sentence be confined within these precise bounds, the disputants must acquiesce in it. They cannot say that it is manifestly unjust, since it is pronounced on a question which they have themselves rendered doubtful by the discordance of their claims, and which has been referred, as such, to the decision of the Arbitrators. Before they can evade such a sentence they must prove, by incontestable facts, that it was the offspring of corruption or flagrant partiality.

Arbitration is a very reasonable mode, and one that is perfectly conformable to the law of nature, for the decision of every dispute which does not directly concern the safety of the nation. Though the claim of justice may be mistaken by the Arbitrators, it is still more to be feared that it will be overpowered in an appeal to arms.

décision n'est pas contraire à la nature de la soumission ou du compromis. Il ne peut y avoir de difficulté que dans le cas d'une soumission vague et illimitée, dans laquelle on n'auroit point déterminé précisément ce qui fait le sujet du différend, ni marqué les limites des prétentions opposées. Il peut arriver alors, comme dans l'exemple allégué tout-à-l'heure, que les arbitres passent leur pouvoir et prononcent sur ce qui ne leur a point été véritablement soumis. Appelés à juger de la satisfaction qu'un Etat doit pour une offense, ils le condamneront à devenir sujet de l'offensé. Assurément cet Etat ne leur a jamais donné un pouvoir si étendu, et leur sentence absurde ne le lie point. Pour éviter toute difficulté, pour ôter tout prétexte à la mauvaise foi, il faut déterminer exactement dans le compromis le sujet de la contestation, les prétentions respectives et opposées, les demandes de l'un et les oppositions de l'autre.

Voilà ce qui est soumis aux arbitres, ce sur quoi on promet de s'en tenir à leur jugement. Alors, si leur sentence demeure dans ces bornes précises, il faut s'y soumettre. On ne peut point dire qu'elle soit manifestement injuste, puisqu'elle prononce sur une question que le dissentiment des parties rendoit douteuse, qui a été soumise comme telle. Pour se soustraire à une pareille sentence, il faudroit prouver par des faits indubitables qu'elle est l'ouvrage de la corruption ou d'une partialité ouverte.

L'arbitrage est un moyen très raisonnable et très conforme à la loi naturelle, pour terminer tout différent qui n'intéresse pas directement le salut de la nation. Si le bon droit peut être méconnu des arbitres, il est plus à craindre encore qu'il ne succombe par le sort des armes.

JEREMY BENTHAM ON AN INTERNATIONAL TRIBUNAL.

Bentham's Scheme is derived from "The Fragments of an Essay on International Law by Jeremy Bentham," published from MSS. bearing date from 1786-1789. These fragments consist of four short Essays :—1. On the objects of International Law. 2. On the subjects ; or personal extent of the dominion of the laws of any State. 3. On War, considered in respect to its causes and consequences. 4. A PLAN FOR AN UNIVERSAL AND PERPETUAL PEACE.

AN INTERNATIONAL CODE, he declares, ought to regulate the conduct of nations in their mutual intercourse. Its objects for any given nation would be—(1) general utility, so far as it consists in doing no injury, and (2) in doing the greatest possible good to other nations, to which two objects, he says, the *duties* which the given nation ought to recognise may be referred ; and (3) general utility, in so far as it consists in not receiving injury, or (4) in receiving the greatest possible benefit from other nations, to which the *rights* it ought to claim may be referred.

But if these rights be violated there is, at present, no mode of seeking compensation but that of *War*, which is not only an evil, it is the complication of all other evils.

The fifth object of an International Code would be to make such arrangements that the least possible evil may be produced by War consistently with the acquisition of the good which is sought for.

"The laws of Peace would be the substantive laws of the International Code : the laws of War would be the adjective laws of the same Code."

PREVENTION OF WAR.

For this he proposes a plan for an universal and perpetual Peace.

This plan is grounded upon two fundamental propositions, both of which he deems indispensable to its success:—

1. The reduction and fixation of the forces of the several nations that compose the European system;

2. The emancipation of the colonial dependencies of each State.

In treating of these he lays down fourteen Pacific Propositions, which he discusses in detail within the limits of his notes.

The elaboration of the thirteenth of these includes his scheme. It is as follows:—

Proposal XIII.—That the maintenance of such a permanent pacification might be considerably facilitated by the establishment of a Common Court of Judicature for the decision of differences between the several nations, although such Court were not to be armed with any coercive powers.

I. "It is an observation of somebody's, that no nation ought to yield any evident point of justice to another.

"This must mean, evident in the eyes of the nation that is to judge, evident in the eyes of the nation called upon to yield. What does this amount to? That no nation is to give up any thing of what it looks upon as its rights:—no nation is to make any concessions. Wherever there is any difference of opinion between the negotiators of the two nations, war is to be the consequence.

"While there is no common tribunal, something might be said for this. Concession to notorious injustice invites fresh injustice."

II. But, "Establish a common tribunal, the necessity for war no longer follows from difference of opinion. Just or unjust, the decision of the Arbiters will save the credit, the honour of the contending party."

III. "Can the arrangement proposed be justly styled visionary, when it has been proved of it that—

1. "It is the interest of the parties concerned;

2. "They are already sensible of that interest;

3. "The situation it would place them in is no new one, nor any other than the original situation they set out from."

IV. "Difficult and complicated Conventions have been [already] effectuated:" *e.g.*, "(1) The Armed Neutrality, (2) the American Confederation, (3) the German Diet, (4) the Swiss League. Why should not the European fraternity subsist as well as the German Diet or the Swiss League?"

"These latter have no ambitious views. Be it so; but is not this already become the case with the former?

"How then shall we concentrate the approbation of the people, and obviate their prejudices?

"One main object of the plan is to effectuate a reduction, and that a mighty one, in the contributions of the people. The amount of the reduction for each nation should be stipulated in the treaty; and even previous to the signature of it, laws for the purpose might be prepared in each nation, and presented to every other, ready to be enacted, as soon as the treaty should be ratified in each State.

"By these means the mass of people, the part most exposed to be led away by prejudices, would not be sooner apprised of the measure, than they would feel the relief it brought them. They would see it was for their advantage it was calculated, and that it could not be calculated for any other purpose.

V. "Such a Congress or Diet might be constituted by each Power sending two deputies to the place of meeting: one of these to be the principal, the other to act as an occasional substitute.

VI. "The proceedings of such Congress or Diet should be all public.

VII. "Its power would consist:—

1. "In reporting its opinion.

2. "In causing that opinion to be circulated in the dominion

of each State. Manifestoes are in common use. A manifesto is designed to be read either by the subjects of the State complained of, or by other States, or by both. It is an appeal to them. It calls for their opinion. The difference is, that in that case (of a manifesto) nothing of proof is given; no opinion regularly made known.

3. "After a certain time, in putting the refractory State under the ban of Europe.

"There might, perhaps, be no harm in regulating as a last resource, the contingent to be furnished by the several States for enforcing the decrees of the Court. But the necessity for the employment of this resource would, in all human probability, be superseded for ever by having recourse to the much more simple and less burthensome expedient of introducing into the instrument by which such Court was instituted a clause, guaranteeing the liberty of the press in each State, in such sort, that the Diet might find no obstacle to its giving, in every State, to its decrees, and to every paper whatever, which it might think proper to sanction with its signature, the most extensive and unlimited circulation."—WORKS, VOL. II., pp. 546 and *seq.*

KANT ON A PERMANENT CONGRESS OF NATIONS.

A True Peace Status.

Since the natural state of peoples, like that of individuals, is one that must be abandoned in order to enter a state regulated by law, before this can take place, every public right and every external Mine-and-Thine of States, which can be acquired and preserved by War, are merely *provisional*, and can become effectively authoritative, and so form a true Peace Status, only in a Universal Union of States (by a process analagous to that whereby a people becomes a State). But because so great an extension of such an Association of States over wide districts must render even Government itself, and consequently the protection of every member, at length impossible, and because a number of such Corporations will lead again to a State of War, therefore, *Perpetual Peace* (the final goal of International Law), is really an impracticable idea. The political principles, however, which tend to that result, viz., to such a Union of States as shall serve as continual approximation thereto, are not themselves impossible; but as this approximation is a matter founded upon duty, and consequently upon the rights of men and of States, it is certainly practicable.

A Permanent Congress of Nations.

Such a Union of single States, having for its object the preservation of Peace, might be termed the Permanent Congress of Nations, to which every neighbouring State might be at liberty to associate itself. Such (at least so far as concerned the formalities of International Law in regard to the maintenance of Peace) was the Diplomatic Conference formed at the Hague during the first half of this century (the eighteenth), where the Ministers of most of the European Courts and even of the

EIN PERMANENTER STAATEN-CONGRESS.

VON IMMANUEL KANT, 1796.

EIN WAHRER FRIEDENSZUSTAND.

Da der Naturzustand der Völker ebensowohl, als einzelner Menschen, ein Zustand ist, aus dem man herausgehen soll, um in einen gesetzlichen zu treten, so ist vor diesem Ereigniss alles Recht der Völker und alles durch den Krieg erwerbliche oder erhaltbare äussere Mein und Dein der Staaten blos *provisorisch*, und kann nur in einem allgemeinen *Staatenverein* (analogisch mit dem, wodurch ein Volk Staat wird), *peremtorisch* geltend und ein wahrer *Fridenszustand* werden. Weil aber, bei gar zu grosser Ausdehnung eines solchen Völkerstaats über weite Landstriche, die Regierung desselben, mithin auch die Beschützung eines jeden Gliedes endlich unmöglich werden muss; eine Menge solcher Corporationen aber wiederum einen Kriegszustand herbeiführt; so ist der *ewige Friede*, (das letzte Ziel des ganzen Völkerrechts,) freilich eine unausführbare Idee. Die politischen Grundsätze aber, die darauf abzwecken, nämlich solche Verbindungen der Staaten einzugehen, als zur continuirlichen *Annäherung* zu demselben dienen, sind es nicht, sondern, so wie diese eine auf der Pflicht, mithin auch auf dem Rechte der Menschen und Staaten gegründete Aufgabe ist, allerdings ausführbar.

EIN PERMANENTER STAATEN-CONGRESS.

Man kann einen solchen *Verein* einiger *Staaten*, um den Frieden zu erhalten, den *permanenten Staatencongress* nennen, zu welchem sich zu gesellen, jedem benachbarten unbenommen bleibt; dergleichen, (wenigstens was die Förmlichkeiten des Völkerrechts in Absicht, auf die Erhaltung des Friedens betrifft), smallest Republics brought their complaints respecting Acts of War which occurred between them. In this manner they formed the whole of Europe into one federal State, which they accepted as Arbitrator in their political differences. Later on, the Law of Nations, which had vanished from the Cabinets, was preserved merely in books, or was confided to the obscurity of Archives, in the form of deductions, after force had been already employed.

A Revocable Association.

But by a Congress will be here understood only a Voluntary Association of the various States, which should be at all times revocable, and not, like that of the States of America, a Union founded on a formal Constitution, and therefore indissoluble. It is in this way only that the idea can be realised of establishing a public Law of Nations which may determine their differences by a civil method, like the judicial proceedings among individuals (Process) and not by a barbarous one (after the manner of savages), that is to say, by War.—Kant, "Rechtslehre," Part II., § 61.

in der ersten Hälfte dieses Jahrhunderts in der Versammlung der Generalstaaten im Haag noch stattfand; wo die Minister der meisten europäischen Höfe, und selbst der kleinsten Republiken, ihre Beschwerden über die Befehdungen, die einem von dem anderen widerfahren waren, anbrachten, und so sich ganz Europa als einen einzigen föderirten Staat dachten, den sie in jener ihren öffentlichen Streitigkeiten gleichsam als Schiedsrichter annahmen, statt dessen späterhin das Völkerrecht blos in Büchern übrig geblieben, aus Cabinetten aber verschwunden, oder nach schon verübter Gewalt, in Form der Deductionen, der Dunkelheit der Archive anvertraut worden ist.

Eine ablösliche Zusammentretung.

Unter einem *Congress* wird hier aber nur eine willkührliche, zu aller Zeit *ablösliche* Zusammentretung verschiedener Staaten, nicht eine solche Verbindung, welche (so wie die der amerikanischen Staaten,) auf einer Staatsverfassung gegründet und daher unauflöslich ist, verstanden; — durch welchen allein die Idee eines zu errichtenden öffentlichen Rechts der Völker, ihre Streitigkeiten auf civile Art, gleichsam durch einen Process, nicht auf barbarische (nach Art der Wilden), nämlich durch Krieg zu entscheiden, realisirt werden kann.—Kant, "Rechtslehre," II. Theil, § 61.

LE CONGRÈS PERMANENT.

Par Emm. Kant.

Un Véritable État de Paix.

Puisque l'état naturel des peuples, comme celui des hommes en particulier, doit être quitté pour entrer dans un état légal,—avant qu'il en soit ainsi, tout droit des peuples, tout Mien-et-Tien extérieur des Etats qui peut être acquis ou conservé par la guerre, est seulement *provisoire ;* il ne peut valoir *péremptoirement* et devenir un véritable *état de paix* que dans l'universelle *union des cités* (par analogie avec les moyens par lesquels un peuple devient un Etat). Mais comme une trop grande étendue d'une pareille cité de peuples à la surface du globe en rendrait impossible le gouvernement, par conséquent aussi la protection de chaque membre de cette cité universelle, attendu qu'ils sont trop disséminés, trop loin les uns des autres, il ne se forme que des corporations partielles, ce qui entraîne un nouvel état de guerre. Ainsi une *paix perpétuelle* (fin dernière de tout droit des gens) est sans doute une idée impraticable. Mais les principes politiques qui tendent à opérer de telles réunions de cités, comme pour favoriser l'*approximation* sans fin de cet état de paix perpétuelle, ne sont pas eux-mêmes impossibles ; et comme cette approximation est une question fondée sur le devoir, par conséquent aussi une question fondée sur le droit des hommes et des Etats, elle est sans doute pratiquable.

Le Congrès Permanent.

On peut appeler cette *alliance* de quelques *Etats*, pour le maintien de la paix, le *congrès permanent* auquel chaque Etat voisin est libre de s'adjoindre ; ce qui (au moins quant aux formalités du droit des gens à l'égard du maintien de la paix) a eu lieu dans la première moitié de ce siècle lors de l'assemblée des Etats généraux à La Haye, où les ministres de la plupart des cours de l'Europe et même des plus petites républiques, portèrent leurs plaintes sur les hostilités commises les unes contre les autres, et firent ainsi de toute l'Europe une confédération qu'ils prirent pour arbitre dans leurs différends politiques. Plus tard le droit des gens, abandonné aux écoles, disparut des cabinets, ou fut confié à l'obscurité des archives, sous forme de déductions, après qu'on eut déjà fait usage de la force.

UNE UNION DISSOLUBLE.

Mais, dans un *congrès* de plusieurs Etats, il ne s'agit que d'une union arbitraire, *dissoluble* en tout temps, et non d'une union qui (comme celle des Etats d'Amérique) serait fondée sur une constitution publique, et par conséquent indissoluble. Ce n'est que de cette façon que l'Idée de la fondation d'un droit des gens, au nom duquel se décideraient les intérêts internationaux à la manière civile, c'est-à-dire, comme par un procès, et non d'une manière barbare (celle des sauvages) par la guerre, peut recevoir une exécution.—"Principes Métaphysiques du Droit," traduit par M. JOSEPH TISSOT, pages 237, 238.

NOTE.—That part of Kant's Rechtslehre relating to International Law was also translated into French and published at Paris in 1814, under the title of "Traité du droit des gens, dédié aux puissances alliées et leurs ministres, extrait d'un ouvrage de Kant." See also Kant, "Doctrine du Droit (Rechtslehre) traduit par Barni § LXI. p. 228."

ZUM EWIGEN FRIEDEN.

EIN PHILOSOPHISCHER ENTWURF

VON IMMANUEL KANT.

(Nach der zweiten Ausgabe von 1796).

ERSTER ABSCHNITT,

welcher die Präliminarartikel zum ewigen Frieden unter Staaten enthält.

1.—Es soll kein Friedensschluss für einen solchen gelten, der mit dem geheimen Vorbehalt des Stoffs zu einem künftigen Kriege gemacht worden.

2.—Es soll kein für sich bestehender Staat (klein oder gross, das gilt hier gleichviel) von einem andern Staate durch Erbung, Tausch, Kauf oder Schenkung erworben werden können.

3.—Stehende Heere *(miles perpetuus)* sollen mit der Zeit ganz aufhören.

4.—Es sollen keine Staatsschulden in Beziehung auf äussere Staatshändel gemacht werden.

5.—Kein Staat soll sich in die Verfassung und Regierung eines andern Staates gewaltthätig einmischen.

6.—Es soll sich kein Staat im Kriege mit einem andern solche Feindseligkein erlauben, welche das wechselseitige Zutrauen im künftigen Frieden unmöglich machen müssen; als da sind, Anstellung der Meuchelmörder (*percussores*), Giftmischer (*venefici*), Brechung der Capitulation, Anstiftung des Verraths (*perduellio*) in dem bekriegten Staat etc.

ZWEITER ABSCHNITT,

welcher die Definitivartikel zum ewigen Frieden unter Staaten enthält.

1.—Die bürgerliche Verfassung in jedem Staat soll republicanisch sein.

1. Die erstlich nach Principien der Freiheit der Glieder einer Gesellschaft (als Menschen;
2. zweitens nach Grundsätzen der Abhängigkeit Aller von einer einzigen gemeinsamen Gesetzgebung (als Unterthanen;

3. und drittens, die nach dem Gesetz der Gleichheit derselben (als Staatsbürger) gestiftete Verfassung;

ist die republicanische.

2.—Das Völkerrecht soll auf einen Föderalismus freier Staaten gegründet sein.

3.—Das Weltbürgerrecht soll auf Bedingungen der allgemeinen Hospitalität eingeschränkt sein.

Erster Zusatz.

Von der Garantie des ewigen Friedens.

Das, was diese Gewähr (Garantie) leistet, ist nichts Geringeres, als die grosse Künstlerin, Natur *(natura dædala rerum)*.

Ihre provisorische Veranstaltung besteht darin: dass sie

1. für die Menschen in allen Erdgegenden gesorgt hat, daselbst leben zu können;
2. sie durch Krieg allerwärts hin, selbst in die unwirthbarsten Gegenden, getrieben hat, um sie zu bevölkern;
3. durch eben denselben sie in mehr oder weniger gesetzliche Verhältnisse zu treten genöthigt hat.

Zweiter Zusatz.

Geheimer Artikel zum ewigen Frieden.

Der einzige Artikel dieser Art ist in dem Satze enthalten: "Die Maximen der Philosophen über die Bedingungen der Möglichkeit des öffentlichen Friedens sollen von den zum Kriege gerüsteten Staaten zu Rathe gezogen werden."

Anhang.

I. Über die Misshelligkeit zwischen der Moral und der Politik, in Absicht auf den ewigen Frieden.

II. Von der Einhelligkeit der Politik mit der Moral nach dem transcendentalen Begriffe des öffentlichen Rechts.

* * *

Wenn es Pflicht, wenn zugleich gegründete Hoffnung da ist, den Zustand eines öffentlichen Rechts, obgleich nur in einer ins Unendliche fortschreitenden Annäherung wirklich zu machen, so ist der ewige Friede, der auf die bisher fälschlich so genannten Friedensschlüsse (eigentlich Waffenstillstände) folgt, keine leere Idee, sondern eine Aufgabe, die nach und nach aufgelöst, ihrem Ziele (weil die Zeiten, in denen gleiche Fortschritte geschehen, hoffentlich immer kürzer werden) beständig näher kommt.

KANT'S "PERPETUAL PEACE."

Kant's scheme was published in the year 1795, when the author, accordingly, was 71 years of age. The immediate occasion of its publication was undoubtedly the Congress of Bâle, which took place in the year 1795, and by which the war carried on between Germany and France, for the preceding four years, was brought to a brief termination.

The scheme contains no reference to a Tribunal. It consisted of two sections :—

First Section,

which contains the Preliminary Articles for a perpetual Peace between States.

Art. 1.—No conclusion of Peace shall be considered valid which has been made with the secret reservation of material for a future war.

Art. 2.—No State having an independent existence (whether small or large), may be acquired by another State by inheritance, exchange, purchase, or gift.

Art. 3.—Standing armies shall in the course of time be entirely abolished.

Art. 4.—No national debts shall be contracted in connection with the foreign affairs of the State.

Art. 5.—No State shall interfere by force with the Constitution or Government of another State.

Art. 6.—No State at war with another shall permit such hostilities as would make mutual confidence impossible in a

LA PAIX PERPÉTUELLE, PAR EMMANUEL KANT.

Le Projet de Kant a été publié en 1795, quand l'auteur avait 71 ans, et quand la paix de Bâle, signée en 1795, mit fin à la lutte engagée, pendant quatre ans, par la Prusse contre la République française. La traduction française fut faite en 1796, sur la deuxième édition allemande.

Le Projet ne fait pas mention d'un Tribunal. Il comprend deux sections :

Première Section.

Articles préliminaires d'une paix perpétuelle entre les Etats.

Article 1er.—Nul traité de paix ne peut mériter ce nom s'il contient des réserves secrètes qui permettent de recommencer la guerre.

Art. 2.—Nul Etat, qu'il soit grand ou petit, ce qui est ici tout à fait indifférent, ne pourra jamais être acquis par un autre Etat, ni par héritage, ni par échange, ni par achat, ni par donation.

Art. 3.—Les armées permanentes (*miles perpetuus*) doivent entièrement disparaître avec le temps.

Art. 4.—On ne doit point contracter de dettes nationales pour soutenir au dehors les intérêts de l'Etat.

Art. 5.—Aucun Etat ne doit s'ingérer de force dans la constitution ni dans le gouvernement d'un autre Etat.

Art. 6.—On ne doit pas se permettre, dans une guerre, des hostilités qui seraient de nature à rendre impossible la confiance future peace; such as the employment of assassins (*percussores*) or poisoners (*venefici*), the violation of a capitulation, the instigation of treason in a State (*perduellio*) against which it is making war, and such like.

SECOND SECTION,

which contains the Definitive Articles for a perpetual Peace between States.

ART. 1.—The civil constitution in every State ought to be republican.

A Republican Constitution is one that is founded—

(1.) On the principle of the *Liberty* of the members of a society (as men);

(2.) On the principle of the *Dependence* of all on a single common Legislation (as subjects);

(3.) And thirdly, on the law of *Equality* of its members (as citizens).

ART. 2.—International right should be founded on a federation of Free States.

ART. 3.—The rights of men as citizens of the world should be restricted to conditions of universal hospitality.

FIRST SUPPLEMENT
OF THE GUARANTEE OF PERPETUAL PEACE.

This guarantee is furnished by nothing less than the great artist Nature herself (*Natura dædala rerum*).

The provisional arrangements of Nature are these:—

(1.) She has made it possible for men to live in all parts of the earth.

réciproque quand il sera question de la paix. Tels seraient l'usage que l'on ferait d'assassins (*percussores*), ou d'empoissonneurs (*venefici*), la violation d'une capitulation, l'encouragement secret à la rébellion (*perduellio*), etc. etc.

Deuxième Section.

Articles définitifs d'un Traité de Paix perpétuelle entre les Etats.

Article 1er.—La Constitution civile de chaque Etat doit être républicaine.

Elle seule est établie sur des principes compatibles :

1°. Avec la liberté qui doit appartenir à tous les membres d'une société en leur qualité d'hommes ;

2°. Avec l'égale soumission de tous à une législation commune comme sujets ;

3°. Enfin, avec le droit d'égalité qui appartient à tous et à chacun comme membres de l'Etat.

Art. 2.—Le Droit international doit être fondé sur une fédéra tion d'Etats libres.

Art. 3.—Le Droit cosmopolitique doit se borner aux conditions d'une hospitalité universelle.

Premier Supplément

de la garantie de la Paix perpétuelle.

Nous avons pour garant de la Paix perpétuelle l'ingénieuse et grande ouvrière, la Nature elle-même (*natura dædala rerum*).

Voici ses dispositions préparatoires :

1°. Elle a mis les hommes en état de vivre dans tous les climats ;

(2.) She has dispersed them everywhere by means of war, so that they might populate even the most inhospitable regions.

(3.) By this same means she has compelled them to enter into relations more or less of a judicial character.

Second Supplement.

Secret Article for Securing Perpetual Peace.

The only Article of this kind is contained in the following proposition: *The maxims of philosophers as to the conditions of the possibility of a public Peace must be taken into account by the States that are armed for war.*

Appendix.

I. On the disagreement between Morality and Politics in reference to Perpetual Peace.

II. Of the Agreement between Politics and Morality according to the transcendental conception of Public Right.

If it is a duty to bring about a state of Public Right (*i.e.*, a juridical status), if at the same time there is a well-grounded hope of doing so, though only by an approximation that seems altogether indefinite, then is Perpetual Peace, which is to follow the hitherto falsely-named *Treaties of Peace* (strictly speaking, only armistices), no empty idea, but a practical problem which, by being gradually solved, is ever coming nearer to its consummation, because these times of progress are, let us hope, hastening its approach.

2°. Elle les a dispersés au moyen de la guerre, afin qu'ils peuplassent les régions les plus inhospitalières ;

3°. Elle les a forcés par la même voie à contracter des relations plus ou moins juridiques.

DEUXIÈME SUPPLÉMENT.

Article secret d'un Traité de Paix perpétuelle.

Ici le seul article de ce genre sera le suivant :

" *Les maximes des philosophes sur les conditions qui rendent possible la Paix perpétuelle doivent être consultées par les Etats armés pour la guerre.*"

APPENDICE.

I. De l'opposition qui se trouverait entre la morale et la politique au sujet de la Paix perpétuelle.

II. De l'accord que l'idée transcendante du droit établit entre la politique et la morale.

S'il est de devoir, si même on peut concevoir l'espérance fondée de réaliser, quoique par des progrès sans fin, le règne du droit public, la paix perpétuelle qui succédera aux *Trèves*, jusqu'ici nommées *Traités de Paix*, n'est donc pas une chimère, mais un problème dont le temps, vraisemblablement abrégé par l'accélération de la marche progressive de l'esprit humain, nous promet la solution.

A FEDERAL SUPREME COURT.

By John Stuart Mill, 1806-1873.

In his treatise on Representative Government, Mr. Mill has the following "considerations" :—

To render a Federation advisable several conditions are necessary.

1. That there should be a sufficient amount of mutual sympathy among the populations.

2. That the separate States be not so powerful as to be able to rely for protection against foreign encroachments on their individual strength.

3. A third condition, not less important than the two others, is that there be not a very marked inequality of strength among the several contracting States.

There are two different modes of organising a Federal Union :—

1. The federal authorities may represent the Governments solely, and then acts may be obligatory only on the Governments as such :

2. Or, they may have the power of enacting laws and issuing orders which are binding directly on individual citizens.

The former is the plan of the German so-called Confederation, and of the Swiss Constitution previous to 1847 ; and it was tried in America for a few years, immediately following the War of Independence. The other principle is that of the existing constitutions of the United States and of the present Swiss Confederacy.

A Supreme Court of Justice.

Under the more perfect mode of federation, where every citizen of each particular State owes obedience to two Governments, that of his own State, and that of the Federation, it is evidently necessary not only that the constitutional limits of the authority of each should be precisely and clearly defined, but that the power to decide between them in any case of dispute should not reside in either of the Governments, or in any functionary subject to it, but in an umpire independent of both. There must be a Supreme Court of Justice, and a system of subordinate Courts in every State of the Union, before whom such questions shall be carried, and whose judgment on them, in the last stage of appeal, shall be final.

2. Every State of the Union, and the Federal Government itself, as well as every functionary of each, must be liable to be sued in those Courts for exceeding their powers, or for non-performance of their federal duties, and must in general be obliged to employ those Courts as the instrument for enforcing their federal rights.

3. This involves the remarkable consequence, actually realised in the United States, that a Court of Justice, the highest Federal tribunal, is supreme over the various Governments, both State and Federal; having the right to declare that any law made, or act done by them, exceeds the powers assigned to them by the Federal Constitution, and, in consequence, has no legal validity.

4. The tribunals which act as umpires between the Federal and the State Governments naturally also decide all disputes between two States, or between a citizen of one State and the Government of another. The usual remedies between nations, war and diplomacy, being precluded by the federal union, it is necessary that a judicial remedy should supply their place.

5. The Supreme Court of the Federation dispenses international law, and is the first great example of what is now one of the most prominent wants of civilised society, a real International Tribunal.

6. The powers of a Federal Government naturally extend not only to Peace and war, and all questions which arise between the country and foreign Governments, but to making any other arrangements which are, in the opinion of the States, necessary to their enjoyment of the full benefits of union.

THE POSSIBLE MEANS OF PREVENTING WAR IN EUROPE.

By the Late Professor Sir J. R. Seeley, K.C.M.G., Litt.D.

(*From a Lecture delivered February 28th*, 1871.)

Civil Society has for its principal object the prevention of private war, and if war between individuals, between townships, between countries, between particular nations can be prevented, can be permanently abolished, why not between nations generally?

Compared with any properly organised legal system, what is deemed the justice of war is simply deplorable. If there is some justice in war there is not anything like enough of it. A proper legal decision is not one in which justice enters; but one in which nothing but justice enters.

The proper cure for popular indifference is a feasible and statesmanlike scheme of Arbitration, such a scheme as should take account of details, and provide contrivances to meet practical difficulties.

The object of this lecture is to offer some suggestions to those who may wish to find out in what way a system of International Arbitration can practically be realised.

The introduction of such a system involves a vast number of political changes, but is not on that account to be considered Utopian, because a Utopian scheme is not merely a vast one, but one which proposes an end disproportionate to the means at command, whilst the means available here, the forces, the influences that may be called in for the accomplishment of this work, are as enormous as the difficulty of the work itself.

I. The international system wanted is something essentially different from, and cannot be developed out of, the already existing system by which European affairs are settled in Congresses of the Great Powers.

What is wanted is something in the nature of a Law-court for international differences. Now, a European Concert has nothing of the nature of a Law-court, and when people call it an Areopagus, or apply to it other epithets proper to judicial assemblies, they are surely guilty of an inadvertence which needs only to be briefly indicated. A Law-court may, of course, have many defects, and yet not cease to be a law-court; but the defect of the European Congress is not an incidental and venial, but a radical, and, therefore, fatal defect. What should we think of a judicial bench every member of which was closely connected by interests with the litigants, and on which, in the most important cases, the litigants themselves invariably sat?

That the judges should be avowedly partial is quite enough to strip them of all judicial character; but when the litigants are among the great European powers they are *judges in their own cause*. An ambassador cannot be at the same time a judge; and a Congress of plenipotentiaries cannot possibly be a Law-court. There ought to be no representation of interests on a judicial bench. A good court is, not where both parties are represented on the bench, but where neither is.

II. The system wanted necessarily involves a Federation of all the Powers that are to reap the benefits of it.

We have a problem of Federation before us, and not merely of constituting a law-court. The law-court is not only historically found invariably within the State, but it also takes all its character and efficiency from the State. It is a matter of demonstration that a State is implied in a law-court, and as a necessary consequence, that an international law-court implies an international State. The nations of Europe must therefore constitute themselves into some sort of federation, or the international court can never come into existence. Judges cannot constitute themselves, and a judicial assembly is inconceivable without a legislative assembly of some kind executing its sentences.

III. In order to be really vigorous and effectual, such a system absolutely requires a federation of the closer kind; that is, a federation not after the model of the late German Bund, but after the model of the United States, a federation with a complete apparatus of powers, legislative, executive, and judicial, and raised above all dependence upon State Governments.

In spite of their one internal war the American Union may be said to have solved the problem of the abolition of war, and we may see there the model which Europe should imitate in her international relations. Now this great triumph of the Union was achieved on the very ground upon which an earlier confederation had conspicuously failed in the same undertaking; and a comparison of the two federations shows that where the federal organisation was lax, and not decisively disentangled from the State organisation, the federation failed; it succeeded when the federal bond was strengthened.

IV. The indispensable condition of success in such a system, is that the power of levying troops be assigned to the Federation only, and be absolutely denied to the individual States.

The special lesson which is taught by the experience of the Americans is, that the decrees of the Federation must not be handed over for execution to the officials of the separate States, but that the Federation must have an independent and separate executive, through which its authority must be brought to bear directly upon individuals. The individual must be distinctly conscious of his obligations to the Federation, and of his membership in it; all federations are mockeries that are mere understandings between governments.

"There has been found hitherto but one substitute for war. It has succeeded over and over again; it succeeds regularly in the long run wherever it can be introduced. This is, to take the disputed question out of the hands of the disputants, to refer it to a third party, whose intelligence, impartiality, and diligence have been secured, and to impose his decision upon the parties with overwhelming force. The last step in this process, the power of enforcing the decisions by the federal union only, is just as essential as the earlier ones, and if you omit it you may just as well omit them too."

[But, happily, historical fact does not agree with this statement of Professor Seeley; for in the instances of successful arbitration, to which he has just referred, there is not a single one in which force has had to be employed in order to compel obedience to the decision of the arbitrator. This follows from the nature of the reference to Arbitration, in which it is essential that the contending parties should agree together to refer the matter in dispute to Arbitrators, and should, by implication if not formally, as is sometimes done, bind themselves to carry out the award, which then becomes a matter of honour and good faith.—ED.]

ARBITRATION PROCEEDINGS

BY DR. J. C. BLUNTSCHLI.

1867.

1. Parties, between whom differences have arisen, may refer the settlement of their dispute to Arbitration.

2. As a rule, the parties who desire Arbitration have the right of freely appointing the Arbitrator.

3. If the parties cannot agree in the choice of Arbitrators, each of them is allowed to choose an equal number. In the absence of a special agreement, the choice of an umpire is made by the Arbitrators themselves or remitted by them to some neutral person or power.

4. The Arbitral Tribunal, when it is composed of several persons, acts as a corporate body. It hears the parties, examines witnesses and experts, weighs the important facts and considers the evidence.

5. The Tribunal is authorised, in case of doubt, to make to the parties equitable proposals with a view to the adjustment of the difference.

6. The Tribunal decides on the interpretation of the Arbitration Agreement, and, as to its own competency in conformity therewith.

7. The decision of the majority has the force of a decision of the whole Tribunal.

8. The decision of the Tribunal has for the parties the force of an Agreement or Treaty.

SCHIEDSRICHTERLICHES VERFAHREN.

Von Dr. J. C. Bluntschli.

1867.

1. Die streitenden Parteien können auch die Erledigung ihres Streites einem Schiedsgericht übertragen.

2. In der Regel steht es den Parteien, welche ein Schiedsgericht berufen, frei, zu bestimmen, wem das Schiedsrichteramt übertragen werde.

3. Vertragen sich die Parteien nicht über gemeinsam zu ernennende Schiedsrichter, so ist anzunehmen, jede Partei wähle ihre Schiedsmänner frei, aber in gleicher Anzahl, wie die Gegenpartei. Ist nicht verabredet, wie der Obmann zu bezeichnen sei, so steht es den beiderseitigen Schiedsrichtern zu, entweder den Obmann gemeinsam zu wählen oder einem unparteiischen Dritten die Wahl desselben anheim zu geben.

4. Das aus mehreren Personen bestehende Schiedsgericht handelt gemeinsam als Ein Körper. Es vernimmt die Parteien und je nach Umständen auch Zeugen und Sachverständige, prüft die erheblichen Thatsachen und erhebt die erforderlichen Beweise.

5. Das Schiedsgericht gilt im Zweifel als ermächtigt, den Parteien billige Vergleichsvorschläge zu machen.

6. Das Schiedsgericht urtheilt über die Auslegung des Compromisses der Parteien und demgemäss über seine Competenz.

7. Der Spruch der Mehrheit gilt als Spruch des ganzen Schiedsgerichts.

8. Der Spruch des Schiedsgerichts wirkt für die Parteien, wie ein Vergleich.

9. The decision of the Tribunal may be considered, by either of the parties, invalid—

(*a*) In so far as the Tribunal has exceeded its powers;

(*b*) Through any dishonest proceeding on the part of the Arbitrators;

(*c*) If the Arbitrators have refused to hear the parties or openly violated some other fundamental principle of legal procedure;

(*d*) If the substance of the decision is incompatible with International Law or human rights;

but the arbitral decision cannot be attacked on the ground of its being wrong or unfair towards one of the litigants. The rectification of mere miscalculation remains reserved.

10. In Confederations of States, such as Federal Republics, Monarchies or Empires, the differences which arise between the different States of the Confederation, or between these and the Federal, Central, or Imperial Power, are, as a matter of course, referred either to an Arbitration Tribunal provided for in the constitution, or to the ordinary Federal or, Imperial Tribunal, for disposal and decision. In the first case, the Arbitration Tribunal exercises a jurisdiction derived not merely from the agreement between the parties, but also from the constitution itself.

11. Provision may be made beforehand, in treaties relating to the differences which may arise between independent States, for the mode of nominating the Arbitrators and the procedure to be adopted by them; and the Tribunal thus constituted will possess an actual jurisdiction.

12. It is reserved for the further development of a genuine International Law, even through the solidarity it secures, to provide generally for the establishment of a regulated Arbitration procedure, particularly in regard to differences arising from claims for indemnity, questions of precedence, and others, which do not affect the existence and the development of the State.

9. Der Spruch des Schiedsgerichts kann von einer Partei als ungültig angefochten werden:

(*a.*) Wenn und soweit das Schiedsgericht dabei seine Vollmachten überschritten hat.

(*b.*) Wegen unredlichen Verfahrens der Schiedsrichter.

(*c.*) Wenn das Schiedsgericht den Parteien das Gehör verweigert oder sonst die Fundamentalgrundsätze alles Rechtsverfahrens offenbar verletzt hat.

(*d.*) Wenn der Inhalt des Spruchs mit den Geboten des Völker- und Menschenrechts unverträglich ist.

Aber der Schiedsspruch darf nicht aus dem Grunde angefochten werden, dass er unrichtig oder für eine Partei unbillig sei. Vorbehalten bleibt die Berichtigung blosser Rechnungsfehler.

10. In zusammengesetzten Staaten (Staatenbünden, Bundesstaaten, Staatenreichen, Bundesreichen) werden die Streitigkeiten der Einzelnstaten unter sich oder mit der Bundes- oder Central- oder Reichsgewalt je nach Umständen an verfassungsmässige Schiedsgerichte oder an festgeordnete Bundes- oder Reichsgerichte zur Verhandlung und Entscheidung verwiesen. Im erstern Fall übt das Schiedsgericht eine Gerichtsbarkeit aus, welche nicht bloss auf dem Compromiss der Parteien, sondern zugleich auf der Verfassung beruht.

11. Durch Staatenverträge können ebenso für vorgesehene Streitigkeiten, welche unter den von einander unabhängigen Staaten entstehen würden, zum Voraus nähere Vorschriften über ein schiedsrichterliches Verfahren festgesetzt und das Schiedsgericht mit einer wirklichen Gerichtsbarkeit ausgerüstet werden.

12. Der Fortbildung eines gesicherten Völkerrechts bleibt es vorbehalten, auch durch völkerrechtliche Vereinbarungen überhaupt für ein geordnetes schiedsrichterliches Verfahren zu sorgen, insbesondere bei Streitigkeiten über Entschädigungsforderungen, ceremonielle Ansprüche und andere Dinge, welche nicht die Existenz und Entwicklung des Staates selbst betreffen.

ARBITRAGES.

Par M. le Docteur J. C. Bluntschli.

1867.

1. Les parties peuvent remettre à un tribunal arbitral la décision de la question qui les divise.

2. Les parties ont dans la règle le droit de désigner librement celui auquel elles veulent confier les fonctions d'arbitre.

3. Si les parties ne peuvent tomber d'accord sur le choix des arbitres, on admet que chaque partie en nomme le même nombre. A moins de conventions spéciales, les arbitres désigent eux-mêmes un sur-arbitre, ou remettent à un tiers le soin de le désigner.

4. Le tribunal arbitral forme un corps indépendant et agit comme collège, lorsqu'il est composé de plusieurs juges. Il entend les parties, fait comparaître les témoins ou les experts, et rassemble toutes les preuves nécessaires.

5. Le tribunal arbitral est autorisé, dans le doute, à faire aux parties des propositions équitables dans le but d'arriver à une transaction.

6. Le tribunal arbitral statue sur l'interprétation du compromis entre les parties, et par conséquent sur sa propre compétence.

7. La décision est prise à la majorité des voix, et oblige le tribunal entier.

8. La décision des arbitres a pour les parties les mêmes effets qu'une transaction.

9. La décision du tribunal arbitral peut être considérée comme nulle :

(*a.*) Dans la mesure en laquelle le tribunal arbitral a dépassé ses pouvoirs ;

(*b.*) En cas de déloyauté et de déni de justice de la part des arbitres ;

(*c.*) Si les arbitres ont refusé d'entendre les parties ou violé quelque autre principe fondamental de la procédure ;

(*d.*) Si la décision arbitrale est contraire au droit international. Mais la décision des arbitres ne peut être attaquée sous le prétexte qu'elle est erronée ou contraire à l'équité. Les erreurs de calcul demeurent réservées.

10. Dans les confédérations d'états et dans les républiques ou monarchies fédératives, les difficultés qui s'élèvent entre les divers états de la confédération ou entre ceux-ci et le pouvoir central, sont renvoyées soit à un tribunal arbitral, soit aux tribunaux ordinaires de la confédération. Dans le premier cas, la compétence du tribunal arbitral repose non seulement sur un compromis des parties, mais encore sur la constitution.

11. On peut aussi régler à l'avance, par des traités, le mode de nomination des arbitres et la procédure à suivre pour trancher les difficultés qui pourraient s'élever entre deux états indépendants ; le tribunal arbitral aura dans ce cas de véritables droits de juridiction.

12. Le droit international, en se développant, ne tardera pas à régulariser le mode de nomination des arbitres, et à fixer la procédure à suivre pour aplanir certaines difficultés, spécialement les questions de dédommagements, d'étiquette et autres, qui ne menacent ni l'existence, ni le développement des états.

THE ORGANISATION OF A EUROPEAN FEDERATION.

BY DR. J. C. BLUNTSCHLI.

A glance at the early political history of Europe shows that the idea of the organisation of the European States into a Union has been familiar to its princes and peoples for centuries, and is by no means chimerical; and a glance at the present conditions of existence amongst the European nations reveals a natural growth of the desire for a better organisation of Europe which shall secure and strengthen both its Peace and its real interests.

. . . .

If the great problem of a constitution for the commonwealth of Europe is to be solved, the indispensable principle of its solution is the *careful preservation of the independence and freedom of the Associated States.*

. . . .

In order to form a proper organisation, the problems which the Union is called upon to solve must be further discussed.

These problems may be grouped in the following manner:—

1. Establishment and Enunciation of a *Code of International Law, International Legislation.*

2. Preservation of the *Peace of the Nations* and the Exercise of the *Higher International Politics.*

3. Management of matters of International Administration.

4. International Administration of Justice.

DIE ORGANISATION DES EUROPÄISCHEN STATENVEREINES.

VON J. C. BLUNTSCHLI.

Ein Blick auf die frühere Statengeschichte Europas überzeugt uns, dass der Gedanke einer Organisation des europäischen Statenvereines den europäischen Fürsten und Völkern schon seit Jahrhunderten bekannt und keineswegs ein chimärischer ist; und ein Blick auf die heutige europäische Lebensgemeinschaft zeigt uns ein naturgemässes Wachsthum des Verlangens nach einer besseren Organisation Europas, welche den europäischen Frieden sichere und stärke und die europäischen Interessen wirksam schütze.

. . . .

Soll das grosse Problem einer Verfassung für die europäische Statengenossenschaft gelöst werden, so ist die unerlässliche Grundbedingung dieser Lösung die *sorgfältige Wahrung der Selbständigkeit und Freiheit der verbündeten Staten.*

. . . .

Um eine richtige Organisation zu bilden, müssen ferner die Aufgaben erwogen werden, welche der Bund zu lösen berufen ist.

Diese Aufgaben lassen sich übersichtlich nach folgenden Gruppen ordnen:

(1) Festsetzung und Aussprache *völkerrechtlicher Normen, völkerrechtliche Gesetzgebung;*

(2) Bewahrung des *Völkerfriedens* und Ausübung der *grossen völkerrechtlichen Politik;*

(3) Besorgung der internationalen Verwaltungssachen;

(4) Internationale Rechtspflege.

International Legislation and High Politics.

For the enunciation and promulgation of a General International Code, a meeting of the Heads of States or of their ministers or representatives is, in our opinion, not sufficient: but the co-operation and concurrence of the Representative Assemblies, which also represent the opinions and views of the people, is indispensable.

I. The Legislative Organisation must therefore be formed from the Representatives of the collective European Governments, which together form the *European United Council.*

(1.) It might without hesitation be left to each Power to appoint and empower its *Representatives*; also the question whether a State should send one or more Representatives.

(2.) But the *Voting Power* to which each State shall lay claim in the United Council must be constitutionally fixed. It might answer the purpose if each State as a rule had one vote, or the States collected together might have one vote each, and only the Great Powers two.

In the United Council there would then be twenty-four votes, half for the Great Powers, and the other half for the other States.

(3.) The *European House of Representatives* or the *European Senate* which as Representatives of the European peoples, acts side by side with the United Council, should not, in my opinion, be very numerous, if it is to accomplish its work. Only men who are conversant with International Law and High Politics are suitable for it. Such men are all too few.

I would give to each of the Great Powers eight or ten Representatives, and to every other State four or five. This would give an Assembly of ninety-six or one hundred and twenty members.

Völkerrechtliche Gesetzgebung und grosse Politik.

Zur Aussprache und Verkündung allgemeiner völkerrechtlicher Normen (Gesetze) genügt nach unseren heutigen Begriffen nicht der Zusammentritt der Statshäupter oder ihrer Minister und Gesanten, sondern ist die Mitwirkung und Zustimmung von repräsentativen Versammlungen unerlässlich, welche die Meinungen und Rechtsansichten auch der Völker vertreten.

(1) Desshalb wird das Organ für die Gesetzgebung zusammen gesetzt sein müssen: aus Vertretern der sämmtlichen europäischen Statsregierungen, welche zusammen den *europäischen Bundesrath* bilden.

Man könnte es ohne Bedenken den Regierungen überlassen, ihre Vertreter zu bezeichnen und zu ermächtigen, gleichviel ob ein Stat einen oder mehrere Vertreter entsendet. Aber die Stimmenzahl, auf welche jeder Stat Anspruch hat in dem Bundesrathe, muss verfassungsmässig bestimmt sein. Es dürfte den Verhältnissen entsprechen, wenn jeder Stat in der Regel Eine Stimme, auch die zusammengesetzten Staten nur Eine Stimme führen und nur die Grossmächte jede zwei Stimmen haben.

In dem Bundesrathe gäbe es dann 24 Stimmen, die eine Hälfte der Grossmächte, die andere Hälfte der anderen Staten.

Das *europäische Repräsentantenhaus* oder der *europäische Senat*, welcher als Vertreter der europäischen Völker dem Bundesrathe an die Seite tritt, darf meines Erachtens nicht sehr zahlreich sein, wenn er seiner Aufgabe gewachsen sein soll. Nur Männer, welche des Völkerrechtes und der grossen politischen Verhältnisse in Europa kundig sind, passen dahin. Solche Männer gibt es nicht allzu viele.

Ich würde jeder Grossmacht etwa acht oder zehn Abgeordnete zutheilen und jedem anderen State vier oder fünf. Das gäbe eine Versammlung von 96 oder 120 Mitgliedern.

(4.) The *Mode of Election* of this European Senate would be left to the individual States; where, however, the Representatives of the people sit in one or two chambers, these should attend to the election.

(5.) *Actual* Voting in the Council must be according to States, and not according to individual members; in the Senate, on the other hand, individual voting is possible, and to be preferred. Members of the Council vote according to their instructions and powers; Senators according to their personal convictions.

(6.) The *difficulty of language* in such an international assembly is not insuperable. In the present state of culture, most educated men understand one or two foreign languages, besides their mother tongue, at least so far as to understand printed matter or a speech. In any case no one should be prevented from speaking in his native tongue. If the speakers wish to be understood by all or even the majority, they will have to speak in French or English or German. These three languages are most widely spread at the present day in Europe, and almost every educated man knows at least one of them. But if by exception a Senator can only speak in his mother tongue, care will have to be taken that his speech shall be translated into one of these universal tongues. This has been the procedure for some time now in Switzerland and at International Conferences.

(7.) The *place* of the sittings of the Senate may be suitably determined by the United Council, and would very well be changed from time to time into different countries. A regular meeting every two or three years is sufficient, as extraordinary meetings may be convened as necessity requires.

(8.) In the interest of the *Independence* of the separate States,

Die Wahl dieser europäischen Senatoren wäre den einzelnen Staten zu überlassen, so jedoch, dass wo Volksvertretungen in Einer oder in zwei Kammern bestehen, diese die Wahl vorzunehmen hätten.

Die Abstimmung im Bundesrathe müsste nach Staten, nicht nach Individuen geschehen, im Senate dagegen wäre die individuelle Abstimmung möglich und vorzuziehen. Die Mitglieder des Bundesrathes stimmen gemäss ihrer Instruktion und Vollmacht, die Senatoren frei nach ihrer persönlichen Ueberzeugung.

Die Schwierigkeit der Sprache einer solchen internationalen Versammlung ist nicht unüberwindlich. Auf der heutigen Bildungsstufe kennen die meisten hochgebildeten Männer ausser ihrer Muttersprache noch eine oder einige fremde Kultursprachen wenigstens so weit, dass sie gedruckte Werke derselben und auch eine Rede verstehen. Es dürfte allerdings Niemandem verwehrt werden, in seiner Muttersprache zu reden. Wenn aber die Redner wünschen, von allen oder doch der Mehrzahl verstanden zu werden, so werden sie französisch oder englisch oder deutsch sprechen müssen. Diese drei Nationalsprachen haben jedenfalls heute in Europa die meiste Verbreitung und fast jeder Gebildete kennt eine derselben. Würde daher ausnahmsweise ein Senator nur in seiner Muttersprache reden können, so wäre dafür zu sorgen, dass seine Rede in einer dieser allgemeinen Sprachen verdolmetscht würde. Man hilft sich in der Schweiz und auf internationalen Konferenzen und Vereinen schon lange auf diese Weise.

Der Ort für die Sitzungen des Senates kann füglich von dem Bundesrathe bestimmt werden und mag schicklich abwechseln zwischen verschiedenen Ländern. Eine regelmässige Versammlung je zu zwei oder drei Jahren ist genügend, da ausserordentliche Versammlungen durch dringende Bedürfnisse gefordert werden können.

Im Interesse der Selbständigkeit der Einzelstaten darf dem

the Council should be subject to no taxation or financial liability, nor to any military liability. The *cost* of the Assembly shall be defrayed by the States in proportion to their voting power. It should, however, be decided what allowance, in addition to travelling expenses, should be made to each Representative, so that in this respect there should be equality.

(9.) International Rules upon which the Council and Senate, each house by a majority of representative votes, are agreed, shall be promulgated by the Council as International Law.

The right of bringing forward a motion in the Council for the publication of an International Law belongs to every Government, and the same applies to the representation of the different nations in the Senate. The decisions in each body must, however, be made by an absolute majority of votes of the representative States and peoples.

(10.) The *presidency* of the Council rotates every year among the Representatives of the Great Powers, that of the Senate may be determined by the free election of the assembly until a new election be made at the next ordinary session. Each Great Power will therefore take precedence in the Council one year in every six. Only formal powers, however, are granted to the President, not essential prerogatives.

(11.) Either a permanent *residence* should be assigned to the Council or a change made every few years amongst a few selected towns; and the same for the general European Bureau. For this purpose the large world-cities are unsuitable, nor should the capital towns of the Great Powers be chosen, but only towns where the inhabitants can exercise no sort of pressure over the discussions, and which, while outside the quiet but real influence of political salons, can yet offer much general information with regard to foreign affairs. Such towns are, *e.g.*, Brussels and Ghent in Belgium, Zurich and Geneva in Switzerland, Baden and Leipzig in Germany, Nancy and Orleans in

Bunde kein Steuerrecht und keine eigentliche Finanzhoheit zukommen, so wenig als eine militärische Hoheit. Die Kosten der Versammlung sind von den Staten beizutragen, je nach ihrem Stimmrechte. Aber es sollte doch bestimmt werden, was für Diäten ausser den Reiseauslagen die Senatoren zu beziehen haben, damit in dieser Hinsicht gleiches Recht gewahrt bleibe.

Völkerrechtliche Normen, über welche sich der Bundesrath und der Senat, jedes Haus mit Mehrheit der vertretenen Stimmen geeinigt haben, werden von dem Bundesrathe als völkerrechtliches Gesetz verkündet.

Jeder Statsregierung müsste das Recht zustehen, in dem Bundesrathe einen Antrag auf Erlassung eines völkerrechtlichen Gesetzes zu stellen, und ebenso jeder Vertretung der verschiedenen Völker in dem Senate. Die Beschlüsse in beiden Körpern werden aber mit absoluter Stimmenmehrheit der vertretenen Staten und Völker gefasst.

Das Präsidium im Bundesrathe wechselt alljährlich unter den Grossmächten, das des Senates kann von der Versammlung frei gewählt werden bis zur Neuwahl in der nächsten ordentlichen Session. Jede Grossmacht würde also in einer Periode von sechs Jahren während eines Jahres den Vorsitz im Bundesrathe einnehmen. Dem Präsidenten sind aber nur formale Befugnisse, nicht sachliche Vorrechte einzuräumen.

Für den Bundesrath ist eine ständige Residenz zu bezeichnen, oder ein mehrjähriger Wechsel zwischen wenigen bestimmten Städten vorzubehalten, ebenso für die gemeinsame europäische Kanzlei. Dafür taugen aber weder grosse Weltstädte noch die Hauptstädte einer Grossmacht, sondern nur Städte, deren Bevölkerung keinerlei Druck auf die Berathung zu üben vermag, auch nicht den stillen aber wirksamen der politischen Salons, und welche doch mancherlei geistige Hülfsmittel bieten für die Kenntniss fremder Zustände. Von der Art wären z. B. die belgischen Städte Brüssel und Gent, die schweizerischen Zürich und Genf, die deutschen Baden-Baden und Leipzig, die

France, Milan and Florence in Italy, and, although a capital city, the Hague in the Netherlands.

II. The *Preservation of the Peace of Nations* and the discussion and decisions in the *affairs of the Higher European Politics* should be entrusted, preferably, to the *United Council* under the guidance of the *Great Powers* but always with the limitation that a new regulation, of permanent effect, shall be also submitted to the Senate for approval.

Hitherto, the difference between the Higher Politics of International Law and the matters of mere international Administration and Justice has been very little considered. To me it appears to be of very decided importance for the constitution of the Union of States. It is very much easier to provide for International Law Institutions, which shall resolve unimportant matters of administration and law suits, than to construct an organisation which shall be called upon to decide supreme questions pertaining to the State.

To the affairs of High Politics belong all questions which concern the existence, the independence, the freedom of States, and on which the conditions of life of the nations, their safety and development, are dependent. If these high interests are threatened, a manly people will put forth its whole strength to protect them, and will always prefer to sacrifice life and property for the maintenance of their right than to submit to the command of any foreign administration or even to the arbitral or judicial award of an international tribunal.

In regard to such questions the commonwealth of all European States, with the co-operation of a European peoples' representation is alone able to form a decisive authority to which the disputing States will submit, and even then only under certain conditions.

Only when the Governments and peoples work together and where possible are united, or at least when an overwhelming majority agree, will that authority be strong enough to reach any französischen Nancy und Orleans, die italienischen Mailand und Florenz, und, obwohl eine Hauptstadt, Haag in den Niederlanden.

2) Die *Bewahrung* des *Völkerfriedens* und die Berathung und Beschlussfassung in den *Angelegenheiten* der *grossen europäischen Politik* werden vorzugsweise dem *Bundesrathe*, unter Führung der *Grossmächte* anzuvertrauen sein, immer aber mit der Beschränkung, dass eine dauernde Neuordnung auch der Gutheissung des Senates unterbreitet wird.

Bisher ist der Unterschied der grossen Politik im Völkerrechte und der blossen internationalen Verwaltungs- und Justizsachen wenig beachtet worden. Mir scheint er für die Verfassung des Statenbundes von ganz entscheidender Wichtigkeit zu sein. Es ist sehr viel leichter, für völkerrechtliche Institutionen zu sorgen, welche die kleinen Verwaltungssachen und Prozesse erledigen, als Organe zu schaffen, welche die statlichen Lebensfragen zu entscheiden berufen sind.

Zu den Angelegenheiten der grossen Politik gehören alle Fragen, welche die Existenz, die Selbständigkeit, die Freiheit der Staten betreffen, von denen die Lebensbedingungen der Völker, ihre Sicherheit und ihre Entwickelung abhängig sind. Wenn diese höchsten Interessen bedroht erscheinen, dann setzen männliche Völker ihre ganze Kraft dafür ein, dieselbe zu schützen und ziehen es noch immer vor, ihr Gut und Blut im Nothfalle für die Behauptung ihres Rechtes zu opfern, als sich einem Gebote irgend einer fremden Verwaltungsbehörde oder selbst dem schiedsrichterlichen oder richterlichen Spruche internationaler Gerichte zu unterwerfen.

Bei solchen Fragen kann nur die Gemeinschaft aller europäischen Staten unter Mitwirkung einer europäischen Volksvertretung und selbst jene nur unter gewissen Bedingungen zu einer entscheidenden Autorität werden, welcher sich die streitenden Staten fügen. Nur wenn die Regierungen und Völker zusammen wirken und wo möglich einig werden, oder mindestens eine überwältigende Mehrheit zu Stande kommt, wird jene Autorität stark genug conclusion. Were the Council to split into nearly equally strong parties, the disputing States would attach themselves to these parties, and a generally recognised result, a new undisputed legal regulation would not be reached.

Therefore if the actual making of decisions is left to the Council, and it reach its decision by a majority, this decision would not be binding unless the decision and assent of the Senate be added.

Were unanimity demanded in the Council, its competency to form a decision would be too circumscribed, nor would a simple majority in such cases be decisive if an important minority, of say six to eight, vote against it.

International Administration and Justice.

It is quite otherwise with the conduct of the *small* matters of International Administration and Justice. I reckon amongst these all regulations respecting international commercial relations, the interpretation of treaties relating to trades and tariffs, regulations referring to streets, railways, post office, telegraph, shipping traffic on the open sea, in harbours, or on rivers, those relating to the extradition of criminals, to questions of the relations of private individuals with the State, to all international individual rights and penalties, to regulations of boundaries, sanitary matters, controversies regarding damages, weights and measures, coinage, ceremonies, etc.

Such matters of administration and justice can be looked after without danger to individual sovereign States by means of general International Institutions. For example, as has already happened, a general Central Bureau for posts and telegraphs or weights and measures may be created and established in any European werden, um Folge zu bewirken. Würden sich Bundesrath und Senat in nahezu gleich starke Parteien spalten, so würden die streitenden Staten sich an diese Parteien anschliessen und ein allgemein anerkanntes Ergebniss, eine neue unbestrittene Rechtsordnung käme nicht zu Stande.

Wenn daher auch dem Bundesrathe die eigentliche Beschlussfassung überlassen und dieser mit Mehrheit Beschluss fassen würde, so würde dieser Beschluss doch nicht anders rechtsverbindlich und vollziehbar werden, als wenn auch das Gutachten oder die Genehmigung des Senates hinzu käme.

Würde Einstimmigkeit im Bundesrathe gefordert, so würde die Beschlussfähigkeit desselben zu sehr eingeengt. Die einfache Mehrheit kann aber in solchen Fällen auch nicht entscheiden, wenn ihr eine erhebliche Minderheit etwa von 6 bis 8 Stimmen entschlossen entgegen tritt.

Internationale Verwaltung und Rechtspflege.

Ganz anders sind die *kleinen* Angelegenheiten der *völkerrechtlichen Verwaltung* und Justiz zu behandeln. Ich rechne zu diesen alle Anordnungen über internationale Verkehrsverhältnisse, über Auslegung von Handels- und Zollverträgen, über Strassen, Eisenbahnen, Posten, Telegraphenwesen, Schifffahrtsverkehr auf offener See oder in den Seehäfen und auf den Strömen, über Auslieferung von Verbrechern, über die Fragen der Stats- und Landesangehörigkeit von Privaten, das gesammte internationale Privat- und Strafrecht, Grenzregulirungen, Sanitätsinteressen, Entschädigungsstreitigkeiten, Mass und Gewicht, Münzwesen, Ceremoniel u. s. f.

Für solche Verwaltungs- und Justizsachen lässt sich ohne Gefahr für die einzelnen souveränen Staten durch gemeinsame internationale Anstalten sorgen. Es kann so z. B., wie das bereits geschehen ist, ein gemeinsames Centralbureau für die Posten oder die Telegraphen, oder die Masse und Gewichte town. With equal readiness the so-called Arbitration Clause in agreements may be taken up, and the nature and course of Arbitral procedure be determined. Under special circumstances also for certain disputes permanent international tribunals may be established. The reform of the jurisdiction regulating prize money can be accomplished, for example, and the inconveniences of the Consular jurisdiction removed only by means of International Courts of Justice.

All such Administrative Bureaus are naturally subordinate to the European Council as the representative of all the Governments, and in the same way International Tribunals, with their independence in giving awards, are placed under the superintendence of the Council as regards their external relationships. In the Council the States exchange views, and are able easily to reach an understanding in regard to common resolutions and decisions. In such cases also the simple decision of a majority is sufficient.

Questions of High Politics are comparatively rare. The Council therefore need only come together from time to time, as they deem it desirable. On the other hand matters of administration demand a constant, regular activity, so that one or two regular sittings of the Council yearly will be necessary and useful. For a long time to come two yearly sittings of about three weeks will suffice. But a *permanent Bureau of the Council,* in which all business should be transacted, I consider to be indispensable. This Bureau should be under the direction of the President for the time being, and will have charge of all communications with the different States.

The cost of these international establishments will be defrayed by the States according to a proportionate scale which takes fair geschaffen und in irgend eine europäische Stadt verlegt werden Es kann ebenso unbedenklich in Verträge die sogenannte Schiedsgerichtsklausel aufgenommen und die Art und der Prozessgang des schiedsrichterlichen Verfahrens geordnet werden. Unter Umständen können auch für gewisse Streitigkeiten feste völkerrechtliche Tribunale eingesetzt werden, wie denn z. B. die Reform der Prisengerichsbarkeit entschieden dahin drängt und dem Uebelstande der Konsulargerichtsbarkeit auch nicht anders als durch internationale Gerichtshöfe abzuhelfen sein wird.

Alle derartigen internationalen Verwaltungsämter und Bureaus sind naturgemäss dem europäischen Bundesrathe, als der Vertretung aller Statsregierungen unterzuordnen und ebenso auch die internationalen Gerichte neben ihrer Unabhängigkeit in dem Urtheile, mit Bezug auf die äusserliche Zusammensetzung und Ordnung der Oberaufsicht des Bundesrathes unterstellt. In dem Bundesrathe tauschen die Staten ihre Meinungen aus und können sie sich leicht über gemeinsame Entschlüsse und Beschlüsse verständigen. In solchen Fällen wird auch ein einfacher Mehrheitsbeschluss genügen.

Verhältnissmässig selten sind die Fragen der grossen Politik. Der Bundesrath wird daher um ihrer willen nur von Zeit zu Zeit zusammen treten müssen. Dagegen die Verwaltungssachen erfordern eine fortgesetzte regelmässige Thätigkeit, so dass wohl alljährlich eine oder ein paar ordentliche Sitzungen des Bundesrathes nöthig oder zweckmässig sein werden. Noch auf lange hin würden jedenfalls zwei jährliche Sitzungen von ein paar Wochen ausreichen. Aber eine *ständige Bundeskanzlei*, in welcher alle Geschäfte mit ihren Akten zusammen laufen, betrachte ich als unentbehrlich. Dieselbe ist der jeweiligen Präsidialmacht bei- und unterzuordnen. Sie besorgt die Einladungen und Mittheilungen an die verbündeten Staten.

Die Kosten für diese internationalen Anstalten werden von den Staten aufgebracht nach einem Vertheilungsmodus, welcher aut die Zahl der Bevölkerung — etwa nach Millionen und auf die account of the extent of their population and of their commerce and the number of their ships, per million, say, of their inhabitants.

Execution of the European Decisions.

In ordinary matters of administration and justice the execution of decisions shall be left to the discretion of the various States, or, as far as concerns the imparting of those decisions, to the Bureau of the Council.

Only in one class of cases—which indeed will seldom happen, but, if they do happen, will by their great importance be very difficult to handle—is this provision not sufficient. If, in an exceptional case it is necessary to exercise compulsion against a State, then neither the Bureau nor even the Council itself, is the proper organisation to carry this compulsion into effect, for it has neither the necessary financial means, nor the armies and fleets, without which such compulsion is impossible.

For such cases the co-operation of the Great Powers, which have the ability, is necessary to exercise forcible pressure.

Hence from the United Council now springs the *College of Great Powers*, which guarantees the execution of those decisions of the Council which have been pronounced to be necessary and desirable.

In order to secure the protection of any single State against the oppression of the Great Powers, a stipulation is necessary that only such decisions shall be carried out by force as have been declared in the Senate by a majority of votes to be equitable, and for which a two-thirds majority of the Council, and also of the College of Great Powers, has declared. Under this

Ausdehnung ihrer Verkehrsverhältnisse — Zahl der Seeschiffe — billige Rücksicht nimmt.

Vollzug der europäischen Beschlüsse.

In den regelmässigen Verwaltungs- und Justizsachen wird der Vollzug den betheiligten Staten anheim zu geben sein, oder so weit es sich um Mittheilung von Beschlüssen handelt, durch die Bundeskanzlei besorgt werden.

Nur in Einer Klasse von Fällen, die freilich selten eintreten, aber wenn sie eintreten, auch durch ihre hohe Bedeutung schwer wiegen, genügt diese Anordnung nicht. Wenn es ausnahmsweise nöthig wird, auch gegen einen Stat einen Zwang auszuüben, dann ist die Bundeskanzlei und selbst der Bundesrath kein geeignetes Organ, um diesen Zwang durchzuführen, denn auch der Bundesrath hat weder die nöthigen Finanzmittel, noch die Heere und Flotten zur Verfügung, ohne welche dieser Zwang unmöglich ist.

Für solche Falle bedarf es der Mitwirkung der Grossmächte, welche die Macht haben, nach aussen einen gewaltsamen Druck zu üben.

Um desswillen tritt jetzt aus dem Bundesrathe als mächtiger Vollziehungsausschuss das *Kollegium der Grossmächte* hervor und gewährleistet den Vollzug der als nothwendig und vollziehbar erklärten Beschlüsse des Bundesrathes.

Um gegen die Unterdrückung irgend eines Einzelstates durch die Uebermacht der Grossmächte einen Schutz zu gewähren, ist eine Bestimmung nöthig, dass nur solche Beschlüsse nöthigenfalls mit Zwang durchgeführt werden dürfen, welche von dem Senate mit Stimmenmehrheit gebilligt worden sind, und für welche sich eine zwei Drittelsmehrheit im Bundesrathe und zugleich in dem Kollegium der Grossmächte erklärt hat. Unter dieser Voraussetzung schwindet jede Besorgniss vor einem tyrannischen oder hypothesis all fear of a tyrannical oppression, or wanton procedure, on the part of any Great Power against a single State disappears. No State need fear that any unlawful violence will be exercised against its autonomy or freedom.

The possibility of a European war will not be completely excluded by this constitution any more than the danger of a civil war is quite averted by any State constitution. But they are weighty guarantees for a peaceful, and at the same time just, settlement of all disputes among the peoples. As a rule, actual compulsion will not be necessary, and the prospect of compulsion if not amenable to the judgment and will of Europe, will lead to reflection and to compliance. The very exercise of compulsion has more the character of the execution of a legal verdict than of a battle of parties. Wars will therefore become very rare, and frivolous wars, or wars prompted by ambition or lust of conquest, will become actually impossible. As a rule every State will voluntarily submit to the threefold majority of the collective European Governments in Council, of the European Representatives in the Senate, and of the Great Powers, without venturing a useless opposition, just as private individuals in dispute submit to the decision of a judge.

For European Peace, for the acceptance and development of European International Law, and for European well-being, much better care will be taken through such an organisation than is at present the case; and the independence and freedom of the separate States will remain not merely untouched but more secure than before.

A disarmament and disbanding of all standing armies would be by no means an immediate consequence of this organisation. But the present strain of military burdens, the greatest hindrance to European prosperity, would cease. The dread of war, impendherrschsüchtigen oder leichtfertigen Vorgehen einiger Mächte wider einen einzelnen Stat. Es braucht dann kein Stat zu fürchten, dass seiner Eigenart und seiner Freiheit eine rechtswidrige Gewalt angethan werde.

Die Möglichkeit eines europäischen Krieges wird durch diese Verfassung nicht völlig ausgeschlossen, so wenig als durch irgend eine Statsverfassung die Gefahr eines Bürgerkrieges ganz beseitigt wird. Aber es sind wichtige Garantien gewonnen für eine friedliche und zugleich für eine gerechte Erledigung aller Streitigkeiten unter den Völkern. In der Regel wird ein wirklicher Zwang entbehrlich werden, und es wird die Aussicht auf den Zwang, wenn ungebührlich dem Urtheile und Willen Europas getrotzt wird, zur Besinnung führen und zur Folge bestimmen. Die Zwangsübung selber hat eher den Charakter der Exekution eines Rechtsurtheiles als den eines Kampfes von Parteien. Die Kriege werden daher sehr selten, und leichtsinnige, ehrsüchtige, eroberungssüchtige Kriege thatsächlich unmöglich werden. In der Regel wird sich jeder Stat der dreifachen Mehrheit der sämmtlichen europäischen Regierungen im Bundesrathe, der europäischen Völkervertretung im Senate und der Grossmächte, ohne einen fruchtlosen Widerstand zu wagen, ebenso freiwillig unterordnen, wie die streitenden Privatpersonen dem Urtheilsspruche seines Richters.

Für den europäischen Frieden, für die Geltung und Entwickelung des europäischen Völkerrechtes und für die europäische Wohlfahrt wäre durch eine solche Organisation Europas sehr viel besser gesorgt als gegenwärtig und die Selbständigkeit und Freiheit der einzelnen Staten bliebe nicht bloss unversehrt, sondern wäre gesicherter als bisher.

Eine Auflösung und Entwaffnung aller Statenheere wird keineswegs die unmittelbare Folge dieser Verfassung sein. Aber die heutige Ueberspannung der Militärlasten, das schwerste Hinderniss der europäischen Wohlfahrt, würde aufhören. Die Rücksicht auf drohende Kriege der Zukunft würde nicht mehr ing in the future, would no longer, as now, consume the taxable powers of the people. Standing armies would gradually decrease, the time of service would at once be reduced, the outlay for arms, fortresses, ships of war, and barracks would be considerably less. The enormous saving thus made would free the citizens from the oppression of taxation, and at the same time provide financial means for the advancement of peaceful culture.

. . . .

The need of a solution of this problem becomes every year more pressing. . . . .

Whether, and, if so, when, a far-seeing statesman will undertake to develop the idea is not very clear at the present time. But the organisation of the United States of Europe is much less difficult than was the union of the German States into the German Empire, and that it would be at least as fruitful and salutary, and even more efficacious for the development of humanity, is undoubted.

wie gegenwärtig, die Steuerkräfte der Völker aufzehren. Die stehenden Heere würden allmählich vermindert, die Dienstzeit unbedenklich herabgesetzt, die Ausgaben für Waffen, Festungen, Kriegsschiffe, Kasernen sehr erheblich abnehmen. Die enorme Ersparniss an dannzumal unnöthigen Militärausgaben würde die Bürger von dem Steuerdrucke befreien, and zugleich finanzielle Mittel schaffen, um für die friedlichen Kulturinteressen reichlicher sorgen zu können.

. . . .

Das Bedürfniss der Lösung des Problemes wird von Jahr zu Jahr dringender empfunden werden. . . . . . .

Ob und wann ein weitsichtiger und weitherziger Statsmann es unternehmen werde, die Idee zu verwirklichen, ist zur Zeit noch unklar. Dass aber die Organisation des europäischen Statenbundes viel weniger schwierig ist, als die Einigung der deutschen Staten zu dem deutschen Reiche gewesen ist, aber mindestens ebenso fruchtbar und heilbringend und für die Entwickelung der Menschheit noch wirksamer wäre, ist unzweifelhaft.

A HIGH TRIBUNAL OF ARBITRATION.

By David Dudley Field.

1872.

Notice of Dissatisfaction, and Claim of Redress.

532. If any disagreement, or cause of complaint, arise between nations, the one aggrieved must give formal notice thereof to the other, specifying in detail the cause of complaint, and the redress which it seeks.

Answer to be given.

533. Every nation, which receives from another, notice of any dissatisfaction, or cause of complaint, whether arising out of a supposed breach of this Code, or otherwise, must, within three months thereafter, give a full and explicit answer thereto.

Joint High Commission.

534. Whenever a nation complaining of another and the nation complained of do not otherwise agree between themselves, they shall each appoint five members of a Joint High Commission, who shall meet together, discuss the differences, and endeavour to reconcile them, and within six months after their appointment, shall report the result to the nations appointing them respectively.

High Tribunal of Arbitration.

535. Whenever a Joint High Commission, appointed by nations to reconcile their differences, shall fail to agree, or the nations appointing them shall fail to ratify their acts, those nations shall, within twelve months after the appointment of the Joint High Commission, give notice of such failure to the other parties to this Code, and there shall then be formed a High Tribunal of Arbitration, in manner following: Each nation receiving the notice shall, within three months thereafter, transmit to the

nations in controversy the names of four persons, and from the list of such persons the nations in controversy shall alternately, in the alphabetical order of their own names, as indicated in Article 16, reject one after another, until the number is reduced to seven, which seven shall constitute the tribunal.

The tribunal thus constituted shall by writing signed by the members, or a majority of them, appoint a time and place of meeting, and give notice thereof to the parties in controversy; and at such time and place, or at other times and places to which an adjournment may be had, it shall hear the parties, and decide between them, and the decision shall be final and conclusive. If any nation receiving the notice fail to transmit the names of four persons within the time prescribed, the parties in controversy shall name each two in their places; and if either of the parties fail to signify its rejection of a name from the list, within one month after a request from the other to do so, the other may reject for it; and if any of the persons selected to constitute the tribunal shall die, or fail for any cause to serve, the vacancy shall be filled by the nation which originally named the person whose place is to be filled.

Each Nation bound by Tribunal of Arbitration.

536. Every nation, party to this Code, binds itself to unite in forming a Joint High Commission, and a High Tribunal of Arbitration, in the cases hereinbefore specified as proper for its action, and to submit to the decision of a High Tribunal of Arbitration, constituted and proceeding in conformity to Article 535.

Annual Conference of Representatives of Nations.

538. A conference of representatives of the nations, parties hereto, shall be held every year, beginning on the first of January, at the capital of each in rotation, ... for the purpose of discussing the provisions of this Code, and their amendment, averting war, facilitating intercourse, and preserving Peace.

LEONE LEVI'S DRAFT PROJECT OF A COUNCIL AND HIGH COURT OF INTERNATIONAL ARBITRATION.

1. Having regard to the earnest desire felt and expressed in every country to avert as much as possible the evil of war, by reason of the enormous loss of life and treasure, and of the burden of large armies which it entails; and by reason also of the retarding of civilisation and morals, the disorganisation of industry and commerce, and the disorder in public finances which are its necessary attendants;

2. Having regard to the fact that some wars are caused by passing gusts of passion, some by false rumours or allegations, some by sinister interests of individual men, or of small knots of men, and that in all such cases it is most important to give time for passion to subside, and for truth to be ascertained;

3. Having regard to the many instances in which States have submitted their disputes to the judgment of an Arbitrator or Arbitrators—sometimes a sovereign, sometimes a court of justice, sometimes a committee of jurists, sometimes a congress, sometimes (as in the Alabama Arbitration) publicists and jurists; and to the success and satisfaction which have resulted, in some cases immediately, in others after a short time allowed for irritation to pass away; in all more quickly and completely than after a war;

4. And, having regard to the fact that Arbitration clauses have been inserted in treaties of commerce—(See Treaties of Commerce and Navigation between the United Kingdom and Italy, June 15, 1885, and Greece, November 16, 1883)—and to the advantage of providing some permanent organisation for giving effect to the same in all cases where arbitration is decided upon by contending parties, thus avoiding the danger and difficulty of long negotiations or the purpose of creating a new method on the occurrence of every emergency. (See papers on the Reasonableness of

AVANT-PROJET RELATIF À LA CRÉATION D'UN CONSEIL ET D'UNE HAUTE COUR D'ARBITRAGE INTERNATIONAUX DE M. LEONE LEVI.

1. Considérant le désir sérieusement manifesté dans toutes les contrées du monde civilisé, de mettre fin, le plus tôt possibles, aux souffrances qui ont pour cause la préparation de la guerre, la permanence des armées, et, par suite inévitable, l'arrêt de tout progrès, la démoralisation et la ruine publique ;

2. Considérant que les conflits internationaux naissant souvent de prétentions ou d'effervescences momentanées, de fausses nouvelles ou d'ambitions personnelles, il est de la plus grande importance de laisser du temps à la réflexion et à la vérité pour produire leur influence conciliatrice ;

3. Considérant que, dans de nombreuses occasions, les nations ont soumis leurs différends au jugement d'un arbitre ou d'un conseil arbitral, — soit qu'elles aient accepté la décision d'un souverain, d'une Cour de Justice ou d'une assemblée de Jurisconsultes, comme dans le cas célèbre de l'Alabama ; que les sentences rendues ont presque toujours été exécutées à la satisfaction de tous. (Voir GLÜBER, *Droit des Gens*, page 318, note *A*, avec les précédents y mentionnés) ;

4. Ayant égard à ce fait, acquis à l'histoire des traités de commerce, que la clause d'arbitrage se trouve insérée dans un certain nombre des plus récents. (Voir *Traité de commerce et de navigation entre le Royaume-Uni et celui d'Italie*, 15 juin 1885 ; avec la Grèce, 16 novembre 1883) ; que cette clause a pour avantage à la fois, d'offrir une organisation permanente du tribunal auquel, en cas de contestations, les parties auraient à recourir, et d'éviter les pertes de temps, les difficultés, les dangers d'une Constitution à faire pour chaque cas particulier. (Voir les documents commu-

International Arbitration, read before the Association for the Reform and Codification of International Law, 1886 and 1887, by Henry Richard, Esq., M.P.)

5. The Committees of the Peace Society and of the International Arbitration and Peace Association earnestly urge the Governments of the several States of Europe and America to enter into communication among themselves with a view to appointing a Permanent Council of International Arbitration, a possible form of which is hereinafter suggested.

6. Each State to nominate a given equal number of members, publicists, and jurists, or other persons of high reputation and standing, to constitute a Council of International Arbitration, to undertake the settlement of international disputes by means of mediation or arbitration, and to take measures whereby international differences may be removed or settled in a friendly manner.

7. Such a Council may be formed by any group of States, even two only, for international affairs relating to themselves—*e.g.*, the United Kingdom may agree with the United States of America to form a joint Council, having the same functions upon questions between them as the more comprehensive body provided by Arts. 5 and 6 would have over the larger area of disputes.

8. If such a beginning is once made, even by two States only, it is probable that others will follow the example. And it will be one of the duties of the Council to extend the sphere of its influence beyond its Constituent States as opportunity occurs.

9. The Council will at its first meeting appoint its Secretaries.

10. On the occurrence of any grave dispute between any States represented on the Council, the Secretaries, at the request of any two members of the Council, shall summon a meeting to consider what steps may be adopted for preventing, if possible, a resort to war measures, and for offering the aid of the Council in the shape of Arbitration.

niqués par M. Henry Richard, M.P., *à l'Association pour la réforme et la codification de la Loi internationale en* 1886 *et* 1887 en faveur de l'arbitrage entre nations.)

5. Par ces motifs :

Les Comités réunis de la Société de la Paix et de l'Association internationale de l'Arbitrage et de la Paix invitent instamment les gouvernements de tous les Etats du monde civilisé à se concerter en vue de la constitution d'un Conseil permanent ayant mandat d'arbitrage international, dont les pouvoirs et l'action seraient établis comme suit :

6. Chaque État choisit, parmi ses publicistes, ses jurisconsultes, ses citoyens les plus considérés, les membres en nombre égal (à déterminer) du Conseil international d'arbitrage qui a pour mission de faire cesser les contestations, au moyen de la médiation, de l'arbitrage et des mesures propres à écarter ou à résoudre pacifiquement les difficultés internationales.

7. Conformément à l'esprit du présent avant-projet, on peut donc admettre que la création du Conseil résulterait de la Convention arrêtée entre deux États de recourir à l'arbitrage pour tout différend surgissant entre eux ; et que si, par exemple, le Royaume-Uni convenait avec les États-Unis d'Amérique de former un conseil commun pour l'arbitrage, ce Conseil aurait, dès sa formation, la compétence la plus étendue conformément aux attributions édictées par les articles 5 et suivants.

8. Le Conseil étant constitué par deux ou plusieurs États, il invitera les autres États à élire leurs délégués afin de se les adjoindre.

9. Le Conseil devra, dès sa première réunion, procéder à la désignation de ses secrétaires.

10. Dès qu'il surgira une difficulté entre des États représentés dans le Conseil, les secrétaires, à la requête des deux membres, convoqueront une réunion chargée d'examiner les mesures à prendre immédiatement en vue d'arrêter les préparatifs de guerre et d'offrir les bons offices du Conseil sous forme d'arbitrage.

11. On the occurrence of any grave dispute to which a State not represented on the Council is a party, the Council may be summoned in the same way to consider whether it is feasible and useful to offer the aid of the Council in the shape of Mediation.

12. When the contending States agree to leave their disputes to Arbitration, the Council will appoint some of its members, and some other persons specially nominated by the contending States, to be a High Court of International Arbitration, and its award in the case shall be binding on the contending States.

13. The appointment of the members of the High Court shall be made with special regard to the character and locality of the dispute, and shall terminate on the settlement of the dispute or abandonment of the arbitration.

14. It is not contemplated to provide for the exercise of physical force in order to secure reference to the Council, or to compel compliance with the award of the Court when made. The authority of the Council is moral, not physical. Nevertheless, when the award of its regularly approved Court is set at nought by the contending parties, it shall be the duty of the Council to communicate the facts of the case, and the award of the Court thereon, to all the States represented in the same.

15. Where, likewise, on the occurrence of any dispute, the action of the Council is ignored by either or both, or all the contending States, it will be within the competency of the Council to review the facts in dispute, and to report thereon to the States which it represents.

16. The Council will make rules for its own conduct and for the procedure of the High Court of International Arbitration. The rules adopted in the Alabama Arbitration, and those proposed by the Institute of International Law, may supply valuable suggestions in the framing of the same.

11. En cas de différends survenus entre des États non représentés au Conseil, les Secrétaires, de la même manière, provoqueront une réunion du Congrès pour offrir l'intervention avec l'espoir d'arriver à une médiation.

12. Lorsque les États en désaccord consentiront à soumettre leur différend à l'Arbitrage, le Conseil déléguera un certain nombre de ses membres pour former, avec les personnes désignées à cet effet par les États en litige, une Haute-Cour d'Arbitrage internationale dont la décision sera obligatoire.

13. Pour le choix des membres de la Haute-Cour, à constituer, il y aura lieu de tenir compte de la nature du conflit et de la contrée où il s'est produit. Leur mandat prendra fin aussitôt la sentence rendue ou l'arbitrage abandonné.

14. Aucune force armée ne peut être employée pour contraindre les Etats en litige à s'en rapporter à la décision de la Haute-Cour, ni pour amener l'exécution de la sentence rendue. L'autorité du Conseil est toute morale. Néanmoins, si, après acceptation de la juridiction les parties refusaient de se soumettre au jugement, il serait du devoir du Conseil de donner, à tous les Etats représentés dans ce Conseil, communication du jugement, en point de fait et décision, ainsi que de la constatation du refus d'exécution.

15. De même aussi, dans le cas où l'un ou l'autre des Etats en litige n'aurait pas invoqué l'intervention du Conseil, celui-ci n'en aurait pas moins le devoir de soumettre les faits litigieux à son examen et de faire son rapport aux Etats représentés par lui.

16. Le Conseil établira lui-même les règlements de son action et de la procédure de la Haute-Cour d'arbitrage internationale.

(Les règles adoptées dans l'arbitrage de l'Alabama et celles qui ont été proposées par l'Institut de Droit international fourniront, à cet effet, de précieuses indications.)

17. It is suggested that the seat of the Council shall be a neutral city, such as Berne or Brussels.

18. The appointment of members of Council should be for a definite number of years, provision being made for the appointment by the respective States of new members to fill the place of those who may cease to be members by retirement or death.

19. The cost of maintaining the Council shall be borne equally by every State concurring in its organisation. The cost of any reference to Arbitration shall be borne by the contending parties in equal shares, regardless of the result of the award on the same on the contending parties.

20. The preparation of a Code of International Law will be of great value for the guidance of the Council and High Court of International Arbitration. It will be the duty of the Council to prepare such a Code as far as possible.

LEONE LEVI,
Of Lincoln's Inn, *Barrister at Law.*

October, 1887.

Revised by LORD HOBHOUSE,
October, 1889.

17. On devra, de préférence, choisir pour siège du Conseil une ville située dans un pays neutre : Berne ou Bruxelles, par exemple.

18. Les membres du Conseil nommés pour un nombre d'années à déterminer, seraient remplacés en cas de démission ou de décès.

19. Les dépenses d'entretien du Conseil seront supportées également entre les Etats qni ont concouru à son organisation.

Les frais auxquels chaque décision arbitrale donnera lieu seront répartis également entre les adversaires quel que soit le résultat de l'arbitrage à l'égard de chacun d'eux.

20. La préparation d'un code de droit international sera d'une grande utilité pour guider le Conseil et la Haute-Cour d'Arbitrage International. Ce sera le devoir du Conseil de pousser aussi loin que possible le travail commencé.

LEONE LEVI,
Avocat, Lincoln's Inn.

Octobre, 1887.

Revisé par LORD HOBHOUSE,
Octobre, 1889.

NOTES ON A PERMANENT INTERNATIONAL TRIBUNAL OF ARBITRATION.

BY SIR EDMUND HORNBY.

1. By appointing its Members for a sufficiently long term—*i.e.*, ten years—absolving them from allegiance to any State whilst in office, rendering them capable of re-election (providing them with salaries and retiring pensions sufficient to place them for life beyond the necessity of truckling to Governments), and assuring them a social rank sufficient to satisfy the highest ambition (whilst denying them the power to accept during life any position, honour, or reward), not only will the services of men of the highest educational attainments be secured, but their ambition and talents will be devoted to rendering the tribunal the object of universal confidence and respect.

2. By confiding to them the elaboration of a system of international jurisprudence they will be induced to devote themselves to perfecting it, not only by research and study, but by care in administering and applying it in the special cases submitted to their decision, upon principles which will secure universal acceptance.

3. Although nominated by Governments, the Senators or Judges should in no sense be regarded as the representatives or mouthpieces of Governments; and, having nothing to hope for, and nothing to fear from the authority nominating them, they will alone look for reward in the confidence and esteem their devotion to the interests of humanity in general—as distinguished from more isolated national interests—will earn for them.

4. The Tribunal must itself establish a procedure, having for its sole object the presentment and development of distinct and clear issues upon which its judgment is sought. It must have powers to indicate and procure all such evidence as it considers necessary to enable it fully to elucidate the facts presented. It must safe-

LE TRIBUNAL INTERNATIONAL

PROPOSITION DE SIR EDMOND HORNBY

(*Traduction libre.*)

1. En donnant aux fonctions de ses membres une durée suffisante et en les dégageant de toute attache avec un État quelconque pendant qu'ils sont en office, en les faisant rééligibles en leur assurant des honoraires suffisants et des pensions libérales, et en leur donnant un rang qui satisfasse à toute légitime ambition, on assurerait au Tribunal la confiance et le respect universels.

2. Chargés d'élaborer une jurisprudence internationale, ils se dévoueraient à son perfectionnement, non seulement par des recherches et des études, mais encore par l'application intelligente des principes de cette jurisprudence aux causes qu'ils auraient à juger.

3. Bien que nommés par les gouvernements, les Sénateurs ou Juges ne pourront pas être considérés comme leurs représentants ou leurs instruments, et comme ils n'auront rien à espérer ni à craindre d'eux, ils ne s'occuperont que des intérêts généraux et humanitaires qui leur seront confiés.

4. La Cour internationale d'arbitrage établira elle-même sa procédure, en ayant pour unique préoccupation de la rendre claire et pratique. Elle indiquera les moyens de preuve qui lui paraîtront nécessaires pour élucider les allégués des parties. Elle empêchera

guard all possibility of masterful will amongst its members prejudicially or mischievously influencing the corporate mind of the tribunal, by a rigid system specially framed to secure the fullest and freest expression of individual thought. Under no circumstances must the judgment be other than that of the Tribunal—be it unanimous or only that of a majority—provision being made for recording the separate or dissenting judgments as interesting memorials of individual opinions, to be published, after a certain lapse of time, when deemed expedient.

5. The *detailed* reasons of an award or judgment should not be given until it has been complied with. With compliance or non-compliance, the Tribunal, however, should have nothing to do. It is *functus officio quoad* the particular case submitted, the moment the award for judgment is communicated, under the seal of the court, by its chief Secretary.

6. The enforcement of an award or judgment is matter of consideration alone for the *Concurring Parties* to the establishment of the tribunal. It is open to them individually or collectively to remonstrate on non-compliance; to compel performance by withdrawal or suspension of diplomatic relations (Consular or trade relations remaining unaffected), by the infliction of a pecuniary penalty, by seizure and occupation of territory, and even in extreme cases, by war.

7. Under no circumstances must any member of the Tribunal enter into communication, direct or indirect, with the Sovereign, Government, or the Press of any nation; the Tribunal, in its corporate character and through its chief Secretary, alone being able to enter into such communications.

8. No member should reside in the country by the Government of which he is nominated. For nine months of each year every member must reside within the College grounds, or within twenty miles thereof.

9. No member of the Tribunal, by virtue of his position, should

toute influence prédominante sur ses membres et assurera la libre expression des opinions individuelles. En aucun cas le jugement ne sera autre que celui de l'unanimité ou de la majorité de la Cour, réserve faite de la mention des votes de minorité, qui pourront être publiés après un certain laps de temps si on le juge à propos.

5. Les considérants d'un jugement ne seront pas donnés avant que le jugement lui-même ait été exécuté. Les membres de la Cour n'auront pas à s'occuper de cette exécution. Ses fonctions cesseront dès que la notification du jugement aura été faite par le Chef-secrétaire sous le sceau du Tribunal.

6. L'exécution d'un jugement sera l'affaire des parties qui auront concouru à la constitution du Tribunal. C'est à elles qu'il incombera de réclamer individuellement ou collectivement contre un refus de se soumettre au jugement et d'en exiger l'exécution, par la rupture, provisoire ou définitive, des relations diplomatiques, par une amende, par la saisie et l'occupation d'un territoire, et, dans des cas extrêmes, par la force armée.

7. En aucun cas un membre du Tribunal ne pourra entrer directement ou indirectement en communication avec le souverain, le gouvernement ou la presse d'un pays ; la Cour seule comme collectivité et par son Chef-secrétaire pourra entretenir des relations de ce genre.

8. Aucun membre de la Cour ne pourra résider dans le pays dont le gouvernement l'a nommé. Durant 9 mois de l'année tout membre de la Cour sera tenu de résider au siége du Tribunal où à 20 milles de ce siége au maximum.

9. En vertu de sa position aucun membre de la Cour ne pourra

be entitled to any official title beyond that of "Senator," but he should be awarded precedence, in every nation, over all laymen not being sovereign rulers.

10. The "Chief Secretary" of the Tribunal should rank on a footing of equality with the principal Secretaries of State of all nations.

11. The site of the College grounds should be declared extra-territorial and neutral, and all persons residing, employed or found therein, should be within the sole jurisdiction of the Tribunal, exercisable, at the discretion of the same, by itself or, at its request, by the judicial authorities of the Government of the State within the territorial boundaries of which the College is situated.

12. To the Government of such State should be entrusted the collection and custody of the funds. Each Concurring State should—in certain fixed proportions to be determined on—contribute towards the maintenance of the Tribunal and College, the payment of salaries and other expenses, and such Government should expend the same in accordance with the requisitions of the Chief Secretary, countersigned by the President of the Tribunal and two members thereof.

13. The Tribunal should consist of not less than thirteen Senators (not necessarily jurists by profession, but statesmen and diplomatists, or men who have filled judicial offices), to be nominated as hereinafter mentioned, and at the commencement of each year such members should elect by ballot one of their number to act as president.

14. There should be appointed a Chief Secretary of the Tribunal, who alone should be in official communication with the Concurring Powers. The duties of this officer should be, amongst others, to regulate the sittings of the Tribunal, to receive all documents, and generally act as keeper of the archives.

15. In addition there should be a Bursar, assistant secretaries,

accepter un autre titre officiel que celui de "Sénateur". Il lui sera accordé en chaque pays la plus haute position après celui du souverain d'un pays.

10. Le Chef-secrétaire sera mis sur le même rang que les principaux secrétaires d'Etat de toutes les nations.

11. Le siège de la Cour sera déclaré ex-territorial et neutre, les employés du Tribunal étant justiciables de lui-même, ou, sur sa demande, placés sous la juridiction de l'Etat dans les limites territoriales duquel le Tribunal a son siège.

12. Le Gouvernement de cet Etat aura à recueillir et à gérer le fonds du Tribunal. Chacun des Etats contractants contribuera, dans des proportions à déterminer, aux frais du Tribunal, au paiement des honoraires et aux autres dépenses. Le gouvernement chargé de la gérance du fonds opérera les paiements sur mandats du Chef-secrétaire visés par le Président et deux membres de la Cour.

13. Le Tribunal se composera, en minimum, de treize Sénateurs, qui ne seront pas nécessairement juristes de profession, mais aussi hommes d'Etat et diplomates ou magistrats ayant rempli des fonctions judiciaires. Ces Sénateurs seront nommés dans la forme prescrite ci-dessous. Chaque année ils éliront un d'entre eux comme président au scrutin secret.

14. Ils nommeront un Chef-secrétaire du Tribunal, qui aura seul à entrer en relations officielles avec les gouvernements contractants. Le Chef-secrétaire aura entre autres à convoquer les séances du Tribunal à recevoir toutes les pièces et à tenir en ordre les archives.

15. Il y aura aussi un caissier, des secrétaires adjoints, un biblio-

a librarian, and such clerks, interpreters, short-hand writers, printers, messengers, servants, etc., as shall be necessary.

16. All and every person employed should on appointment be sworn to keep secret all such information or knowledge as he may acquire by virtue of his office, under penalty of dismissal, forfeiture of pension, and incapability of holding any public appointment anywhere in the service of any one of the Concurring Powers.

17. Every Concurring Nation should be entitled to name one member of the Tribunal, such member not necessarily being a citizen of such nation.

18. In the event of a Concurring Nation not nominating a member, the Tribunal itself should, if the number of members be under thirteen, nominate and by ballot elect a member.

19. Every member of the Tribunal should on his acceptance, and previous to entering on the duties of his office, solemnly renounce and be absolved from allegiance to the country of his birth or adoption, or to the Sovereign of the same, and take an oath to perform his duties without fear, favour, or affection, and with perfect impartiality—undertaking to hold no communication with any Ruler or Government, and not to apply for or receive during life any rank, income, reward, decoration, or office from any Ruler or Government; and any member guilty of infraction of such undertaking should *ipso facto* cease to be a member, and should forfeit all right or title to any pension.

20. The first duty of the Tribunal should be to frame a Code of procedure, providing for the mode in which disputes and differences between nations should be submitted to it.

21. This Code should provide that, immediately on it being shown that any difference cannot be satisfactorily settled by ordinary diplomatic action, as evidenced by the proposal of one of the parties to refer the same to arbitration, the Tribunal be seized with the determination of the same.

thécaire et le nombre voulu d'interprètes, de calligraphes, de commis, de facteurs, etc.

16. Tout employé prêtera serment en entrant en fonctions, de garder le secret sur tout ce qu'il peut avoir appris dans l'exercice de sa charge, sous peine de perdre sa place et sa pension et d'être déclaré incapable de remplir aucun office au service d'un des gouvernements contractants.

17. Toute nation contractante a le droit de nommer un membre du Tribunal, qui ne sera pas nécessairement citoyen de cette nation.

18. Si l'une des nations contractantes ne nomme pas un membre du Tribunal et que le nombre des membres soit inférieur à treize, le Tribunal lui-même fera cette nomination au scrutin secret.

19. En acceptant sa nomination et avant d'entrer en fonctions, tout membre du Tribunal doit renoncer solennellement à tout engagement vis-à-vis de son pays d'origine ou d'adoption, ainsi que vis-à-vis de l'autorité souveraine de ce pays, et en être entièrement libéré ; il doit prêter serment de remplir son office sans crainte, sans favoritisme et avec une parfaite impartialité, en s'engageant à ne solliciter et à n'accepter pendant sa vie, aucun rang, aucun revenu, aucune récompense, aucune décoration et aucun office d'un prince ou d'un gouvernement, sous peine de perdre sa charge de membre du Tribunal, ainsi que tout droit ou titre à une pension.

20. Le premier devoir du Tribunal sera d'élaborer un code de procédure fixant la manière en laquelle les différends entre nations doivent lui être soumis.

21. Ce code stipulera qu'aussitôt qu'on verra qu'un différend ne peut pas être réglé d'une façon satisfaisante par la voie diplomatique et qu'une des parties recourra à l'arbitrage, le Tribunal se considérera comme saisi du litige.

22. From that moment neither party to the difference should directly or indirectly do anything which could be interpreted as an attempt or indication of persistence in the conduct or acts which led to the difference.

23. If the nature of the difference is such that a *modus vivendi* pending the settlement is necessary and cannot be arrived at by mutual agreement, the Tribunal should be requested to arrange the same, each of the two disputant nations sending in writing, within a time to be limited, its view of what the character of the *modus vivendi* should be.

24. On receipt of the same the Tribunal should nominate a Committee of itself, consisting of three members, *not* being of the nationality of the disputants, to arrange the terms of the *modus*, and should, if the same be not accepted, sit as a Court of Appeal from the decision of such Committee, and finally determine the same.

25. The Tribunal should appoint a time within which the disputant powers should prepare and send in their respective cases and counter-cases.

26. On receipt of such cases the Tribunal should consider the same, and therefrom frame distinct issues of facts and law for decision.

27. Such issues should then be communicated to the disputants for their observations and assent. If they agree, then a day should be appointed, when the Tribunal will hear the case. If the parties do not agree on the issues, the hearing must be deferred until, with the assistance of the Tribunal, they are framed to meet the views of the litigants.

28. The disputant Powers should, if either think fit, nominate agents to represent them, as also counsel to argue the respective cases on the hearing.

29. All documents, including cases and counter-cases, may be

22. A partir de ce moment, chacune des parties en cause s'abstiendra de tout acte qui, directement ou indirectement, pourrait être interprété comme une agression de sa part ou comme indiquant qu'elle persiste dans la conduite ou les faits qui ont provoqué le litige.

23. Si le différend est de telle nature qu'un *modus vivendi*, en attendant sa solution, soit nécessaire et ne puisse être fixé à l'amiable, le Tribunal sera invité à le déterminer, après que chacune des nations litigantes lui aura fait connaître par écrit, dans un délai limité, sa manière de voir sur le caractère que doit revêtir le *modus vivendi*.

24. A la réception de ces pièces, le Tribunal nommera une commission de trois membres, dont aucun ne peut être ressortissant d'un des Etats en cause, et la chargera d'arranger les termes du *modus vivendi*; si ce dernier n'est pas accepté, le tribunal siégera comme cour d'appel et prononcera en dernier ressort.

25. Le tribunal fixera aux Etats litigants un terme avant l'expiration duquel ils devront préparer et envoyer leurs mémoires pour et contre.

26. Après réception de ces mémoires, le tribunal les examinera et rédigera un exposé des questions de fait et de droit, soulevées dans l'espèce.

27. Cet exposé sera soumis aux parties pour qu'elles l'acceptent ou fassent leurs observations. S'il est accepté, on fixera le jour où la cause sera appelée. S'il n'est pas accepté, la cause doit être ajournée jusqu'à ce que, avec le concours du Tribunal, il soit rédigé conformément aux vues des parties en cause.

28. Les Etats litigants peuvent, s'ils le jugent à propos, désigner des agents pour les représenter et des avocats pour soutenir leur cause devant le Tribunal.

29. Tous les documents, y compris les mémoires des deman-

in the respective languages of the disputants, but must be accompanied by verified translations in French, and all oral arguments must be in French.

30. The Tribunal should have full power to call for the production of any documents it may require, and for such other evidence as it may desire; and it should be empowered *proprio motu* to issue commissions for the purpose of obtaining evidence, appoint commissioners, and enable them to administer oaths; and to receive and consider the evidence thus obtained, if it thinks desirable, in private; the same being preserved, under the seal of the Court, in the archives thereof.

31. On the settlement of the issues, the Tribunal should possess the power to permit the intervention of third Powers on due and sufficient cause being shown that their interests are affected, or likely to be affected, by any decision the Tribunal may arrive at, and in its decisions on the main issue between the original parties to the dispute the Tribunal should be empowered to make such terms as regards such intervening parties as will safeguard their interests.

32. The mode in which the decisions or judgments of the Tribunal are to be given should be as follows:—

After consultation and discussion, each member of the Tribunal should draw up his judgment in the first instance in *draft*, and each judgment should be identified by a private mark, so that the author of the same should be unknown to his colleagues. Copies of each judgment, unmarked and unauthenticated, should be supplied by the chief Secretary to every member of the tribunal, each member thus having the opportunity of becoming acquainted with the views and opinions of his colleagues before the same are finally settled, without however knowing *whose* views and opinions they are, so that each Senator may have the opportunity of considering such views and opinions, of pointing out fallacies and errors, or correcting or modifying his own views. Then each deurs et des défendeurs, peuvent être rédigés dans la langue des parties, mais ils doivent être accompagnés de traductions vidimées en langue française et tous les débats oraux doivent avoir lieu en français.

30. Le tribunal a le droit d'exiger la production des documents qu'il juge utiles et des autres moyens de preuves qu'il peut désirer; il peut nommer de son propre chef des commissions pour s'assurer de certains faits et nommer des commissaires ayant la faculté d'assermenter des témoins; et de recevoir et apprécier à huis clos les preuves ainsi obtenues. Les rapports de ces commissaires sont conservés dans les archives sous le sceau de la Cour.

31. Dans ses exposés, le Tribunal peut permettre l'intervention de tierces parties lorsqu'il est évident pour lui que leurs intérêts sont ou seront vraisemblablement mis en cause par le jugement qui sera rendu, et, dans la décision sur la partie essentielle du litige entre les litigants primitifs, il a le droit de faire des stipulations en vue de sauvegarder les intérêts des intervenants.

32. Les jugements seront rendus dans les formes suivantes:

Après la consultation et la discussion, chaque membre du Tribunal opinera en première instance par écrit et sous pli cacheté portant un signe connu de lui seul, de telle sorte que ses collègues ne sachent pas quel a été son jugement. Le Chef-secrétaire remettra une copie de ces avis à chacun des membres du Tribunal, de manière à ce qu'il connaisse les opinions de ses collègues avant le vote définitif, sans toutefois savoir lequel d'entre eux a émis tel ou tel avis De cette façon, chaque Sénateur pourra apprécier ce qu'il y a de juste ou d'erroné dans les appréciations des autres membres de la Cour et aura la possibilité de corriger ou de modifier sa propre opinion. Chaque membre du member should draw up his *final* judgment, affixing thereto his private mark, and send the same in a sealed envelope to the chief Secretary.

33. The chief Secretary should then, after perusing the same, determine in whose favour the majority of the judgments is, and should draw up from the same minutes, and submit the same to the authors of the majority of the judgments, which minutes as finally settled, should constitute the judgment of the Tribunal.

34. Such judgment should then be officially delivered to the disputants, and within one month of such delivery to all the Concurring Nations. If the judgment be complied with, then the judgments, accompanied by a precis of the case and counter-case, should be communicated *in extenso*, so that every nation may know the views of the Tribunal on the law and the facts.

35. No appeal should lie from such judgment. All the judgments—as well those of the minority as those of the majority, together with the final judgment—should be made matter of record, and should be published, with the names of the respective authors, together with the precis of the case and counter-case, at the end of a term—say—of three years.

36. The Tribunal, besides hearing and deciding judicially matters in difference, should be also prepared at the instance of any two or more nations to express an extra-judicial opinion on any question of law or interpretation of treaties, with the object of preventing differences arising in the future.

37. It should also be ready, in view of Conferences or Congresses of Sovereigns and Statesmen, to suggest modifications and alterations with reference to international law on points of difference which remain unsettled—such as privateering, right of search, neutral rights, blockade, &c., &c.—and on which differences of opinion exist.

38. The Concurring Powers should also confer on the Tribunal in its character of a "College of International Law," a faculty to

Tribunal émettra ensuite par écrit son jugement *définitif*, en y apposant sa marque particulière et en l'envoyant sous pli cacheté au Chef-secrétaire.

33. Le Chef-secrétaire déterminera la majorité après avoir lu ces avis, au moyen desquels il rédigera le jugement, dont il soumettra le projet aux membres qui ont formé la majorité; ce projet, après avoir été revisé et approuvé, constituera le jugement définitif du Tribunal.

34. Ce jugement sera alors notifié aux parties litigantes, puis, dans le délai d'un mois, à tous les Etats contractants. Dès qu'il aura été accepté, les avis des membres du tribunal seront portés *in extenso* à la connaissance des Etats avec un résumé de la demande et de la réplique, de manière à ce que chaque nation puisse se rendre compte de l'opinion du Tribunal sur les questions de droit et de fait.

35. Le jugement rendu sera sans appel. Au bout d'un certain temps, trois ans par exemple, les avis de tous les membres du Tribunal, majorité et minorité, feront l'objet d'un rapport, qui sera publié avec les noms des opinants et avec le résumé de la demande et de la réplique.

36. Outre le devoir de trancher par voie juridique les litiges qui lui sont soumis, le Tribunal aura celui d'exprimer, sur la demande de deux ou plusieurs nations, son opinion sur des questions de droit ou sur l'interprétation de traités, en vue de prévenir des litiges dans l'avenir.

37. Il devra aussi se préparer à faire des propositions aux conférences ou congrès de souverains et d'hommes d'Etat pour des modifications aux lois internationales sur des points qui n'ont pas encore été réglés, en matière de lettres de marque, de perquisitions, de droit des neutres, de blocus, etc., etc., et sur lesquels les opinions diffèrent.

38. Les Etats contractants donneront aussi au Tribunal, en sa qualité de "Collège de droit international", la faculté de conférer

grant the "degree" of "Doctor of International Law," which should only be conferable on students who had obtained the degree of Doctor of Laws, or its equivalent, in the national colleges of the several Concurring Countries, and this degree should rank as the highest degree in the faculties of law, and should entitle the holder thereof to precedence according to date in all courts.

39. Switzerland seems a central and accessible locality in which to locate the Tribunal or college. The building should be worthy of the object, and, since the Senators should be in residence at least nine months of the year, sufficiently spacious to accommodate them and the staff. The site and grounds should be extra-territorialised, the whole being placed under the guardianship of the Republic, the Cantonal Government being entrusted with the necessary funds for the purchase of the selected site, for the erection of the building, and for the disbursement of all the expenses of maintenance.

40. The first cost would hardly exceed a sum of one million sterling, whilst the annual expenditure may be put at about £200,000 a year.

This first cost and annual expenditure might be defrayed by the concurring Powers in proportion and according to their rank as first, second, or third class Powers.

Thus, if for instance, six First-class Powers contributed to the Capital Fund £100,000 each, eight Second-class Powers £50,000 each, and eight or ten Third-class Powers £25,000 each, a sum of £1,200,000 would be provided, sufficient to purchase the site and defray the cost of buildings, &c., &c.

If then these Powers—which may be called the "Concurring Powers"—agreed to contribute each of them annually—the First-class £20,000, the Second-class £10,000, and the Third-class £5,000, an income of £240,000 would be raised, sufficient to provide amply for salaries and all other expenses, as well as to form the nucleus of a Pension Fund.

le grade de " Docteur en droit international ", exclusivement à des étudiants qui ont obtenu le grade de docteur en droit ou son équivalent dans les Universités des dits Etats ; ce grade sera considéré comme supérieur à tous les autres dans les facultés de droit et donnera à celui qui le porte la préséance dans toutes les Cours de justice.

39. La Suisse semble être un point central et accessible pour servir de siège au Tribunal. L'édifice doit être digne de sa destination et suffisamment spacieux pour les juges, qui doivent y résider au moins neuf mois de l'année, et pour le personnel. Il doit jouir de l'exterritorialité et être placé sous la garde de la République. Le gouvernement cantonal doit être pourvu des fonds nécessaires pour l'achat du terrain, pour la construction de l'édifice et pour toutes les dépenses d'entretien.

40. Les premiers frais excéderaient à peine vingt-cinq millions francs et les dépenses d'entretien peuvent être évaluées à cinq millions par année.

Les premiers fonds doivent être fournis par les Etats contractants en proportion de leur rang comme puissances de premier, de second ou de troisième ordre.

Si, par exemple, six puissances de premier ordre contribuent pour 2,500,000 fr. chacune, huit de second ordre pour 1,250,000 fr. et huit ou dix de troisième ordre pour 625,000 fr., on réunira ainsi une somme de 30,000,000 fr., amplement suffisante pour couvrir les frais d'achat du terrain, de construction de l'édifice, etc., etc.

Si ensuite ces puissances, que nous appellerons "puissances contractantes", consentent à participer annuellement aux frais à raison de 500,000 fr. pour la première classe, 250,000 fr. pour la seconde et 125,000 fr. pour la troisième, cela suffira pleinement pour les honoraires et toutes les autres dépenses, de même que pour former le noyau d'un fonds de pensions.

TREATY OF WASHINGTON,

BETWEEN GREAT BRITAIN AND THE UNITED STATES OF AMERICA.

Signed at Washington, May 8th, 1871.

Ratifications exchanged at London, June 17th, 1871.

Her Britannic Majesty and the United States of America, being desirous to provide for an amicable settlement of all causes of difference between the two countries, have for that purpose appointed their respective Plenipotentiaries, that is to say:—

For Great Britain: Earl de Grey and Ripon, Lord President of the Privy Council; Sir Stafford Henry Northcote, Bart., M.P.; Sir Edward Thornton, Ambassador to the U.S.A.; Sir John Alexander Macdonald, Attorney-General for Canada, and Professor Mountague Bernard; and for the United States: Hamilton Fish, Secretary of State; Robert Cumming Schenck, American Minister to Great Britain; Samuel Nelson, Judge of the Supreme Court; Ebenezer Rockwood Hoar, Esq., of Massachusetts, and George Henry Williams, Esq., of Oregon.

And the said Plenipotentiaries, after having exchanged their full powers, which were found to be in due and proper form, have agreed to and concluded the following Articles:—

SECTION I.—VIOLATION OF NEUTRALITY.

ART. 1.—Whereas differences have arisen between the Government of the United States and the Government of Her Britannic Majesty, and still exist, growing out of the acts committed by the several vessels which have given rise to the claims generically known as the "Alabama" claims:

And whereas Her Britannic Majesty has authorised Her High Commissioners and Plenipotentiaries to express, in a friendly spirit, the regret felt by Her Majesty's Government for the escape, under whatever circumstances, of the "Alabama" and other vessels from British ports, and for the depredations committed by those vessels:

Now, in order to remove and adjust all complaints and claims on the part of the United States, and to provide for the speedy settlement of such claims, which are not admitted by Her Britannic Majesty's Government, the High Contracting Parties agree that all the said claims, growing out of acts committed by the aforesaid vessels, and generically known as the "Alabama" claims, shall be referred to a Tribunal of Arbitration to be composed of five Arbitrators to be appointed in the following manner, that is to say: one shall be named by Her Britannic Majesty; one shall be named by the President of the United States; His Majesty the King of Italy shall be requested to name one; the President of the Swiss Confederation shall be requested to name one; and His Majesty the Emperor of Brazil shall be requested to name one.

In case of the death, absence, or incapacity to serve of any or either of the said Arbitrators, or in the event of either of the said Arbitrators omitting or declining or ceasing to act as such, Her Britannic Majesty, or the President of the United States, or His Majesty the King of Italy, or the President of the Swiss Confederation, or His Majesty the Emperor of Brazil, as the case may be, may forthwith name another person to act as Arbitrator in the place and stead of the Arbitrator originally named by such head of a State.

And in the event of the refusal or omission for two months after receipt of the request from either of the High Contracting Parties of His Majesty the King of Italy, or the President of the Swiss Confederation, or His Majesty the Emperor of Brazil, to name an Arbitrator either to fill the original appointment or in the place of one who may have died, be absent, or incapacitated, or who may omit, decline, or from any cause cease to act as such Arbitrator, His Majesty the King of Sweden and Norway shall be requested to name one or more persons, as the case may be, to act as such Arbitrator or Arbitrators.

ART. 2.—The Arbitrators shall meet at Geneva, in Switzerland, at the earliest convenient day after they shall have been named, and shall proceed impartially and carefully to examine and decide all questions that shall be laid before them on the part of the Governments of Her Britannic Majesty and the United States respectively. All questions considered by the Tribunal, including the final award, shall be decided by a majority of all the Arbitrators.

Each of the High Contracting Parties shall also name one person to attend the Tribunal as its Agent to represent it generally in all matters connected with the Arbitration.

ART 3.—The written or printed case of each of the two Parties accompanied by the documents, the official correspondence, and other evidence on which each relies, shall be delivered in duplicate to each of the Arbitrators and to the Agent of the other Party as soon as may be after the organisation of the Tribunal, but within a period not exceeding six months from the date of the exchange of the ratifications of this Treaty.

ART. 4.—Within four months after the delivery on both sides of the written or printed case, either Party may, in like manner, deliver in duplicate to each of the said Arbitrators, and to the Agent of the other Party, a counter case and additional documents, correspondence, and evidence, in reply to the case, documents, correspondence, and evidence, so presented by the other Party.

The Arbitrators may, however, extend the time for delivering such counter case, documents, correspondence, and evidence, when, in their judgment, it becomes necessary, in consequence of the distance of the place from which the evidence to be presented is to be procured.

If in the case submitted to the Arbitrators either Party shall have specified or alluded to any report or document in its own exclusive possession without annexing a copy, such Party shall be bound, if the other Party thinks proper to apply for it, to furnish that Party with a copy thereof; and either Party may call upon the other, through the Arbitrators, to produce the originals or certified copies of any papers adduced as evidence, giving in each instance such reasonable notice as the Arbitrators may require.

ART. 5.—It shall be the duty of the Agent of each Party, within two months after the expiration of the time limited for the delivery of the counter case on both sides, to deliver in duplicate to each of the said Arbitrators and to the Agent of the other Party a written or printed argument showing the points and referring to the evidence upon which his Government relies; and the Arbitrators may, if they desire further elucidation with regard to any point, require a written or printed statement or argument or oral argument by counsel upon it; but in such case the other Party shall be entitled to reply either orally or in writing, as the case may be.

ART. 6. — In deciding the matters submitted to the Arbitrators they shall be governed by the following three rules, which are agreed upon by the High Contracting Parties as rules to be taken as applicable to the case, and by such principles of international law not inconsistent therewith as the Arbitrators a ll determine to have been applicable to the case:—

RULES.

A neutral Government is bound—

First:—To use due diligence to prevent the fitting out, arming or equipping, within its jurisdiction, of any vessel which it has reasonable ground to believe is intended to cruise or to carry on war against a Power with which it is at peace; and also to use like diligence to prevent the departure from its jurisdiction of any vessel intended to cruise or carry on war as above, such vessel having been specially adapted, in whole or in part, within such jurisdiction, to warlike use.

Secondly:—Not to permit or suffer either belligerent to make use of its ports or waters as the base of naval operations against the other, or for the purpose of the renewal or augmentation of military supplies or arms, or the recruitment of men.

Thirdly:—To exercise due diligence in its own ports and waters, and, as to all persons within its jurisdiction, to prevent any violation of the foregoing obligations and duties.

Her Britannic Majesty has commanded her High Commissioners and Plenipotentiaries to declare that Her Majesty's Government cannot assent to the foregoing rules as a statement of principles of international law which were in force at the time when the claims mentioned in Article I. arose, but that Her Majesty's Government, in order to evince its desire of strengthening the friendly relations between the two countries and of making satisfactory provision for the future, agrees that, in deciding the questions between the two countries arising out of those claims, the Arbitrators should assume that Her Majesty's Government had undertaken to act upon the principles set forth in these rules.

And the High Contracting Parties agree to observe these rules as between themselves in future, and to bring them to the knowledge of other maritime Powers and to invite them to accede to them.

ART. 7.—The decision of the Tribunal shall, if possible, be made within three months from the close of the argument on both sides.

It shall be made in writing and dated, and shall be signed by the Arbitrators who may assent to it.

The said Tribunal shall first determine as to each vessel separately whether Great Britain has, by any act or omission, failed to fulfil any of the duties set forth in the foregoing three rules, or recognised by the principles of international law not inconsistent with such rules, and shall certify such fact as to each of the said vessels. In case the Tribunal find that Great Britain has failed to fulfil any duty or duties as aforesaid, it may, if it think proper, proceed to award a sum in gross to be paid by Great Britain to the United States for all the claims referred to it; and in such case the gross sum so awarded shall be paid in coin by the Government of Great Britain to the Government of the United States at Washington within twelve months after the date of the award.

The award shall be in duplicate, one copy whereof shall be

delivered to the Agent of Great Britain for his Government, and the other copy shall be delivered to the Agent of the United States for his Government.

ART. 8.—Each Government shall pay its own Agent and provide for the proper remuneration of the Counsel employed by it, and of the Arbitrator appointed by it, and for the expense of preparing and submitting its case to the Tribunal. All other expenses connected with the Arbitration shall be defrayed by the two Governments in equal moieties.

ART. 9.—The Arbitrators shall keep an accurate record of their proceedings, and may appoint and employ the necessary officers to assist them.

ART. 10.—(1.) In case the Tribunal finds that Great Britain has failed to fulfil any duty or duties as aforesaid, and does not award a sum in gross, the High Contracting Parties agree that a Board of Assessors shall be appointed to ascertain and determine what claims are valid, and what amount or amounts shall be paid by Great Britain to the United States on account of the liability arising from such failure as to each vessel, according to the extent of such liability as decided by the Arbitrators.

(2.) The Board of Assessors shall be constituted as follows: One member thereof shall be named by Her Britannic Majesty, one member thereof shall be named by the President of the United States, and one member thereof shall be named by the Representative at Washington of His Majesty the King of Italy; and in case of a vacancy happening from any cause, it shall be filled in the same manner in which the original appointment was made.

(3.) As soon as possible after such nominations the Board of Assessors shall be organised in Washington, with power to hold their sittings there, or in New York, or in Boston.

(4.) The members thereof shall severally subscribe a solemn declaration that they will impartially and carefully examine and decide, to the best of their judgment and according to justice and equity, all matters submitted to them, and shall forthwith proceed, under such rules and regulations as they may prescribe, to the investigation of the claims which shall be presented to them by the Government of the United States, and shall examine and decide upon them in such order and manner as they may think proper, but upon such evidence or information only as shall be furnished by or on behalf of the Governments of Great Britain and of the United States respectively.

(5.) They shall be bound to hear on each separate claim, if required, one person on behalf of each Government as Counsel or Agent.

(6.) A majority of the Assessors in each case shall be sufficient for a decision.

(7.) The decision of the Assessors shall be given upon each claim in writing, and shall be signed by them respectively, and dated.

(8.) Every claim shall be presented to the Assessors within six months from the day of their first meeting; but they may, for good cause shown, extend the time for the presentation of any claim to a further period not exceeding three months.

(9.) The Assessors shall report to each Government, at or before the expiration of one year from the date of their first meeting, the amount of claims decided by them up to the date of such report; if further claims then remain undecided, they shall make a further report at or before the expiration of two years from the date of such first meeting; and in case any claims remain undetermined at that time, they shall make a final report within a further period of six months.

(10.) The report or reports shall be made in duplicate, and one copy thereof shall be delivered to the Representative of Her Britannic Majesty at Washington, and one copy thereof to the Secretary of State of the United States.

(11.) All sums of money which may be awarded under this Article shall be payable at Washington, in coin, within twelve months after the delivery of each report.

(12.) The Board of Assessors may employ such clerks as they shall think necessary.

(13.) The expenses of the Board of Assessors shall be borne equally by the two Governments, and paid from time to time, as may be found expedient, on the production of accounts certified by the Board. The remuneration of the Assessors shall also be paid by the two Governments in equal moieties in a similar manner.

ART. 11.—The High Contracting Parties engage to consider the result of the proceedings of the Tribunal of Arbitration and of the Board of Assessors, should such Board be appointed, as a full, perfect, and final settlement of all the claims hereinbefore referred to; and further engage that every such claim, whether the same may or may not have been presented to the notice of, made, preferred, or laid before the Tribunal or Board, shall, from and after the conclusion of the proceedings of the Tribunal or Board, be considered and treated as finally settled, barred, and thenceforth inadmissible.

SECTION II.—MARITIME CAPTURES.

ART. 12.—The High Contracting Parties agree that all claims on the part of Corporations, Companies, or private individuals, citizens of the United States, upon the Government of Her Britannic Majesty, arising out of acts committed against the persons or property of citizens of the United States during the period between the 13th of April, 1861, and the 9th of April, 1865, inclusive, not being claims growing out of the acts of the vessels referred to in Article 1 of this Treaty; and all claims, with the like exception, on the part of Corporations, Companies, or private individuals, subjects of Her Britannic Majesty, upon the Government of the United States, arising out of acts committed against the persons or property of subjects of Her Britannic Majesty during the same period, which may have been presented to either Government for its interposition with the other, and which yet remain unsettled, as well as any other such claims which may be presented within the time specified in Article 14 of this Treaty, shall be referred to three Commissioners, to be appointed in the following manner, that is to say:—One Commissioner shall be named by Her Britannic Majesty, one by the President of the United States, and a third by Her Britannic Majesty and the President of the United States conjointly; and in case the third Commissioner shall not have been so named within a period of three months from the date of the exchange of the ratifications of this Treaty, then the third Commissioner shall be named by the Representative at Washington of His Majesty the King of Spain. In case of the death, absence, or incapacity of any Commissioner, or in the event of any Commissioner omitting or ceasing to act, the vacancy shall be filled in the manner hereinbefore provided for making the original appointment, the period of three months in case of such substitution being calculated from the date of the happening of the vacancy.

The Commissioners so named shall meet at Washington at the earliest convenient period after they have been respectively named; and shall, before proceeding to any business, make and subscribe a solemn declaration that they will impartially and carefully examine and decide, to the best of their judgment, and according to justice and equity, all such claims as shall be laid before them on the part of the Governments of Her Britannic Majesty and of the United States, respectively; and such declaration shall be entered on the record of their proceedings.

ART. 13.—The Commissioners shall then forthwith proceed to the investigation of the claims which shall be presented to them. They shall investigate and decide such claims in such order and such manner as they may think proper, but upon such evidence or information only as shall be furnished by or on behalf of their respective Governments. They shall be bound to receive and consider all written documents or statements which may be presented to them by or on behalf of their respective Governments in support of, or in answer to, any claim; and to hear, if required, one person on each side, on behalf of each Government, as Counsel or Agent for such Government, on each and every separate claim. A majority of the Commissioners shall be sufficient for an award in each case. The award shall be given upon each claim in writing, and shall be signed by the Commissioners assenting to it. It shall be competent for each Government to name one person to attend the Commissioners as its Agent to present and support claims on its behalf, and to answer claims made upon it, and to represent it generally in all matters connected with the investigation and decision thereof.

The High Contracting Parties hereby engage to consider the decision of the Commissioners as absolutely final and conclusive, upon each claim decided upon by them, and to give full effect to such decisions without any objection, evasion, or delay whatsoever.

ART. 14.—Every claim shall be presented to the Commissioners within six months from the day of their first meeting, unless in any case where reasons for delay shall be established to the satisfaction of the Commissioners; and then, and in any such case, the period for presenting the claim may be extended by them to any time not exceeding three months longer.

The Commissioners shall be bound to examine and decide upon every claim within two years from the day of their first meeting. It shall be competent for the Commissioners to decide in each case whether any claim has or has not been duly made, preferred, and laid before them, either wholly or to any and what extent, according to the true intent and meaning of this Treaty.

ART. 15.—All sums of money which may be awarded by the Commissioners on account of any claim shall be paid by the one Government to the other, as the case may be, within twelve months after the date of the final award, without interest, and without any deduction save as specified in Art. 16 of this Treaty.

ART. 16.—The Commissioners shall keep an accurate record,

and correct minutes or notes of all their proceedings, with the dates thereof, and may appoint and employ a Secretary, and any other necessary officer or officers, to assist them in the transaction of the business which may come before them.

Each Government shall pay its own Commissioner and Agent or Counsel. All other expenses shalt be defrayed by the two Governments in equal moieties.

The whole expenses of the Commission, including contingent expenses, shall be defrayed by a rateable deduction on the amount of the sums awarded by the Commissioners; provided always that such deduction shall not exceed the rate of five per cent. on the sums so awarded.

ART. 17.—The High Contracting Parties engage to consider the result of the procceedings of this Commission as a full, perfect, and final settlement of all such claims as are mentioned in Article 12 of this Treaty upon either Government; and further engage that every such claim, whether or not the same may have been presented to the notice of, made, preferred, or laid before the said Commission, shall, from and after the conclusion of the proceedings of the said Commission, be considered and treated as finally settled, barred, and thenceforth inadmissible.

SECTION III.—FISHERY RIGHTS.

ART. 18.—It is agreed between the High Contracting Parties that liberty, which "applies solely to the sea fishery," be given to the United States fishermen to fish, etc., in places defined therein for the term of years mentioned in Art. 33 of this Treaty.

ART. 19.—It is agreed that similar rights be conceded in places defined therein to British subjects for the same term of years.

ART. 20.—Relates to places reserved from the common right of fishing under the Treaty of Washington, of the 5th June, 1854, and provides that should any question arise in regard to these, a Commission shall be appointed to designate such places, constituted in the same manner, and having the same powers, duties, and authority as the Commission appointed under the first Article of the Treaty of the 5th of June, 1854.

ART. 21.—It is agreed that, for the term of years mentioned in Article 33, the produce of the fisheries shall be admitted into each country, respectively, free of duty.

ART. 22.—It is further agreed that Commissioners shall be appointed to determine the amount of any compensation which, in their opinion, ought to be paid by the Government of the United States in return for the privileges accorded under Article 18 of this Treaty; and that any sum of money which the said Commissioners may so award shall be paid by the United States Government, in a gross sum, within twelve months after such award shall have been given.

ART. 23.—The Commissioners referred to in the preceding Article shall be appointed in the following manner, that is to say: One Commissioner shall be named by Her Britannic Majesty, one by the President of the United States, and a third by Her Britannic Majesty and the President of the United States, conjointly; and in case the third Commissioner shall not have been so named within a period of three months from the date when this Article shall take effect, then the third Commissioner shall be named by the Representative at London of His Majesty the Emperor of Austria and King of Hungary. In case of the death, absence, or incapacity of any Commissioner, or in the event of any Commissioner omitting or ceasing to act, the vacancy shall be filled in the manner hereinbefore provided for making the original appointment, the period of three months in case of such substitution being calculated from the date of the happening of the vacancy.

The Commissioners so named shall meet in the city of Halifax, in the province of Nova Scotia, at the earliest convenient period after they have been respectively named, and shall, before proceeding to any business, make and subscribe a solemn declaration that they will impartially and carefully examine and decide the matters referred to them, to the best of their judgment, and according to justice and equity; and such declaration shall be entered on the record of their proceedings.

Each of the High Contracting Parties shall also name one person to attend the Commission as its Agent, to represent it generally in all matters connected with the Commission.

ART. 24.—The proceedings shall be conducted in such order as the Commissioners appointed under Articles 22 and 23 of this Treaty shall determine. They shall be bound to receive such oral or written testimony as either Government may present. If either Party shall offer oral testimony, the other Party shall have the right of cross-examination, under such rules as the Commissioners shall prescribe.

If in the case submitted to the Commissioners either Party shall have specified or alluded to any report or document in its own exclusive possession, without annexing a copy, such Party shall be bound, if the other Party thinks proper to apply for it, to furnish that Party with a copy thereof; and either Party may call upon the other, through the Commissioners, to produce the originals or certified copies of any papers adduced as evidence, giving in each instance such reasonable notice as the Commissioners may require.

The case on either side shall be closed within a period of six months from the date of the organisation of the Commission, and the Commissioners shall be requested to give their award as soon as possible thereafter. The aforesaid period of six months may be extended for three months in case of a vacancy occurring among the Commissioners under the circumstances contemplated in Article 23 of this Treaty.

ART. 25.—The Commissioners shall keep an accurate record and correct minutes or notes of all their proceedings, with the dates thereof, and may appoint and employ a Secretary and any other necessary officer or officers to assist them in the transaction of the business which may come before them.

Each of the High Contracting Parties shall pay its own Commissioner and Agent or Council; all other expenses shall be defrayed by the two Governments in equal moieties.

SECTION IV.—DELIMITATIONS.

ART. 26.—Refers to the free and open navigation of the rivers St. Lawrence, Yukon, Porcupine, and Stikine.

ART. 27.—Refers to the use on terms of equality of certain canals, both in the Dominion and in the States.

ART. 28.—Stipulates the free and open navigation of Lake Michigan for the term of years mentioned in Art. 33.

ART. 29.—Relates to Custom duties and transit of goods for the same term of years.

ART. 30.—Regulates the transportation of goods, export duties, etc., for the same term of years.

ART. 31.—Relates to the removal, by the Parliament of the Dominion of Canada, and the Legislature of New Brunswick, of duties on lumber and timber for the same term of years.

ART. 32.—Agrees that the provisions and stipulations of Articles 18 to 25 of this Treaty inclusive, shall extend to the Colony of Newfoundland, so far as they are applicable.

ART. 33. — The foregoing Articles 18 to 25 inclusive, and Article 30 of this Treaty, shall take effect as soon as the laws required to carry them into operation shall have been passed by the Imperial Parliament of Great Britain, by the Parliament of Canada, and by the Legislature of Prince Edward's Island on the one hand, and by the Congress of the United States on the other. Such assent having been given, the said Articles shall remain in force for the period of ten years from the date at which they may come into operation, and further, until the expiration of two years after either of the High Contracting Parties shall have given notice to the other of its wish to terminate the same; each of the High Contracting Parties being at liberty to give such notice to the other at the end of the said period of ten years or at any time afterward.

ART. 34.—It is agreed that the respective claims of the two Governments in regard to the boundary line between the United States and Canada, running south through the middle of the Channel which separates the Continent and Vancouvers Island and thence through the middle of Fuca Straits to the Pacific Ocean, which by Article 1 of the Treaty concluded at Washington June 15th, 1846, was referred to Commissioners who were unable to agree upon the same, "shall be submitted to the Arbitration and award of His Majesty the Emperor of Germany, who, having regard to the above-mentioned Article of the said Treaty, shall decide thereupon, finally and without appeal, which of those claims is most in accordance with the true interpretation of the Treaty of June 15th, 1846."

ART. 35.—The award of His Majesty the Emperor of Germany shall be considered as absolutely final and conclusive; and full effect shall be given to such award without any objection, evasion, or delay whatsoever. Such decision shall be given in writing and dated; it shall be in whatsoever form His Majesty may choose to adopt; it shall be delivered to the Representatives or other public Agents of Great Britain and of the United States respectively, who may be actually at Berlin, and shall be considered as operative from the day of the date of the delivery thereof.

ART. 36.—The written or printed case of each of the two Parties, accompanied by the evidence offered in support of the same, shall be laid before His Majesty the Emperor of Germany within six months from the date of the exchange of the ratifications of this Treaty, and a copy of such case and evidence shall be communicated by each Party to the other, through their respective Representatives at Berlin.

The High Contracting Parties may include, in the evidence to be considered by the Arbitrator, such documents, official correspondence, and other official or public statements bearing on the subject of the reference as they may consider necessary to the support of their respective cases.

After the written or printed case shall have been communicated by each Party to the other, each Party shall have the power of drawing up and laying before the Arbitrator a second and definitive statement, if it think fit to do so, in reply to the case of the other Party so communicated, which definitive statement shall be so laid before the Arbitrator, and also be mutually communicated in the same manner as aforesaid, by each Party to the other, within six months from the date of laying the first statement of the case before the Arbitrator.

ART. 37.—If in the case submitted to the Arbitrator either Party shall specify or allude to any report or document in his own exclusive possession without annexing a copy, such Party shall be bound, if the other Party thinks proper to apply for it, to furnish that Party with a copy thereof, and either Party may call upon the other, through the Arbitrator, to produce the originals or certified copies of any papers adduced as evidence, giving in each instance such reasonable notice as the Arbitrator may require. And if the Arbitrator should desire further elucidation or evidence with regard to any point contained in the statements laid before him, he shall be at liberty to require it from either Party, and he shall be at liberty to hear one Counsel or Agent for each Party, in relation to any matter, and at such time, and in such manner as he may think fit.

ART. 38.—The Representatives or other public Agents of Great Britain, and of the United States, at Berlin respectively, shall be considered as the Agents of their respective Governments to conduct their cases before the Arbitrator, who shall be requested to address all his communications, and give all his notices, to such Representatives or other public Agents who shall represent their Governments generally in all matters connected with the Arbitration.

ART. 39.—It shall be competent to the Arbitrator to proceed

in the said Arbitration, and all matters relating thereto, as and when he shall see fit, either in person, or by a person or persons named by him for that purpose, either in the presence or absence of either or both Agents, and either orally or by written discussion, or otherwise.

ART. 40.—The Arbitrator may, if he think fit, appoint a Secretary or Clerk, for the purposes of the proposed Arbitration, at such rate of remuneration as he shall think proper. This and all other expenses of and connected with the said Arbitration shall be provided for as hereinafter stipulated.

ART. 41.—The Arbitrator shall be requested to deliver, together with his award, an account of all the costs and expenses which he may have been put to, in relation to this matter, which shall forthwith be repaid by the two Governments in equal moieties.

ART. 42.—The Arbitrator shall be requested to give his award in writing as early as convenient after the whole case on each side shall have been laid before him, and to deliver one copy thereof to each of the said Agents.

ART. 43.—The present Treaty shall be duly ratified by Her Britannic Majesty, and by the President of the United States of America, by and with the advice and consent of the Senate thereof, and the ratifications shall be exchanged either at London or at Washington within six months from the date hereof, or earlier if possible.

TRAITE DE WASHINGTON

du 8 Mai 1871.

Les Quatre Cas d'Arbitration.

Le Traité de Washington de 1871 contient quatre cas d'Arbitrage :

Le premier relatif à des faits de violation de neutralité (Art. I à XI) déféré à un Tribunal d'Arbitrage siégeant à Genève ;

Le deuxième relatif à des questions de validité de prises maritimes (Art. XII à XVII) déféré à un Tribunal d'Arbitrage siégeant à Washington ;

Le troisième relatif à des droits de pêche (Art. XVIII à XXV) déféré à un Tribunal d'Arbitrage siégeant à Halifax ;

Le quatrième relatif à une contestation de limites (Art. XXXIV à XLII) déféré à la décision arbitrale de Sa Majesté l'Empereur d'Allemagne.

Les Trois Règles.

Première Règle.—Un gouvernement neutre est obligé de faire toutes les diligences nécessaires (due diligence) pour s'opposer, dans les limites de sa juridiction territoriale, à ce qu'un vaisseau soit mis en mesure de prendre la mer, soit armé on équipé, quand ce gouvernement a des motifs suffisants pour penser que ce vaisseau est destiné à croiser ou à faire des actes de guerre contre une puissance avec laquelle il est lui-même en paix. Ce gouvernement doit faire également toutes diligences nécessaires pour s'opposer à ce qu'un vaisseau destiné à croiser ou à faire des actes de guerre, comme il est dit ci-dessus, quitte les limites de sa juridiction territoriale, dans le cas où il aurait été spécialement adapté, soit en totalité soit en partie, à des usages belligérants.

Deuxième Règle.—Un gouvernement neutre ne doit ni permettre ni tolérer que l'un des belligérants se serve de ses ports ou de ses eaux comme d'une base d'opérations navales contre l'autre belligérant ; il ne doit ni permettre ni tolérer non plus que l'un des belligérants renouvelle ou augmente ses approvisionnements militaires, qu'il se procure des armes, ou bien encore qu'il recrute des hommes.

Troisième Règle.—Un gouvernement neutre est obligé de faire toutes les diligences nécessaires dans ses ports et dans ses eaux, pour prévenir toute violation des obligations et des devoirs ci-dessus énoncés ; il agira de même à l'égard de toutes les personnes qui se trouveront dans sa juridiction.—Conf. Martens, "Nouveau Recueil," XX, 698.

MEMORIAL OF THE BAR ASSOCIATION OF THE STATE OF NEW YORK.

Adopted in the City of Albany, 22nd January, 1896.

To the President:—

The Petition of the Bar Association of the State of New York respectfully shows:—

That, impelled by a sense of duty to the state and nation and a purpose to serve the cause of humanity everywhere, your Petitioner at its annual session held in the city of Albany on the 22nd day of January, 1896, appointed a committee to consider the subject of International Arbitration and to devise and submit to it a plan for the organisation of a tribunal to which may hereafter be submitted controverted international questions between the Governments of Great Britain and the United States.

That said committee entered upon the performance of its duty at once, and, after long and careful deliberation, reached the conclusion that it is impracticable, if not impossible, to form a satisfactory Anglo-American Tribunal, for the adjustment of grave international controversies, that shall be composed only of representatives of the two Governments of Great Britain and the United States.

That, in order that the subject might receive more mature and careful consideration, the matter was referred to a sub-committee, by whom an extended report was made to the full committee. This report was adopted as the report of the full committee, and, at a Special Meeting of the State Bar Association called to consider the matter, and held at the State Capitol in the city of

Albany on the 16th day of April, 1896, the action of the committee was affirmed and the plan submitted fully endorsed. As the report referred to contains the argument in brief, both in support of the contention that it is impracticable to organise a court composed only of representatives of the Governments of Great Britain and the United States, and in support of the plan outlined in it, a copy of the report is hereto appended, and your Petitioner asks that it be made and considered a part of this Petition.

That your Petitioner cordially endorses the principle of Arbitration for the settlement of all controversies between civilised nations, and it believes that it is quite within the possibility of the educated intellects of the leading Powers of the world to agree upon a plan for a great central World's Court that, by the common consent of nations, shall eventually have jurisdiction of all disputes arising between Independent Powers that cannot be adjusted by friendly diplomatic negotiations. Holding tenaciously to this opinion and, conscious that there must be a first step in every good work, else there will never be a second, your Petitioner respectfully but earnestly urges your early consideration of the subject that ultimately—at least during the early years of the coming century—the honest purpose of good men of every nation may be realised in devising means for the peaceful solution of menacing disputes between civilised nations. Your Petitioner therefore submits to you the following recommendations :—

First.—The establishment of a permanent International Tribunal, to be known as "The International Court of Arbitration."

Second.—Such Court shall be composed of nine members, one each from nine independent states or nations, such representative to be a member of the Supreme or Highest Court of the nation he shall represent, chosen by a majority vote of his associates, because of his high character as a publicist and judge, and his recognised ability and irreproachable integrity. Each judge thus selected to hold office during life or the will of the Court selecting him.

THIRD.—The Court thus constituted shall make its own rules of procedure, shall have power to fix its place of sessions and to change the same from time to time as circumstances and the convenience of litigants may suggest, and to appoint such clerks and attendants as the Court may require.

FOURTH.—Controverted questions arising between any two or more Independent Powers, whether represented in said "International Court of Arbitration" or not, at the option of said Powers, may be submitted by treaty between said Powers to said Court, providing only that said treaty shall contain a stipulation to the effect that all parties thereto shall respect and abide by the rules and regulations of said Court, and conform to whatever determination it shall make of said controversy.

FIFTH.—Said Court shall be opened at all times for the filing of cases and counter cases under treaty stipulations by any nation, whether represented in the Court or not, and such orderly proceedings in the interim between sessions of the Court, in preparation for argument, and submission of the controversy, as may seem necessary, to be taken as the rules of the Court provide for and may be agreed upon between the litigants.

SIXTH.—Independent Powers not represented in said Court, but which may have become parties litigant in a controversy before it and, by treaty stipulation, have agreed to submit to its adjudication, shall comply with the rules of the Court and shall contribute such stipulated amount to its expenses as may be provided for by its rules, or determined by the Court.

SEVENTH.—Your Petitioner also recommends that you enter a

once into correspondence and negotiation, through the proper diplomatic channels, with representatives of the Governments of Great Britain, France, Germany, Russia, The Netherlands, Mexico, Brazil and the Argentine Republic, for a union with the Government of the United States in the laudable undertaking of forming an International Court substantially on the basis herein outlined.

Your Petitioner presumes it is unnecessary to enter into further argument in support of the foregoing propositions than is contained in the report of its committee, which is appended hereto and which your Petitioner has already asked to have considered a part of this Petition. Your Petitioner will be pardoned, however, if it invite especial attention to that part of the report emphasising the fact that the plan herein outlined is intended, if adopted, at once to meet the universal demand among English-speaking people for a permanent tribunal to settle contested international questions that may hereafter arise between the Governments of Great Britain and the United States.

While it is contended that it is wholly impracticable to form such a tribunal without the friendly interposition of other nations on the joint invitation of the Powers who unite in its organization, it is very evident that a most acceptable permanent International Court may be speedily secured by the united and harmonious action of said Powers as already suggested. Should obstacles be interposed to the acceptance, by any of the Powers named by your Petitioner, of the invitation to name a representative for such a court on the plan herein generally outlined, some other equally satisfactory Power could be solicited to unite in the creation of such a court.

Believing that, in the fulfilment of its destiny among the civilised nations of the world, it has devolved upon the younger of the two Anglo-Saxon Powers, now happily in the enjoyment of nothing but future peaceful prospects, to take the first step looking to the permanency of peace among nations, your Petitioner, representing the Bar of the Empire State, earnestly appeals to you as the Chief Executive Officer of the Government of the United States, to take such timely action as shall lead eventually to the organisation of such a tribunal as has been outlined in the foregoing recommendations. While ominous sounds of martial preparations are in the air, the shipbuilder's hammer is industriously welding the bolt, and arsenals are testing armour-plates, your Petitioner, apprehensive for the future, feels that delays are dangerous, and it urgently reccommends that action be taken at once by you to compass the realisation of the dream of good men in every period of the world's history, when nations shall learn war no more and enlightened Reason shall fight the only battles fought among the children of men.

And your Petitioner will ever pray.

Attested in behalf of the New York State Bar Association at the Capitol in the City of Albany, N.Y., April 16th, 1896.

ED. G. WHITAKER, President.

L. B. PROCTOR, Secretary.

CONVENTION

CONCLUDED THE 15TH JANUARY, 1880, BETWEEN FRANCE AND THE UNITED STATES OF AMERICA, RELATIVE TO CERTAIN CLAIMS FOR DAMAGES CAUSED BY WAR.

The French Republic and the United States of America, animated by the desire of settling, by a friendly arrangement, the claims made by the citizens of each of the two countries against the Government of the other, and arising from acts committed during the state of war or insurrection, by the civil and military authorities of either country, under the circumstances specified below, have resolved to take measures to this effect, by means of a Convention, and have appointed as their plenipotentiaries for conferring and establishing an agreement, Mr. George Maxim Outrey, Envoy Extraordinary and Minister Plenipotentiary of France at Washington (appointed by the President of the French Republic), and Mr. William Maxwell Evarts, Secretary of State to the United States (appointed by the President of the United States), who, after having communicated their respective plenary powers and having found them in good and due order, have agreed to the following articles :—

ART. 1.—All the claims raised by corporations, companies, or individuals, citizens of the United States, against the French Government, and resulting from acts committed on the high seas or on the territory of France, her colonies and dependencies, during the last war between France and Mexico, or during that of 1870-1871 between France and Germany, and during the subsequent civil troubles known under the name "Insurrection of the Commune," by the French civil or military authorities, to the prejudice of the persons or property of citizens of the United States not in the service of the enemies of France and who have not voluntarily lent them aid or assistance, and, on the other hand, all the claims raised by corporations, companies or individual French citizens, against the Government of the United States and founded on acts committed on the high seas

CONVENTION
CONCLUE LE 15 JANVIER 1880 ENTRE LA FRANCE ET LES ÉTATS-UNIS D'AMÉRIQUE, RELATIVE A CERTAINES RÉCLAMATIONS POUR DOMMAGES DE GUERRE.

La République française et les États-Unis d'Amérique, animés du désir de régler, par un arrangement amical, les réclamations élevées par les citoyens de chacun des deux pays contre le gouvernement de l'autre et résultant d'actes commis pendant l'état de guerre ou d'insurrection par les autorités civiles et militaires de l'un ou de l'autre pays, dans les circonstances spécifiées ci-après, ont résolu de prendre des mesures à cet effet, au moyen d'une convention, et ont désigné comme leurs plénipotentiaires pour conférer et établir un accord, savoir : M. le Président de la République française, M. George-Maxime Outrey, envoyé extraordinaire et Ministre plénipotentiaire de France à Washington, et le Président des États-Unis ; M. William Maxwell Evarts, secrétaire d'État aux États-Unis, lesquels, après s'être communiqué leurs pleins pouvoirs respectifs et les avoir trouvés en bonne et due forme, sont convenus des articles suivants :

ART. 1.—Toutes les réclamations élevées par des corporations, des compagnies ou de simples particuliers, citoyens des Etats-Unis, contre le Gouvernement français et résultant d'actes commis en haute mer ou sur le territoire de la France, de ses colonies et dépendances, pendant la dernière guerre entre la France et le Mexique ou pendant celle de 1870-1871 entre la France et l'Allemagne et pendant les troubles civils subséquents connus sous le nom " d'insurrection de la commune," par les autorités civiles ou militaires françaises, au préjudice des personnes ou de la propriété de citoyens des Etats-Unis non au service des ennemis de la France et qui ne leur ont prêté volontairement ni aide ni assistance, et d'autre part, toutes les réclamations élevées par des corporations, des compagnies ou de simples particuliers citoyens français, contre le Gouvernement des Etats-Unis et fondées sur and on the territory of the United States during the period comprised between the 13th April, 1861, and the 20th August, 1866, by the civil or military authorities of the United States Government, to the prejudice of the persons or property of French citizens not in the service of the enemies of the United States Government, and who have not voluntarily lent them aid or assistance, shall be submitted to three Commissioners, one of whom shall be appointed by the French Government, another by the President of the United States, and the third by His Majesty the Emperor of Brazil.

ART. 2.—The said Commission, thus constituted, shall have the right and duty of deciding upon all claims having the character indicated above, presented by the citizens of each of the two countries, except upon those which either Government shall have caused to be settled diplomatically, judicially or otherwise by competent authorities. But no claim or item of injury or damages based on the loss or emancipation of slaves shall be examined by the said Commission.

ART. 3.—In the case of death, prolonged absence, or inability to serve, of one of the said Commissioners, or in case of one of the said Commissioners neglecting, refusing, or ceasing to fulfil his functions, the French Government, or the President of the United States, or His Majesty the Emperor of Brazil, according to the circumstances, shall fill the vacancy thus caused, by appointing a new Commissioner in three months from the day when the vacancy was produced.

ART. 4.—The Commissioners, appointed according to the preceding arrangements, shall meet in the City of Washington, as soon as possible within the six months following the exchange of ratification of this Convention; and their first act, immediately after their meeting, shall be to make and sign a solemn declaration that they will examine and decide with care and impartiality, to the best of their judgment, in conformity with Public Law, Justice and Equity, without fear, favour or affection, all the claims comprised in the terms and the true signification of des actes commis en haute mer et sur le territoire des Etats-Unis pendant la période comprise entre le 13 avril 1861 et le 20 août 1866, par les autorités civiles ou militaires du Gouvernement des Etats-Unis, au préjudice des personnes ou de la propriété de citoyens français non au service des ennemis du Gouvernement des Etats-Unis et qui ne leur ont prêté volontairement ni aide ni assistance, seront soumises à trois commissaires, dont un sera nommé par le Gouvernement français, un autre par le Président des Etats-Unis et le troisième par S.M. l'Empereur du Brésil.

ART. 2.—La dite commission ainsi constituée aura compétence et devra statuer sur toutes les réclamations ayant le caractère ci-dessus indiqué, présentées par les citoyens de chacun des deux pays, sauf sur celles que l'un ou l'autre gouvernement aurait déjà fait régler diplomatiquement, judiciairement ou autrement par des autorités compétentes. Mais aucune réclamation ni article de torts ou de dommages fondés sur la perte ou l'émancipation d'esclaves ne seront examinés par la dite commission.

ART. 3.—Dans le cas de mort, d'absence prolongée, d'incapacité de servir de l'un des dits commissaires, ou dans le cas où l'un des dits commissaires négligerait, refuserait ou cesserait de remplir ses fonctions, le Gouvernement français, ou le Président des Etats-Unis, ou S. M. l'Empereur du Brésil, suivant le cas, devra remplir la vacance ainsi occasionnée, en nommant un nouveau commissaire dans les trois mois à dater du jour où la vacance se serait produite.

ART. 4.—Les commissaires, nommés conformément aux dispositions précédentes, se réuniront dans la ville de Washington, aussitôt qu'il leur sera possible, dans les six mois qui suivront l'échange des ratifications de cette convention, et leur premier acte, aussitôt après leur réunion, sera de faire et de signer une déclaration solennelle qu'ils examineront et décideront avec soin et impartialité, au mieux de leur jugement, conformément au droit public, à la justice et à l'équité, sans crainte, faveur ni affection, toutes les réclamations comprises dans les termes et la véritable signification des articles 1 et 2, qui leur seront soumises de la

Articles 1 and 2, which shall be submitted to them by the two Governments of France and the United States respectively; this declaration shall be entered on the minutes of their proceedings. It is further understood that the decision given by two of the Commissioners shall be sufficient for all the intermediate decisions which they may have to make in the accomplishment of their duty, as for each final decision.

ART. 5.—The Commissioners shall proceed without delay, after the organisation of the Commission, to the examination of, and decision on, the claims specified by the preceding articles. They shall advise the respective Governments of the day on which the Court is constituted, informing them that they are in a position to proceed with the work of the Commission. They shall examine and decide on the said claims in such order and in such fashion as they shall judge suitable, but only on the proofs and information furnished by the respective Governments, or in their name. They shall be bound to receive and take into consideration all the documents or written statements, which shall be presented to them by the respective Governments, or in their name, in support of, or in reply to, every claim, and to hear, if so required, one person on each side, whom the two Governments shall have the right to appoint as their Council or Agent to present and uphold the claims in their name in each affair taken separately. Each of the two Governments shall, at the request of the Commissioners or of two of them, furnish the documents in its possession which may be important for the just determination of every claim brought before the Commission.

ART. 6.—The unanimous decisions of the Commissioners or of two of them shall be conclusive and definitive. The said decisions shall, in each matter, be given in writing, separately on each claim, and fix, in the case where a pecuniary indemnity is awarded, the amount, or the equivalent value of this indemnity, in gold coinage of France or the United States, according to circumstances, and, if the judgment allow interest, the rate and the time for which interest should be calculated shall be likewise fixed, this period not to extend beyond the duration of the Com-part des deux gouvernements de France et des Etats-Unis respectivement ; cette déclaration sera consignée au procès-verbal de leurs travaux. Il est entendu d'ailleurs que le jugement rendu par deux des commissaires sera suffisant pour toutes les décisions intermédiaires qu'ils auront à prendre dans l'accomplissement de leurs fonctions, comme pour chaque décision finale.

ART. 5.—Les commissaires devront procéder sans délai, après l'organisation de la commission, à l'examen et au jugement des réclamations spécifiées par les articles précédents. Ils donneront avis aux gouvernements respectifs du jour de leur organisation, en leur faisant savoir qu'ils sont en mesure de procéder aux travaux de la commission. Ils devront examiner et juger les dites réclamations en tel ordre et de telle façon qu'ils jugeront convenable, mais seulement sur les preuves et informations fournies par les gouvernements respectifs ou en leur nom. Ils seront tenus de recevoir et de prendre en considération tous les documents ou exposés écrits qui leur seront présentés par les gouvernements respectifs ou en leur nom à l'appui de ou en réponse à toute réclamation et d'entendre, s'ils en sont requis, une personne de chaque côté que les deux gouvernements auront le droit de désigner comme leur conseil ou agent pour présenter et soutenir les réclamations en leur nom dans chaque affaire prise séparément. Chacun des deux gouvernements devra fournir à la requête des commissaires ou de deux d'entre eux, les pièces en sa possession qui peuvent être importantes pour la juste détermination de toute réclamation portée devant la commission.

ART. 6.—Les décisions unanimes des commissaires ou de deux d'entre eux seront concluantes et définitives. Les dites décisions devront, dans chaque affaire, être rendues par écrit, séparément sur chaque réclamation, et fixer, dans le cas où une indemnité pécuniaire serait accordée, le montant ou la valeur équivalente de cette indemnité en monnaie d'or de France ou des Etats-Unis, suivant le cas, et, si le jugement allouait des intérêts, le taux et la période pour laquelle ils devront être comptés seront également déterminés, cette période ne pouvant s'étendre au-delà de la durée de la commission ; les dites mission; these decisions shall be signed by the Commissioners who have concurred in them.

ART. 7. — The High Contracting Parties engage, by these presents, to consider the decision of the Commissioners, or of two of them, as absolutely definitive and conclusive in each matter decided by them, and to give full effect to these decisions, without objection or evasive delays of any kind.

ART. 8.—All claims shall be presented to the Commissioners within six months from the day whereon they meet to begin their labours, after notice given to the respective Governments, agreeably to the directions of Article 5 of this Convention. However, in any case where just cause for delay can be shown to the satisfaction of the Commissioners or of two of them, the time during which the claim shall be effectively presented may be extended by them to a period which must not exceed an additional term of three months.

The Commissioners shall be obliged to examine, and deliver an award on, all the claims, within two years, to date from the day of their first meeting as above; this period cannot be extended except where the labours of the Commission have been interrupted by death, inability to serve, dismissal or repeal of appointment of one of the Commissioners. In this contingency, the time such interruption actually lasts shall not be counted in the term of two years fixed above.

It shall be for the Commissioners to decide, in each matter, whether the claim has or has not been duly made, presented and submitted, whether in its entirety or in part, in conformity with the spirit and true signification of the Convention.

ART. 9.—All sums of money which may be awarded by the Commissioners, in virtue of the preceding arrangements, shall be paid by one of the Governments to the other, as the case may be, in the capital of the Government which is to receive the payment, within twelve months following the date of the final award, without interest or other deductions than those specified in Article 10.

décisions devront être signées par les commissaires qui y auront concouru.

Art. 7.—Les hautes parties contractantes s'engagent, par le présent acte, à considérer la décision des commissaires ou de deux d'entre eux, comme absolument définitive et concluante dans chaque affaire réglée par eux, et à donner plein effet à ces décisions, sans objection ni délais évasifs d'aucune nature.

Art. 8.—Toutes les réclamations devront être présentées aux commissaires dans une période de six mois à dater du jour où ils se seront réunis pour commencer leurs travaux, après avis donné aux gouvernements respectifs, conformément aux dispositions de l'article 5 de cette convention. Toutefois, dans tous les cas où l'on ferait valoir de justes motifs de délai à la satisfaction des commissaires ou de deux d'entre eux, le temps où la réclamation sera valablement présentée, pourra être étendu par eux à une période qui ne devra point excéder un terme additionel de trois mois.

Les commissaires seront tenus d'examiner et de rendre une décision sur toutes les réclamations, dans les deux ans à dater du jour de leur première réunion comme ci-dessus, ce délai ne pourra être étendu que dans le cas où les travaux de la commission seraient interrompus par la mort, l'incapacité de servir, la démission ou la cassation des fonctions de l'un des commissaires. Dans cette éventualité, le temps où une pareille interruption aura existé de fait ne sera point compté dans le terme de deux ans ci-dessus fixé.

Il appartiendra aux commissaires de décider, dans chaque affaire, si la réclamation a ou n'a pas été dûment faite, présentée et soumise, soit dans son entier, soit en partie, conformément à l'esprit et à la véritable signification de la Convention.

Art. 9.—Toutes les sommes d'argent qui pourraient être allouées par les commissaires, en vertu des dispositions précédentes, devront être versées par l'un des gouvernements à l'autre, suivant le cas, dans la capitale du Gouvernement qui devra recevoir le paiement, dans les douze mois qui suivront la date du jugement final, sans intérêts ni autres déductions que celles spécifiées dans l'article 10.

Art. 10.—The Commissioners shall keep an exact record, and preserve correct and dated minutes or notes of all their proceedings; the Governments of France and the United States may each appoint and employ a Secretary acquainted with the languages of both countries; and the Commissioners may appoint such other employés as they may deem necessary to aid them in the despatch of the matters that shall come before them.

Each Government shall pay its own Commissioners, Secretary and Counsel, and the compensation which shall be granted them shall be equal or equivalent, so far as possible, on both sides, for the functionaries of the same rank.

All the other expenses, including the allowance of the third Commissioner, shall be borne by the two Governments in equal shares.

The general expenses of the Commission, including contingent expenses, shall be covered by a proportional deduction on the total of the sums awarded by the Commissioners. It is understood, however, that this deduction shall not exceed five per cent. of the sums awarded. If the general expenses exceed this rate, the surplus shall be borne conjointly and in equal shares by the two Governments.

Art. 11.—The High Contracting Parties have agreed to consider the result of the Commission co-instituted by this Convention as a complete settlement, perfect and definitive, of all and each of the claims against either one of them, in conformity with the terms and the true signification of Articles 1 and 2, so that every claim of this nature, whether it has or has not been brought to the knowledge of the Commissioners, whether it has or has not been presented and submitted to them, shall, from and after the termination of the proceedings of the said Commission be held and considered as definitively settled, decided and concluded.

Art. 12. The present Convention shall be ratified by the President of the French Republic and by the President of the United States, by and with the advice and consent of the Senate; and the ratifications shall be exchanged at Washington on the earliest possible day in the nine months following the date of this document.

ART. 10.—Les commissaires devront tenir un procès verbal exact et conserver des minutes ou notes correctes et datées de tous leurs travaux; les gouvernements de France et des Etats-Unis pourront chacun nommer et employer un secrétaire versé dans le langage des deux pays, et les commissaires pourront nommer tels autres employés qu'ils jugeront nécessaires pour les aider dans l'expédition des affaires qui viendront devant eux.

Chaque Gouvernement paiera ses propres commissaires, secrétaire et agent de conseil et la compensation qui leur sera allouée devra être égale ou équivalente, autant que possible, des deux côtés, pour les fonctionnaires de même rang.

Toutes les autres dépenses, y compris l'allocation du troisième commissaire, seront supportées par les deux gouvernements en parties égales.

Les dépenses générales de la Commission, y compris les dépenses éventuelles, seront couvertes par une déduction proportionnelle sur le montant des sommes allouées par les commissaires. Il est bien entendu, toutefois, que cette retenue ne devra pas excéder cinq pour cent des sommes accordées. Si les dépenses générales excédaient ce taux, le surplus serait supporté conjointement et en parties égales par les deux gouvernements.

ART. 11.—Les hautes parties contractantes sont convenues de considérer le résultat de la commission instituée par cette convention comme un règlement complet, parfait et définitif de toutes et de chacune des réclamations contre l'une d'elles, conformément aux termes et à la vraie signification des articles 1 et 2, de telle sorte que toute réclamation de cette nature, qu'elle ait été ou non portée à la connaissance des commissaires, qu'elle leur ait ou non été présentée et soumise, devra, à dater de la fin des travaux de la dite commission, être tenue et considérée comme définitivement réglée, décidée et éteinte.

ART. 12.—La présente convention sera ratifiée par le Président de la République française et par le Président des Etats-Unis, par et avec l'avis et consentement du Sénat, et les ratifications seront échangées à Washington, au jour le plus rapproché qu'il sera possible dans les neuf mois à partir de la date du présent acte.

CONVENTION

CONCLUDED NOVEMBER 2, 1882, BETWEEN FRANCE AND CHILI, RELATING TO CERTAIN CLAIMS FOR DAMAGE CAUSED BY WAR.

The President of the French Republic and His Excellency the President of the Republic of Chili, desiring to settle in a friendly way the claims advanced by French citizens, supported by the Legation of the French Republic in Chili, and founded on the acts and operations accomplished by the forces of the Republic of Chili, on the territories and coasts of Peru and Bolivia, during the present war, have resolved to conclude an Arbitration Convention. For this purpose they have appointed as their respective plenipotentiaries :—

The President of the French Republic appointed Adolph, Baron d'Avril, Minister Plenipotentiary of the First Class, Officer of the national order of the Legion of Honour, and His Excellency the President of the Republic of Chili, Señor Luis Aldunate, Minister for Foreign Affairs of the Republic.

Which plenipotentiaries, after having examined and exchanged their authorisations, and having found them in good and due form, agreed to the following Articles :—

ART. 1.—An Arbitral Tribunal, or International mixed Commission, shall, in the form and according to the rules which shall be laid down in the present Convention, examine all the claims which, founded on the acts and operations accomplished by the Chilian sea and land forces, on the territories and coasts of Peru and Bolivia, during the present war, have been presented up to the present, or shall be presented later, by French citizens under the patronage of the Legation of the French Republic in Chili, within the time named hereafter.

CONVENTION
CONCLUE LE 2 NOVEMBRE 1882, ENTRE LA FRANCE ET LE CHILI, RELATIVE À CERTAINES RÉCLAMATIONS POUR DOMMAGES DE GUERRE.

Le Président de la République française et S. E. le Président de la République du Chili, désirant mettre amicalement un terme aux réclamations introduites par des citoyens français, appuyées par la légation de la République française au Chili, et motivées par les actes et opérations accomplis par les forces de la République du Chili, sur les territoires et côtes du Pérou et de la Bolivie, durant la présente guerre, ont résolu de conclure une convention d'arbitrage. A cet effet, ils ont nommé pour leurs plénipotentiaires respectifs :

Le Président de la République française, le sieur Adolphe baron d'Avril, ministre plénipotentiaire de 1re classe, officier de l'ordre national de la Légion d'honneur, et S. E. le Président de la République du Chili, le sieur Luis Aldunate, ministre des relations extérieures de la République.

Lesquels plénipotentiaires, après avoir examiné et échangé leurs pouvoirs et les avoir trouvés en bonne et due forme, sont convenus des articles suivants :

ART. 1.—Un tribunal arbitral ou commission mixte internationale jugera en la forme et suivants les termes qui seront établis dans la présente convention toutes les réclamations, qui motivées par les actes et les opérations accomplis par les forces chiliennes de mer et de terre, sur les territoires et côtes du Pérou et de la Bolivie, durant la présente guerre, ont été introduits jusqu'à présent ou seront introduits ultérieurement par des citoyens français sous le patronage de la légation de la République française au Chili, dans le délai qui sera indiqué ci-après.

Art. 2.—The Commission shall be composed of three members, one appointed by the President of the French Republic, another by the President of the Republic of Chili, and the third by the Emperor of Brazil, either directly or by the intermediary of the diplomatic agent accredited by His Majesty to Chili.

In case of death, absence or incapacity, through whatever cause, of one or more of the members of the Commission, provision shall be made for replacing him, in the forms and conditions respectively expressed in the preceding paragraph.

Art. 3.—The mixed Commission shall examine and decide on the claims which the French citizens have presented up to the present time or shall present later by their diplomatic representative, and which are founded on the acts and operations accomplished by the armies and fleets of the Republic, since February 14th, 1879, the date of the opening of hostilities, up to the day when a Treaty of Peace or an Armistice shall be concluded between the belligerent nations, *i.e.*, up to the time when the hostilities between the three nations at war shall have actually ceased.

Art. 4.—The mixed Commission shall receive such proofs and evidence as shall, in the opinion and proper judgment of its members, best conduce to throw light on the facts in dispute, and especially to settle the status and neutral character of the claimants.

The Commission shall receive alike verbal statements and written documents from the two Governments or their respective Agents or Counsel.

Art. 5.—Each Government may appoint an agent to watch over the interests of its constituents and take up their case; to present petitions, documents, interrogatories; propose motions or reply to them, support its counter-affirmations, furnish proofs of them, and, before the Commission, by himself or by means of a lawyer, verbally or by writing, conformably to the rules of procedure and the ways which the Commission itself

ART. 2.—La commission se composera de trois membres, un nommé par le Président de la République française, un autre par le Président de la République du Chili, et le troisième, par l'Empereur du Brésil, soit directement, soit par l'intermédiaire de l'agent diplomatique accrédité par Sa Majesté au Chili.

Dans le cas de mort, absence ou incapacité, pour quelques motifs que ce soit, d'un ou de plusieurs des membres de la commission, il sera pourvu à son remplacement dans les formes et conditions respectivement exprimées au paragraphe précédent.

ART. 3.—La commission mixte examinera et jugera les réclamations que les citoyens français ont introduites jusqu'à aujourd'hui ou introduiront ultérieurement par leur organe diplomatique, et motivées par les actes ou les opérations accomplis par les armées et escadres de la République, depuis le 14 février 1879, date de l'ouverture des hostilités, jusqu'au jour où il sera conclu de traité de paix ou des armistices entre les nations belligérantes jusqu'au jour où auront cessé de fait les hostilités entre les trois nations en guerre.

ART. 4.—La commission mixte accueillera les moyens probatoires ou d'investigation qui, d'après l'appréciation et le juste discernement de ses membres, pourront le mieux conduire à l'éclaircissement des faits controversés et spécialement à la détermination de l'état et du caractère neutre des réclamants.

La commission recevra également les allégations verbales et écrites des deux gouvernements ou de leurs agents ou défenseurs respectifs.

ART. 5.—Chaque gouvernement pourra constituer un agent qui veille aux intérêts de ses commettants et en prenne la défense ; qui présente des pétitions, documents, interrogatoires ; qui pose des conclusions ou y réponde, qui appuie ses affirmations contraires, qui en fournisse les preuves et qui, devant la commission, par lui-même ou par l'organe d'un homme de loi, verbalement ou par écrit, conformément aux règles de procédure et aux voies que la commission elle-même arrêtera en commenshall determine when commencing its proceedings, set forth the doctrines, legal principles or precedents which suit his case.

ART. 6.—The mixed Commission shall decide on the claims according to the value of the proof furnished, and in conformity with the principles of International Law, as also with the practice and jurisprudence established by recent similar tribunals having the most authority and prestige; and its decisions, whether interlocutory or definitive, shall be arrived at by a majority of votes.

In each definitive award the Commission shall briefly put forth the facts and causalities of the claim, the motives alleged in support or in contradiction, and the grounds on which its resolutions rest.

The resolutions and awards of the Commission shall be in writing, signed by all its members and authenticated by its Secretary. The original documents shall remain, with their respective dossiers, at the Chilian Ministry of Foreign Affairs, where certified copies shall be delivered to those parties demanding them.

The Commission shall keep a register in which shall be entered the procedure followed, the demands of the claimants, and the awards and decisions rendered. The Commission shall hold its sittings at Santiago.

ART. 7.—The Commission shall have the power to provide itself with secretaries, reporters and such other employés, as it shall deem necessary for the satisfactory accomplishment of its duties.

It belongs to the Commission to propose the persons who will have to fulfil these functions and to fix the terms and salaries.

The appointment of these different employés will be made by His Excellency the President of the Republic of Chili.

The decisions of the mixed Commission, which have to be carried out in Chili, will have the support of the public force in the same manner as those which are rendered by the ordinary çant ses fonctions, expose les doctrines, principes légaux ou précédents qui conviennent à sa cause.

Art. 6.—La commission mixte jugera les réclamations d'après la valeur de la preuve fournie et conformément aux principes de droit international, ainsi qu'à la pratique et à la jurisprudence établies par les tribunaux récents analogues ayant le plus d'autorité et de prestige, en prenant ses résolutions, tant interlocutoires que définitives, à la majorité des votes.

Dans chaque jugement définitif, la commission exposera brièvement les faits et causalités de la réclamation, les motifs allégués à l'appui ou en contradiction, et les bases sur lesquelles s'appuient ses résolutions.

Les résolutions et jugements de la commission seront écrits, signés par tous ses membres et revêtus de la forme authentique par son secrétaire. Les actes originaux resteront, avec leurs dossiers respectifs, au ministère des relations extérieures du Chili, où il sera délivré des copies certifiées aux parties qui les demanderont.

La commission tiendra un livre d'enregistrement dans lequel on inscrira la procédure suivie, les demandes des réclamants et les jugements et décisions rendus. La commission fonctionnera à Santiago.

Art. 7.—La commission aura la faculté de se pourvoir de secrétaires, rapporteurs et autres employés qu'elle estimera nécessaire pour le bon accomplissement de ses fonctions.

Il appartient à la commission de proposer les personnes qui auront à remplir respectivement ces emplois et de fixer les traitements et rémunérations à leur assigner.

La nomination de ces divers employés sera faite par S. E. le Président de la République du Chili.

Les décisions de la commission mixte qui devront être exécutées au Chili, auront l'appui de la force publique de la même manière que celles qui sont rendues par les tribunaux ordinaires tribunals of the country; the decisions which have to be carried out abroad will have their effect in conformity with the rules and usages of private International Law.

ART. 8.—The claims shall be presented to the mixed Commission in the six months following the date of its first sitting, and those presented at the expiration of that time shall not be admitted. For the carrying out of the provision contained in the preceding paragraph, the mixed Commission shall publish in the official journal of the Republic of Chili a notice by which it shall indicate the date of its installation.

ART. 9.—The Commission, to terminate its mission, with regard to all the claims submitted for its examination and decision, shall be allowed a period of two years counted from the day when it shall be declared installed.

When this time has passed, the Commission shall have the power to prolong its proceedings for a new period which must not exceed six months, if, through illness or temporary incapacity of one of its members, or for any other reason of acknowledged weight, it would be unable to complete its mission in the time fixed in the first paragraph.

ART. 10.—Each of the contracting Governments shall provide for the expenses of its own Agents or Counsel.

The expenses of the organisation of the mixed Commission, the honorariums of its members, the salaries of the secretaries, reporters, and other employés, and all costs and expenses of common service shall be paid, half by each of the two Governments; but if any sum is awarded to the claimants, there shall be deducted from it the said common costs and expenses provided they do not exceed 6 per cent. of the amount which the Treasury of Chili may have to pay for the sum total of the admitted claims.

The sums which the mixed Commission shall assign in favour of the claimants shall be paid by the Government of Chili to the du pays, les décisions qui auront à être exécutées à l'étranger sortiront leurs effets conformément aux règles et usages de droit international privé.

ART. 8.—Les réclamations seront présentées à la commission mixte dans les six mois qui suivront la date de sa première séance, et celles qu'on présenterait à l'expiration de ce délai ne seront pas admises. Pour les effets de la disposition contenue au paragraphe précédent, la commission mixte publiera dans le *Journal officiel* de la République du Chili, un avis par lequel elle indiquera la date de son installation.

ART. 9.—La commission aura, pour terminer sa mission, à l'égard de toutes les réclamations soumises à son examen et décision, un délai de deux années comptées depuis le jour où elle sera déclarée installée.

Passé ce délai, la commission aura la faculté de proroger ses fonctions pour une nouvelle période qui ne pourra excéder six mois, dans le cas où, pour cause de maladie ou d'incapacité temporaire de quelqu'un de ses membres ou pour tout autre motif de gravité reconnue, elle ne serait parvenue à terminer sa mission dans le délai fixé au premier paragraphe.

ART. 10.—Chacun des gouvernements contractants pourvoiera aux frais de ses propres agents ou défenseurs.

Les dépenses d'organisation de la commission mixte, les honoraires de ses membres, les appointements des secrétaires, rapporteurs et autres employés et tous frais et dépens de service commun seront payés de moitié par les deux gouvernements, mais s'il y a des sommes allouées en faveur des réclamants, il en sera déduit les dits frais et dépenses communs en tant qu'ils n'excèdent pas le 6% des valeurs que le Trésor du Chili ait à payer pour la totalité des réclamations admises.

Les sommes que la commission mixte assignera en faveur des réclamants seront versées par le gouvernement du Chili au

French Government through the intermediary of its Legation at Santiago or through the person designated by this Legation, within one year reckoning from the date of the resolution relating thereto, and so that during this time the said sums shall be liable to no interest in favour of the claimants.

ART. 11.—The High Contracting Parties engage themselves to consider the award of the mixed Commission organised by this present Convention, as a satisfactory, complete and irrevocable solution of the difficulties which it has had under settlement; and it is understood that all the claims of the French citizens, whether presented or not in the conditions set forth in the preceding articles, shall be held to be decided and settled definitively and in such a manner that they can, for no motive and under no pretext, be the subject of a new examination or discussion.

ART. 12.—The present Convention shall be ratified by the High Contracting Parties, and the exchange of ratifications shall be made at Santiago.

gouvernement français par l'entremise de sa légation à Santiago ou de la personne désignée par cette légation, dans le délai d'une année à compter de la date de la résolution y afférente, sans que durant ce délai les dites sommes soient passibles d'aucun intérêt en faveur des réclamants.

ART. 11.—Les hautes parties contractantes s'obligent à considérer les jugements de la commission mixte organisée par la présente convention, comme une solution satisfaisante, parfaite et irrévocable des difficultés qu'elle a eu en vue de régler, et il est bien entendu que toutes les réclamations des citoyens français, présentées ou non présentées dans les conditions signalées aux articles précédents, seront tenues pour décidées et jugées définitivement et de manière que, pour aucun motif ou prétexte, elles ne puissent être l'objet d'un nouvel examen ou d'une nouvelle discussion.

ART. 12.—La présente convention sera ratifiée par les hautes parties contractantes et l'échange des ratifications s'effectuera à Santiago.

PROJECT OF A PERMANENT TREATY OF ARBITRATION BETWEEN THE UNITED STATES AND SWITZERLAND, ADOPTED BY THE SWISS FEDERAL COUNCIL, JULY 24TH, 1883.

1. The Contracting Parties agree to submit to an arbitral tribunal all difficulties which may arise between them during the existence of the present treaty, whatever may be the cause, the nature or the object of such difficulties.

2. The Arbitral Tribunal shall be composed of three persons. Each party shall designate one of the arbitrators. It shall choose him from among those who are neither citizens of the State nor inhabitants of its territory. The two arbitrators thus chosen shall themselves choose a third arbitrator; but if they should be unable to agree, the third arbitrator shall be named by a neutral Government. This Government shall be designated by the two arbitrators, or, if they cannot agree, by lot.

3. The Arbitral Tribunal, when called together by the third arbitrator, shall draw up a form of agreement which shall determine the object of the litigation, the composition of the tribunal and the duration of its powers. The agreement shall be signed by the representatives of the parties and by the arbitrators.

4. The Arbitrators shall determine their own procedure. In order to secure a just result, they shall make use of all the means of information which they may deem necessary, the contracting parties engaging to place them at their disposal. Their judgment shall be communicated to the parties, and shall become executory one month after its communication.

5. The Contracting Parties bind themselves to observe and loyally to carry out the arbitral sentence.

6. The present treaty shall remain in force for a period of thirty years after the exchange of ratifications. If notice of its abrogation is not given before the beginning of the thirtieth year, it shall remain in force for another period of thirty years, and so on.

PROJET DE TRAITÉ GÉNÉRAL D'ARBITRAGE ENTRE LA SUISSE ET LES ETATS-UNIS.

Entre les Etats-Unis de l'Amérique du Nord et la Confédération Suisse, il a été conclu un traité permanent d'arbitrage comme suit :

Art. 1.—Les deux Etats contractants s'engagent à soumettre à un tribunal arbitral toutes les difficultés qui pourraient naître entre eux pendant la durée du présent traité, quels que puissent être la cause, la nature ou l'objet de ces difficultés.

Art. 2.—Le tribunal arbitral sera composé de trois personnes. Chacun des Etats désignera l'un des arbitres. Il le choisira parmi les personnes qui ne sont ni les ressortissants de l'Etat, ni les habitants de son territoire. Les deux arbitres choisiront eux-mêmes leur sur-arbitre. S'il ne peuvent s'entendre sur ce choix, le sur-arbitre sera nommé par un gouvernement neutre. Ce gouvernement sera lui-même désigné par les deux arbitres, ou à défaut d'entente, par le sort.

Art. 3.—Le tribunal arbitral, réuni par les soins du sur-arbitre fera rédiger un compromis qui fixera l'objet du litige, la composition du tribunal et la durée du pouvoir de ce dernier. Ce compromis sera signé par les représentants des parties et par les arbitres.

Art. 4.—Les arbitres détermineront leur procédure. Ils useront pour éclairer leur justice de tous les moyens d'informations qu'ils jugeront nécessaires, les parties s'engageant à les mettre à leur disposition. Leur sentence sera communiquée aux parties. Elle sera exécutoire de plein droit un mois après cette communication.

Art. 5.—Chacun des Etats contractants s'engage à observer et à exécuter loyalement la sentence arbitrale.

Art. 6.—Le présent traité est fait pour la durée de trente années, à partir de l'échange des ratifications; s'il n'est pas dénoncé avant le commencement de la trentième année, il sera renouvelé pour une nouvelle durée de trente ans et ainsi de suite.

PLAN OF A PERMANENT TRIBUNAL OF ARBITRATION, ADOPTED BY THE INTERNATIONAL AMERICAN CONFERENCE, APRIL 18, 1890.

I.—Plan of Arbitration.

The Delegates from North, Central, and South America in Conference assembled;

Believing that war is the most cruel, the most fruitless, and the most dangerous expedient for the settlement of International differences;

Recognising that the growth of the moral principles which govern political societies has created an earnest desire in favour of the amicable adjustment of such differences;

Animated by the realisation of the great moral and material benefits that Peace offers to mankind, and trusting that the existing conditions of the respective nations are especially propitious for the adoption of Arbitration as a substitute for armed struggles;

Convinced by reason of their friendly and cordial meeting in the present Conference, that the American Republics, controlled alike by the principles, the duties and the responsibilities of popular Government, and bound together by vast and increasing mutual interests, can, within the sphere of their own action, maintain the Peace of the Continent, and the goodwill of all its inhabitants;

And considering it their duty to lend their assent to the lofty principles of Peace which the most enlightened public sentiment of the world approves;

Do solemnly recommend all the Governments by which they are accredited, to celebrate a uniform Treaty of Arbitration in the Articles following:—

Art. 1.—The republics of North, Central, and South America hereby adopt arbitration as a principle of American International

PROJET DE TRAITÉ D'ARBITRAGE ENTRE LES ÉTATS D'AMÉRIQUE

SIGNÉ À WASHINGTON LE 18 AVRIL 1890.

I.—Plan d'Arbitrage.

Les délégués de l'Amérique du Nord, de celle du Centre et de celle du Sud, assemblés en conférence :

Croyant que la guerre est le plus cruel, le plus infructueux et le plus dangereux expédient pour l'arrangement des différends internationaux ;

Reconnaissant que le développement des principes moraux qui gouvernent les sociétés politiques a donné naissance à un ardent sentiment en faveur de l'arrangement amical de ces différends ;

Animés par la conviction des grands bénéfices moraux et matériels que la paix offre à l'humanité, et comptant que les conditions actuelles des nations sont spécialement propices à l'adoption de l'arbitrage à la place des luttes armées ;

Convaincus, en raison de leur amicale et cordiale rencontre à la présente conférence, que les Républiques américaines, pareillement soumises à des principes, des devoirs et des responsabilités de gouvernement populaire, et liées ensemble par de vastes et toujours croissants intérêts mutuels, peuvent, dans la sphère de leur propre action, maintenir la paix sur le continent et la bonne volonté parmi tous ses habitants ;

Et considérant qu'il est de leur devoir de prêter leur assentiment aux grands principes de la paix que le sentiment public le plus éclairé approuve ;

Recommandent solennellement à tous les Governements près lesquels ils sont accrédités, de conclure un traité uniforme d'arbitrage dont les articles suivent :

Art. 1. — Les Républiques de l'Amérique du Nord, de l'Amerique du Centre et de l'Amérique du Sud adoptent, par

Law for the settlement of the differences, disputes or controversies that may arise between two or more of them.

ART. 2.—Arbitration shall be obligatory in all controversies concerning diplomatic and consular privileges, boundaries, territories, indemnities, the right of navigation, and the validity, construction and enforcement of treaties.

ART. 3.—Arbitration shall be equally obligatory in all cases other than those mentioned in the foregoing article, whatever may be their origin, nature, or object, with the single exception mentioned in the next following article.

ART. 4.—The sole questions excepted from the provisions of the preceding articles, are those which, in the judgment of any one of the nations involved in the controversy, may imperil its independence. In which case for such nation arbitration shall be optional; but it shall be obligatory upon the adversary power.

ART. 5.—All controversies or differences, whether pending or hereafter arising, shall be submitted to arbitration, even though they may have originated in occurrences antedating the present treaty.

ART. 6.—No question shall be revived by virtue of this treaty, concerning which a definite agreement shall already have been reached. In such cases, arbitration shall be resorted to only for the settlement of questions concerning the validity, interpretation or enforcement of such agreements.

ART. 7.—The choice of arbitrators shall not be limited or confined to American States. Any Government may serve in the capacity of arbitrator, which maintains friendly relations with the nation opposed to the one selecting it. The office of Arbitrator may also be entrusted to tribunals of justice, to scientific bodies, to public officials, or to private individuals, whether citizens or not of the states selecting them.

ART. 8.—The Court of Arbitration may consist of one or more persons. If of one person, he shall be selected jointly by the ces présents, l'arbitrage comme un principe de la loi internationale américaine pour l'arrangement des différends, des disputes ou des controverses qui peuvent s'élever entre deux ou plusieurs d'entre elles.

ART. 2.—L'arbitrage sera obligatoire dans toutes les controverses relatives aux privilèges diplomatiques ou consulaires, aux frontières, territoires, indemnités, au droit de navigation et à la validité, à l'interprétation et à la violation des traités.

ART. 3.—L'arbitrage sera également obligatoire dans tous les autres cas que ceux mentionnés dans le précédent article, quelle que puisse être leur origine, leur nature ou leur objet avec la seule exception mentionnée dans l'article suivant.

ART. 4.—Le seul cas excepté des clauses des articles précédents est celui qui, dans le jugement d'une des nations enveloppées dans la controverse, peut mettre en péril son indépendance. Dans ce cas, pour cette nation, l'arbitrage sera facultatif, mais il sera obligatoire pour la puissance adverse.

ART. 5.—Toutes les controverses, tous les différends pendant actuellement ou qui s'élèveront dans la suite, seront soumis à l'arbitrage, même s'ils provenaient d'occurrences antérieures au présent traité.

ART. 6.—En vertu de ce traité, aucune question qui aura été déjà réglée définitivement ne pourra être renouvelée. Dans un tel cas, on n'aurait recours à l'arbitrage que pour l'arrangement des questions relatives à la validité, à l'interprétation ou à la violation des engagements.

ART. 7.—Le choix des arbitres ne sera pas limité ou confiné aux Etats américains. Tout gouvernement peut servir en qualité d'arbitre s'il entretient d'amicales relations avec la nation adverse de celle qui l'a choisi. L'office d'arbitre peut aussi être confié à des tribunaux de justice, à des corps scientifiques, à des officiers publics ou à de simples particuliers, citoyens ou non des Etats les choisissant.

ART. 8.—La Cour d'arbitrage peut consister en une seule ou plusieurs personnes. Si elle se compose d'une personne, elle nations concerned. If of several persons, their selection may be jointly made by the nations concerned. Should no choice be agreed upon, each nation showing a distinct interest in the question at issue shall have the right to appoint one arbitrator on its own behalf.

ART. 9.—Whenever the Court shall consist of an even number of arbitrators, the nations concerned shall appoint an umpire, who shall decide all questions upon which the arbitrators may disagree. If the nations interested fail to agree in the selection of an umpire, such umpire shall be selected by the arbitrators already appointed.

ART. 10.—The appointment of an umpire, and his acceptance, shall take place before the arbitrators enter upon the hearing of the questions in dispute.

ART. 11.—The umpire shall not act as a member of the Court, but his duties and powers shall be limited to the decision of questions, whether principal or incidental, upon which the arbitrators shall be unable to agree.

ART. 12.—Should an arbitrator or an umpire be prevented from serving by reason of death, resignation, or other cause, such arbitrator or umpire shall be replaced by a substitute to be selected in the same manner in which the original arbitrator or umpire shall have been chosen.

ART. 13.—The Court shall hold its sessions at such place as the parties in interest may agree upon, and in case of disagreement or failure to name a place the Court itself may determine the location.

ART. 14.—When the Court shall consist of several arbitrators, a majority of the whole number may act, notwithstanding the absence or withdrawal of the minority. In such case the majority shall continue in the performance of their duties, until they shall have reached a final determination of the questions submitted for their consideration.

sera choisie conjointement par les nations intéressées. Si elle se compose de plusieurs personnes, leur choix doit être fait conjointement par les nations intéressées. Si on ne pouvait tomber d'accord pour aucun choix, chaque nation ayant un intérêt distinct dans le résultat de la question, aura le droit de désigner un arbitre pour sa propre défense.

ART. 9.—Lorsque la Cour consistera en un nombre égal d'arbitres, les nations intéressées désigneront un tiers arbitre qui décidera toutes les questions sur lesquelles les arbitres ne seraient pas d'accord. Si les nations intéressées ne tombent pas d'accord pour le choix d'un tiers-arbitre, ce tiers-arbitre sera choisi par les arbitres déjà désignés.

ART. 10.—Le choix du tiers-arbitre et son acceptation devront avoir lieu avant que les arbitres n'entrent en audience sur les questions de la dispute.

ART. 11.—Le tiers-arbitre n'agira pas comme membre de la Cour; mais ses devoirs et ses pouvoirs seront limités à la décision des questions, soit principales, soit secondaires, sur lesquelles les arbitres ne pourront tomber d'accord.

ART. 12.—Si un arbitre ou un tiers-arbitre était empêché de remplir ses fonctions par suite de décès, de renonciation ou pour toute autre cause, cet arbitre ou tiers-arbitre sera remplacé par un substitut qui devra être choisi de la même manière que l'aurait été le premier arbitre ou tiers-arbitre.

ART. 13.—La Cour tiendra des sessions en tel lieu que les nations intéressées s'accorderont à désigner, et, dans le cas de désaccord, ou si elles manquaient de désigner le lieu, la Cour elle-même pourra déterminer la localité.

ART. 14.—Lorsque la Cour consistera en plusieurs arbitres, une majorité de tous les membres pourra agir malgré l'absence ou le départ de la minorité. Dans un tel cas, la majorité continuera à remplir ses devoirs jusqu'à ce qu'elle soit parvenue à une détermination finale dans toutes les questions soumises à l'examen des arbitres.

ART. 15.—The decision of a majority of the whole number of arbitrators shall be final, both on the main and incidental issues, unless in the agreement to arbitrate it shall have been expressly provided that unanimity is essential.

ART. 16.—The general expenses of arbitration proceedings shall be paid in equal proportions by the Governments that are parties thereto; but expenses incurred by either party in the preparation and prosecution of its case shall be defrayed by it individually.

ART. 17.—Whenever disputes arise, the nations involved shall appoint courts of arbitration in accordance with the provisions of the preceding articles. Only by the mutual and free consent of all such nations may those provisions be disregarded, and courts of arbitration appointed under different arrangements.

ART. 18.—This treaty shall remain in force for twenty years from the date of the exchange of ratifications. After the expiration of that period, it shall continue in operation until one of the contracting parties shall have notified all the others of its desire to terminate it. In the event of such notice, the treaty shall continue obligatory upon the party giving it for one year thereafter, but the withdrawal of one or more nations shall not invalidate the treaty with respect to the other nations concerned.

ART. 19.—This treaty shall be ratified by all the nations approving it according to their respective constitutional methods; and the ratifications shall be exchanged in the city of Washington on or before the 1st day of May, A.D. 1891. Any other nation may accept this treaty and become a party thereto by signing a copy thereof and depositing the same with the Government of the United States; whereupon the said Government shall communicate this fact to the other contracting parties.

ART. 15.—La décision de la majorité des arbitres sera définitive aussi bien sur les questions principales que sur les questions incidentes, à moins que, dans les conditions de l'arbitrage, on n'ait expressément déterminé que l'unanimité serait indispensable.

ART. 16.—Les dépenses générales du procédé d'arbitrage seront payées en proportions égales par les gouvernements qui sont parties intéressées; mais les dépenses faites par chacune des parties pour la préparation et la poursuite de sa défense seront payées par chacune d'entre elles individuellement.

ART. 17.—Lorsque des disputes s'élèveront, les nations intéressées désigneront les Cours d'Arbitrage d'après les clauses des précédents articles. Seulement, dans le cas où ces nations y consentiraient mutuellement et librement, ces clauses pourraient être mises de côté, et les Cours d'Arbitrage seraient désignées d'après d'autres arrangements.

ART. 18.—Ce traité restera en vigueur pendant vingt ans à partir du jour où il sera ratifié. Après l'expiration de cette période, il continuera à être valable jusqu'à ce qu'une des parties contractantes notifie à toutes les autres un désir d'y mettre fin. Dans le cas de cette notification, le traité continuera à être obligatoire pendant un an pour la partie l'abandonnant; mais l'action d'une ou de plusieurs nations renonçant à ce traité ne l'invalidera pas pour les autres nations en faisant partie.

ART. 19.—Ce traité sera ratifié par toutes les nations l'approuvant, chacune selon sa méthode constitutionnelle et les ratifications seront échangées dans la ville de Washington le premier jour de mai A.D. 1891, ou avant si c'est possible. Toute autre nation peut accepter ce traité et devenir une partie contractante, en signant une copie de traité et en la déposant entre les mains du Gouvernement des Etats-Unis, sur quoi le dit Gouvernement communiquera le fait aux autres parties contractantes. En foi de quoi, les plénipotentiaires soussignés ont apposé leur signature et leur sceau.

II.—Recommendation to European Powers.

The International American Conference resolves:—

That this Conference, having recommended Arbitration for the settlement of disputes among the Republics of America, begs leave to express the wish that controversies between them and the nations of Europe may be settled in the same friendly manner.

It is further recommended that the Government of each nation herein represented communicate this wish to all friendly Powers.

NON-RATIFICATION OF THE TREATY.

The Treaty was signed by the Representatives of eleven States, as follows: Bolivia, Ecuador, Guatemala, Haiti, Honduras, Nicaragua, Salvador, the United States of America, the United States of Brazil, the United States of Venezuela, and Uruguay.

It was provided by Article XIX that "this Treaty shall be ratified by all the nations approving it, according to their respective constitutional methods; and the ratifications shall be exchanged, in the City of Washington, on or before the first day of May, A.D. 1891."

The Treaty, however, *lapsed, through the failure of all its signatories to exchange ratifications within the prescribed time; the United States being one of the signatories who did not sign the Treaty.*

An attempt has since been made to revive the Treaty. A form of extension was agreed upon and submitted to all the Signatory Powers, October 29th, 1891. The following Governments signified their acceptance of the proposal to revive the lapsed Treaty, viz., Ecuador, Guatemala, Honduras, Venezuela, Nicaragua, Salvador, and Bolivia.

The matter never progressed beyond this latter stage, and so the Treaty never became operative between the States concerned.

II. Recommendation aux Puissances Européennes.

La Conférence internationale américaine résout : Que cette Conférence ayant recommandé l'arbitrage, pour l'arrangement des différends entre les Républiques Américaines, demande la permission d'exprimer le désir que les controverses entre elles et les nations de l'Europe puissent être terminées de la même manière amicale. Il est de plus recommandé que le Gouvernement de chaque nation, représentée dans ce traité, communique ce désir à toutes les puissances amies.

NON-RATIFICATION DU TRAITÉ.

Le traité était signé par les représentants de onze États, c'est à dire : Bolivie, l'Equateur, Guatemala, Haïti, Honduras, Nicaragua, Salvador, les États-Unis d'Amérique, les États-Unis de Brésil, les Etats-Unis de Venezuela, et Uruguay.

Il était pourvu dans l'Article XIX, que : "Ce traité sera ratifié par toutes les nations l'approuvant, chacune selon sa méthode constitutionelle ; et les ratifications seront échangées dans la ville de Washington le premier jour de mai A.D. 1891, ou avant si c'est possible."

Cependant ce Traité *faillit, car tous les signataires, les Etats-Unis mêmes, manquèrent d'échanger les ratifications dans le temps prescrit.*

On a tenté depuis de renouveler le Traité. On a convenu sur une forme d'extension, qui fut soumise à toutes les Puissances signataires, 29 Octobre 1891. Les gouvernements ci-dessous acceptaient la proposition, savoir : l'Equateur, Guatemala, Honduras, Venezuela, Nicaragua, Salvador et Bolivie.

La chose ne s'avança plus, et ainsi le Traité n'est jamais devenu efficace entre les Etats.

THE ANGLO-AMERICAN ARBITRATION TREATY.

SIGNED AT WASHINGTON, 11TH JANUARY, 1897, BUT NOT RATIFIED.

PREAMBLE.

The Governments of Great Britain and the United States, desirous of consolidating the relations of amity so happily existing, and of consecrating by treaty the principle of International Arbitration, have therefore concluded the following Treaty :—

ART. 1.—The High Contracting Parties agree to submit to Arbitration, in accordance with the provisions and subject to the limitations of the Treaty, all questions in difference between them which may fail to adjust themselves by diplomatic negotiations.

ART. 2.—All pecuniary claims or groups of pecuniary claims which do not in the aggregate exceed £100,000 in amount, and which do not involve the determination of territorial claims, shall be dealt with and decided by an Arbitral Tribunal constituted as provided in the next following article.

In this article, and in Article 4, the words "groups of pecuniary claims" mean pecuniary claims by one or more persons arising out of the same transactions or involving the same issues of law and of fact.

ART. 3.—Each of the High Contracting Parties shall nominate one Arbitrator, who shall be a jurist of repute, and the two Arbitrators so nominated shall within two months of the date of nomination select an Umpire. In case they shall fail to do so within a limit of time, the Umpire shall be appointed by agreement between the members for the time being of the Supreme Court of the United States, and the members for the time being of the Judicial Committee of the Privy Council of Great Britain, each nominating body acting by a majority. In case they fail to agree upon an Umpire within three months of the date of the application being made to them in that behalf by the High Con-

TRAITÉ D'ARBITRAGE ANGLO-AMÉRICAIN.

SIGNÉ À WASHINGTON, LE 11me JANVIER 1897, MAIS NON RATIFIÉ.

Voici le texte du traité d'arbitrage signé récemment à Washington par MM. Olney, secrétaire d'État et Pauncefote, ambassadeur de la Grande-Bretagne :

Les gouvernements de la Grande-Bretagne et des États-Unis, désirant consolider les relations d'amitié qui existent entre les deux États et consacrer par un traité le principe de l'arbitrage international, ont conclu la convention suivante :

ARTICLE PREMIER.—Les hautes parties contractantes conviennent de soumettre à l'arbitrage, sous les réserves ci-après, toutes les questions litigieuses qui surgiront entre elles et qui ne pourront être réglées par la voie diplomatique.

ART. 2.—Les réclamations pécuniaires ou les groupes de réclamations pécuniaires, dont le total n'excède pas la somme de 100,000 livres sterling et qui n'ont pas en même temps le caractère de réclamations territoriales, seront soumises au jugement d'un tribunal arbitral constitué comme il est dit à l'article suivant.

L'expression "groupe de réclamations pécuniaires" mentionnée dans le présent article et dans l'art. 4, signifie les réclamations d'argent faites par une ou plusieurs personnes à raison des mêmes transactions ou résultant des mêmes positions de droit ou de fait.

ART. 3.—Chacune des hautes parties contractantes désignera un arbitre dans la personne d'un juriste de renom ; ces deux arbitres choisiront, dans le délai de deux mois à partir de leur nomination, un sur-arbitre. Dans le cas où ils négligeraient de le faire dans le délai prescrit, le sur-arbitre sera désigné d'un commun accord par les membres de la Cour suprême des États-Unis et par les membres de la Commission judiciaire du Conseil privé de la Grande-Bretagne, la nomination incombant à chacun de ces corps ayant lieu à la majorité. Si ceux-ci ne peuvent s'entendre sur le choix du sur-arbitre dans le délai de trois mois à partir du jour où ils auront été invités par les hautes parties contractantes ou par l'une tracting Parties, or either of them, the Umpire shall be selected in the manner provided for in Article 10.

The person so selected shall be President of the Tribunal, and the award of the majority of the members shall be final.

ART. 4.—All pecuniary claims or groups of pecuniary claims which shall exceed £100,000 in amount, and all other matters in difference in respect of which either of the High Contracting Parties shall have rights against the other under treaty or otherwise, provided such matters in difference do not involve the determination of territorial claims, shall be dealt with and decided by an Arbitral Tribunal constituted as provided in the next following Article.

ART. 5.—Any subject of Arbitration described in Article 4 shall be submitted to the Tribunal provided for by Article 3, the award of which Tribunal, if unanimous, shall be final; if not unanimous, either of the contracting parties may within six months from the date of the award demand a review thereof. In such case the matter in controversy shall be submitted to an Arbitral Tribunal consisting of five jurists of repute, no one of whom shall have been a member of the Tribunal whose award is to be reviewed, and who shall be selected as follows, viz., two by each of the High Contracting Parties, and one, to act as Umpire, by the four thus nominated, and to be chosen within three months after the date of their nomination.

In case they fail to choose an Umpire within the limit of time mentioned, the Umpire shall be appointed by agreement between the nominating bodies designated in Article 3, acting in the manner therein provided.

In case they fail to agree upon an Umpire within three months of the date of an application made to them by the High Contracting Parties or either of them, an Umpire shall be selected, as provided for in Article 10.

The person so selected shall be President of the Tribunal, and the award of the majority of members shall be final.

d'elles à procéder à cette nomination, le sur-arbitre sera désigné de la manière prévue à l'article 10.

La personne désignée remplira les fonctions de président du tribunal et la sentence rendue par la majorité des membres sera définitive.

ART. 4.—Les réclamations pécuniaires ou groupes de réclamations pécuniaires dont le total excède 100,000 livres sterling, de même que tous autres différends au sujet desquels l'une des hautes parties contractantes peut invoquer contre l'autre des droits résultant d'un traité ou de toute autre cause, pourvu que ces différends n'aient pas le caractère de réclamations territoriales, seront soumises au jugement d'un tribunal arbitral constitué comme il est dit à l'article suivant.

ART. 5.—Les litiges mentionnés à l'article 4 seront soumis au jugement d'un tribunal constitué comme il est dit à l'article 3. Si le jugement de ce tribunal est rendu à l'unanimité des voix, il sera définitif; dans le cas contraire, chacune des parties contractantes pourra en demander la révision dans les six mois de sa date. Dans ce cas, le différend sera soumis à un tribunal arbitral, composé de cinq juristes de renom, à l'exclusion de ceux dont la sentence doit être révisée; chacune des hautes parties contractantes nommera deux arbitres et les quatres réunis désigneront un sur-arbitre dans le délai de trois mois à partir du jour de leur nomination.

Dans le cas où ils négligeraient de le désigner dans le délai prescrit, le sur-arbitre sera choisi d'un commun accord par les corps mentionnés à l'article 3, comme il est expliqué à cet article.

Si ceux-ci ne peuvent s'entendre sur le choix du sur-arbitre dans le délai de trois mois à partir du jour où ils auront été invités par les hautes parties contractantes, ou par l'une d'elles, à procéder à cette nomination, le sur-arbitre sera désigné de la manière prévue à l'article 10.

La personne désignée remplira les fonctions de président du tribunal et la sentence rendue par la majorité des membres sera définitive.

ART. 6.—Any Controversy which shall involve the determination of territorial claims shall be submitted to a Tribunal composed of six members, three of whom, subject to the provisions of Article 8, shall be judges of the Supreme Court of the United States or Justices of Circuit Courts, to be nominated by the President of the United States; and the other three, subject to the provisions of Article 8, shall be judges of the British Supreme Court of Judicature, or members of the Judicial Committee of the Privy Council, to be nominated by her Britannic Majesty, whose award by a majority of not less than five to one shall be final.

In case of the Award being made by less than the prescribed majority, the award shall also be final unless either Power shall, within three months after the award has been reported, protest that the same is erroneous, in which case the award shall be of no validity.

In the event of the Award being made by less than the prescribed majority, and protested against as above provided, or if members of the Arbitral Tribunal shall be equally divided, there shall be no recourse to hostile measures of any description until the mediation of one or more friendly Powers has been invited by one or both of the High Contracting Parties.

ART. 7.—Objections to the jurisdiction of an Arbitral Tribunal constituted under the Treaty shall not be taken except as provided in this Article.

If, before the close of the hearing upon the claim submitted to an Arbitral Tribunal constituted under Article 3 or Article 5, either of the High Contracting Parties shall move such Tribunal to decide, and thereupon it shall decide, that the determination of such a claim necessarily involves the decision of a disputed question of principle, of grave general importance affecting the national rights of such party as distinguished from private rights, whereof it is merely an international representative, the jurisdiction of

Art. 6.—Tout différend ayant le caractère d'une réclamation territoriale sera soumis à un tribunal de six membres, dont trois seront désignés par le président des États-Unis sous réserve de ce qui est dit à l'art. 8, parmi les juges de la Cour suprême des États-Unis ou des Cours d'arrondissement, et les trois autres, sous la même réserve, par S. M. la reine de la Grande-Bretagne, parmi les juges de la Cour suprême britannique ou les membres de la Commission judiciaire du Conseil privé. La sentence du tribunal sera définitive, pourvu qu'elle ait été rendu à l'unanimité ou par cinq voix contre une.

Dans le cas de majorité insuffisante, le jugement sera également définitif, à moins qu'une des puissances ne déclare, dans les trois mois de sa date, le considérer comme faux, laquelle déclaration annule le jugement.

Lorsqu'un jugement, rendu à une majorité insuffisante, a été déclaré nul comme il vient d'être dit, ou lorsque les voix des membres du tribunal arbitral se sont partagées par moitié, les parties contractantes ne recourront à aucune mesure d'hostilité de quelle nature que ce soit avant d'avoir, ensemble ou séparément, requis la médiation d'une ou de plusieurs puissances amies.

Art. 7.—La compétence du tribunal arbitral, constitué conformément aux dispositions du présent traité ne pourra être attaquée que dans le cas suivant :

Lorsque avant la clôture de l'instruction d'une réclamation soumise à un tribunal arbitral constitué conformément aux articles 3 ou 5, ce tribunal reconnaît, à la demande de l'une des hautes parties contractantes, que la qualification de cette réclamation entraînera nécessairement une décision sur une question de principe contestée d'une importance grave et générale concernant des droits nationaux, la partie qui les revendique n'agissant pas en réalité pour la poursuite de droits privés, mais plutôt comme agent international, le tribunal arbitral sera incompétent pour such Arbitral Tribunal over such claim shall cease, and the same shall be dealt with by Arbitration under Article 6.

ART. 8.—Where the question involved concerns a particular State or Territory of the United States, the President may appoint a judicial officer of such State or territory to be one of the Arbitrators. Where the question involved concerns a British colony or possession, her Majesty may appoint a judicial officer of such colony or possession to be one of the Arbitrators.

ART. 9.—Territorial claims in the Treaty shall include all claims to territory and all other claims involving questions of servitude, rights of navigation, and of access to fisheries, and all rights and interests necessary to the control and enjoyment of territory claimed by either of the high contracting parties.

ART. 10.—If, in any case, the nominating bodies designated in Articles 3 and 5 shall fail to agree upon an Umpire, the Umpire shall be appointed by his Majesty the King of Sweden and Norway.

Either of the High Contracting Parties may at any time give notice to the other that by reason of material changes in the conditions as existing at the date of the Treaty, it is of opinion that a substitute for his Majesty should be chosen. The substitute may be agreed upon.

ART. 11.—In case of the death, &c., of any Arbitrator, the vacancy shall be filled in the manner provided for in the original appointment.

ART. 12.—This Article provides for each Government paying its own counsel and Arbitrators, but in the case of an essential matter of difference submitted to Arbitration it is the right of one of the parties to receive disavowals of or apologies for acts or defaults of the other, not resulting in substantial pecuniary injury. The Arbitral Tribunal, finally disposing of the matter, shall direct statuer sur cette réclamation et celle-ci sera soumise à l'arbitrage prévu par l'art 6.

ART. 8.—Lorsque le différend concerne un des Etats ou territoires des États-Unis, le président pourra désigner comme arbitre un officier judiciaire de cet État ou territoire. Lorsque le différend concerne une colonie ou possession britannique, Sa Majesté pourra désigner comme arbitre un officier judiciaire de cette colonie ou possession.

ART. 9. — Les réclamations territoriales comprennent, aux termes du présent traité, outre celles concernant un territoire, toute question de servitude, de droit de navigation, de pêcherie, et tous les droits et intérêts dont l'exercice est nécessaire pour la surveillance ou la jouissance du territoire réclamé par l'une des hautes parties contractantes.

ART. 10.—Lorsque les corps désignés aux art. 3 et 5 ne pourront s'entendre au sujet de la nomination du sur-arbitre, celui-ci sera désigné par S. M. le roi de Suède et de Norvège.

Chacune des hautes parties contractantes pourra aviser en tout temps l'autre État, qu'à raison de la modification matérielle des circonstances sous l'empire desquelles le présent traité est conclu, elle estime qu'il est opportun de désigner un remplaçant à Sa Majesté. Le remplaçant pourra être consulté à ce sujet.

ART. 11.—En cas de décès, etc., d'un arbitre, il sera pourvu à son remplacement de la même manière que pour sa nomination.

ART. 12.—Chaque gouvernement paiera son conseil et ses arbitres. Cependant, dans les cas importants soumis à l'arbitrage, de une partie pourra accepter des actes de désaveu, de défense ou défaut, sans que ses charges au sujet des dépens s'en trouvent aggravées. Le tribunal arbitral décidera, dans sa sentence finale, whether any of the expenses of the successful party shall be borne by the unsuccessful party, and to what extent.

ART. 13.—The time and place of the meeting of the Arbitral Tribunal, and all arrangements for the hearing, and all questions of procedure shall be decided by the Tribunal itself.

This Article also provides for the keeping of a record and employment of agents, &c., and stipulates that the decision of the Tribunal shall, if possible, be made within three months from the close of the arguments on both sides, and shall be in writing and dated and signed by the Arbitrators who assent to it.

ART. 14.—This Treaty shall remain in force for five years from the date it shall come into operation, and, further, until the expiration of twelve months after either of the High Contracting Parties shall have given notice to the other of its wish to terminate it.

ART. 15.—This Treaty shall be ratified by the President of the United States and her Majesty the Queen of Great Britain and Ireland, and the exchange of ratifications shall take place in Washington or London within six months of the date hereof, or earlier if possible.

si et dans quelles proportions les frais de la partie qui obtient gain de cause seront mis à la charge de la partie adverse.

ART. 13.—Le tribunal fixera lui-même l'époque et le lieu de ses séances; il arrêtera également le mode d'instruction, ainsi que toutes les questions de procédure. La sentence du tribunal sera rendue si possible dans le délai de trois mois après la clôture de l'instruction; elle sera écrite, datée et signée par les arbitres qui y ont adhéré.

ART. 14.—Le présent traité restera en vigueur pendant cinq années à partir du jour où il en sera fait application et continuera aussi longtemps que l'une des hautes parties contractantes n'aura pas signifié à l'autre État, douze mois à l'avance, qu'elle désire le résilier.

ART. 15.—Le présent traité sera ratifié par le président des États-Unis et par S. M. la reine de la Grande-Bretagne et d'Irlande. L'échange des ratifications aura lieu à Washington ou à Londres dans les six mois de sa date, ou plus tôt si possible.

THE ARBITRATION TREATY BETWEEN ITALY AND THE ARGENTINE REPUBLIC.

The following is the text of the Arbitration Treaty between the kingdom of Italy and the Argentine Republic, which was signed at Rome on July 23rd, 1898.

ART. 1.—The High Contracting Parties hereby bind themselves to submit to an Arbitration decision all the disputes, whatever may be their nature or cause, which may arise between the said parties, when such cannot be adjusted in a friendly way by the ordinary course of diplomacy. This provision for Arbitration shall extend even over disputes which may have arisen prior to the negotiation of this Treaty.

ART. 2.—Should Arbitration be necessary, the parties shall make a special Convention to determine the object of the litigation, the scope of the powers of the Arbitrators, and any other matters having reference to procedure.

In default of such a Convention, the tribunal under the instruction of the parties shall determine the points of law and of fact which must be decided in order to adjust the dispute. In default of a convention, or in case the point in question has not been foreseen, the following rules shall be observed:—

ART. 3.—The tribunal shall be composed of three judges. Each of the States shall appoint one. The two Arbitrators shall choose the third. If they fail to agree in a choice, the third Arbitrator shall be chosen by the head of a third State, to be named. If the parties shall not agree upon the head of the State to be named, the President of the Swiss Confederation and the King of Sweden and Norway shall be asked in turn to name the third Arbitrator.

The third Arbitrator thus chosen shall be president of the

TRAITE D'ARBITRAGE PERMANENT ENTRE LE ROYAUME D'ITALIE ET LA REPUBLIQUE ARGENTINE

Le texte du traité d'arbitrage permanent, signé le 23 juillet 1898 à Rome, entre le représentant de la République Argentine et le ministre des affaires étrangères du royaume d'Italie, au nom de leurs gouvernements :

Article premier.—Les hautes parties contractantes se sont obligées à soumettre à un jugement arbitral tous les litiges, quelles qu'en soient la nature et la cause, qui viendraient à surgir entre les dites parties, si l'on n'a pu les vider amiablement par voie diplomatique directe. La clause d'arbitrage s'étend même aux litiges qui peuvent avoir une origine antérieure à la stipulation du dit traité.

Art. 2.—Le cas échéant, les parties stipuleront une convention spéciale pour déterminer l'objet du litige, la portée des pouvoirs des arbitres et toute autre modalité relative à la procédure.

A défaut d'une telle convention, le tribunal, sur les déductions des parties, déterminera les points de droit et de fait qui doivent être résolus pour vider le litige.

A défaut de convention, ou si elle n'a pas prévu le point en question, on observera les règles suivantes :

Art. 3.—Le tribunal sera composé de trois juges. Chacun des Etats en désignera un. Les deux arbitres choisiront le troisième arbitre. S'ils ne se mettent pas d'accord sur ce choix, le tiers-arbitre sera choisi par le chef d'un Etat-tiers qui en sera requis. Si ces parties ne sont pas d'accord sur le chef d'Etat à choisir, la demande de nomination sera faite alternativement au président de la confédération suisse et au roi de Suède et de Norvège.

Le tiers-arbitre élu dans ces circonstances sera président de droit du tribunal.

tribunal. The same person cannot be named as third Arbitrator more than once in succession.

The Arbitrators cannot be citizens of the contracting States nor reside, nor have homes, in their territories. They must have no interest in the question which constitutes the ground for the Arbitration.

ART. 4.—If an Arbitrator, for any reason whatever, cannot perform, or continue in, the office of Arbitrator to which he has been named, his place shall be filled according to the same procedure used in his nomination.

ART. 5.—In default of a special agreement between the parties the tribunal shall designate the time and the place of the meeting, outside of the territories of the contracting States, and shall choose the language which shall be employed. It shall determine the methods of procedure, the forms and the delays to be observed by the parties, the procedures to be followed, and, in general, it shall adopt all the measures which it shall judge necessary for its action, and suitable for the solving of all the difficulties of procedure which may arise in the course of the discussion.

The parties, on their part, pledge themselves to put at the disposal of the Arbitrators all the means of information within their power.

ART. 6.—An Agent of each of the parties shall be present at the sittings, and he shall represent his Government in all matters pertaining to the Arbitration.

ART. 7.—The Tribunal shall be competent to decide upon the regularity of its constitution, the validity of the Arbitration Agreement and its interpretation.

ART. 8.—The Tribunal shall render its decisions according to the principles of International Law, unless the Agreement provides for the application of special rules, and authorises the Arbitrators to render their decision as friendly counsellors.

ART. 9.—Unless provision is made to the contrary, the

Il est défendu de nommer tiers-arbitre plusieurs fois de suite la même personne.

Les arbitres ne peuvent être ni citoyens des Etats contractants, ni domiciliés ou résidents dans leurs territoires. Ils doivent n'avoir aucun intérêt dans les questions qui font l'objet de l'arbitrage.

ART. 4.— Si un arbitre, pour une raison quelconque, ne peut remplir ou continuer l'office d'arbitre auquel il avait été nommé, on le remplacera suivant la même procédure adoptée pour sa nomination.

ART. 5.— A défaut d'un accord spécial entre les parties, le tribunal désignera l'époque et le lieu des séances loin des territoires des Etats contractants, et choisira la langue dont on devra faire usage ; il déterminera les moyens de procédure, les formes et les délais à fixer aux parties, les procédures à suivre, et en général, il prendra toutes les mesures qu'il jugera nécessaires à son action et propres à résoudre toutes les difficultés de procédure qui pourraient surgir dans le cours du débat.

Les parties, de leur côté, s'engagent à mettre à la disposition des arbitres tous les moyens d'information qui dépendent d'elles.

ART. 6.—Un mandataire de chacune des parties assistera aux séances, et il représentera son gouvernement dans toutes les affaires qui se rapporteront à l'arbitrage.

ART. 7.— Le tribunal est compétent pour statuer sur la régularité de sa constitution, sur la validité du compromis et sur son interprétation.

ART. 8.—Le tribunal devra prononcer d'après les principes du Droit international, à moins que le compromis n'impose l'application de règles spéciales et n'autorise les arbitres à statuer comme amiables compositeurs.

ART. 9.—Sauf le cas de dispositions contraires, toutes les

decisions of the tribunal shall be made by a majority vote of the Arbitrators.

ART. 10.—The Award rendered shall decide definitely every point of the dispute. Two copies of it shall be drawn up and signed by all the Arbitrators. If one of the Arbitrators refuses to sign, a note of the refusal shall be made in the Award, which shall be carried into effect, if it bears the signature of a majority of the Arbitrators. The Award shall not contain any counter-arguments. Each of the parties shall be notified of the Award by its representative before the tribunal.

ART. 11.—Each of the parties shall bear its own expenses and one-half of the expenses of the Arbitral Tribunal.

ART. 12.—The Award, legally pronounced, shall settle, within the limits of its applicability, the matters in dispute between the parties. It shall indicate the limit of time within which it is to be executed. The Tribunal shall have the power to settle any questions which shall arise as to the execution of he decree.

ART. 13.—There shall be no appeal from the Award, and its execution shall be confided to the honour of the nations signing this Treaty.

The revision of the Award before the same Tribunal which has pronounced it may be asked for before the execution of the sentence: First, if the judgment has been based upon a false or erroneous document; and, second, if the decision in whole or in part has resulted from an error of fact, positive or negative, resulting from the acts or documents of the trial.

ART. 14.—This Treaty shall continue in force for a period of ten years from the exchange of ratifications. If the Treaty is not denounced six months before the date of its expiration, it shall be understood that it is renewed for a new period of ten years, and so thereafter.

délibérations du tribunal seront valables quand elles auront la majorité des voix des arbitres.

ART. 10.—La sentence devra décider définitivement tout point du litige. Elle sera rédigée en deux exemplaires et signée par tous les arbitres. Si l'un des arbitres s'y refuse, on donnera acte du refus dans la sentence qui aura effet, si elle porte la signature de la majorité absolue des arbitres. Il est défendu de joindre à la sentence des motifs contraires. La sentence devra être notifiée à chacune des parties par son représentant auprès du tribunal.

ART. 11.—Chacune des parties supportera ses propres frais et la moitié des frais du tribunal arbitral.

ART. 12.—La sentence, légalement prononcée, tranche dans les limites de sa portée, la contestation entre les parties. Elle devra contenir l'indication du terme dans lequel elle doit être exécutée.

Le tribunal a le pouvoir de vider les questions qui pourraient surgir sur l'exécution de l'arrêt.

ART. 13.—Le jugement n'est pas susceptible d'appel et il est confié à l'honneur des nations signataires du pacte.

Est reconnu le droit d'en demander, avant que la sentence ne soit exécutée, la revision devant le même tribunal qui a prononcé le jugement : 1° si on a jugé sur un document faux ou erroné ; 2° si la sentence, en tout ou en partie, a été l'effet d'une erreur de fait, positif ou négatif, résultant des actes ou des documents du procès.

ART. 14.—Le traité est conclu pour la durée de dix ans à partir de l'échange des ratifications. Si le traité n'est pas dénoncé six mois avant la date de l'échéance, il est entendu qu'il est renouvelé pour une nouvelle période de dix ans, et ainsi de suite.

ARGENTINA E ITALIA IL TESTO UFFICIALE DEL TRATTATO ARBITRALE TRA L'ITALIA E L'ARGENTINA.

S. M. il Re d'Italia e S. E. il Presidente della Repubblica Argentina, animati dal desiderio di sempre più favorire i cordiali rapporti esistenti fra i loro Stati, hanno risoluto di concludere un trattato generale di arbitrato, ed hanno a tal fine nominato come loro plenipotenziari :

SUA MAESTÀ IL RE D'ITALIA

Sua Eccellenza il conte Napoleone Canevaro, senatore del Regno, vice ammiraglio nella Real Marina, Suo Ministro Segretario di Stato per gli affari esteri, e

SUA ECCELLENZA IL PRESIDENTE DELLA REPUBBLICA ARGENTINA.

Sua Eccellenza Don Enrico B. Moreno, Suo Inviato straordinario e Ministro plenipotenziario presso Sua Maestà il Re d'Italia, i quali, avendo riconosciuto perfettamente regolari i respettivi loro pieni poteri, hanno convenuto quanto segue :

ART. 1.—Le Alte Parti contraenti si obbligano di sottoporre a guidizio arbitrale tutte le controversie, di qualunque natura, che per qualsiasi causa sorgessero fra di esse nel periodo di durata del presente trattato, e per le quali non si sia potuto ottenere un' amichevole soluzione mercè trattative dirette. Nulla importa che tali controversie abbiano la loro origine in fatti anteriori alla stipulazione del presente trattato.

ART. 2.—Caso per caso le Alte Parti contraenti concluderanno una speciale Convenzione con lo scopo di determinare il preciso oggetto della controversia, l'estensione dei poteri degli arbitri, e ogni altra opportuna modalità relativa al procedimento.

Mancando tale convenzione, spetterà al tribunale di specificare, in base alle reciproche pretese delle parti, i punti di diritto e di fatto che dovranno essere risoluti per decidere la controversia.

Per ogni altro provvedimento varranno, nell'assenza di speciale Convenzione, o nel suo silenzio, le regole qui sotto enunciate.

ART. 3.—Il tribunale sarà composto di tre guidici. Ognuno

degli Stati contraenti ne designerà uno. Gli arbitri cosi nominati sceglieranno il terzo arbitro. Se non potranno accordarsi nella scelta, il terzo arbitro sarà nominato dal capo di un terzo Stato a cui ne sarà fatta richiesta. Tale Stato sarà designato dagli arbitri già nominati. In mancanza di accordo, per la nomina del terzo arbitro, la richiesta sarà fatta al presidente della Confederazione Svizzera ed al Re di Svezia e Norvegia alternativamente.

Il terzo arbitro cosi eletto sarà di diritto presidente del tribunale.

A terzo arbitro non potrà mai venir nominata successivamente la medesima persona.

Nessuno degli arbitri potrà essere cittadino degli Stati contraenti, nè domiciliato o residente nei loro territorii. Non dovranno avere interesse nelle questioni che sono oggetto dell'arbitrato.

ART. 4.—Qualora un arbitro, per qualunque ragione, non possa assumere o non possa continuare l'ufficio a cui fu nominato, si provvederà alla sua sostituzione con il medesimo procedimento adoperato per la sua nomina.

ART. 5.—Nella mancanza di speciali accordi fra le parti spetta al tribunale: di designare l'epoca ed il luogo delle proprie sedute, fuori dei territorii degli Stati contraenti; di scegliere la lingua, di cui dovrà essere fatto uso; di determinare i modi di istruzione, le forme e i termini da prescrivere alle parti, le procedure da seguirsi, e in generale di prendere tutti i provvedimenti che siano necessari per il proprio funzionamento, e di risolvere tutte le difficoltà procedurali che potessero sorgere nel corso del dibattimento.

Le parti si obbligano, dal canto loro, di porre a disposizione degli arbitri tutti i mezzi di informazione che da loro dipendono.

ART. 6.—Un mandatario di ognuna delle parti assisterà alle sedute e rappresenterà il proprio governo in tutti gli affari che hanno rapporto con l'arbitrato.

ART. 7.—Il Tribunale è competente a decidere sulla regolarità della propria costituzione, sulla validità del compromesso e sulla sua interpretazione.

ART. 8—Il Tribunale dovrà decidere secondo i principii del diritto internazionale a meno che il compromesso non imponga l' applicazione di regole speciali, o non autorizzi gli arbitri a decidere come amichevoli compositori.

ART. 9.—A meno di espresse disposizioni contrarie, tutte le deliberazioni del tribunale saranno valide quando ottengano la maggioranza dei voti di tutti gli arbitri.

ART. 10.—La sentenza dovrà decidere definitivamente ogni punto del litigio. Dovrà essere redatta in doppio originale e sottoscritta da tutti gli arbitri. Ricusando alcuno di essi di sottoscriverla, ne dovrà esser fatta menzione dagli altri, e la sentenza avrà effetto perchè sottoscritta dalla maggioranza assoluta degli arbitri. Non potranno essere allegati alla sentenza voti motivati contrarii. La sentenza dovrà essere notificata a ciascuna dalle parti, per mezzo del suo rappresentante presso il tribunale.

ART. 11.—Ognuna delle parti sapporterà le spese proprie e metà delle spese generali del tribunale arbitrale.

ART. 12.—La sentenza legalmente pronunciata decide, nei limiti della sua portata, la contestazione fra le parti. Essa dovrà contenere l'indicazione del termine entro cui dovrà essere eseguita. Sulle questioni che potessero insorgere nella esecuzione della sentenza, dovrà decidere il tribunale medesimo che la pronunciò.

ART. 13.—La sentenza è inappellabile, e la sua esecuzione è affidata all' onore delle nazioni firmatarie di questo patto.

E' ammessa peraltro la domanda di revisione dinanzi al medesimo tribunale che la pronunciò, e prima che la sentenza medesima sia stata eseguita: 1° se sia stato giudicato sopra un documento falso od errato; 2° se la sentenza sia stata, in tutto o in parte, l'effetto di un errore di fatto, positivo o negativo, che risulti dagli atti o documenti della causa.

ART. 14.—Il presente trattato avrà la durata di dieci anni a partire dallo scambio delle ratifiche. Se non sarà denunciato sei mesi prima della sua scadenza, lo si intenderà rinnovato per un nuovo periodo di dieci anni e cosi di seguito.

ART. 15.—Il presente trattato sarà ratificato e le ratifiche saranno scambiate a Buenos Ayres entro sei mesi dalla presente data.

Fatto a Roma in doppio esemplare, addi ventitrè luglio dell'anno mille ottocento novantotto.

(L. S.) CANEVARO. (L. S.) ENRIQUE MORENO.

A CONGRESS AND COURT OF NATIONS.

By the American Peace Society, 1840.

A Congress of Nations was a favourite plan with the American Peace Society, from its first organisation at New York in 1828. At its first annual meeting it offered a prize for the best essay on the subject. Thirty-five essays were written in response, of which five were selected for publication. The President of the Society, Mr. William Ladd, examined the other essays, and a sixth was written and published by him, which contained all the matter relevant to the subject from the rejected essays.

The practical scheme in this essay is the following:—

1. Our plan is composed of two parts, viz., a Congress of Nations, and a Court of Nations, either of which might exist without the other, but they would tend much more to the happiness of mankind if united in one plan though not in one body.

Such a Congress would provide for the organisation of such a Court; but they would not constitute that Court, which would be permanent, like the Supreme Court of the United States, while the Congress would be transient or periodical like the Congress or Senate of the United States.

THE CONGRESS OF NATIONS.

2. The Congress of Nations would be organised by a Convention, composed of Ambassadors from all those Christian or civilised nations who should concur in the measure, each nation having one vote, however numerous may be the Ambassadors sent to the Convention.

This Convention would organise themselves into a Congress of Nations by adopting such regulations and bye-laws as might appeal expedient to the majority.

The Congress thus constituted would choose its president, vice-presidents, secretaries, clerks and such other officers as may be seen fit.

New members might be received, at any time subsequent to the first organisation of the Congress, by their embracing the rules already adopted, and also the laws of nations enacted by the Congress, and duly ratifying these before becoming members of the Congress.

3. After organisation, the Congress would proceed to the consideration of the first principles of the law of nations—no principle to be established unless it had the unanimous consent of all the nations represented at the Congress and were ratified by all the Governments of those nations—each principle thus ratified having the force of a treaty between them.

4. The [formation of the] Court of Nations need not be delayed until all the points of International Law were settled; but its organisation might be one of the first things for the Congress of Nations to do, and in the meantime the Court of Nations might decide cases brought before it, on principles generally known and accepted.

5. The Congress of Nations is to have nothing to do with the internal affairs of nations, or with insurrections, revolutions or contending factions of people or princes or with forms of government, but shall solely concern itself with the intercourse of nations [in relation] to Peace and war.

The four great divisions of its labours shall be: —

1. To define the rights of belligerents towards each other, and [to] endeavour, as much as possible, to abate the horrors of war, lessen its frequency and promote its termination.

2. To settle the rights of neutrals, and thus abate the evils which war inflicts on those nations that are desirous of remaining in Peace;

3. To agree on measures of utility to mankind in a state of Peace;

4. And to organise—

A COURT OF NATIONS.

I.—Organisation and Powers.

1. The Court shall be composed of as many members as the Congress of Nations shall previously agree upon, say two from each of the Powers represented at the Congress.

2. The power of this Court shall be merely advisory. It shall act as a High Court of Admiralty, but without its enforcing powers. There shall be no sheriff or posse to enforce its commands. It shall take cognisance only of such cases as shall be referred to it by the free and mutual consent of both parties concerned, like a Chamber of Commerce; and shall have no more power to enforce its decisions than an Ecclesiastical Court in this country (U.S.A.).

II.—Members and Meetings.

3. The members of this Court shall be appointed by the Governments represented in the Congress of Nations, and shall hold their places according to the tenure previously agreed upon in the Congress notably during good behavour.

4. Whether they should be paid by the Governments sending them, or by the nations represented in the Congress conjointly, according to the ratio of their population or wealth, may be agreed on in the Congress.

5. The Court should organise itself by choosing a president and vice-presidents from among its members, and they should appoint the necessary clerks, secretaries, reporters, etc.

6. The Court should hear counsel on both sides of the questions to be judged.

7. Its members might meet once a year for the transaction of business, and adjourn till such time, and to such place, as they think proper.

8. Their meeting should never be in a country which had a case on trial.

9. These persons should enjoy the same privileges and immunities as ambassadors.

III.—Awards.

10. Their verdicts, like those of other great Courts, should be decided by a majority, and need not be, like the decrees of the Congress, unanimous.

11. The majority should appoint one of their number to make out their verdict, giving a statement of facts from the testimony presented to the Court, and the reasoning on those facts by which they come to a conclusion.

IV.—Methods and Functions.

12. All cases submitted to the Court should be judged by the true interpretation of existing Treaties, and by the Laws enacted by the Congress and ratified by the nations represented; and where these Treaties and Laws fail of establishing the point at issue, they should judge the cause by the principles of equity and justice.

13. In cases of disputed boundary, the Court should have the power to send surveyors, appointed by themselves, but at the expense of the parties, to survey the boundaries, collect facts on the spot, and report to the Court.

14. This Court should not only decide on all cases brought before it by any two or more independent, contending nations, but it should be authorised to offer its MEDIATION where war actually exists, or in any difficulty arising between any two or more nations which would endanger the Peace of the world.

Its members should act as conservators of the Peace of Christendom, and watch over the welfare of mankind, both of the nations of the Confederacy and the world at large.

Often nations go to war on a point of honour, and having begun to threaten [each other], think they cannot recede without disgrace; at the same time, they would be glad to catch at such an excuse for moderation. And often, when nations are nearly exhausted by a protracted war, they would be glad to make Peace, but they fear to make the first advances, lest it should be imputed to weakness. In such cases they would welcome a mediator.

In cases where ambassadors would neither be sent nor accepted, the members of this Court might go as heralds of Peace.

15. Should the Court be applied to to settle any internal disputes between contending factions, such as the right of succession to the throne, it would be its duty to hear the parties, and give its opinion according to the laws and usages of the country asking its advice, but it should never officiously [officially] offer an *ex parte* verdict though it might propose [suggest] terms of reconciliation.

16. It should be the duty of a Court of Nations, from time to time, to suggest topics for the consideration of the Congress, as new or unsettled principles, favourable to the Peace and welfare of nations, would present themselves to the Court, in the adjudication of cases.

17. There are many other cases, besides those above mentioned, in which such a Court would either prevent war or end it.

A nation would not be justified, in the opinion of the world, in going to war, when there was an able and impartial umpire to judge its case; and many a dispute would be quashed at the outset if it were known that the world would require an impartial investigation of it by able judges.

NOTE.—In the same essay occurs the statement: "The London Peace Society" [which was always in accord with its sister society in America,] "has always been friendly to the plan of a Court or Congress of Nations, as appears by the following extract from the *Herald of Peace*, which is their organ:— "The Court of Nations [*i.e.* a permanent Court of Arbitration] is the end of the operations of the Peace Societies. . . . . . The *Herald of Peace* for July, 1839, contains a Petition to Parliament on the subject of a Congress of Nations, which was presented on the 12th of April preceding, by Edward Baines, Esq., Member for Leeds, and in the House of Lords by I know not whom. I mention this event in this place for the purpose of preserving the connection."

THE HIGH TRIBUNAL OF PUBLIC INTERNATIONAL JUDICATURE,

BY A. P. SPRAGUE.

From First Prize Essay, "*Pro pace nationum*," on the Codification of Public International Law, in "Internationalism," 1876.

PRELIMINARY.

1. The department of judicative public international law is the most positive and constructive of the departments.

2. It is, in some respects, the most important; for it is considered the international *desideratum* of the age that there should be a Tribunal for the settlement of international controversies.

3. The judicative branch of the Code being of a constructive character, should be prepared with a care and judgment quite equal to that required in the substantive branch.

4. Judicative law includes the constitution and jurisdiction of a Tribunal for the settlement of claims and controversies and the mode of procedure in the cases which shall come before the tribunal.

5. The constitution of a Tribunal of an international and public character is, obviously, of more importance than the rules of procedure.

The latter must, necessarily, be special and technical, and can be easily determined; and, whatever mode of procedure may be adopted, would be likely to give general satisfaction.

THE CONSTITUTION OF THE PUBLIC INTERNATIONAL TRIBUNAL OF JUDICATURE OR ARBITRATION.

6. It is essential to the dignity and influence of the Tribunal that it be composed of persons of an international and judicial character.

7. It is desirable that the Tribunal should possess variability or elasticity combined with permanence and cohesion.

This cannot be the case where the Tribunal consists of judges appointed as occasion may require, to sit only in the cause for which they are required (*tribunal ad hoc*); the tribunal would lack permanence and cohesion.

Whereas, if the Tribunal should be composed of a number of judges, appointed by each of the associated Powers, to hold office during life, and all the judges to sit upon each case, the tribunal would be rather unwieldy, so to speak, and there would not be sufficient variability of judicial talent and international representation; although the permanence of the tribunal would, of course, be assured under such a system, and the results of the decisions would be a great body of international interpretive law.

8. A medium must, therefore, be sought, such as—

A Tribunal consisting of a number of judges appointed for a long period (for life), one or more from each Power, only a part of whom shall sit in any single cause.

By this means the number of judges may be large enough to represent effectually the different interests of the various associated Powers; and by a selection from this number the acting court or tribunal may be sufficiently small to be efficient.

9. If the selection is given to the contending Powers, as it should be, each cause will be heard and decided by judges especially representing the parties to the controversy.

10. The location of the Tribunal should be left to the choice of the judges, with the limitation that the Tribunal shall not have its sittings at any place within the territory of either of the contending parties, nor outside of the territory of the Association of Powers.

The Jurisdiction of the Tribunal.

In respect to the jurisdiction of the Tribunal various schemes may be devised:—

11. It has been proposed by some writers to erect a tribunal which shall have power to settle all disputes between nations.

This was the scheme of Emery de la Croix, in his "Nouveau Cynée"; of Castel de St. Pierre, in his "Projet de la Paix"; and also the Plan of Bentham.

12. But the Tribunal here proposed is not a common-law tribunal, but a statutory one, a tribunal whose jurisdiction should be defined.

I have already considered the impracticability of submitting all questions to an international tribunal for settlement in the present state of international sentiment; and, under a partial, political codification (of international law), such as that here proposed, there is no necessity or propriety for a tribunal having a jurisdiction any more extensive than the extent of the substantive rules.

13. For the purpose, however, of indirectly including the unwritten public international law in the code of judicative law, it may be expedient to establish or recommend an additional tribunal.

14. This additional tribunal might be termed a Tribunal of Arbitration, and have jurisdiction over all questions which the parties in controversy shall agree to submit to it.

15. From this tribunal appeals might lie, in cases involving an interpretation of the code, to the principal tribunal, which might be denominated the High Tribunal of International Judicature, and have not only appellate, but original jurisdiction in matters arising under the code.

16. Thus, let it be provided that there shall be a High Tribunal of public international judicature, having power to hear and determine questions arising under the Code, and having both an appellate and an original jurisdiction in respect to such questions; also that there shall be Tribunal of public International Arbitration, having its constitution or existence in the option of the contending Powers, and its jurisdiction co-extensive with the option of the contending Powers; that from this tribunal appeals shall lie to the High Tribunal in causes involving the construction or interpre-

tation of the Code—that in all other cases, or in cases where the parties so agree, the decision of the tribunal of arbitration shall be final.

17. By such a scheme the Code would encourage, though not require, adjudication or arbitration upon the unwritten as well as written law.

Arrangement of the whole Scheme.

The whole scheme of judicative law will then be susceptible of the following arrangement:—

1. The High Tribunal of Public International Judicature shall consist of at least as many judges as there are Powers, and, under some conditions of the Association of Powers, of more judges than Powers.

2. If there are fifteen or more Powers, there shall be one judge appointed from each Power; if less than fifteen and more that six Powers, there shall be two judges appointed from each Power; if less than seven Powers, there shall be four judges appointed from each Power.

3. The hearing of a cause or question and its decision shall be by nine judges—four to be chosen from all the judges by each party, and the ninth, by the eight so chosen, from the remaining judges.

4. If at any time, by the accession of new Powers to the Association of Powers, the number of judges shall become too great, one (or more) shall be retired by each of the Powers; or if, at any time, the number of judges shall become too small, by the withdrawal of Powers from the Association, each Power shall appoint an additional number.

5. In the event of the death of a judge, the Power by which he was appointed would, of course, be required to fill the vacancy.

6. The original jurisdiction of the High Tribunal of Public

International Judicature shall be limited to the interpretation of the Code, and the administration of the substantive law embodied therein.

7. Where the settlement of a controverted point, or claim under the Code is desired by either of the contending Powers, such Power may give notice to the adverse Power that it intends to bring the point or claim before the High Tribunal of Public International Judicature for adjudication; and such notice shall require the adverse Power to join the complaining Power in selecting the judges and preparing the cause for adjudication, according to the rules of the Code.

8. *It is recommended* that wherever the Powers contending can agree upon the submission of a disputed point or claim, of whatever nature, to arbitration, that they submit their cause to a Tribunal of public International Arbitration, such tribunal to be constituted in any manner in which the contending powers may agree.

9. The Tribunal of Arbitration shall give its decision upon all questions which may be submitted to it, and shall decide upon principles and rules not inconsistent with the Code.

10. In cases where the interpretation of the Code is involved, the decision of the Tribunal of Arbitration shall not be final, unless the parties so agree beforehand; but an appeal in such cases may be taken to the High Tribunal of Judicature, which shall have power to hear and decide such appeal.

Remarks on Preceding.

On examining this scheme, it will be seen that it allows the utmost latitude to the Powers, consistent with any kind of permanence and stability. It will be seen also that while all questions *may* be submitted for settlement to an appropriate public international tribunal under this scheme, yet the Code only *requires* that questions involving an interpretation and application of the principles of the codified law shall be submitted for settlement.

This scheme contemplates both adjudication and arbitration; but it must be observed that the adjudication proposed is, essentially, arbitration, the voluntary element in the submission of causes to adjudication being concentrated in the act of adopting the Code.

And while the High Tribunal of Public International Judicature may not be, nominally, a Tribunal of Arbitration, but a Court of Adjudication, it nevertheless differs from the ordinary, or municipal, court of adjudication, in which the involuntary element is predominant, and the voluntary element, in the submission of causes, is remote and obscure.

The similarity of the proposed High Tribunal of Judicature to a Tribunal of Arbitration will be more apparent when we come to consider the method of executing its decrees, and the consequences of a violation of the provisions of the Code. It will only be expedient to state now that any tribunal which has not an accessory physical power sufficient to procure the execution of its decrees, must be, essentially, a Tribunal of Arbitration, no matter what it may be denominated.

CODE OF INTERNATIONAL ARBITRATION.

Approved by the Peace Congress, held at Antwerp, at its sitting of 30th August, 1894.

CHAPTER I.

DEFINITION OF INTERNATIONAL ARBITRATION, AND THE MODE OF INSTITUTING IT.

1. International Arbitration is a voluntary and contentious jurisdiction which consists in the investment, by two or more nations, of private individuals, or rulers, with the power of pronouncing on the differences which have arisen, or which may arise between them.

2. All disputes, of whatever kind, are capable of being settled by arbitration, provided that they do not affect the autonomy or the independence of the disputant nations.

3. International Arbitration is occasional or permanent. Occasional Arbitration is that which has for its object to settle a specific dispute in accordance with rules agreed on for this particular dispute. Permanent Arbitration is that which has for its object the settlement, according to certain rules previously agreed on, of all the disputes which shall arise between two or more nations.

4. Occasional Arbitration is governed by the terms of the special convention which establishes it, unless the disputant nations declare that they refer to the rules determined in the following articles.

5. Occasional Arbitration shall nevertheless be considered as invalid, if the convention which establishes it does not specify the points of the dispute, if it does not provide for the appointment of the arbitrators, and if it does not bear the signatures of the plenipotentiaries validly appointed for this purpose by the disputant nations.

CODE DE L'ARBITRAGE INTERNATIONAL.

Approuvé par le sixième Congrès de la Paix, tenu à Anvers, en sa séance du 30 *août* 1894.

CHAPITRE PREMIER

DE LA DÉFINITION DE L'ARBITRAGE INTERNATIONAL ET DE LA MANIÈRE DE L'INSTITUER.

1. L'arbitrage international est une juridiction contentieuse et volontaire qui consiste dans le fait, par deux ou plusieurs nations, d'investir des particuliers ou des gouvernants du pouvoir de prononcer sur les différends qui ont surgi ou qui peuvent surgir entre elles.

2. Tous les différends, quels qu'ils soient, sont susceptibles de recevoir une solution arbitrale, à moins qu'ils ne touchent à l'autonomie ou à l'indépendance des nations litigantes.

3. L'arbitrage international est occasionnel ou permanent. L'àrbitrage occasionnel est celui qui a pour objet de résoudre un différend déterminé suivant des règles fixées pour ce seul différend. L'arbitrage permanent est celui qui a pour objet de résoudre, suivant certaines règles fixées préalablement, tous les différends qui surgiront entre deux ou plusieurs nations.

4. L'arbitrage occasionnel est régi par les termes de la convention spéciale qui l'institue, à moins que les nations litigantes ne déclarent s'en référer aux règles déterminées dans les articles suivants.

5. L'arbitrage occasionnel sera néanmoins considéré comme nul, si la convention qui l'institue ne désigne pas les objets du litige, si elle ne règle pas la nomination des arbitres et si elle ne porte pas les signatures des plénipotentiaires valablement délégués à cet effet par les nations litigantes.

6. Permanent Arbitration is constituted by a Convention between two or more nations: this convention determines the rules to be followed for appointing the arbitrators who shall be called on to determine the differences which shall arise between them, as also the procedure which shall be observed by the arbitral courts.

7. The Convention which constitutes the Permanent Arbitration shall be general or limited. Such a convention is *limited* if no foreign nation may become a party to it without the consent of the previously contracting parties; it is *general* if any nation may become a party to it by a simple expression of its willingness.

8. In default of special provisions, the Convention which constitutes a Permanent Arbitration is considered to refer to the rules determined in the following articles.

9. The question in dispute shall be precisely specified: the arbitrators shall be forbidden, under pain of their award being considered invalid, to enlarge their powers beyond the fixed limits. In any case, when there is a doubt as to the scope of the reference, the least strict interpretation should be allowed.

10. The arbitrators shall be at least three in number: one to be chosen by each of the disputant nations: these two arbitrators shall choose the umpire.

11. In case of the disputant nations desiring to have a dispute referred to more than three arbitrators, the number of these arbitrators shall always be unequal, and the umpire shall always be chosen by the arbitrators appointed in equal numbers by the disputant nations.

12. When a dispute arises between more than two nations the number of the arbitrators shall be fixed in such a way that their total shall always be an odd number, and that the umpire be chosen by the arbitrators appointed in equal numbers by each of the disputant nations.

13. If the arbitrators do not arrive at an understanding on the

6. L'arbitrage permanent est institué par une convention entre deux ou plusieurs nations : cette convention détermine les règles à suivre pour désigner les arbitres appelés à trancher les différends qui surgiront entre elles ainsi que la procédure qui sera observée au cours de l'arbitrage.

7. La convention qui institue l'arbitrage permanent sera ouverte ou fermée. Une telle convention est fermée si aucune nation étrangère ne peut y accéder que du consentement des contractants antérieurs ; elle est ouverte si toute nation peut y accéder par une simple manifestation de sa volonté. Dans le doute, une convention d'arbitrage permanent sera considérée comme ouverte.

8. A défaut de stipulations spéciales, la convention qui institue un arbitrage permanent est censée s'en référer aux règles déterminées dans les articles suivants.

9. L'objet de chaque différend sera nettement circonscrit : il est interdit aux arbitres, sous peine de nullité de leur sentence, d'étendre leur compétence en dehors des limites qui leur seront fixées. Toutefois, dans le doute sur la portée du litige, l'interprétation la moins stricte doit prévaloir.

10. Les arbitres seront au moins au nombre de trois. Il en sera choisi un par chacune des nations litigantes : ces deux arbitres choisiront le sur-arbitre.

11. Dans le cas où les nations litigantes désirent qu'un différend soit soumis à plus de trois arbitres, le chiffre de ces arbitres sera toujours impair et le sur-arbitre sera toujours choisi par les arbitres nommés en nombre égal par chacune des nations litigantes.

12. Dans le cas où un différend surgit entre plus de deux nations, le nombre des arbitres sera fixé de manière à ce que leur total soit toujours impair et à ce que le sur-arbitre soit choisi par les arbitres nommés en nombre égal par chacune des nations litigantes.

13. Si les arbitres ne parviennent pas à s'entendre sur le choix

choice of an umpire, he shall be chosen by the ruler of some neutral state, which shall be determined by lot.

14. The following are not eligible for the office of arbitrators: those who are under the jurisdiction of the disputant nations; those of bad character; incapables and minors.

15. The arbitrators appointed may refuse to accept the mission with which they have been charged, but their consent is definitively obtained. This consent may be made known expressly or tacitly.

16. Any arbitrator who withdraws without legitimate excuse from the mission which he has undertaken shall be condemned to payment of an indemnity equal to the expenses incurred by the disputant nations.

17. The nation which desires to resort to arbitration shall signify its wish by diplomatic channels to the nation with which it finds itself in dispute, and shall notify to it the name of the arbitrator chosen by it.

18. The nation affected by this notice shall be obliged to appoint its arbitrator within one month. The two arbitrators appointed shall be obliged, within one month, to appoint the umpire or to declare that they have not been able to agree on the choice of one.

19. Within a month from the appointment of the umpire a convention shall be signed by plenipotentiaries specially appointed for this purpose, and by the arbitrators. This convention shall have as its object the exact definition of the dispute, the appointment of the place of meeting of the arbitrators, the fixing of the duration of their powers, and, eventually, the drawing up of the juridical principles admitted by the disputant nations as the basis of the decision to be arrived at.

20. The place of meeting of the arbitrators may not form part of any territory on which one of the disputant nations has any special power.

du sur-arbitre, ce dernier sera choisi par le chef d'une nation neutre désigné par la voie du sort.

14. Ne peuvent remplir l'office d'arbitres, les ressortissants des nations litigantes, les indignes, les incapables et les mineurs.

15. Les arbitres désignés peuvent refuser d'accepter la mission dont ils ont été chargés, mais leur acquiescement est définitivement acquis. Cet acquiescement peut se manifester expressément ou tacitement.

16. L'arbitre qui se soustrait sans motif légitime à la mission qu'il a assumée sera poursuivi en payement d'une indemnité égale aux frais qui auront été faits par les nations litigantes.

17. La nation qui désire recourir à un arbitrage, signifiera sa volonté par la voie diplomatique à la nation avec laquelle elle se trouve en litige et lui notifiera le nom de l'arbitre choisi par elle.

18. La nation touchée par cette signification sera tenue dans le délai d'un mois de désigner son arbitre. Les deux arbitres nommés seront tenus, dans le délai d'un mois, de désigner le surarbitre ou de déclarer qu'ils n'ont pu s'entendre sur le choix de ce dernier.

19. Dans le délai d'un mois, après la désignation du sur-arbitre, un compromis sera signé par des plénipotentiaires spécialement désignés à cet effet, et par les arbitres. Ce compromis aura pour objet de déterminer le différend, de désigner la localité où les arbitres se réuniront, de fixer la durée de leurs pouvoirs et éventuellement de libeller les principes juridiques admis par les nations litigantes comme base de la décision à intervenir.

20. La localité où les arbitres se réuniront ne pourra faire partie d'un territoire sur lequel l'une des nations litigantes a un pouvoir éminent quelconque.

21. If no place of meeting is named the arbitrators shall meet at the residence of the umpire, if this locality meets the conditions of the preceding article, or if not at the residence of one of the two other arbitrators. A place shall be chosen by the arbitrators by common agreement, or by lot, if none of the localities aforementioned fulfils the conditions mentioned above.

22. The arbitrators may not change their location, except when the accomplishment of their mission in it would be impossible or dangerous.

23. The arbitrators shall meet within a month of the signing of the convention.

24. If the duration of the powers of the arbitrators has not been fixed by the convention, it shall be for one year at most, from the date of their first meeting. The extension of the powers of the arbitrators is allowed in all cases, but with the consent of the disputant nations. The duration of the powers of the arbitrators shall be extended by as much time as they may have been forcibly prevented from sitting.

25. The revocation of the arbitrators is not possible during the time of the arbitration, except with the consent of the disputant nations.

CHAPTER II.

The Arbitral Procedure.

26. In principle, the disputant nations and the arbitrators shall follow in the procedure the forms established before the ordinary jurisdictions of civilised countries. In case of differences between the legislations of these countries, those rules shall be applied which are most advantageous to that one of the disputant nations which invokes them.

27. The records of their examination, the drawing up of the minutes of the duties performed by them, the deliberation on and the delivery of the award shall be shared in by all the arbitrators.

21. A défaut de désignation d'une localité, les arbitres se réuniront au domicile du sur-arbitre, si cette localité se trouve dans les conditions de l'article précédent, ou sinon au domicile de l'un des deux autres arbitres. Une localité sera choisie par les arbitres d'un commun accord ou par la voie du sort, si aucune des localités prémentionnées ne remplit les conditions indiquées plus haut.

22. Les arbitres ne pourront changer le siège de leurs délibérations que dans le cas où l'accomplissement de leur mission y deviendrait impossible ou périlleux.

23. Les arbitres se réuniront un mois au plus tard après la signature du compromis.

24. Si la durée des pouvoirs des arbitres n'a pas été fixée par le compromis, elle sera d'un an au plus, à partir de la date de leur première réunion. La prorogation des pouvoirs des arbitres est permise dans tous les cas, mais du consentement des nations litigantes. La durée des pouvoirs des arbitres sera prolongée de tout le temps qu'ils auraient été violemment empêchés de siéger.

25. La révocation des arbitres n'est possible, pendant la durée de l'arbitrage, que du consentement des nations litigantes.

CHAPITRE II.

DE LA PROCÉDURE ARBITRALE.

26. En principe, les nations litigantes et les arbitres suivront, dans la procédure, les formes établies devant les juridictions ordinaires des pays civilisés. En cas de divergences entre les législations de ces pays, les règles les plus avantageuses à celle des nations litigantes qui les invoquera, seront appliquées.

27. Les actes de l'instruction, la rédaction des procès-verbaux des devoirs par eux accomplis, la délibération et le prononcé de la sentence seront réalisés par tous les arbitres.

28. In every case the arbitrators should hear each of the disputant nations on each of the contested points. All documents, of whatever description, produced by one of them, shall be communicated entire. The limits of time allowed to the disputant nations for the completion of the various documents in the case shall be determined by the arbitrators.

29. All oral proceedings before the arbitrators shall be subject to cross-examination.

30. The choice of the languages to be used before them shall be left to the arbitrators. In any case, each of the disputant nations has the right to have any documents which are produced before the Arbitration Court translated into its own language at its own expense by a sworn translator.

31. Each of the disputant nations has the right to be represented before the arbitrators by a special delegate, who shall be obliged to choose a residence at the place where the arbitral tribunal is located. In the absence of any declaration to the contrary, after the opening of the debates, all notifications, in the course of the arbitration, shall be made to the representative chosen by each of the disputant nations.

32. This delegate may be assisted by such persons as each of the disputant nations shall consider qualified to defend its cause.

33. The arbitrators may take the oaths of witnesses and experts.

34. The unopposed claims and declarations of a disputant nation shall be held to be verified.

35. No appeal in warranty shall be allowed by the arbitrators. However, those who are liable to such an appeal may, by a special convention with the appellant in warranty and with the consent of the arbitrators, agree that the latter shall decide by one single award the accessory dispute and the principal dispute.

36. Counter claims may be entertained if they are provided for by the Arbitration Agreement, or in cases where the agreement makes no mention of them, by the consent of the disputant parties and the arbitrators.

28. Dans tous les cas, les arbitres doivent entendre chacune des nations litigantes sur chacun des points litigieux. Tous les documents, quels qu'ils soient, produits par l'une d'elles, seront communiqués intégralement. Les délais à observer par les nations litigantes pour l'accomplissement des divers actes de la procédure seront déterminés par les arbitres.

29. Toute procédure orale devant les arbitres sera contradictoire.

30. Le choix des langues qui seront employées devant eux est abandonné aux arbitres. Toutefois, chacune des nations litigantes a le droit de faire traduire dans sa langue et à ses frais, par un traducteur assermenté, les documents produits au cours de l'arbitrage.

31. Chacune des nations litigantes a le droit de se faire représenter devant les arbitres par un délégué spécial, qui sera tenu d'élire domicile au siège du tribunal arbitral. A moins de déclaration contraire, lors de l'ouverture des débats, toutes les notifications pourront se faire, au cours de l'arbitrage, au représentant choisi par chacune des nations litigantes.

32. Ce délégué pourra se faire assister par telles personnes que chacune des nations litigantes jugera qualifiées pour défendre sa cause.

33. Les arbitres pourront recevoir le serment des témoins et des experts.

34. Les prétentions et déclarations de l'une des nations litigantes, qui ne seront pas contestées seront tenues pour vérifiées.

35. Aucun appel en garantie ne sera admis par les arbitres. Toutefois, ceux qui sont passibles d'un tel appel peuvent, par un compromis spécial avec l'appelant en garantie et du consentement des arbitres, accepter que ces derniers jugent par une seule sentence le différend accessoire et le différend principal.

36. Les demandes reconventionnelles sont recevables si elles sont prévues par le compromis ou, dans le cas où ce dernier serait muet à leur égard, du consentement des parties litigantes et des arbitres.

37. In default of special stipulations in the Agreement, or of a supplementary convention between the disputant nations, the arbitrators shall take as the basis or ground of their award: Firstly, the special international law formulated in the treaties made between the disputant nations; secondly, the general international law formulated or used by civilised nations; thirdly, the public or private law of the disputant nations or of other civilised nations.

38. The arbitrators shall make a constant appeal to equity, both for the interpretation and application of the principles and the texts.

39. The arbitrators may not refuse to give their award, under pretext of the insufficiency of the information supplied by the disputant nations, or the obscurity of the juridical principles to be applied.

40. The arbitrators may, in the absence of any stipulation to the contrary in the Agreement, pronounce successively on the points in dispute, but they should, before separating, pronounce on all the disputed points.

41. Every decision shall be taken by an absolute majority of the arbitrators. If no decision has been able to secure an absolute majority, the arbitrators shall be obliged to draw up the different judgments expressed by them, without indicating the names of those who have shared in them.

42. The award shall contain a statement of the reasons on each of the points in dispute. In case of divided votes, with each of these votes there shall be a statement of reasons.

43. The award shall be drawn up in writing, and signed by each of the arbitrators. In case of the minority of arbitrators refusing to sign it, the other arbitrators should mention the fact, and the award shall have effect as if it had been signed by all the arbitrators.

43*a*. The award is to be drawn up and signed in as many copies as there are disputant nations.

37. A défaut de stipulations spéciales, dans le compromis ou de convention ultérieure entre les nations litigantes, les arbitres, pour asseoir leur sentence, se baseront : en premier lieu, sur le droit international spécial formulé dans les traités intervenus entre les nations litigantes ; en second lieu, sur le droit international général formulé ou usité par les nations civilisées ; en troisième lieu, sur le droit public ou privé tant des nations litigantes que des autres nations civilisées.

38. Les arbitres feront un appel constant à l'équité tant pour l'interprétation que pour l'application des principes et des textes.

39. Les arbitres ne peuvent se refuser à prononcer leur sentence, sous prétexte de l'insuffisance des renseignements fournis par les nations litigantes ou de l'obscurité des principes juridiques à appliquer.

40. Les arbitres peuvent, à moins d'une stipulation contraire dans le compromis, prononcer successivement sur les points en litige, mais ils doivent, avant de se séparer, prononcer sur tous les points litigieux.

41. Toute décision sera prise à la majorité absolue des arbitres. Si aucune décision n'a pu rallier la majorité absolue, les arbitres seront tenus de libeller les différents avis émis par eux, sans indiquer les noms de ceux qui les ont partagés.

42. La sentence sera motivée sur chacun des points en litige. En cas d'avis partagés, chacun de ces avis sera motivé.

43. La sentence sera rédigée par écrit et signée par chacun des arbitres. Au cas où la minorité des arbitres refuserait de la signer, les autres arbitres en feraient mention et la sentence aura effet comme si elle avait été signée par chacun des arbitres.

43*a*. La sentence est rédigée et signée en autant d'expéditions qu'il y a de nations litigantes.

44. The award is notified to the representatives of each of the disputant nations, accredited to the arbitrators, unless there are precise stipulations to the contrary in the agreement.

45. The notification is effected by delivery of copies of the award to the representatives or delegates of the disputant nations. This is done simultaneously in the arbitrators' presence, and a minute of it is drawn up and signed both by the arbitrators and the aforementioned representatives or delegates.

46. The costs of procedure are borne equally by each of the disputant nations. However, the expenses of counsel and proxies shall be borne entirely by the nation that incurs them.

CHAPTER III.

Execution and Nullity of the Award.

47. The execution of the award is in principle left to the good faith of the disputant nations. They may by mutual agreement make such arrangements on this point as may suit them.

48. The disputant nations may, by a special and mutual provision of the Agreement, give the arbitrators the power to enforce their award, and suggest the means.

49. In any case it is forbidden to enforce the award by taking any steps which should in any way have the character of acts of war, or which might lead to war, or to the destruction of human lives or public or private property.

50. Each of the disputant nations has the right to ask for the interpretation of the award arrived at, and the correction of material errors which it may contain.

51. Such a request shall be notified to the arbitrators and to the other nation within 30 days at the most after the delivery of the copy of the award.

52. The arbitrators shall pronounce judgment on this application within a period of two months. The award shall from that time be definitive.

44. La sentence est notifiée au représentant de chacune des nations litigantes, accrédité auprès des arbitres, à moins de stipulation contraire et précise dans le compromis.

45. La notification a lieu par la remise, aux représentants ou aux délégués des nations litigantes, des expéditions de la sentence. La remise a lieu simultanément en présence des arbitres et il en est dressé procès-verbal signé tant par les arbitres que par les représentants ou délégués prémentionnés.

46. Les frais de procédure sont supportés par chacune des nations litigantes, par parts égales. Toutefois, les frais de représentation ou de délégation restent à charge de celle des nations qui les aura exposés.

CHAPITRE III.

DE L'EXÉCUTION ET DE LA NULLITÉ DE LA SENTENCE.

47. L'exécution de la sentence est en principe abandonnée à la bonne foi des nations litigantes. Elles peuvent de commun accord prendre à ce sujet tels arrangements qu'il leur conviendra.

48. Les nations litigantes peuvent, par une disposition spéciale et mutuelle du compromis, donner aux arbitres le pouvoir de sanctionner leur sentence et leur en indiquer les moyens.

49. Toutefois il est interdit de sanctionner la sentence par des mesures d'exécution qui, de quelque manière que ce soit, auraient le caractère d'actes de guerre, ou pourraient conduire à la guerre ou à la destruction de vies humaines ou de propriétés publiques ou privées.

50. Chacune des nations litigantes a le droit de requérir l'interprétation de la sentence intervenue et la réparation des erreurs matérielles qu'elle peut contenir.

51. Une telle réquisition sera notifiée aux arbitres et à la nation défenderesse trente jours au plus tard après la remise de l'expédition de la sentence.

52. Les arbitres prononceront sur cette réquisition dans un délai de deux mois. La sentence sera dès lors définitive.

53. Each of the disputant nations has the right to demand the re-opening of the discussions, if use has been made of forged or altered documents, or if false witnesses have been heard.

54. This demand shall be notified not later than 30 days after the forgeries, the alterations, or the false witnesses have been brought to the notice of the other nation.

55. The arbitrators shall declare the discussions re-opened, and shall make the same regulations as above—in articles 26 to 46.

56. The expenses incurred since the re-opening of the discussions shall be placed to the account of the nation which fails in its case.

57. The award shall be annulled on the demand of one of the disputant nations, if it has contravened articles 5, 9, 22, 27, 28, 42, 45, of the present code.

58. However, nullity, based on the fact that the Arbitration Agreement was not validly concluded, shall be excused if the nation which claims the declaration of nullity has taken part in the procedure before the arbitrators without pleading the invalidity of the Agreement.

59. The award shall still be annulled if the arbitrators have granted to one of the disputant nations more than it asked, if their decision requires an immoral or illegal act, if one of the arbitrators has accepted from one of the disputant nations any advantage whatever, or the promise of any advantage.

60. The same shall be the case if the rules of procedure and the principles of law, whether they have been enumerated in the Arbitration Agreement or in a later convention, or whether they have been laid down by the arbitrators, have been broken by them.

61. Every petition of nullity shall form the subject of a convention concluded according to the rules enumerated in the present code or, in default of the conclusion of a convention, shall be brought before the Supreme Court of the nation on whose territory the Arbitrators have sat.

62. The petition of nullity shall be notified by diplomatic

53. Chacune des nations litigantes a le droit de demander la réouverture des débats, s'il a été fait usage d'actes faux ou altérés ou s'il a été entendu de faux témoins.

54. Cette demande sera notifiée trente jours au plus tard après que les faux, les altérations ou les faux témoignages auront été portés à la connaissance de la nation demanderesse.

55. Les arbitres déclareront les débats réouverts et statueront comme il a été dit plus haut aux articles 26 à 46.

56. Les frais faits depuis la réouverture des débats seront mis à la charge de la nation qui succombe.

57. La sentence sera annulée à la demande d'une des nations litigantes, s'il a été contrevenu aux articles 5, 9, 22, 27, 28, 42, 45 du présent code.

58. Toutefois la nullité, basée sur ce que le compromis n'a pas été valablement conclu, sera couverte si la nation demanderesse a pris part à la procédure devant les arbitres sans avoir opposé l'invalidité du compromis.

59. La sentence sera encore annulée si les arbitres ont accordé à l'une des nations litigantes plus qu'elle ne demandait, si leur décision ordonne un acte immoral ou illégal, si l'un des arbitres a accepté d'une des nations litigantes un avantage quelconque ou la promesse d'un avantage.

60. Il en sera encore ainsi si les règles de procédure et les principes de droit, soit qu'ils aient été énumérés dans le compromis ou dans une convention ultérieure, soit qu'ils aient été posés par les arbitres, ont été violés par ces derniers.

61. Tout recours en nullité fera l'objet d'un compromis conclu d'après les règles énumérées dans le présent code ou, à défaut de la conclusion d'un compromis, sera porté devant la cour suprême de la nation sur le territoire de laquelle les arbitres ont siégé.

62. Le recours en nullité sera notifié par la voie diplomatique

means within three months of the delivery of the copies of the award.

63. Nevertheless the petition of nullity, if it is based on facts contrary to the rules of Articles 27 and 28, or on facts of bribery provided for by Article 59, shall still be receivable after the expiration of the time allowed by the preceding article, if the nation which claims it proves that the facts appealed to by it were not brought to its knowledge till after the expiration of this interval. When this is the case, the appeal shall be notified not later than three months after the facts appealed to have been brought to the knowledge of the appealing nation.

64. Five months after the said notification, the petition of nullity shall be considered as abandoned, if the appealing nation has not presented to the court before which the matter has come a justificatory memorandum explaining all the reasons urged by it, and if it has not at the same time deposited the sum of 10,000 francs by way of possible indemnity.

65. A like interval of five months is allowed to the defendant nation to draw up its arguments in reply.

66. After an interval of one year at most, the Court shall be bound to give its judgment on the grounds of the petition.

67. If one of the arguments is sustained, the arbitral award shall be annulled. If the arbitral award comprises several independent decisions, those decisions which have been successfully attacked shall alone be annulled.

68. If the Court rejects the petition, the indemnity which has been deposited shall be forfeited to the advantage of the defendant nation.

69. The costs of these proceedings shall be charged to the nation which loses its case.

70. The decision on the petition of nullity is definitive.

71. The rules of procedure fixed by Articles 26 to 46 shall be observed during the hearing of the petition of nullity.

trois mois au plus tard après la remise de l'expédition de la sentence.

63. Toutefois le recours en nullité, s'il est basé sur des faits contraires aux prescriptions des articles 27 et 28 ou sur des faits de corruption prévus par l'article 59, sera encore recevable, après l'expiration du délai établi par l'article précédent, si la nation demanderesse établit que les faits invoqués par elle n'ont été portés à sa connaissance que postérieurement à l'expiration de ce délai. Dans cette hypothèse, le recours sera notifié trois mois au plus tard après que les faits invoqués ont été portés à la connaissance de la nation demanderesse.

64. Cinq mois après la dite notification, le recours en nullité sera considéré comme abandonné si la nation demanderesse n'a pas présenté à la juridiction saisie un mémoire justificatif exposant tous les motifs invoqués par elle et si elle n'a pas déposé simultanément une somme de dix mille francs à titre d'amende éventuelle.

65. Un pareil délai de cinq mois est accordé à la nation défenderesse pour faire valoir ses motifs en réponse.

66. Dans le délai d'une année au plus, la juridiction saisie sera tenue de se prononcer sur les motifs du recours.

67. Si l'un des motifs est fondé, la sentence arbitrale sera annulée. Si la sentence arbitrale contient plusieurs décisions indépendantes, les décisions efficacement attaquées seront seules annulées.

68. Si la juridiction saisie rejette le recours, l'amende déposée sera confisquée au profit de la nation défenderesse.

69. Les frais de cette procédure seront mis à charge de la nation qui succombe.

70. La décision sur le recours en nullité est définitive.

71. Les règles de procédure déterminées par les articles 26 à 46 seront observées au cours de l'instance en nullité.

A FORM OF INTERNATIONAL TREATY OF ARBITRATION FOR PERMANENT ADOPTION BETWEEN STATES.

Prepared by the late M. CHARLES LEMONNIER, Doctor of Law, and President of the "Ligue Internationale de la Paix et de la Liberté."

ART. I.—The two contracting parties undertake to submit to a tribunal, endowed with the constitution, jurisdiction, and powers to be described in the following articles, all differences and all difficulties which may arise between the two nations during the term of the present treaty, whatever may be the cause, nature, or subject-matter of such disputes. Moreover, the two States undertake, in the most absolute manner, without restriction or reserve, directly or indirectly, to have no recourse to warlike proceedings of any kind or description.

ART. II.—Every difference which may have arisen, or which may arise, between the two nations shall be submitted to a tribunal composed of three persons; and its decisions shall be final and without appeal. The Power which takes the initiative in such a case, when inviting the other Power to constitute an arbitral tribunal, shall report the name of the arbitrator whom it has selected, and the latter shall reply within fifteen days of this notification by naming a second arbitrator.

Within a month from the time of such nomination, the two arbitrators shall jointly name a third arbitrator.

ART. III.—Within a month from the date when the third arbitrator is selected, the following matters shall be specified in the Agreement:—The constitution of the tribunal; the duties of the arbitrators; the subject of the dispute; the respective claims of the parties; and the place where the tribunal shall be constituted.

This Agreement shall be signed by the representatives of the parties, and by the arbitrators.

FORMULE D'UN TRAITÉ D'ARBITRAGE PERMANENT ENTRE NATIONS

PAR CH. LEMONNIER.

ARTICLE 1er. — Les deux parties contractantes s'engagent à soumettre au tribunal arbitral, dont la constitution, la juridiction et la compétence seront fixées plus bas, tous les différends et toutes les difficultés qui pourront naître entre les deux peuples pendant la durée du présent traité, quels que puissent être la cause, la nature et l'objet de ces difficultés. Les deux nations renonçant de la façon la plus absolue, sans aucune exception, restriction ni réserve, à user, l'une vis-à-vis de l'autre, directement ni indirectement, d'aucun moyen ni procédé de guerre.

ART. 2. — Tout différend né ou à naître entre les deux peuples sera soumis à un tribunal composé de trois personnes, lequel jugera sans appel et en dernier ressort.

La partie la plus diligente, en requérant de l'autre la constitution du tribunal arbitral, lui fera connaître l'arbitre choisi par elle, et celle-ci devra répondre dans la quinzaine de la notification à elle faite, par la désignation d'un autre arbitre. Dans le mois qui suivra cette désignation, les deux arbitres en nommeront un troisième.

ART. 3. — Le compromis qui, dans le mois de l'acceptation du troisième arbitre, constatera par écrit la constitution du tribunal, déterminera la mission des arbitres, en fixant l'objet du litige, les prétentions respectives des parties, et le lieu de la réunion du tribunal. Ce compromis sera signé par les représentants des parties et par les arbitres.

Art. IV.—In the absence of positive international law for their guidance, the contracting parties shall expressly agree that, in all the cases which may be submitted to them, the arbitrators shall be guided by, and apply the following rules and principles, which the parties undertake to recognise as having the force of law:—

(*a*) All nations are in relations of complete equality, whatever may be the number of their population, or the extent of their territory.

(*b*) Every nation possesses sovereign rights, and is responsible to other nations both for its own acts, and for those of its subjects and citizens, as well as for the acts of its Government.

(*c*) The right of a nation to belong to itself and to govern itself is inalienable and imprescriptible.

(*d*) No individual, Government, or people can, under any pretext, legitimately dispose of the fortunes of another people by annexation, by conquest, or by any other means whatever.

(*e*) Four conditions are requisite to the validity of any convention or treaty between nations, as follows:—

(1.) Capacity to enter into contracts with another party.

(2.) Free consent on the part of both.

(3.) A definite object as the subject-matter of the agreement.

(4.) A lawful purpose—that is to say, one which does not affect public order or morals.

(*f*) Any clause, treaty, or agreement shall be null and void, because contrary to public order and morality, which includes any of the following purposes:—

Any infringement of the sovereign rights and independence of one or more nations or persons; a war which is not strictly defensive; any conquest, invasion, hostile occupation,

ART. 4. — En l'absence d'une loi internationale positive qui les régisse, les parties contractantes conviennent expressément que dans tous les cas qui pourront leur être déférés par elles, les arbitres consulteront et appliqueront les règles et les principes qui suivent, auxquels les parties entendent donner entre elles force de loi :

I. Les peuples sont égaux entre eux, sans égard à la superficie des territoires, non plus qu'à la densité des populations.

II. Les peuples s'appartiennent à eux-mêmes ; ils sont responsables les uns envers les autres, tant de leurs propres actes que des actes des sujets ou citoyens qui les composent ainsi que des actes de leurs gouvernements.

III. Le droit des peuples à s'appartenir et à se gouverner eux-mêmes est inaliénable et imprescriptible.

IV. Nul individu, nul gouvernement, nul peuple ne peut légitimement ni sous aucun prétexte disposer d'un autre peuple par annexion, par conquête ou de quelque autre façon que ce soit.

V. Quatre conditions sont requises pour la validité de toute convention et de tout traité entre peuples :

La capacité de contracter chez l'une et l'autre parties;

Le libre consentement de l'une et de l'autre;

Un objet certain qui forme la matière de l'engagement;

Une cause licite, c'est-à-dire qui ne blesse ni l'ordre public ni les bonnes mœurs.

VI. Est nul comme contraire à l'ordre public et aux bonnes mœurs, toute clause, convention ou traité ayant pour objet :

Toute atteinte à l'autonomie d'un ou de plusieurs peuples, ou individus;

Toute guerre qui n'est point strictement défensive;

Toute conquête, invasion, occupation, partage, démembredismemberment, cession, annexation or acquisition, on any grounds or under any circumstances whatever, of the whole or part of a territory occupied by one people, or by any population whatever, if such occupation has not been previously accepted by the inhabitants, both male and female.

(*g*) Every nation which is invaded has the right, for purposes of defence, to make use of all the resources of its territory, and of all the collective or individual forces of its inhabitants; and the exercise of this right is not subject to any conditions whatever.

(*h*) War becomes culpable from the moment that it passes from the defensive to the offensive, and in order to enter upon the illicit course of invasion and conquest.

Moreover, in accordance with the special character of each case referred to arbitrators, the Agreement should, as per Article III., define the constitution of the tribunal and the subject of the dispute. Again, it should if necessary prescribe the special rules, which, like the general rules above stated, will constitute the law to be put in force by the arbitrators.

If it happens that in applying the provisions of this article some difficulty or obscurity occurs, the arbitrators shall supply what is wanted, as their conscience and reason may direct; and they shall not fail to pronounce a decision in any case submitted to them. Nor shall they fail to carry out the principles laid down in the above article.

ART. V.—The Agreement shall prescribe the duration of the functions of the arbitrators; but the term may be extended at the consent of the parties. Should it happen that the treaty ceases to be in force before the expiration of the powers conferred upon the arbitrators by the last agreement between the parties, those powers shall not be thereby terminated or invalidated in any respect whatever.

ART. VI.—The arbitrators shall themselves determine their procedure, fix the periods for the execution of processes, and ment, cession, annexion ou acquisition à quelque titre ou de quelque façon que ce soit, de tout ou partie d'un territoire occupé par un peuple, ou par une population quelconque, qui n'a pas été au préalable consentie par les habitants, sans distinction de sexe.

VII. Tout peuple envahi a le droit, pour repousser l'invasion, d'user de toutes les ressources de son territoire et de toutes les forces collectives ou individuelles de ses habitants ; ce droit n'est subordonné dans son exercice à aucune condition, soit de signe extérieur, soit d'organisation militaire.

VIII. La guerre devient coupable du moment qu'elle passe de la défensive à l'offensive pour entrer dans la voie illicite de l'invasion et de la conquête.

En outre et selon la spécialité des cas litigieux soumis aux arbitres, le compromis qui devra, aux termes de l'article 3, constater la constitution du tribunal et fixer l'objet du litige, devra, s'il y échet, déterminer les règles particulières qui devront, comme les règles générales énoncées ci-dessus, servir de loi aux arbitres.

S'il arrive que dans l'application, les dispositions du présent article offrent quelque obscurité, quelque omission, quelque lacune, les arbitres devront y suppléer par les lumières de leur conscience et de leur raison, sans pouvoir en aucun cas s'abstenir de juger, ni déroger aux principes édictés par le dit article.

Art. 5. — Le compromis fixera la durée des pouvoirs des arbitres. Ces pouvoirs pourront toujours être prorogés du consentement des parties. S'il arrivait que le traité prît fin avant l'expiration des pouvoirs conférés aux arbitres par le dernier compromis passé entre les parties, ces pouvoirs n'en seraient ni détruits, ni diminués en quoi que ce soit.

Art. 6. — Les arbitres règleront eux-mêmes leur procédure, fixeront les délais et règleront la forme en laquelle les parties prescribe the formalities according to which the parties shall present their claims, counterclaims, pleas, and rejoinders.

ART. VII.—The arbitrators shall have recourse to all means of information which they may think necessary for the purpose of ascertaining the facts, and of arriving at a just decision, such as investigations, the services of experts, the production of documents (with or without transfer from their place of custody), examination of documents, the removal of judges from one place to another, commissions of inquiry, &c. Each party shall undertake to place at the service of the judges all facilities and means of information that may be necessary.

ART. VIII.—There shall be no appeal from the decision of the judges, which shall be final. Their award shall be executory, and shall have the force of law a month after it has been notified by them to the two parties. They will be required to make their award known through the medium of official journals or delegates specially authorised to receive legal notices, within eight days of its issue.

The arbitrators shall themselves fix the salaries and emoluments of the persons employed by them. They shall regulate all expenses, including their own honoraria; and they shall specify in the award the proportion of expenses to be paid by the two parties respectively.

ART. IX.—The arbitral decision shall not be annulled, except in the following cases, and for the following reasons:—

(*a*) If the arbitrators have pronounced judgment in reference to matters not referred to them.

(*b*) If the decision has been based upon an Agreement which is null and void, or which has expired.

(*c*) If the forms and periods of time prescribed by the Treaty have not been observed.

devront produire devant eux leurs demandes, requêtes, conclusions et défenses.

Art. 7.—Les arbitres useront, pour éclairer leur justice, de tous les moyens d'informations qu'ils jugeront nécessaires : enquêtes, expertises, production de pièces, avec ou sans déplacement, compulsoires, transports de juges, commissions rogatoires, etc., chaque partie s'obligeant à mettre à leur disposition tous les moyens, ressources et facilités nécessaires.

Art. 8.—Les arbitres jugeront sans appel et en dernier ressort. Leur sentence sera exécutoire, de plein droit, un mois après la notification qui en sera faite par leurs soins aux deux parties. Ils seront tenus de rendre cette sentence publique par la voie des journaux officiels ou délégués pour recevoir les annonces légales dans la huitaine de la dite notification.

Les arbitres fixeront eux-mêmes les salaires et émoluments des personnes qu'ils auront employées ; ils règleront les frais faits par eux, en y comprenant leurs propres honoraires, et détermineront par la sentence la proportion dans laquelle ces frais et honoraires devront être supportés par les parties.

Art. 9.—La sentence arbitrale ne pourra être annulée que dans les cas et pour les causes suivantes :

Si les arbitres ont prononcé sur choses non demandées ;

Si la sentence a été rendue sur compromis nul ou expiré ;

Si les formes et délais prescrits par le présent traité n'ont pas été observés.

In either of these cases, the party desiring to have the award declared null and void, should make a claim to that effect, on pain of forfeiture of the same, within a month of the declaration of the award. Such party should, in his statement of claim, name an arbitrator, and the inquiry into the demand for nullity shall be conducted as in the case of arbitration, and in conformity with the rules above laid down.

ART. X.—Arbitrators conducting an inquiry into the nullity of an award shall confine themselves to a declaration on that point alone; and their decision shall not be called in question, either by way of appeal or in any other manner, it being definite and absolute. In the case of the award in question being annulled, a new arbitral tribunal shall be constituted for the purpose of arriving at a decision, according to the rules laid down in Articles II., III., IV., V., VII., VIII., as above.

If the award whose nullity has been demanded is affirmed, it shall come into full effect within fifteen days of the declaration being notified to the parties.

ART. XI.—The present treaty shall remain in full effect for thirty successive years from the date on which it is signed. Unless one of the parties shall have given notice, in writing, to the contrary at least six months before its expiry, the said treaty shall continue to have effect by tacit renewal ("reconduction"). Each party shall, however, retain full power, by a simple notification, to terminate the treaty at the expiration of the thirty years aforesaid. Such notification, however, shall not take effect until six months afterwards, and shall not invalidate the conditions stated in Article V.

ART. XII.—The two parties pledge their honour faithfully to observe the execution of the preceding treaty, in respect to all its provisions.

L'un de ces cas échéant, celle des parties qui voudra se pourvoir en nullité de la sentence devra le faire, à peine de forclusion, dans le mois de la notification de la sentence. Elle devra, par le même acte, désigner un arbitre, et la procédure de la demande en nullité devra être poursuivie par voie d'arbitrage, et conformément aux règles établies ci-dessus.

ART. 10.—Les arbitres saisis d'une demande en nullité d'une sentence rendue ne devront statuer que sur la question de nullité, leur sentence ne pourra être attaquée ni par voie d'appel, ni par aucune autre voie, elle sera souveraine et définitive. S'ils annulent la sentence à eux déférée, un nouveau tribunal arbitral sera formé pour instruire et statuer selon les règles tracées par les articles 2, 3, 4, 5, 6, 7 et 8 qui précèdent.

Si la sentence arguée de nullité est déclarée valable, elle sortira son plein et entier effet dans la quinzaine de la notification faite aux parties de la sentence qui en aura déclaré la validité.

ART. 11.—Le présent traité aura son plein et entier effet pendant trente années consécutives, à partir de la signature. A moins que l'une des parties n'ait, six mois au moins avant son expiration, notifié par écrit son intention contraire, le dit traité continuera d'avoir effet entre les parties par voie de tacite réconduction. Chaque partie gardant d'ailleurs la faculté d'y mettre fin après l'expiration des trente années ci-dessus indiquées, par une simple déclaration qui n'aura d'effet que six mois après sa notification, et ce, sans dérogation aux dispositions portées en l'article 5.

ART. 12.—Les deux parties engagent leur honneur à exécuter fidèlement et en toutes ses dispositions le traité qui précède.

A MODEL OF A TREATY OF ARBITRATION FOR PERMANENT ADOPTION BETWEEN STATES.

PREPARED BY M. EMILE ARNAUD,

President of the "Ligue Internationale de la Paix et de la Liberté."

Between :

. . . .

. . . .

There is concluded, in the following terms, a permanent treaty of Arbitration :—

I. The contracting States reciprocally recognise their full Autonomy and independence.

II. These States engage to submit to an arbitral tribunal judging without appeal and finally* all the disputes and differences which may arise between them during the time that the present treaty is in force, whatever may be the cause, nature and object of these difficulties: consequently they renounce, without any exception or reserve, the use against each other. whether directly or indirectly, of any means or process of war during this period.

III. The arbitral tribunal shall be composed of three persons, Each of the States shall appoint one of the arbitrators. It shall choose him from amongst persons who are neither under the jurisdiction of one of the contracting States nor inhabitants of their continental or colonial territory. The two arbitrators shall themselves choose the third.

If, three months after being called upon to appoint its arbitrator, one of the States has not proceeded to such appointment, or if the

* It would be easy, if the contracting parties desired it, to constitute a second degree of jurisdiction. It would be sufficient to settle in the treaty the composition of the Arbitration Court (5 or 7 members appointed as the arbitrators of the 1st degree) the time allowed for appeal, and the procedure.

PROJET-MODÈLE D'UN TRAITÉ D'ARBITRAGE PERMANENT ENTRE NATIONS.

PAR M. EMILE ARNAUD,

Président de la Ligue Internationale de la Paix et de la Liberté.

Entre :

. . . .

. . . .

Il est conclu, dans les termes suivants, un traité d'arbitrage permanent :

I. Les Etats contractants reconnaissent réciproquement leur pleine Autonomie et Indépendance.

II. Ces Etats s'engagent à soumettre à un tribunal arbitral jugeant sans appel et en dernier ressort (*) tous les conflits et différends qui pourraient naître entre eux pendant la durée du présent traité, quels que puissent être la cause, la nature et l'objet de ces difficultés ; ils renoncent en conséquence, sans aucune exception ni réserve, à user l'un vis-à-vis de l'autre, soit directement, soit indirectement, d'aucun moyen ni procédé de guerre pendant cette durée.

III. Le tribunal arbitral sera composé de trois personnes. Chacun des Etats désignera l'un des arbitres. Il le choisira parmi les personnes qui ne sont ni ressortissants de l'un des Etats contractants ni habitants de leur territoire continental ou colonial. Les deux arbitres choisiront eux-mêmes le troisième.

Si trois mois après une mise en demeure de désigner son arbitre l'un des Etats n'a pas procédé à cette désignation, ou si

(*) Il serait aisé, si les contractants le désiraient, de constituer un second degré de juridiction. Il suffirait de régler dans le traité, la composition de la Cour d'arbitrage (5 ou 7 membres nommés comme les arbitres du 1er degré), les délais d'appel et la procédure.

two arbitrators cannot agree on the choice of the third arbitrator, this first arbitrator or the third arbitrator shall be appointed by the Swiss Federal Council (*or by any other neutral Government, or by any independent authority of a neutral Power*).

IV. The tribunal called together by the third arbitrator, shall immediately have an Agreement drawn up which shall fix the object of the suit, the composition of the tribunal, the character and duration of this tribunal. This Convention shall be signed by the representatives of the parties and by the arbitrators.

V. The arbitrators shall determine their procedure and the place of meeting of the tribunal, whose sittings shall be public.

To throw light on the question, they shall use all the means of information which they shall judge necessary, the parties engaging to place them at their disposition. Their award shall be notified to the parties within three days; it shall be invested with the force of law one month after this notification.

VI. Each of the parties engages to observe and loyally execute this award.

The parties may, by a special clause of the Agreement, give the arbitrators the power and the means of enforcing their award.

VII. The present treaty is concluded for thirty consecutive years, dating from the exchange of the ratifications. If notice to the contrary is not given before the commencement of the thirtieth year, it will continue to have effect between the parties, by tacit renewal ("reconduction"), during another period of thirty years, and so continuously.

les deux arbitres ne peuvent s'entendre sur le choix du tiers arbitre, ce premier arbitre ou le tiers arbitre sera désigné par le Conseil fédéral helvétique (*ou par tout autre gouvernement neutre, ou par toute autorité indépendante d'une puissance neutre*).

IV. Le tribunal réuni par les soins du tiers arbitre, fera rédiger immédiatement un compromis qui fixera l'objet du litige, la composition du tribunal, le caractère et la durée des pouvoirs de ce dernier. Le compromis sera signé par les représentants des parties et par les arbitres.

V. Les arbitres détermineront leur procédure et le lieu de réunion du tribunal dont les audiences seront publiques.

Ils useront, pour éclairer leur justice, de tous les moyens d'information qu'ils jugeront nécessaires, les parties s'engageant à les mettre à leur disposition. Leur sentence sera notifiée aux parties dans les troix jours; elle sera exécutoire de plein droit un mois après cette notification.

VI. Chacune des parties s'engage à observer et à exécuter loyalement cette sentence.

Les parties pourront, par une clause spéciale du compromis, donner aux arbitres le pouvoir et les moyens de sanctionner leur sentence.

VII. Le présent traité est fait pour trente années consécutives qui courront à partir de l'échange des ratifications. S'il n'est pas dénoncé avant le commencement de la trentième année, il continuera d'avoir effet entre les parties, par voie de tacite réconduction, pendant une autre période de trente ans et toujours ainsi par la suite.

A CHINESE SCHEME FOR UNIVERSAL PEACE.

The *Shih Pao* develops, in a long article, a scheme for securing universal Peace, which, it says, has been suggested by a distinguished Japanese.

Premising that the modern political world may be compared to the ancient contending States of China, the *Shih Pao* says that in the United States an idea is found which may be expanded into a scheme for maintaining Peace and giving effect upon earth to the life-loving virtue of Heaven. The scheme it propounds is thus summarised :—

I. Several great strategical places should be fixed upon in the five continents, which should constitute together the seat of International Dominion.

II. A General Arbiter and a Vice-Arbiter should be chosen, and also four Great Generals, with subordinate officers, by popular vote of all nations; offices to be held for four years, with a possibility of re-election for a second time only.

III. All nations should contribute, according to their size, to the revenue of the Peace Department; and the Department should have a standing army of several hundreds of thousands.

IV. The General Arbiter is to be the absolute exponent of International Law.

V. But it seems his function would be also similar to those of a superintendent of police, for the Great Generals are in every case to proceed at once under his direction to punish any State which commences to use force against another, whether it be in the right or wrong; and then the Arbiter, like a police magistrate, is to settle the terms of peace between the two nations.

VI. The Peace Department is not to interfere with the internal government of States, or even in civil wars, unless called upon to put them down.—*Herald of Peace*, October, 1890.

SKETCH OF A PROPOSED ARBITRATION TREATY.

Prepared for the Alumni Association of Haverford College, and submitted to a convention held at St. George's Hall, Philadelphia, November 27th, 1883.

1. The Powers joining the Arbitration League, shall sign a treaty, binding themselves to submit all disputes to an international tribunal, to abide by the decisions thereof, and to assist in enforcing such decisions upon any recalcitrant member of the Arbitration League.

2. Each signatory shall disarm, reserving only such force as under the treaty such signatory is required to maintain as its contingent in the international police.

3. The contingent to be maintained by each signatory shall be calculated, (1) in the case of land forces, on the basis of population, and (2) in the case of sea forces, on the basis of the tonnage of the shipping entered in the ports of each signatory.

4. Such contingents shall remain under the control of their respective authorities, until summoned by order of the international tribunal on international service, when they shall unite to execute its commands.

5. Upon receipt of such summons, the commanders of both land and sea forces shall elect, by ballot, a Commander-in-chief and Lord High Admiral, who shall thereupon assume the direction of their respective forces.

6. An international tribunal shall be constituted to perform the herein recited functions.

AND OF THE CONSTITUTION OF A PROPOSED

INTERNATIONAL TRIBUNAL.

1. Each signatory to the arbitration treaty shall nominate judges according to population of such signatory. For fifteen millions and under, one judge: between fifteen and twenty-five millions, two judges; over twenty-five millions, three judges and no more.

2. At the first session of the international tribunal, the members thereof shall elect their president by ballot.

3. When any question is submitted, concerning which not more than three nations are at issue, the judges representing such nations shall retire from the bench and shall be at liberty to act as counsel for their respective nations, but all questions affecting more than three nations shall be heard and decided by the entire bench.

4. The salaries of the judges shall be paid by the nations which they represent.

5. Contending nations shall appear by such counsel as they may think fit to employ, but judges may not act as counsel, except as provided in Art. 3.

6. Each nation shall, by its judge or judges, select and name a place of session within its territory. An alphabetical list of such places shall be drawn up, and the tribunal shall sit at each place in rotation, except as provided in Art. 7.

7. The tribunal shall not sit at the place of session of any nation which is a party to the question to be decided, notwithstanding that such nation is next in order on the rota-list, but in such case, the session shall be held at the place of session of the nation immediately following on the rota-list which shall not be a party to the questions to be decided; and places of session

so postponed, shall *pro hâc vice* exchange positions on the rota-list, with places of session so substituted.

8. The judges shall collect existing precedents of international law, to form the basis of a future code.

9. The language of the tribunal shall be the French tongue.*

10. It shall be lawful for the tribunal to interfere in cases of internal disturbances in nations being parties to the arbitration treaty whenever, in their opinion, such disturbances are calculated to lead to internecine conflicts.

11. The international police shall be at the disposal of the tribunal to execute any orders it may think fit to issue.

* The French language has been inserted here as being the recognised medium of diplomatic communications.

RULES PROPOSED BY THE INSTITUTE OF INTERNATIONAL LAW.

ADOPTED AT THE HAGUE, AUGUST 28TH, 1875.

The Institute, desiring that recourse to Arbitration for the settlement of international disputes should be more and more resorted to by civilised peoples, hopes to contribute usefully to the realisation of this progress by proposing the following possible regulations for the Arbitral Tribunals. It recommends it for entire or partial adoption by those State which may form Arbitration Agreements.

ART. 1.—An Agreement to arbitrate is concluded by a valid international treaty.

It may be so concluded:

(*a.*) By anticipation, whether for any and every difference, or for those of a certain class specially to be designated, that may arise between the Contracting States;

(*b.*) For one or more differences already existing.

ART. 2.—The Agreement to arbitrate gives to each of the Contracting Parties the right to appeal to the Arbitration Tribunal which it designates for the decision of the question in dispute. If the Agreement to arbitrate does not designate the number and names of the arbitrators, the Arbitration Tribunal shall proceed according to the provisions laid down in the Agreement to arbitrate, or in some other agreement.

If there be no such provision, each of the Contracting Parties shall choose an arbitrator, and the two arbitrators thus appointed shall choose a third arbitrator, or name a third person who shall appoint him.

If the two arbitrators appointed by the parties cannot agree on the choice of a third arbitrator, or if one of the parties refuses the co-operation which, according to the Agreement to arbitrate, he should give to the formation of the Court of Arbitration, or if the person named refuses to choose, the Agreement to arbitrate is annulled.

ART. 3.—If in the first instance, or because they have not been

PROJET DE RÈGLEMENT POUR LA PROCÉDURE ARBITRALE INTERNATIONALE

ADOPTÉ PAR L'INSTITUT DE DROIT INTERNATIONAL LE 28 AOÛT 1875 À LA HAYE.

L'Institut, désirant que le recours à l'arbitrage pour la solution des conflits internationaux soit de plus en plus pratiqué par les peuples civilisés, espère concourir utilement à la réalisation de ce progrès en proposant pour les tribunaux arbitraux le règlement éventuel suivant. Il le recommande à l'adoption entière ou partielle des Etats qui concluraient des compromis.

ART. 1.—Le compromis est conclu par traité international valable.

Il peut l'être:

(*a.*) *D'avance*, soit pour toutes contestations, soit pour les contestations d'une certaine espèce à déterminer, qui pourraient s'élever entre les Etats contractants:

(*b.*) Pour une contestation ou plusieurs contestations *déjà nées* entre les Etats contractants.

ART. 2.—Le compromis donne à chacune des parties contractantes le droit de s'adresser au tribunal arbitral qu'il désigne pour la décision de la contestation. A défaut de désignation du nombre et des noms des arbitres dans le compromis, le tribunal arbitral se règlera selon les dispositions prescrites par le compromis ou par une autre convention.

A défaut de disposition, chacune des parties contractantes choisit de son côté un arbitre, et les deux arbitres ainsi nommés choisissent un tiers-arbitre ou désignent une personne tierce qui l'indiquera.

Si les deux arbitres nommés par les parties ne peuvent s'accorder sur le choix d'un tiers-arbitre, ou si l'une des parties refuse la coopération qu'elle doit prêter selon le compromis à la formation du tribunal arbitral, ou si la personne désignée refuse de choisir, e compromis est éteint.

ART. 3.—Si dès le principe, ou parce qu'elles n'ont pu tomber able to agree on the choice of arbitrators, the Contracting Parties have agreed that the Arbitration Tribunal should be formed by a third person named by them, and if the person named undertakes the formation of the tribunal, the course to be followed shall depend, first, on the provisions of the Agreement to arbitrate. If there be no such provisions, then the third person so named may either himself appoint the arbitrators, or propose a certain number of persons, among whom each of the parties shall choose.

ART. 4.—The following shall be eligible for appointment as International Arbitrators: Sovereigns and Heads of Governments, without any restriction; and all persons who are competent, according to the law of their country, to exercise the functions of arbitrator.

ART. 5.—If the parties have agreed upon individual arbitrators, the incompetency of, or the allegation of a valid objection to, one of such arbitrators, invalidates the whole agreement to arbitrate, unless the parties can agree upon another competent arbitrator.

If the Agreement to arbitrate does not prescribe the manner of selecting another arbitrator in case of incompetency, or of the allegation of a valid objection, the method prescribed for the original choice must again be followed.

ART. 6.—The acceptance of the office of arbitrator must be in writing.

ART. 7.—If an arbitrator refuses the office, or if he resigns after having accepted it, or if he dies, or becomes mentally incompetent, or if he is validly challenged on account of inability to serve according to the terms of Art. 4, then the provisions of Art. 5 shall be in force.

ART. 8.—If the seat of the Arbitration Tribunal is not named either by the Agreement to arbitrate or by a subsequent agreement of the parties, it shall be named by the arbitrator or by a majority of the arbitrators.

The Arbitration Tribunal is authorised to change the place of its sessions, only in case the performance of its duties at the place agreed upon is impossible or manifestly dangerous.

d'accord sur le choix des arbitres, les parties contractantes son convenues que le tribunal arbitral serait formé par une personne tierce par elles désignée, et si la personne désignée se charge de la formation du tribunal arbitral, la marche à suivre à cet effet se règlera en première ligne d'après les prescriptions du compromis. A défaut de prescriptions, le tiers désigné peut ou nommer lui-même les arbitres ou proposer un certain nombre de personnes parmi lesquelles chacune des parties choisira.

ART. 4.—Seront capables d'être nommés arbitres internationaux les souverains et chefs de gouvernements sans aucune restriction, et toutes les personnes qui ont la capacité d'exercer les fonctions d'arbitre d'après la loi commune de leur pays.

ART. 5.—Si les parties ont valablement compromis sur des arbitres individuellement déterminés, l'incapacité ou la récusation valable, fût-ce d'un seul de ces arbitres, infirme le compromis entier, pour autant que les parties ne peuvent se mettre d'accord sur un autre arbitre capable.

Si le compromis ne porte pas détermination individuelle de l'arbitre en question, il faut, en cas d'incapacité ou de récusation valable, suivre la marche prescrite pour le choix originaire (art. 2, 3).

ART. 6.—La déclaration d'acceptation de l'office d'arbitre a lieu par écrit.

ART. 7.—Si un arbitre refuse l'office arbitral, ou s'il se déporte après l'avoir accepté, ou s'il meurt, ou s'il tombe en état de démence, ou s'il est valablement récusé pour cause d'incapacité aux termes de l'article 4, il y a lieu à l'application des dispositions de l'article 5.

ART. 8.—Si le siège du tribunal arbitral n'est désigné ni par le compromis ni par une convention subséquente des parties, la désignation a lieu par l'arbitre ou la majorité des arbitres.

Le tribunal arbitral n'est autorisé à changer de siège qu'au cas où l'accomplissement de ses fonctions au lieu convenu est impossible ou manifestement périlleux.

ART. 9. — The Arbitration Tribunal, if composed of several members, chooses a president from among its own number, and appoints one or more secretaries.

The Arbitration Tribunal decides in what language or languages its deliberations and the pleadings of the litigants shall be conducted, and the documents and other evidence be presented. It keeps minutes of its sessions.

ART. 10.—The Arbitration Tribunal sits with all its members present. It may, however, delegate one or more of its members, or even commission outside persons, to draw up certain preliminary proceedings.

If the arbitrator is a State, or its head, a commune or other corporation, an authority, a faculty of law, a learned society, or the actual president of the commune, corporation, authority, faculty, or society, all the pleadings may be conducted, with the consent of the parties, before a commission appointed *ad hoc* by the arbitrator. A protocol of such pleadings shall be kept.

ART. 11.—No arbitrator can, without the consent of the litigants, name a substitute for himself.

ART. 12.—If the Agreement to arbitrate, or a subsequent agreement of the parties, prescribes the method of procedure to be followed by the Court of Arbitration, or prescribes to it the observance of a definite and positive law of procedure, the Arbitration Tribunal must conform thereto. If there be no such provision, the procedure to be followed shall be freely prescribed by the Arbitration Tribunal, which is in such case required to conform only to the rules which it has informed the parties it would observe.

The control of the discussions belongs to the President of the tribunal.

ART. 13.—Each of the parties may appoint one or more persons to represent it before the tribunal.

ART. 14.—Exceptions based on the incompetency of the arbitrators must be taken before any others. In case of the silence of the parties, any later contestation is excluded, except for cases of incompetency that have subsequently supervened.

ART. 9.—Le tribunal arbitral, s'il est composé de plusieurs membres, nomme un président, pris dans son sein, et s'adjoint un ou plusieurs secrétaires.

Le tribunal arbitral décide en quelle langue ou quelles langues devront avoir lieu ses délibérations et les débats des parties, et devront être présentés les actes et les autres moyens de preuve. Il tient procès-verbal de ses délibérations.

ART. 10.—Le tribunal arbitral délibère tous membres présents. Il lui est loisible toutefois de déléguer un ou plusieurs membres ou même de commettre des tierces personnes pour certains actes d'instruction.

Si l'arbitre est un Etat ou son chef, une commune ou autre corporation, une autorité, une faculté de droit, une société savante, ou le président actuel de la commune, corporation, autorité, faculté, compagnie, tous les débats peuvent avoir lieu du consentement des parties devant le commissaire nommé *ad hoc* par l'arbitre. Il en est dressé protocole.

ART. 11.—Aucun arbitre n'est autorisé sans le consentement des parties à se nommer un substitut.

ART. 12.—Si le compromis ou une convention subséquente des compromettants prescrit au tribunal arbitral le mode de procédure à suivre, ou l'observation d'une loi de procédure déterminée et positive, le tribunal arbitral doit se conformer à cette prescription. A défaut d'une prescription pareille, la procédure à suivre sera choisie librement par le tribunal arbitral, lequel est seulement tenu de se conformer aux principes qu'il a déclaré aux parties vouloir suivre.

La direction des débats appartient au président du tribunal arbitral.

ART. 13.—Chacune des parties pourra constituer un ou plusieurs représentants auprès du tribunal arbitral.

ART. 14.—Les exceptions tirées de l'incapacité des arbitres doivent être opposées avant toute autre. Dans le silence des parties, toute contestation ultérieure est exclue, sauf les cas d'incapacité postérieurement survenue.

The arbitrators must pronounce upon the exceptions taken to the incompetency of the Court of Arbitration (subject to the appeal referred to in the next paragraph), and must pronounce in accordance with the provisions of the Agreement to arbitrate.

There shall be no appeal from the preliminary judgments on the question of competency, except in connection with the appeal from the final judgment in the arbitration.

In case the doubt on the question of competency depends upon the interpretation of a clause of the Agreement to arbitrate, the parties are deemed to have given to the arbitrators full power to settle the question, unless there be a clause to the contrary.

ART. 15.—Unless there be provisions to the contrary in the Agreement to arbitrate, the Arbitration Tribunal has the right:

1. To determine the forms, and the periods of time, in which each litigant must, by his duly authorised representatives, present his conclusions, support them in fact and in law, lay his proofs before the tribunal, communicate them to his opponent, and produce the documents the production of which his opponent demands.

2. To consider as conceded the claims of each Party which are not plainly contested by his opponent, as, for instance, the alleged contents of documents which the opponent, without sufficient reason, fails to produce.

3. To order new hearings of the Parties, and to demand from each of them the clearing up of doubtful points.

4. To make rules of procedure (for the conduct of the case), to compel the production of evidence, and, if necessary, to require of a Competent Court the performance of judicial acts which the Arbitration Tribunal is not qualified to perform, notably the swearing of experts and of witnesses.

5. To decide with its own free judgment on the interpretation of the documents produced, and in general on the merits of the evidence presented by the litigants.

The forms and the periods of time, mentioned in clauses 1 and 2 of the present article, shall be determined by the arbitrators by a preliminary order.

Les arbitres doivent prononcer sur les exceptions tirées de l'incompétence du tribunal arbitral, sauf le recours dont il est question à l'art. 24, 2me al., et conformément aux dispositions du compromis.

Aucune voie de recours ne sera ouverte contre des jugements préliminaires sur la compétence, si ce n'est cumulativement avec le recours contre le jugement arbitral définitif.

Dans le cas où le doute sur la compétence dépend de l'interprétation d'une clause du compromis, les parties sont censées avoir donné aux arbitres la faculté de trancher la question, sauf clause contraire.

ART. 15.—Sauf dispositions contraires du compromis, le tribunal arbitral a le droit :

1° De déterminer les formes et délais dans lesquels chaque partie devra, par ses représentants dûment légitimés, présenter ses conclusions, les fonder en fait et en droit, proposer ses moyens de preuve au tribunal, les communiquer à la partie adverse, produire les documents dont la partie adverse requiert la production ;

2° De tenir pour accordées les prétentions de chaque partie qui ne sont pas nettement contestées par la partie adverse, ainsi que le contenu prétendu des documents dont la partie adverse omet la production sans motifs suffisants ;

3° D'ordonner de nouvelles auditions des parties, d'exiger de chaque partie l'éclaircissement de points douteux ;

4° De rendre des ordonnances de procédure (sur la direction du procès), faire administrer des preuves et requérir, s'il le faut, du tribunal compétent les actes judiciaires pour lesquels le tribunal arbitral n'est pas qualifié, notamment l'assermentation d'experts et de témoins ;

5° De statuer, selon sa libre appréciation, sur l'interprétation des documents produits et généralement sur le mérite des moyens de preuves présentés par les parties.

Les formes et délais mentionnés sous les numéros 1 et 2 du présent article seront déterminés par les arbitres dans une ordonnance préliminaire.

ART. 16.—Neither the parties nor the arbitrators can officially implead other States or third persons, without the special and express authorization of the Agreement to arbitrate, and the previous consent of such third parties.

The voluntary intervention of a third party can be allowed only with the consent of the parties who originally concluded the Agreement to arbitrate.

ART. 17.—Cross-actions can be brought before the Arbitration Tribunal only so far as they are provided for by the original Agreement to arbitrate, or as the parties and the tribunal may agree to allow them.

ART. 18.—The Arbitration Tribunal decides in accordance with the principles of international law, unless the Agreement to arbitrate prescribes different rules or leaves the decision to the free judgment of the arbitrators.

ART. 19.—The Arbitration Tribunal cannot refuse to pronounce judgment, on the pretext that it is insufficiently informed either as to the facts, or as to the legal principles to be applied.

It must decide finally each of the points at issue. If, however, the Agreement to arbitrate does not require a final decision to be given simultaneously on all the points, the Tribunal may, while deciding finally on certain points, reserve others for subsequent disposition.

The Arbitration Tribunal may render interlocutory or preliminary judgments.

ART. 20.—The final decision must be pronounced within the period of time fixed by the Agreement to arbitrate, or by a subsequent agreement. If there be no other provision, a period of two years, from the day of the conclusion of the Agreement to arbitrate, is to be considered as agreed on. The day of the conclusion of the Agreement is not included, nor the time during which one or more arbitrators have been prevented, by *force majeure*, from fulfilling their duties.

In case the arbitrators, by interlocutory judgments, order preliminary proceedings, the period is to be extended for a year.

ART. 21.—Every judgment, final or provisional, shall be deter-

ART. 16.—Ni les parties, ni les arbitres ne peuvent d'office mettre en cause d'autres Etats ou des tierces personnes quelconques, sauf autorisation spéciale exprimée dans le compromis et consentement préalable du tiers.

L'intervention spontanée d'un tiers n'est admissible qu'avec le consentement des parties qui ont conclu le compromis.

ART. 17.—Les demandes reconventionnelles ne peuvent être portées devant le tribunal arbitral qu'en tant qu'elles lui sont déférées par le compromis, ou que les deux parties et le tribunal sont d'accord pour les admettre.

ART. 18.—Le tribunal arbitral juge selon les principes du droit international, à moins que le compromis ne lui impose des règles différentes ou ne remette la décision à la libre appréciation des arbitres.

ART. 19.—Le tribunal arbitral ne peut refuser de prononcer sous le prétexte qu'il n'est pas suffisamment éclairé soit sur les faits, soit sur les principes juridiques qu'il doit appliquer.

Il doit décider définitivement chacun des points en litige. Toutefois, si le compromis ne prescrit pas la décision définitive simultanée de *tous* les points, le tribunal peut, en décidant définitivement certains points, réserver les autres pour une procédure ultérieure.

Le tribunal arbitral peut rendre des jugements interlocutoires ou préparatoires.

ART. 20.—Le prononcé de la décision définitive doit avoir lieu dans le délai fixé par le compromis ou par une convention subséquente. A défaut d'autre détermination, on tient pour convenu un délai de deux ans à partir du jour de la conclusion du compromis. Le jour de la conclusion n'y est pas compris; on n'y comprend pas non plus le temps durant lequel un ou plusieurs arbitres auront été empêchés, par force majeure, de remplir leurs fonctions.

Dans le cas où les arbitres, par des jugements interlocutoires, ordonnent des moyens d'instruction, le délai est augmenté d'une année.

ART. 21.—Toute décision définitive ou provisoire sera prise à mined by a majority of all the arbitrators appointed, even in case one or more of them should refuse to concur in it.

ART. 22.—If the Arbitration Tribunal finds the claims of neither of the parties justified, it shall so declare, and, unless limited in this respect by the Agreement to arbitrate, shall determine the true state of the law with regard to the parties to the dispute.

ART. 23.—The arbitral Sentence must be drawn up in writing, and contain an exposition of the grounds of the decision, unless exemption from this be stipulated in the agreement to arbitrate. It must be signed by each of the members of the court of arbitration. If a minority refuse to sign it, the signature of the majority is sufficient, with a written statement that the minority refuse to sign.

ART. 24.—The Sentence, together with the grounds, if an exposition of them be given, is formally communicated to each party. This is done by communicating a certified copy to the representative of each party, or to its attorney appointed *ad hoc*.

After the Sentence has been communicated to the representative or attorney of one of the parties, it cannot be changed by the Arbitration Tribunal.

Nevertheless, the tribunal has the right, so long as the time limits of the Agreement to arbitrate have not expired, to correct errors in writing or in reckoning, even though neither of the parties should suggest it; and to complete the Sentence on points at issue not decided, on the suggestion of one of the parties, and after giving the other party a hearing. An interpretation of the Sentence is allowable only on demand of both parties.

ART. 25.—The Sentence duly pronounced decides, within the scope of its operation, the point at issue between the parties.

ART. 26.—Each party shall bear its own costs, and half of the costs of the Arbitration Tribunal, without prejudice to the decision of the Court as to the indemnity that one or the other party may be condemned to pay.

ART. 27.—The Arbitral Sentence shall be void in case of the avoidance of the Agreement to arbitrate, or of an excess of power, or of proved corruption of one of the arbitrators, or of essential error.

a majorité de tous les arbitres nommés, même dans le cas où l'un ou quelques-uns des arbitres refuseraient d'y prendre part.

ART. 22.—Si le tribunal arbitral ne trouve fondées les prétentions d'aucune des parties, il doit le déclarer, et, s'il n'est limité sous ce rapport par le compromis, établir l'état réel du droit relatif aux parties en litige.

ART. 23.—La sentence arbitrale doit être rédigée par écrit et contenir un exposé des motifs sauf dispense stipulée par le compromis. Elle doit être signée par chacun des membres du tribunal arbitral. Si une minorité refuse de signer, la signature de la majorité suffit, avec déclaration écrite que la minorité a refusé de signer.

ART. 24.—La sentence, avec les motifs, s'ils sont exposés, est notifiée à chaque partie. La notification a lieu par signification d'une expédition au représentant de chaque partie ou à un fondé de pouvoirs de chaque partie constitué *ad hoc*.

Même si elle n'a été signifiée qu'au représentant ou au fondé de pouvoirs d'une seule partie, la sentence ne peut plus être changée par le tribunal arbitral.

Il a néanmoins le droit, tant que les délais du compromis ne sont pas expirés, de corriger de simples fautes d'écriture ou de calcul, lors même qu'aucune des parties n'en ferait la proposition, et de compléter la sentence sur les points litigieux non décidés, sur la proposition d'une partie et après audition de la partie adverse. Une interprétation de la sentence notifiée n'est admissible que si les deux parties la requièrent.

ART. 25.—La sentence dûment prononcée décide, dans les limites de sa portée, la contestation entre les parties.

ART. 26.—Chaque partie supportera ses propres frais et la moitié des frais du tribunal arbitral, sans préjudice de la décision du tribunal arbitral touchant l'indemnité que l'une ou l'autre des parties pourra être condamnée à payer.

ART. 27.—La sentence arbitrale est nulle en cas de compromis nul, ou d'excès de pouvoir, ou de corruption prouvée d'un des arbitres, ou d'erreur essentielle.

PROPOSED RULES FOR THE ORGANISATION OF AN INTERNATIONAL TRIBUNAL OF ARBITRATION.

Submitted by Messrs. *Wm. Allen Butler*, *Dorman B. Eaton*, and *Cephas Brainerd*, to the Universal Peace Congress at Chicago, in 1893.

In order to maintain peace between the High Contracting Parties, they agree as follows:

FIRST.—If any cause of complaint arise between any of the nations parties hereto, the one aggrieved shall give formal notice thereof to the other, specifying in detail the cause of complaint and the redress which it seeks.

SECOND.—The nation which receives from another notice of any cause of complaint shall, within one month thereafter, give a full and explicit answer thereto.

THIRD.—If the nation complaining and the nation complained of do not otherwise, within two months after such answer, agree between themselves, they shall each appoint three members of a Joint Commission, who shall confer together, discuss the differences, endeavour to reconcile them, and within one month after their appointment shall report the result to the nations appointing them respectively.

FOURTH.—If the Joint Commissioners fail to agree, or the nations appointing them fail to ratify their acts, those nations shall, within twelve months after the appointment of the Joint Commission, give notice of such failure to the other parties to the treaty, and the cause of complaint shall be referred to the Tribunal of Arbitration, instituted as follows:

1. Each Signatory Nation shall, within one month after the ratification of this treaty, transmit to the other signatory nations the names of four persons as fit to serve on such tribunal.

2. From the list of such persons, the nations at any time in controversy shall alternately, and as speedily as possible, select one after another until seven are selected, which seven shall constitute

PLAN POUR L'ORGANISATION D'UN TRIBUNAL INTERNATIONAL D'ARBITAGE.

(Projet soumis au Ve Congrès universel de la Paix, à Chicago, par MM. *William Allen Butler*, *Dorman B. Eaton*, *et Céphas Brainerd*, tous trois jurisconsultes à New-York.

En vue de maintenir la paix entre elles, les hautes parties contractantes conviennent de ce qui suit :

1° Si un litige survient entre des Etats qui sont parties dans le présent contrat, celui qui croit avoir à se plaindre en informe l'autre en spécifiant ses griefs et les mesures qu'il réclame.

2° La nation qui reçoit d'une autre une notification de ce genre doit y répondre d'une manière complète et explicite dans le délai d'un mois.

3° Si la nation plaignante et l'autre n'en disposent pas autrement et que la réponse n'ait pas mis fin au litige, chacune d'elles nommera trois membres d'une Commission qui discutera les questions litigieuses et cherchera à concilier les parties. Chacune de ces délibérations informera ses mandants du résultat des délibérations.

4° Si les commissaires ne peuvent se mettre d'accord ou que leurs Etats n'acceptent pas leurs propositions, ces Etats en informent dans le délai de douze mois les autres signataires du présent traité, et le litige est alors renvoyé au Tribunal d'arbitrage, institué comme suit :

a. Chacune des nations signataires doit, dans le délai d'un mois, après la signature du présent traité, transmettre aux autres nations signataires les noms de quatre personnes capables de siéger dans le tribunal.

b. Sur la liste de ces personnes, les nations litigantes ont à choisir alternativement et aussi vite que possible, l'une après l'autre celles qui leur agréent, jusqu'à ce qu'il en ait été désigné sept, qui constituent le tribunal appelé à prononcer sur le litige.

the tribunal for the hearing and decision of that controversy. Notice of each selection shall immediately be given to the permanent Secretary, who shall at once notify the person so selected.

3. The tribunal thus constituted shall, by writing signed by the members or a majority of them, appoint a time and place of meeting, and give notice thereof through the permanent Secretary to the parties in controversy; and at such time and place, or at other times and places to which an adjournment may be had, it shall hear the parties and decide between them, and such decision shall be final and conclusive.

4. If either of these parties fail to signify its selection of names from the lists within one month after a request from the other to do so, the other may select for it; and if any of the persons selected to constitute the tribunal shall die or fail from any cause to serve, the vacancy shall be filled by the nation which originally named the person whose place is to be filled.

FIFTH.—Each of the parties to this treaty binds itself to unite, as herein prescribed, in forming a Tribunal of Arbitration for all cases in controversy between any of them not adjusted by a Joint Commission, as hereinbefore provided, except that such arbitration shall not extend to any question respecting the independence or sovereignty of a nation, or its equality with other nations, or its form of government or its internal affairs.

1. The Tribunal of Arbitration shall consist of seven members, and shall be constituted in a manner provided in the foregoing fourth rule; but it may, if the nations in controversy so agree, consist of less than seven persons, and in that case the members of the tribunal shall be selected jointly by them from the whole list of persons named by the signatory nations. Each nation claiming a distinct interest in the question at issue shall have the right to appoint one additional arbitrator on its own behalf.

2. When the tribunal shall consist of several arbitrators a Majority of the whole number may act, notwithstanding the absence

Chaque choix sera immédiatement porté à la connaissance du Secrétaire permanent, qui en avisera chaque fois la personne ainsi élue.

c. Le Tribunal ainsi constitué désigne par écrit et avec la signature de ses membres ou de la majorité de ceux-ci, la date et le lieu de sa réunion et en donne connaisance aux parties en cause par l'intermédiaire du Secrétaire permanent. A cette date et à ce lieu ou à une autre date et à un autre lieu s'il y a ajournement, il entend les parties et prononce entre elles. Son jugement est définitif et sans appel.

d. Si l'une des parties n'a pas indiqué les choix qu'elle a faits sur la liste dans le délai d'un mois après en avoir été requise par l'autre partie, c'est celle-ci qui fera les choix pour elle, et si l'une des personnes choisies pour constituer le tribunal était empêchée par suite de décès ou pour toute autre cause, la lacune serait comblée par la nation qui avait désigné primitivement la personne à remplacer.

5° Chacune des parties signataires du présent traité s'engage à contribuer, comme il est dit plus haut, à la formation d'un tribunal d'arbitrage pour tous les différends qui viendraient à surgir entre elles et n'auraient pu être réglés par la Commission de conciliation prévue ci-dessus, sauf que l'arbitrage ne peut s'étendre à des questions touchant l'indépendance ou la souveraineté d'une nation, son égalité avec d'autres nations, la forme de son gouvernement ou ses affaires intérieures.

a. Le tribunal d'arbitrage se composera de sept membres et sera constitué de la manière prévue dans les quatre articles qui précèdent; mais il peut se composer de moins de sept personnes, si cela convient aux parties, et dans ce cas les membres du tribunal seront choisis conjointement sur toute la liste des noms désignés par les nations signataires. Toute nation qui déclare avoir un intérêt spécial dans la question litigieuse a le droit d'adjoindre un arbitre au tribunal pour sa propre défense.

b. Quand le tribunal se compose de plusieurs arbitres, la majorité de ses membres délibère valablement nonobstant l'absence or withdrawal of the minority. In such case the majority shall continue in the performance of their duties until they shall have reached a final determination of the question submitted for their consideration.

3. The Decision of a majority of the whole number of arbitrators shall be final, both on the main and incidental issues, unless it shall have been expressly provided by the nations in controversy that unanimity is essential.

4. The Expenses of an arbitration proceeding, including the compensation of the arbitrators, shall be paid in equal proportions by the nations that are parties thereto, except as provided in subdivision 6 of this article; but expenses of either party in the preparation and prosecution of its case shall be defrayed by it individually.

5. Only by the mutual consent of all the signatory nations may the provisions of these articles be disregarded and Courts of Arbitration appointed under different arrangements.

6. A permanent Secretary shall be appointed by agreement between the signatory nations, whose office shall be at Berne, Switzerland, where the records of the tribunal shall be preserved. The permanent Secretary shall have power to appoint two assistant secretaries, and such other assistants as may be required for the performance of the duties incident to the proceedings of the tribunal.

The Salary of the permanent secretary, assistant secretaries and other persons connected with his office shall be paid by the signatory nations, out of a fund to be provided for that purpose, to which each of such nations shall contribute in a proportion corresponding to the population of the several nations.

7. Upon the Reference of any controversy to the tribunal, and after the selection of the arbitrators to constitute the tribunal for the hearing of such controversy, it shall fix the time within which the case, the counter-case, reply, evidence and arguments of the

ou la retraite de la minorité. Dans un cas de ce genre, la majorité doit suivre à l'exécution du mandat confié au tribunal jusqu'à ce qu'une détermination définitive ait été prise sur les questions soumises à l'arbitrage.

c. La décision de la majorité des arbitres est valable, soit sur la question principale, soit sur les questions incidentes, à moins que les nations en cause n'aient expressément exigé l'unanimité.

d. Les frais d'un arbitrage, y compris les honoraires des arbitres, sont mis par parts égales à la charge des nations en cause, sauf ce qui est prévu au chiffre 6 du présent article ; les dépenses faites par chacune des parties pour la préparation et la poursuite de sa cause sont exclusivement supportées par elle.

e. Il ne peut être dérogé aux dispositions des articles ci-dessus et les tribunaux d'arbitrage ne peuvent être constitués sur d'autres bases qu'avec l'assentiment de toutes les nations signataires.

f. Un secrétaire permanent sera nommé d'un commun accord entre les nations signataires. Son siège sera à Berne (Suisse), où es archives du Tribunal seront conservées. Le Secrétaire permanent peut s'adjoindre deux secrétaires et autant d'autres auxiliaires que l'exigeront les travaux se rapportant à la procédure devant le Tribunal.

Les honoraires du secrétaire permanent, de ses secrétaires auxiliaires et des autres employés de son bureau sont payés par les nations signataires ou au moyen d'un fonds à prévoir à cet effet et à la formation duquel chacune des nations contribuera au prorata de sa population.

g. Quand une cause est portée devant l'arbitrage et après le choix des arbitres qui doivent constituer le tribunal appelé à prononcer sur le litige, les délais pour la demande, la défense, la réplique et les autres moyens à présenter par les parties seront respective parties shall be submitted to it, and shall make rules regulating the proceedings under which that controversy shall be heard.

8. The tribunal as first constituted, for the determination of a controversy, may establish general Rules for practice and proceeding before all tribunals assembled for the hearing of any controversy submitted under the provisions of these articles, which rules may from time to time be amended or changed by any subsequent tribunal; and all such rules shall immediately, upon their adoption, be notified to the various signatory powers.

SIXTH.—If any of the parties to this treaty shall begin Hostilities against another party without having first exhausted the means of reconciliation herein provided for, or shall fail to comply with the decisions of the Tribunal of Arbitration, within one month after receiving notice of the decision, the chief executive of every other nation, party hereto, shall issue a proclamation declaring (such) hostilities or failure, to be an infraction of this treaty, and at the end of thirty days thereafter, the ports of the nations from which the proclamation proceeds shall be closed against the offending or defaulting nation, except upon condition that all vessels and goods coming from or belonging to any of its citizens shall, as a condition, be subjected to double the duties to which they would otherwise have been subjected. But the exclusion may be at any time revoked by another proclamation of like authority, issued at the request of the offending nation declaring its readiness to comply with this treaty in its letter and spirit.

SEVENTH.—A Conference of representatives of the nations, parties to this treaty, shall be held every alternate year, beginning on the first of January, at the capital of each in rotation, and in the order of the signatures to this treaty, for the purpose of discussing the provisions of the treaty, and desired amendments thereof, averting war, facilitating intercourse, and preserving peace.

fixés et des règles seront établies pour déterminer la procédure à suivre.

h. Le Tribunal constitué le premier pour juger un litige peut établir des règles générales de procédure pour tous les Tribunaux appelés à arbitrer des différends en conformité des dispositions ci-dessus. Ces règles peuvent être modifiées ou changées en tout temps par des tribunaux subséquents ; elles doivent être notifiées aux pouvoirs signataires aussitôt après leur adoption.

6° Si l'une des parties signataires du présent traité entamait des hostilités contre une autre partie avant d'avoir essayé des moyens de réconciliation prévus dans ce traité, ou si elle refuse de se soumettre aux décisions du Tribunal d'arbitrage dans le délai d'un mois après que ces décisions lui ont été notifiées, le pouvoir exécutif de chacune des autres nations en cause lancera une proclamation déclarant que les hostilités ou le refus constitue une infraction au traité, et à l'expiration du 30e jour après cette proclamation, les ports de la nation de laquelle provient la proclamation seront fermés à la nation agressive ou réfractaire, en ce sens que tous les vaisseaux et toutes les marchandises en provenance ou à destination des citoyens de cette dernière nation seront frappés d'un droit double de celui auquel ils auraient été soumis sans cela. Toutefois cette exclusion peut en tout temps être révoquée par une autre proclamation de la même autorité, faite à la requête de la nation agressive se déclarant prête à se soumettre au traité dans sa lettre et dans son esprit.

7° Une conférence de représentants des nations signataires du présent traité se tiendra tous les deux ans ; elle s'ouvrira le 1er janvier alternativement dans la capitale de chacune de ces nations en suivant l'ordre des signatures, en vue de discuter les mesures d'application du traité et les amendements au traité qui peuvent être proposés, de prévenir les guerres, de faciliter les relations et de sauvegarder la paix.

RESOLUTION ADOPTED BY THE INTER-PARLIAMENTARY CONFERENCE AT BRUSSELS, IN 1895, CONCERNING THE ESTABLISHMENT OF A PERMANENT COURT OF INTERNATIONAL ARBITRATION.

The Inter-Parliamentary Conference, assembled at Brussels, considering the frequency of cases of International Arbitration and the number and extension of arbitral clauses in treaties, and desiring to see an International Justice and an International Jurisdiction established on a stable basis, charges its President to recommend to the favourable consideration of the governments of civilised states the following provisions, which may be made the subject of a diplomatic conference or of special conventions:

1. The High Contracting Parties constitute a PERMANENT COURT OF INTERNATIONAL ARBITRATION to take cognisance of differences which they shall submit to its decision.

In cases in which a difference shall arise between two or more of them, the parties shall decide whether the contest is of a nature to be brought before the Court, under the obligations which they have contracted by treaty.

2. The Court shall sit at..

Its seat may be transferred to another place by the decision of a majority of three-fourths of the adhering Powers.

The government of the State in which the Court is sitting guarantees its safety as well as the freedom of its discussions and decisions.

3. Each signatory or adhering Government shall name two members of the Court.

Nevertheless, two or more Governments may unite in designating two members in common.

The members of the Court shall be appointed for a period of five years, and their powers may be renewed.

COUR D'ARBITRAGE INTERNATIONAL.

RÉSOLUTION ADOPTÉE PAR LA VIe CONFÉRENCE INTERPARLEMENTAIRE.

La Conférence interparlementaire réunie à Bruxelles, considérant la fréquence des cas d'arbitrage international, le nombre et l'extension des clauses compromissoires dans les traités, désirant voir s'établir sur des bases stables une justice et une juridiction internationales,

Charge son président de recommander à l'examen bienveillant des gouvernements des Etats civilisés les dispositions suivantes qui pourront faire l'objet d'une conférence diplomatique ou de conventions spéciales.

1. Les parties contractantes constituent une *Cour permanente d'arbitrage international* pour connaître des différends qui seront soumis à sa décision.

Dans le cas où un différend surgirait entre deux ou plusieurs d'entre elles, les parties contractantes décideront si le litige est de nature à être porté devant la Cour, sous réserve des obligations qu'elles peuvent avoir contractées par traité.

2. La cour siège à...

Le siège en pourra être transféré ailleurs par décision prise à la majorité des trois quarts des puissances adhérentes.

Le gouvernement de l'Etat dans lequel siège la Cour garantit sa sûreté, ainsi que la liberté de ses discussions et décisions.

3. Chaque gouvernement signataire ou adhérent nomme deux membres de la Cour. Néanmoins, deux ou plusieurs Etats peuvent se réunir pour désigner en commun deux membres. Les membres de la Cour sont nommés pour une durée de cinq ans ; leurs pouvoirs peuvent être renouvelés.

4. The support and compensation of the members of the Court shall be defrayed by the State which names them.

The expenses of the Court shall be shared equally by the adhering States.

5. The Court shall elect from its members a President and a Vice-president for a period of a year. The president is not eligible for re-election after a period of five years. The vice-president shall take the place of the president in all cases in which the latter is unable to act.

The Court shall appoint its Clerk and determine the number of employees which it deems necessary.

The clerk shall reside at the seat of the Court, and have charge of its archives.

6. The parties may, by common accord, lay their suit directly before the Court.

7. The Court is invested with jurisdiction by means of a notification given to the clerk, by the parties, of their intention to submit their difference to the Court.

The clerk shall bring the notification at once to the knowledge of the president.

If the parties have not availed themselves of their privilege of bringing their suit directly before the Court, the president shall designate two members who shall constitute a tribunal to act in the first instance.

On the request of one of the parties, the members called to constitute this tribunal shall be designated by the Court itself.

The members named by the States that are parties to the suit shall not be a part of the tribunal.

The members designated to sit cannot refuse to do so.

8. The form of the submission shall be determined by the disputing governments, and, in case they are unable to agree, by the Tribunal, or, when there is occasion for it, by the Court.

There may also be formulated a Counter case.

4. Les traitements ou indemnités des membres de la Cour sont payés par l'Etat qui les nomme.

Les frais de la Cour sont supportés par parts égales par les Etats adhérents.

5. La cour élit dans son sein un président et un vice-président pour une durée d'une année. Le président n'est rééligible qu'après une période de cinq ans. Le vice-président remplace le président dans tous les cas où celui-ci est empêché.

La Cour nomme son greffier et fixe le nombre d'employés qu'elle juge nécessaire.

Le greffier réside au siège de la Cour et a le soin des archives.

6. Les parties peuvent, de commun accord, porter directement leur litige devant la Cour.

7. La Cour est saisie au moyen d'une notification faite au greffier par les parties de leur intention de soumettre leur différend à la Cour.

Le greffier porte immédiatement cette notification à la connaissance du président.

Si les parties n'ont pas usé de la faculté de porter directement leur litige devant la Cour, le président désigne les membres de la Cour qui devront constituer un tribunal appelé à prononcer en première instance.

A la requête d'une des parties, les membres appelés à constituer ce tribunal devront être désignés par la Cour elle-même.

Les membres nommés par les Etats en litige ne peuvent faire partie du tribunal.

Les membres désignés pour siéger ne peuvent s'y refuser.

8. Le compromis est arrêté par les gouvernements litigants ; à défaut d'entente, il est arrêté par le tribunal ou, s'il y a lieu, par la Cour.

Il peut être formulé une demande reconventionnelle.

9. The Judgment shall disclose the reasons on which it is based, and it shall be pronounced within a period of two months after the close of the discussions. It shall be notified to the parties by the clerk.

10. Each party has the right to interpose an Appeal within three months after the notification of the judgment.

The Appeal shall be brought before the Court. The members named by the States concerned in the litigation, and those who formed part of the tribunal, cannot sit in the appeal.

The case shall proceed as in the first instance. The Judgment of the Court shall be definitive. It shall not be attacked by any means whatsoever.

11. The Execution of the decisions of the Court is committed to the honour and good faith of the litigating States.

The Court shall make a proper application of the agreements of parties who, in an arbitration, have given it the means of attaching a pacific sanction to its decisions.

12. The Nominations prescribed by Article 3 shall be made within six months from the exchange of the ratifications of the Convention. They shall be brought by diplomatic channels, to the knowledge of the adhering powers.

The Court shall assemble and fully organise one month after the expiration of that period, whatever may be the number of its members. It shall proceed to the election of a president, of a vice-president, and of a clerk, as well as to the formulation of rules for its internal regulation.

13. The Contracting Parties shall formulate the organic Law of the Court. It shall be an integral part of the Convention.

14. States which have not taken part in the Convention may adhere to it in the ordinary way.

Their adhesion shall be notified to the Government of the country in which the Court sits, and by that to the other adhering Governments.

9. Le jugement est motivé ; il est prononcé dans un délai de deux mois après la clôture des débats. Il est notifié aux parties par le greffier.

10. Chaque partie a le droit d'interjeter appel dans les trois mois de la notification.

L'appel est porté devant la Cour. Les membres nommés par les Etats en litige et ceux qui ont fait partie du tribunal ne peuvent y siéger.

Il est procédé comme en première instance. L'arrêt de la Cour est définitif. Il ne peut être attaqué par un moyen quelconque.

11. L'exécution des décisions de la Cour est confiée à l'honneur et à la bonne foi des Etats en litige.

La Cour fera application des conventions des parties qui, dans un compromis, lui auraient donné les moyens de sanctionner pacifiquement ses décisions.

12. Les nominations prescrites sous le chiffre III seront faites dans les six mois de l'échange des ratifications de la convention. Elles seront portées, par la voie diplomatique, à la connaissance des Etats adhérents.

La Cour sera instituée et se réunira de plein droit à son siège un mois après l'expiration de ce délai, quel que soit le nombre de ses membres. Elle procédera à l'élection d'un président, d'un vice-président et d'un greffier, ainsi qu'à l'élaboration de son règlement d'ordre intérieur.

13. Les parties contractantes formuleront le règlement organique de la Cour. Il fera partie intégrante de la convention.

14. Les Etats qui n'ont point pris part à la convention sont admis à y adhérer dans les formes habituelles.

Leur adhésion sera notifiée au gouvernement du pays où siège la Cour et par celui-ci aux autres gouvernements adhérents.

RULES FOR INTERNATIONAL ARBITRATION.

By Professor the Marquis Corsi.

Section I.—Form and Object of Arbitration Conventions.

Art. 1.—The Agreement for Arbitration is a Convention by which two or more international juridical personalities engage to submit to the decision of one or more Arbitrators all the disputes, or a specified class of disputes, which might arise between them, as also one or some disputes already existent; and by which they formulate the conditions for the validity of their decision, and engage to conform thereto.

This Convention may result, either from a general Treaty, or a special Treaty (called an Arbitration Treaty), or from a clause (termed an Arbitral Clause) inserted in a Treaty, or in a protocol of an International Congress, to which the same States have been parties.

Art. 2.—The Agreement is valid when it has been ratified by the chiefs of the signatory States in the conditions and forms required by their respective laws, and if such is the case, by the treaties which limit their liberty in regard to other States.

Art. 3.—The Agreement should specify the questions of fact or law which the Arbitrators are called on to settle, and the extent of their powers.

In case of doubt as to the object of the Agreement, the Arbitrators may, at the opening of their sittings, invite the parties to state definitely their intentions. But, especially if the Agreement is not limited to one or several specified questions, lack of precision in the definition of the object of the Agreement gives the Arbitrators the right to interpret it, and to refer, for the extension of their powers, to previous Arbitrations and the following Articles.

PROJET DE RÈGLEMENT POUR LES ARBITRAGES INTERNATIONAUX.

PAR LE PROF. LE MARQUIS A. CORSI.

SECTION I.— FORME ET OBJET DES CONVENTIONS D'ARBITRAGES.

ARTICLE 1er. — Le compromis est une convention par laquelle deux ou plusieurs personnes juridiques internationales s'engagent à soumettre à la décision d'un ou de plusieurs arbitres tous les conflits, ou une espèce déterminée de conflits, qui pourraient s'élever entre eux, aussi bien qu'une ou certaines contestations déjà nées ; et par laquelle ils réglent les conditions pour la validité de leur décision et ils s'engagent à s'y conformer.

Cette convention peut résulter, soit d'un traité général ou spécial (dit traité d'arbitrage), soit d'une clause (dite compromissoire) insérée dans un traité, ou dans un protocole de Congrès international auquel les mêmes Etats aient adhéré.

ART. 2. — Le compromis est valide lorsqu'il a été ratifié par les chefs des Etats signataires dans les conditions et dans les formes requises par leurs lois respectives, et, si tel est le cas, par les traités qui limitent leur liberté vis-à-vis d'autres Etats.

ART. 3. — Le compromis doit spécifier les questions de fait ou de droit que les arbitres sont appelés à résoudre, et l'extension de leurs pouvoirs.

En cas de doute sur l'objet du compromis les arbitres à l'ouverture de leurs séances peuvent inviter les parties à préciser leurs intentions.

Au reste, surtout si le compromis n'est pas limité à une ou à plusieurs questions déterminées, le manque de précision dans la définition de l'objet du compromis attribue aux arbitres la faculté de l'interpréter et de s'en rapporter, pour l'extension de leurs pouvoirs, aux arbitrages précédents et aux articles qui suivent :

ART. 4.—Disputes as to whether a question which may arise between the States united by a Treaty of Arbitration, is comprised amongst those intended by the Treaty, should be submitted to the decision of the Arbitrators, if one of the States requires it ; only the other signatory States may require the judgment to be limited to the admissibility of the demand for Arbitration, reserving the right to raise the question afresh by a new Arbitration later on, if need be.

SECTION II.—APPOINTMENT OF ARBITRATORS—REFUSAL TO SERVE—FRESH APPOINTMENTS.

ART. 5.—The Arbitrators may be one only, or several, constituting an Arbitral Tribunal, or Arbitration Court.

Whatever be their number, they are appointed conjointly by the contracting States, in accordance with the stipulations of the Agreement.

In default of such stipulations, or in case of disagreement as to the manner of choosing, each of the parties chooses two Arbitrators, and the Arbitrators thus nominated choose another, or appoint a third person who shall choose him.

ART. 6.—When it is agreed that, the Arbitrators being an even number, if they do not succeed in coming to an agreement, the question shall be submitted to an Umpire, the latter should be nominated and accepted before the Arbitrators begin to treat of the questions which form the object of the Arbitral Agreement ; but he shall not act as a member of the Tribunal, but shall only be called on to give an award on their invitation, and for the principal or incidental questions in which they shall have been unable to agree.

ART. 7.—If the Arbitrators are nominated or appointed in the Agreement, either one of the contracting parties may take the initiative in calling them together, while inviting the other party to join them in taking the necessary steps.

ART. 4. — Les contestations sur le point de savoir si une question qui s'agite entre les Etats liés par un traité d'arbitrage est comprise parmi celles prévues par ce traité, doivent être soumises à la décision des arbitres, si l'un des Etats l'exige ; seulement les autres Etats signataires peuvent exiger que le jugement soit limité à l'admissibilité de la demande d'arbitrage, se réservant à provoquer ensuite, s'il en sera le cas, par un nouvel arbitrage, la décision de la question de fond.

SECTION II. — DÉSIGNATION, RÉCUSATION ET SUBSTITUTION DES ARBITRES.

ART. 5. — Les arbitres peuvent être un seul, ou plusieurs constituant un Tribunal arbitral, ou Cour d'arbitrage.

Quel que soit leur nombre, ils sont nommés conjointement par les Etats contractants, suivant les dispositions du compromis.

A défaut de ces dispositions, ou en cas de désaccord dans la forme du choix, chacune des parties choisit deux arbitres, et les arbitres ainsi nommés en choisissent un autre, ou désignent une personne tierce qui l'indiquera.

ART. 6. — Lorsqu'il est convenu que, les arbitres étant en nombre pair, s'ils ne réussissent à se mettre d'accord, la question soit soumise à un sur-arbitre (*umpire*), celui-ci devra être nommé et accepté avant que les arbitres commencent à traiter les questions qui font l'objet du compromis ; mais il n'agira pas comme membre du tribunal, étant appelé à prononcer sa décision seulement d'après leur invitation, et pour les questions principales ou incidentelles dans lesquelles ils n'auront pu tomber d'accord.

ART. 7. — Si les arbitres sont nommés ou désignés dans le compromis, chacune des parties contractantes peut prendre l'initiative de leur réunion, en invitant l'autre à faire ensemble les démarches nécessaires.

The express or tacit refusal to provide for the formation or the first convocation of the Tribunal, shall be considered tantamount to a withdrawal from the Treaty by the State which thus refuses; so that it shall no longer be able to profit thereby when it may choose to appeal to it.

If the third person charged with the choice of the Arbitrators refuses to make a choice, the Treaty obligation is suspended until the parties have substituted another in his place.

ART. 8.—All those persons are eligible for appointment as Arbitrators who, according to the law of the country by which, or in the name of which, they are appointed, might be charged, if they were under its jurisdiction, with a diplomatic or judicial mission.

ART. 9.—The name of the Arbitrators chosen in accordance with the last paragraph of Art. 5 should be notified immediately by the party which has chosen them, to all the others.

Each of these will (for the space of fifteen days) have the right to object to them on any of the following grounds:—

(1.) If they are subjects of one of the contracting States;

(2.) If they have a personal interest in the questions which are the object of the Arbitration;

(3.) If they have published their opinion on these same questions by pamphlets, or by speeches in public meetings, or even as members of some national or international tribunal, which has already pronounced its verdict.

ART. 10.—If the Arbitrators are individually appointed in the Agreement, and they become incapacitated for one of the reasons mentioned above before they enter upon their duties, the Agreement is thereby invalidated, unless the parties can agree upon another suitable Arbitrator.

But if the Agreement does not contain an individual appointment of the Arbitrators, the objection to an Arbitrator made by one Government to the other, by means of a note containing the reasons for the objection, obliges the nominating Government to appoint another without discussing the validity of the objection.

Le refus exprès ou tacite de pourvoir à la formation ou à la première convocation du tribunal donne lieu à considérer le compromis, ou la clause compromissoire, comme dénoncés par l'Etat qui refuse ; en sorte que celui-ci ne pourra plus se prévaloir de cette clause lorsqu'il lui arrivait de l'invoquer en sa faveur.

Si la tierce personne chargée du choix des arbitres refuse de choisir, l'obligation de compromettre est suspendue jusqu'à ce que les parties lui en aient substitué une autre.

ART. 8.—Sont capables d'être nommés arbitres toutes les personnes qui, d'après la loi du pays par lequel, ou au nom duquel, elles sont désignées, pourraient être chargées, si elles étaient ses ressortissants, d'une mission diplomatique ou judiciaire.

ART. 9.—Le nom des arbitres choisis suivant le dernier alinéa de l'art. 5 doit être immédiatement notifié par la partie qui les a désignés à toutes les autres.

Chacune d'elles pourra les récuser dans le délai de quinze jours pour un des motifs suivants :

1° s'ils sont sujets d'un des Etats contractants ;

2° s'ils ont un intérêt personnel dans les questions qui sont l'objet de l'arbitrage ;

3° s'ils ont publié leur opinion sur ces mêmes questions par des brochures, ou par des discours dans des conférences publiques, ou bien comme membres de quelque tribunal national ou international qui ait déjà prononcé son arrêt.

ART. 10.—Si les arbitres sont individuellement déterminés dans le compromis, l'incapacité survenue pour un des motifs précédents, avant qu'ils commencent leurs fonctions, infirme le compromis pour autant que les parties ne se mettent d'accord sur un autre arbitre capable.

Mais, si le compromis ne contient pas détermination individuelle des arbitres, la récusation faite par une note motivée d'un gouvernement à l'autre, oblige celui qui l'a nommé à en désigner un autre sans discuter sur la validité de la récusation.

ART. 11.—The successive challenging of more than three Arbitrators by a Government is equivalent to refusal to carry out the Agreement, and produces as a consequence the effect provided for by the second paragraph of Art. 7.

ART. 12.—The acceptance of the office of Arbitrator must be by writing, and should be notified to the other parties in the same manner as his nomination.

ART. 13.—The Arbitrators who have been nominated by one party and accepted by the other may not be represented by substitutes, nor removed from their office unless by reason of death, or an incurable malady within one month, or a like case of *force majeure.*

In making new appointments the same forms and conditions must be observed as in the original appointment.

No Arbitrator is authorised to appoint a substitute unless with the consent of all the parties, or of all the other Arbitrators, if he has been chosen by them.

ART. 14.—If one of the Arbitrators chosen is a State, a township, or other corporation, a religious authority, a faculty of law, a learned society, or the actual head of one of these bodies, the arbitral functions may be performed entirely or in part by a Commissioner appointed *ad hoc* by this Arbitrator.

This Commissioner once invested with his functions, should preserve them, in the measure that they have been confided to him, during the whole course of the Arbitration, unless changes regarding the person he represents were such as could justify him in replacing him, or giving him fresh instructions, or modifying the extent of his powers.

SECTION III.—PLACE AND PRIVILEGES OF THE TRIBUNAL.

ART. 15.—If the Arbitral Tribunal has to be formed expressly for a particular dispute, its place of meeting will be arranged for in the Agreement, or by the Arbitrators, possibly outside the territory of the parties.

ART. 11.—La récusation successive de plus de trois arbitres de la part d'un gouvernement, équivaut à refus d'exécuter le compromis et produit à sa charge l'effet prévu par le 2e al. de l'art. 6.

ART. 12.—L'acceptation de l'office d'arbitre a lieu par écrit et doit être notifiée aux autres parties dans la même forme que sa nomination.

ART. 13.—Les arbitres qui ont été nommés d'une part et acceptés de l'autre ne peuvent être substitués, ni éloignés de leur office, si ce n'est à cause de mort, ou d'une maladie incurable dans un mois, ou d'un cas semblable de force majeure.

Alors pour les remplacer on doit observer les formes et les conditions adoptées pour leur nomination.

Aucun arbitre n'est autorisé à se nommer lui-même un substitut, si ce n'est avec le consentement de toutes les parties, ou de tous les autres arbitres, s'il a été choisi par ces derniers.

ART. 14.—Si un des arbitres choisis est un Etat, une commune ou autre corporation, une autorité religieuse, une faculté de droit, une société savante, ou le chef actuel d'une de ces personnes morales, ses fonctions d'arbitre peuvent être remplies entièrement ou en partie par un commissaire nommé *ad hoc* par cet arbitre.

Ce commissaire une fois investi de ses fonctions doit les conserver, dans la mesure qu'elles lui ont été confiées, pendant toute la durée de l'arbitrage, sans que les changements survenus à l'égard de la personne qu'il représente puissent autoriser cette dernière à le remplacer, ou à lui donner des instructions nouvelles, ou à modifier l'extension de ses pouvoirs.

SECTION III.—SIÈGE ET IMMUNITÉS DU TRIBUNAL.

ART. 15.—Si le tribunal arbitral doit être constitué exprès pour un conflit déterminé, le lieu de ses réunions sera établi dans le compromis ou par les arbitres, possiblement en dehors du territoire des parties.

Even when the seat of the Tribunal has been fixed beforehand by the Agreement, the Arbitrators, by a simple majority, may resolve to transfer it elsewhere, when the accomplishment of their functions at the place agreed has become manifestly perilous for their health, or if it no longer presents the guarantees of independence which are necessary to them.

ART. 16.—In all cases the Arbitral Tribunal should be treated as a diplomatic mission of the first rank, both as to the honours to be paid to the members and the immunities which they enjoy in the exercise of their functions, and also as to the punishment of offences which might be directed, even through the Press, against their deliberations or against their persons.

SECTION IV.—CONSTITUTION AND ORGANISATION OF THE ARBITRAL TRIBUNAL.

ART. 17.—Each of the parties in the case may appoint an Agent who shall watch over its interests or the interests of those under its jurisdiction, and undertake their defence; who shall present petitions, documents, and interrogatories, state conclusions, or reply to them, and furnish the proofs of his statements, and who by himself or through the medium of a lawyer, verbally or in writing, according to the rules of procedure (which the Commission itself shall publish when beginning its functions), shall state the points of his case, and the legal principles or the precedents which support his case.

ART. 18.—The Arbitrators, in their first meetings, shall take the following steps:—

(1.) They shall choose from their own number a President; they shall name the Secretaries and other officers charged with the editing of the minutes of their conferences, the transmission of documents, the care of archives, &c.; they shall recognise the agents and the counsel appointed by the parties for their defence, as appears in the previous article; and see to other matters necessary for the conduct of business.

Même dans le cas où le siège du tribunal a été fixé d'avance par le compromis, les arbitres, à la simple majorité, peuvent délibérer de le transférer ailleurs, lorsque l'accomplissement de leurs fonctions au lieu convenu est devenu manifestement périlleux pour leur santé, ou bien s'il ne présente plus les garanties d'indépendance qui leur sont nécessaires.

ART. 16.—Dans tous les cas le tribunal arbitral doit être traité comme une mission diplomatique de premier rang, soit quant aux honneurs qui lui sont dûs et aux immunités dont jouissent ses membres dans l'exercice de leurs fonctions, soit quant à la punition des offenses qui pourraient être dirigées, même au moyen de la presse, contre leurs délibérations, ou contre leurs personnes.

SECTION IV.—CONSTITUTION ET ORGANISATION DU TRIBUNAL ARBITRAL.

ART. 17.—Chacune des parties en cause pourra constituer un agent qui veille à ses intérêts ou à ceux de ses ressortissants et qui en prenne la défense; qui présente des pétitions, documents, interrogatoires, qui pose des conclusions ou y réponde, qui fournisse les preuves de ses affirmations, qui, par lui-même, ou par l'organe d'un homme de loi, verbalement ou par écrit, conformément aux règles de procédure que la Commission elle-même arrêtera en commençant ses fonctions, expose les doctrines, les principes légaux ou les précédents qui conviennent à sa cause.

ART. 18.—Les arbitres dans leurs premières réunions accomplissent les opérations suivantes :

1° Ils choisissent dans leur sein un président; ils nomment les secrétaires et autres officiers chargés de la rédaction des procès-verbaux des séances, de la transmission des actes, de la conservation des archives, etc.; ils reconnaissent les agents, et les conseils délégués par les parties pour leur défense comme il est dit à l'article précédent; et ils pourvoient aux autres conditions nécessaires pour fonctionner.

(2.) They shall investigate the object of the Arbitration, and where this is not clearly specified in the Agreement, invite the parties to define its scope and the limits of their powers.

(3.) They shall decide in what language their records should be drawn up, the means of proof or defence, and oral discussions; and also whether the public may be admitted at all to be present at these discussions, and which of their documents can be published, and in what form.

(4.) When accessory questions have been presented since the commencement, they shall decide whether they ought to settle them apart from the main question: and in general they shall decide all preliminary questions of competence, while keeping in view the principle that the aim and object of the Agreement is to efface all traces of the conflict which the parties have submitted to them.

(5.) They shall establish the procedure to be followed, whether by taking note of the rules contained in the Agreement, or by agreeing to rules adopted by other tribunals, or in enacting new rules.

ART. 19.—The Arbitrators are not bound in their opinion, nor in the measure of their jurisdiction by previous decrees of the Tribunals of a State on the questions which are proposed to them. In this respect they should place themselves in the position of a constituted Authority outside of every judicial hierarchy, to settle these questions *de novo*, in the first and last resort, relatively to the contesting Governments, as much as to their Tribunals and their citizens.

ART. 20.—The decision of the majority of the Arbitrators will be definitive both on the principal questions and on those of minor importance, unless it has been expressly settled in the conditions of the Arbitration that unanimity is indispensable.

In the latter case there will be drawn up a minute of the decision proposed by the majority, and the reasons which prevent the minority from concurring.

2° Ils reconnaissent l'objet de l'arbitrage, et dans le cas qu'il ne soit clairement spécifié dans le compromis ils invitent les parties à déclarer sa portée et les limites de leurs pouvoirs.

3° Ils établissent dans quelle langue doivent être rédigés leurs actes, les moyens de preuve ou de défense et les discussions orales; et ils décident si le public pourra être admis en quelque partie à assister à ces discussions, et lesquels parmi leurs actes pourront être publiés, et en quelle forme.

4° Les questions accessoires ayant été présentées dès le commencement, ils décident s'ils doivent les résoudre séparément de la question principale ; et en général ils décident toute question *préliminaire* de compétence, en tenant compte du principe que le but du compromis est celui d'effacer toutes les traces du conflit que les parties leur ont soumis.

5° Ils établissent la procédure à suivre, soit en prenant acte des règles contenues dans le compromis, soit en se rapportant à des règlements adoptés par d'autres tribunaux, soit en édictant des règles nouvelles.

ART. 19.—Les arbitres ne sont pas liés dans leur opinion, ni dans la mesure de leur juridiction, par les arrêts précédents des tribunaux d'un Etat sur les questions qui leur sont proposées. A cet égard ils doivent se placer dans la condition d'une autorité constituée, en dehors d'une hiérarchie judiciaire quelconque, pour résoudre ces questions *ex novo* en premier et en dernier ressort, tant relativement aux gouvernements en conflit, qu'à leurs tribunaux et à leurs citoyens.

ART. 20.—La décision de la majorité des arbitres sera définitive aussi bien sur les questions principales que sur celles secondaires, à moins que dans les conditions de l'arbitrage on ait expressément déterminé que l'unanimité serait indispensable.

Dans ce dernier cas il sera rédigé procès-verbal de la décision proposée par la majorité et des raisons qui empêchent à la minorité d'y adhérer.

In the former case the dissentient members shall be allowed to insert in the records their dissent, with the reasons therefor, only if the majority has expressly refused to take cognisance of some document, fact, or argument on which their dissent is based.

SECTION V.—REGULATIONS FOR DEBATE—ADMISSION OF PROOFS—INCIDENTAL DEMANDS.

ART. 21.—If the Convention does not prescribe a mode of procedure, the following rules are adopted :—

The Tribunal, at its opening meeting, fixes the forms and the periods of time in which each party shall, by its accredited agents, present simultaneously its arguments or counter-arguments in matters of fact and law, state its means of proof (written or oral), present its documents and communicate them to the opposing party.

In like manner a suitable period of time shall be fixed for each party, after the examination of the case and the reply, to present its replies on matters of fact and points of law, or, after the admission of some other evidence, to explain or modify its demands, and, if occasion arise, a preliminary discussion shall be allowed on the points of fact or law on which the written argument seems insufficient.

Finally, a time limit shall be fixed at the beginning for the final discussion and the termination of the pleadings, so that the award may be given within the time fixed in the Agreement.

ART. 22.—The periods of time fixed by the Tribunal may be prolonged by it, provided that all the parties be admitted to profit by it in an equal degree.

ART. 23.—The rules of procedure approved by the Tribunal cannot be modified or annulled, except with the consent of all parties, if they were fixed in the Arbitration Convention, or with the consent of the majority of the Arbitrators if they were framed by them.

Dans le premier cas les membres de la minorité pourront faire insérer dans les actes un vœu contraire motivé, seulement si la majorité a expressément refusé de prendre connaissance de quelque document, fait, ou argument sur lequel est basé son dissentiment.

SECTION V.—INSTRUCTION DU DÉBAT.—ADMISSION DES PREUVES.—DEMANDES INCIDENTELLES.

ART. 21.—Dans le silence des conventions, les règ'es suivantes sont adoptées :

Le tribunal, dans sa séance préliminaire, fixe les formes et délais dans lesquels chaque partie devra, par ses agents accrédités auprès du tribunal, présenter simultanément ses mémoires ou contre-mémoires en fait et en droit, proposer ses moyens de preuve écrite ou orale, produire ses documents et les communiquer à la partie adverse.

Egalement un délai convenable sera établi afin que chaque partie, après l'examen des mémoires et des moyens de défense de l'adversaire, présente ses répliques en fait et en droit, ou après l'admission de quelque autre preuve, éclaircisse ou modifie ses demandes, et, le cas échéant, soit admise à une discussion préliminaire sur les points de fait ou de droit sur lesquels le débat écrit semble insuffisant.

Enfin un délai sera établi d'avance pour la discussion finale et pour la clôture du débat, en sorte que la décision puisse être rendue dans le délai convenu dans le compromis.

ART. 22.—Les délais établis par le tribunal pourront être prolongés par lui-même, à condition que toutes les parties soient admises à en profiter en égale mesure.

ART. 23.—Les règles de procédure approuvées par le tribunal ne peuvent être modifiées ou abrogées, si ce n'est avec le consentement de toutes les parties, si elles étaient établies dans les conventions d'arbitrage,—ou avec le consentement de la majorité des arbitres si elles étaient leur œuvre.

The Tribunal may always, by a simple majority of votes, interpret these rules so as to render the application of them easier, and develop them by others which might appear necessary for the accomplishment of their task.

ART. 24.—The rules relative to the nature of the proofs admissible, and the conditions and formalities necessary to render them admissible, whether fixed in the Agreement or announced by the Arbitrators at the commencement of their meetings, may not be changed during the pleadings.

But if there is nothing in the Agreement or the Rules of Procedure to forbid, or in case of doubt as to the force of the provisions, the Tribunal shall admit, by General Orders, those means of proof which are not excluded by the Rules or the Agreement, and which are not irreconcilable with the character of the questions to be decided, or with the principles of international public order.

ART. 25.—Each party may demand of the other the production of any reserved documents at its disposal, which the Tribunal declares to be vital to the question.

But no party shall have the right to submit to examination those documents (hereinafter called "domestic documents") which, having existed before the difference arose, and being since then in the possession of, or known by, one party or its predecessors in title, have not been communicated to the other party or its predecessors in title, before the difference arose.

ART. 26.—Solemn written statements, made in due form by a witness before a public officer, should be admissible in evidence as proof of relevant facts, subject to the right of cross-examining the witness. The probative value of such statements would always be for the Tribunal.

ART. 27.—Each party should be entitled to require the other to produce, for oral examination before the Tribunal, any witness making on behalf of that other party such a written statement as is mentioned in Art. 26.

Le tribunal pourra toutefois, à la simple majorité des voix, interpréter ces règles pour en rendre l'application plus facile, et les développer par d'autres qui paraîtraient nécessaires pour l'accomplissement de leur tâche.

ART. 24.—Les règles relatives à la nature des preuves admissibles et aux conditions de formes requises pour les admettre, qu'elles soient établies dans le compromis ou édictées par les arbitres au début de leurs séances, ne pourront être changées pendant le débat.

Mais en cas de silence du compromis et du règlement de procédure, ou en cas de doute sur la valeur de leurs dispositions, le tribunal admettra, par des arrêts d'ordre général, ces moyens de preuve qui n'ont été défendus par le règlement ni par le compromis, et qui ne sont pas inconciliables avec le caractère des questions à résoudre ou avec les principes d'ordre public international.

ART. 25.—Chaque partie pourra exiger de l'autre qu'elle produise les documents réservés dont elle dispose et que le tribunal juge décisifs pour la question.

Mais aucune partie n'aura le droit de soumettre à l'examen ces documents (que nous appellerons *privés*) dans le cas que,—ayant existé avant le conflit, et étant dès lors dans le domaine ou à connaissance d'une partie ou de ses auteurs,—ils n'aient été communiqués à l'autre ou à ses auteurs avant l'origine du conflit.

ART. 26.—Les dépositions écrites faites en due forme par un témoin devant un officier public devront être acceptées comme preuve des faits pertinents, avec le droit pour l'autre partie de contre-interroger le témoin.

Le tribunal sera pourtant toujours souverain dans l'appréciation de la valeur probante de ses dépositions.

ART. 27.—Chaque partie pourra exiger que l'autre présente, pour l'examen oral devant le tribunal, les témoins qui ont fait en faveur de l'autre partie les dépositions écrites mentionnées à l'art. 26.

When a witness cannot be produced before the Arbitral Tribunal, the Tribunal may commission the judicial authorities exercising jurisdiction over the place of the domicile of the witness to hold the necessary cross-examination. Domestic documents, and the statements of witnesses who, though required by one party, have not been produced for oral examination by the other party, may, on the application of the party (against which they are adduced) be expunged from the evidence, and not be included in the records which the Tribunal may have reprinted, if it please.

ART. 28.—When the Tribunal is forming its award, no one but the Secretaries who have the charge of recording the Minutes shall be present at the meetings of the Tribunal.

ART. 29.—Neither the parties nor the Arbitrators may bring into the Arbitration other States, or third persons, unless with the previous consent of all the parties and of this third person or State.

The spontaneous intervention of a third party is not admissible, except with the consent of the parties in the case.

ART. 30.—Cross claims may not be brought before the Tribunal unless they have been submitted to it by the Agreement, or the parties are agreed to submit them to its decision.

SECTION VI.—FORMATION AND PUBLICATION OF AWARDS, AND CONDITIONS OF THEIR VALIDITY.

ART. 31.—Interlocutory judgments need not be published, being notified to the agents of the parties, or their Governments.

Definitive awards, whether they decide one question only, or all the questions at once which were submitted to the Arbitrators, shall not be published until the final sitting of the Tribunal, by their being read on that occasion, and by notification to the agents, or to their Governments, in the periods of time fixed by the rules.

Lorsque ces témoins ne peuvent être traduits avant le tribunal arbitral, celui-ci pourra requérir à cet effet l'autorité judiciaire compétente d'après la loi de leur domicile.

Les documents privés et les dépositions des témoins qui, malgré les instances d'une partie, n'ont pas été présentés par l'autre à l'examen oral, peuvent être sur sa demande éliminés du procès, et ne pas être compris dans les actes, que le tribunal peut faire réimprimer à sa volonté.

ART. 28.—Lorsque le tribunal prend ses décisions, personne, excepté les secrétaires chargés de la rédaction des procès-verbaux, ne pourra assister aux séances du tribunal.

ART. 29.—Ni les parties ni les arbitres d'office ne peuvent appeler en cause d'autres Etats ou des tierces personnes, si ce n'est avec le consentement préalable de toutes les parties et de cette tierce personne ou Etat.

L'intervention spontanée d'un tiers n'est admissible qu'avec le consentement des parties en cause.

ART. 30.—Les demandes reconventionnelles ne peuvent être portées devant le tribunal que si elles lui sont déférées par le compromis, ou que les parties sont d'accord pour les soumettre à sa décision.

SECTION VI.—FORMATION, PUBLICATION DES ARRÊTS ET CONDITIONS DE LEUR VALIDITÉ.

ART. 31.—Les arrêts interlocutoires n'ont pas besoin d'être publiés, étant notifiés aux agents des parties, ou à leurs gouvernements.

Les arrêts définitifs, soit qu'ils décident une seule, ou toutes à la fois les questions soumises aux arbitres, ne seront publiés que le jour de la clôture des séances, par la lecture qu'il en sera donnée, et par la notification aux agents, ou à leurs gouvernements dans les délais établis par le règlement.

Nevertheless, when the Tribunal decides the questions separately, it may give the President the power to communicate a certified copy of such award to the parties who shall prove that delay in the publication is dangerous to their interests.

ART. 32.—The Tribunal should definitively decide all the points of the dispute, and should not be allowed to decline giving an award under any pretext.

Nevertheless, if the Agreement does not insist on a simultaneous definitive award on all points, the Tribunal may, whilst definitively deciding certain points, reserve the others for further hearing.

If the Tribunal does not find that the claims of any of the parties are well founded, it should declare so, establishing in its award the real state of the law between the parties on the subject of the dispute.

ART. 33.—The majority of the total number of the Arbitrators shall be able to act in spite of the absence or the departure of the minority. The decisions of this majority shall be definitive both on the principal questions and on the secondary questions, unless, in the conditions of the Arbitration, it is expressly stipulated that unanimity is indispensable.

ART. 34.—All the awards of the Tribunal should be drawn up in writing, and contain a recital of the reasons, unless the opposite is expressly stipulated in the Agreement.

They should be signed by each of the Arbitrators; if some refuse, there should be added to the signatures of the others the declaration that such members have refused to sign; and if they require it, a record shall be made in a separate Minute of the reasons by which they justify their refusal.

ART. 35.—The definitive award should be given within the period of time fixed by the Agreement or by the rules adopted at the commencement of the labours of the Tribunal.

Toutefois lorsque le tribunal décide les questions séparément, il pourra attribuer au président la faculté d'en donner communication par extrait, comme document authentique, aux parties qui prouveront que le retard dans la publication est dangereux pour leurs intérêts.

ART. 32.—Le tribunal doit décider définitivement tous les points du litige, ne pouvant refuser de prononcer sous aucun prétexte.

Toutefois, si le compromis ne prescrit pas la décision définitive simultanée de tous les points, le tribunal peut, en décidant définitivement certains points, réserver les autres pour une procédure ultérieure.

Si le tribunal ne trouve fondées les prétentions d'aucune des parties, il doit le déclarer établissant dans son arrêt l'état réel du droit entre les parties sur l'objet du litige.

ART. 33.—La majorité du nombre total des arbitres pourra agir malgré l'absence ou le départ de la minorité. Les décisions de cette majorité seront définitives aussi bien sur les questions principales que sur les questions secondaires, à moins que, dans les conditions de l'arbitrage, on ait expressément déterminé que l'unanimité serait indispensable.

ART. 34.—Tous les arrêts du tribunal doivent être rédigés par écrit et contenir un exposé des motifs, sauf dispense stipulée dans le compromis.

Ils doivent être signés par chacun des arbitres ; si quelques-uns s'y refusent, on ajoutera à la signature des autres la déclaration que les tels membres ont refusé de signer ; et on prendra acte, s'ils l'exigent, dans un procès-verbal à part, des raisons par lesquelles ils justifient leur refus.

ART. 35.—La décision définitive doit être prononcée dans le délai fixé par le compromis ou par le règlement adopté au début des travaux du tribunal.

There may be deducted, however, the time during which the Tribunal has been prevented by *force majeure* from continuing its work. In the case where the time (fixed by the Agreement or by the Arbitrators) has proved insufficient for full examination, or from some unforeseen circumstance, it cannot be extended except by a subsequent convention, or, respectively, by a decree of the Arbitrators, containing the reasons therefor.

SECTION VII.—EXECUTION AND REVISION OF THE AWARD.

ART. 36.—On the demand of one of the parties, the Award shall fix a limit of time within which it should be executed; and, if the Agreement expressly gives the Arbitrators this authority, it should further impose guarantees (either pecuniary or territorial or personal) which the condemned party must furnish in order to assure the acomplishment of the obligations imposed by the award.

If no limit of time or guarantee is specified, the award is to be executed immediately and spontaneously.

ART. 37.—If it be necessary for a third Power, which had not signed the Agreement, to conform to the award or to accomplish some act to enable it to be carried into effect, it must be notified to that Power by the more active party; but that Power may confine itself to taking note of this communication.

ART. 38.—In case of refusal or voluntary delay in the execution of the award, the President of the Tribunal or the Umpire, if it is he who has drawn it up, shall, on the demand of that party which complains of the delay or refusal, as soon as possible, invite the other party to present its defence within a fixed period of time.

Except in the cases where this proves a demand for revision according to Art. 40, the Tribunal or the Umpire will confine themselves to deciding whether the reasons on which the contesting party relies have been already considered implicitly or explicitly in the award.

On pourra toutefois faire déduction du temps pendant lequel le tribunal, par force majeure, aura été empêché de continuer ses fonctions.

Dans le cas où les moyens d'instruction ou quelque circonstance imprévue auraient rendu insuffisant le délai fixé par le compromis ou par les arbitres, il ne pourra être prolongé que par une convention subséquente, où, respectivement, par un arrêt motivé des arbitres.

Section VII. — Exécution et Révision de la Sentence.

Art. 36. — Sur la demande de l'une des parties, la sentence établira un délai dans lequel elle devra être exécutée ; et, si le compromis donne expressément aux arbitres cette autorité, elle devra en outre établir les garanties (soit pécuniaires, soit territoriales ou personnelles) que la partie condamnée devra fournir pour assurer l'accomplissement des obligations imposées par la sentence.

A défaut de délai et de garanties, la sentence devra être exécutée immédiatement et spontanément.

Art. 37. — S'il est nécessaire qu'une puissance tierce, qui n'avait pas signé le compromis, se conforme à la sentence ou accomplisse quelque acte, pour qu'elle puisse être exécutée, elle devra lui être notifiée par la partie plus diligente ; mais elle pourra se limiter à prendre acte de cette communication.

Art. 38. — En cas de refus ou de retard volontaire dans l'exécution de la sentence, le président du tribunal ou le sur-arbitre (si c'est lui qui l'a rédigée), sur la demande de cette partie qui se plaint du retard ou de refus, invitent, aussitôt que possible, l'autre partie à présenter ses défenses dans un délai déterminé.

Sauf les cas où celle-ci conclut à une demande en révision conforme à l'article 40, le tribunal ou le sur-arbitre se limitent à décider si les motifs sur lesquels s'appuie la partie contestante ont été déjà envisagés implicitement ou explicitement dans la sentence.

If these reasons have not been considered they will provide for this by an additional declaration, which shall form an integral part of the award.

In the contrary case, they declare by a new judgment, which shall be published in all forms, the refusal or voluntary delay in the execution of the award, and they fix a peremptory limit of time, after which the contesting party shall be exposed to the consequences provided for in the following article.

ART. 39.—Refusal to submit to the Award provided for by the preceding Article is not only the gravest violation of a treaty law, but a direct offence against the principles of law on which rests the society of States.

The Government which incurs this guilt exposes itself to all the consequences which may be arranged for in the Agreement, amongst others that Arbitral Clauses contained in other treaties with the same State can no longer be appealed to by it, and these treaties may be considered by the other party as lapsed *ipso iure* without any regard to the limits of time fixed for their lapsing.

It is, furthermore, liable to have the other States, with which it is united by Arbitration Treaties, refuse to observe their clauses unless it presents special guarantees for their execution.

ART. 40.—If the Agreement does not forbid it, there may be admitted before the same Arbitrators the demands for correction or revision of the award, presented by one of the parties, provided they are founded on one of the following reasons, and without prejudice to the rights acquired by interlocutory awards, or parts of the definitive award already executed :

(*a*) Contradiction in the purview, between the different parts of the definitive award, or between these and other awards published by the same Tribunal in the same case.

(*b*) Forgeries in the documents or in the proofs on which the award is expressly founded—on condition that the party which sustains the falsification of these means of evidence did not

Si ces motifs n'ont été envisagés, ils y pourvoient par une déclaration additionnelle qui fera partie intégrale de la sentence.

En cas contraire, ils constatent par un nouvel arrêt, qui sera publié en toutes formes, le refus ou le retard volontaire dans l'exécution de la sentence, et ils établissent un délai péremptoire, au delà duquel la partie contestante sera exposée aux conséquences prévues dans l'article suivant.

ART. 39. — Le manque de soumission à l'arrêt prévu par l'article précédent implique non seulement la plus grave violation d'un droit conventionnel, mais une offense directe aux principes de droit sur lesquels repose la société des Etats.

Le gouvernement qui s'en rend coupable s'expose à toutes les conséquences qui pourront être établies dans le compromis, entre autres à celle, que les clauses compromissoires contenues dans d'autres traités avec ce même Etat, ne pourront plus être invoquées par lui, et ces traités pourront être considérés par l'autre partie comme dissous *ipso jure* sans aucun égard aux délais établis pour pouvoir les dénoncer.

Il s'expose en outre à voir les autres Etats, avec lesquels il est lié par des traités d'arbitrage, refuser d'en observer les clauses s'il ne présente des garanties spéciales pour leur exécution.

ART. 40. — Si le compromis ne l'interdit pas, on pourra admettre devant les mêmes arbitres les demandes de correction ou de révision de la sentence présentées par l'une des parties, à condition qu'elles soient fondées sur l'un des motifs suivants, et sans préjudice des droits acquis par effet des arrêts interlocutoires, ou des parties de la sentence définitive, qui auraient été déjà exécutées :

(*a*) Contradiction dans le dispositif, entre les différentes parties de la sentence définitive, ou entre celles-ci et d'autres sentences publiées par le même tribunal dans la même cause.

(*b*) Faux dans les documents ou dans les preuves sur lesquelles est expressément fondée la décision, — à condition que la partie qui soutient la falsification de ces moyens d'instruction n'en ait pas possess the knowledge of it during the argument, and that it has been declared by an authority whose competence is not, or cannot be contested, according to the principles of Common Law, by any of the parties in the case.

(*c*) Error of Fact; provided that the award is founded expressly on the existence or on the want of a document or a fact, whose existence or want has not been observed before the Tribunal, or could not be proved, whereas after the publication of the award success has been attained in giving such proofs of it that all the parties must admit them as decisive.

ART. 41.—The demand for revision or correction should be notified by writing, with the reasons and the copies of the documents to all the Arbitrators, as also to each of the parties, with such a number of copies that they may be communicated immediately to their agents before the Arbitral Tribunal. Within one month after this notification each party must notify to the others and to the Arbitrators its reply or its defence with reasons, which shall not confer any right to further replies.

On these materials the Arbitrators shall pronounce their final award, fixing a positive period for its execution, that it may produce the same effects as that provided for by Art. 39.

ART. 42.—The costs of Arbitration procedure shall be paid in equal proportions by the Governments interested; but the expenses incurred by the parties for the preparation and carrying on of their case shall be paid by each of them individually.

On the demand of the parties, the Tribunal may charge the one which has been condemned with the total, or the greater part, of the costs of the Arbitration.

eu connaissance pendant le débat, et qu'elle ait été déclarée par une autorité dont la compétence n'est, ou ne peut-être contestée, selon les principes de droit commun, par aucune des parties en cause.

(*c*) Erreur de fait, — à condition que la sentence soit fondée expressément sur l'existence ou sur le défaut d'un acte ou d'un fait, dont l'existence ou le défaut n'ait pas été observé avant le tribunal, ou n'ait pu être prouvé, tandis qu'après la publication de l'arrêt, on réussit à en donner de telles preuves que toutes les parties doivent les admettre comme décisives.

ART. 41.—La demande de révision ou correction doit être notifiée par écrit, avec les motifs et les copies des documents, à tous les arbitres, aussi bien qu'a chacune des parties, en tel nombre d'exemplaires qu'elle puisse être immédiatement communiquée à leurs agents auprès du tribunal arbitral.

Dans le délai d'un mois après cette notification, chaque partie devra notifier aux autres et aux arbitres sa réponse, ou sa défense motivée, qui ne donnera droit à d'autres répliques.

Sur ces éléments les arbitres prononceront leur dernier arrêt, établissant un délai péremptoire pour son exécution, afin qu'il puisse produire les mêmes effets que celui prévu par l'article 39.

ART. 42.—Les frais de procédure d'arbitrage seront payés en proportions égales par les gouvernements intéressés ; mais les dépenses faites par les parties pour la préparation et la poursuite de leur défense seront payées par chacune d'elles individuellement.

Sur la demande des parties, le tribunal pourra mettre à la charge de celle qui a été condamnée le total, ou une portion plus grande, des frais de l'arbitrage.

THE ARBITRATION TRIBUNAL.

BY SIGNOR P. FIORE,

Professor of International Law in the University of Naples, etc.

1897.

1. The Arbitration tribunal is composed of persons appointed in the capacity of arbiters to decide any particular difference arising between two or more States, or to pronounce a judgment thereon, according to the principles of Public Law, or any special law agreed upon by the parties by means of a Treaty stipulated between them.

2. Submission to the jurisdiction of the Arbitration tribunal is either voluntary or compulsory.

The former is that which follows from a stipulation in a Treaty by which the parties have agreed to submit to Arbitration any dispute which may arise respecting its interpretation or execution; or from a general Treaty by which they have bound themselves to refer to arbitrators any question between them; or from a special agreement (*compromis*) by which they combine to refer any particular question to arbitrators for their adjudication.

Compulsory submission to arbitral jurisdiction might arise from the deliberation of a Conference which had decided that a question of fact or particular law between the parties should be submitted to Arbitration; or if, in the absence of an agreement (*compromis*), should one of the parties consider it a case for arbitral jurisdiction and declare itself prepared to submit thereto, the Conference might consider that an Arbitration tribunal should be formed to decide the dispute in question.

3. It is incumbent on States, even if they have not previously

DEL TRIBUNALE ARBITRALE.

DI PASQUALE FIORE,

Professore ordinario di Diritto Internazionale, e di Diritto Privato comparato dell' Universita di Napoli, Membro dell' Instituto di Dirito Internazionale.

1897.

1. Il tribunale arbitrale è costituito dalle persone nominate in qualità di arbitri per decidere una controversia d'interesse particolare nata fra due o più Stati, e per sentenziare intorno ad essa applicando i principii del Diritto comune, o il Diritto particolare stabilito fra le parti mediante i trattati fra di esse stipulati.

2. La sottomissione alla giurisdizione del tribunale arbitrale sarà volontaria o forzata.

La prima è quella che nasce in conseguenza del patto espresso concordato in un trattato, col quale le parti abbiano convenuto di sottomettere agli arbitri le controversie che possano nascere nella sua interpretazione, o nell'esecuzione; o quando con un trattato avessero assunto in generale l'obbligo reciproco di sottomettere ad arbitri qualunque vertenza fra di loro; o quando, con compromesso speciale, avessero convenuto di sottomettersi ad arbitri per far risolvere da essi una particolare controversia di ordine giuridico.

La giurisdizione arbitrale forzata potrà derivare dalla deliberazione di una Conferenza, con la quale, decisa la questione principale, fosse stata deferita agli arbitri la decisione d'una questione di fatto o di Diritto particolare fra le parti stesse; ovvero quando, mancando il compromesso, e sostenendo una delle parti che fosse il caso della giurisdizione arbitrale, e dichiarandosi pronta a sottomettersi, la Conferenza riconoscesse fondata tale istanza e decidesse che dovesse essere costituito un tribunale arbitrale per decidere sulla determinata controversia.

3. Incombe agli Stati, anche quando non si siano a ciò pre-

bound themselves to do so, to recognise the evident general utility of submitting to the decision of an arbitral tribunal all the differences of a juridical nature which may arise between them, which concern their particular interests, and which, according to the principles of Public Law might form matter for a reference to arbitration (*compromis*).

Formation of the Arbitral Tribunal.

4. The arbitral tribunal shall be considered constituted when the arbitrators have been appointed, according to the agreement (*compromis*) entered into between the parties, or according to the following regulations; and they have accepted the mandate.

5. The constitution of an arbitral tribunal might also be effected by means of an arbitration clause in a Treaty by which the parties have agreed to refer all differences arising between them to Arbitration, if such differences can be considered a subject of reference, and to submit themselves to the regulations of International Public Law by means of the Arbitration.

6. The choice of the arbitrators must, in general, be left with the parties intending to submit themselves to the arbitral tribunal, or it may be made by persons invited by them to do so, these persons, of course, adhering strictly to the arrangement previously entered into in virtue of the Agreement.

7. The number of arbitrators ought generally to be restricted to three, but may, by agreement of the parties, be extended to five. The parties, however, may agree to refer the decision of the dispute to one person chosen by themselves to act as arbitrator.

8. If the parties have, by agreement, appointed the arbitrator or arbitrators, their functions must be personally exercised by the person or persons appointed; and if one of these persons should be unable, or should decline, to act, he cannot be represented by a substitute, unless a new agreement (*compromis*) be made between the parties for that purpose.

cedentemente obbligati, il riconoscere l'evidente comune utilità di sottoporre alla decisione di un tribunale arbitrale tutte le differenze di ordine giuridico che nascano fra di loro, e che concernano loro particolari interessi, e che, secondo i principii del Diritto comune, possano formar materia di compromesso.

Formazione del Tribunale Arbitrale.

4. Il tribunale arbitrale si reputerà costituito quando gli arbitri siano stati nominati a norma del compromesso concluso fra le parti o delle regole seguenti, ed essi abbiano accettato il mandato.

5. La costituzione del tribunale arbitrale potrà effettuarsi altresì in forza della clausola compromissoria contenuta in un trattato, con la quale le parti si siano obbligate di deferire agli arbitri tutte le controversie che potessero sorgere tra di loro, idonee ad essere oggetto di compromesso, rimettendosi poi alle regole del Diritto comune internazionale per l'attuazione dell'arbitrato.

6. La scelta degli arbitri dovrà ritenersi in massima deferita alle parti stesse che intendano sottomettersi al tribunale arbitrale, ovvero potrà essere fatta dalle persone designate da esse per fare tale scelta, attenendosi in ordine a ciò a quanto sia stato previamente stabilito in virtù del compromesso.

7. Il numero degli arbitri dovrà ritenersi in massima fissato a tre, e potrà per accordo delle parti essere esteso a cinque.

Potranno nonpertanto le parti convenire di deferire la decisione della controversia ad uno scelto da esse per decidere in qualità di arbitro.

8. Se le parti abbiano designato d'accordo l'arbitro, o gli arbitri, le funzioni dovranno essere esercitate individualmente dalla persona o dalle persone da esse determinate; e qualora una di dette persone non fosse capace o essendo tale ricusasse, non potrà procedersi a sostituirla, se non quando sia intervenuto tra le parti stesse un nuovo compromesso in ordine a ciò.

9. If the parties should not agree in the choice of arbitrators, or should no arbitral clause, previously stipulated as regards such choice, be in existence; and if they cannot arrive at an agreement (*compromis*) for that purpose; or if they have already severally appointed arbitrators, one of whom has proved unable or unwilling to serve; generally speaking each of the parties retains the right to appoint an equal number of arbitrators, and the arbitrators thus nominated shall appoint an umpire, unless the parties are able to agree upon the appointment, as umpire, of a person selected by them. If it is left to the arbitrators themselves to appoint an umpire, they are at liberty to remit the choice to a third person.

Qualifications of an Arbitrator.

10. The juridical qualification of an arbitrator, according to Public Law, is the ability to exercise the functions of an Arbitrator in private matters.

11. The moral qualification attaches by preference to those persons who, from their independent position, and their recognised judicial experience, inspire full confidence that they will decide with uprightness and impartiality; and who have no interest whatever, directly or indirectly, in regard to the dispute in question.

12. The functions of an arbitrator may be confided to Sovereigns, jurisconsults, and publicists, on condition that the person accepting the appointment shall himself exercise the duties required, and cannot delegate them to some one else.

13. Regularly constituted bodies (such as a Faculty of Law or an appointed Tribunal) may be chosen as Arbitrators.

Refusal to Submit to Arbitral Jurisdiction.

14. The party which desires a reference to Arbitration, and declares itself ready to submit thereto for the settlement of the

9. Qualora le parti non arrivino ad accordarsi sulla scelta degli arbitri, o che non esista fra di esse una clausola compromissoria previamente stipulata per procedere alla scelta, e che non arrivino a concordare un compromesso in ordine a ciò, o che essendosi accordate sulla scelta di arbitri individualmente designati una delle persone scelta sia divenuta incapace, o non abbia accettato, dovrà ritenersi in massima che ciascuna delle parti abbia diritto di nominare lo stesso numero di arbitri, e che gli arbitri da esse nominati debbano designare il terzo arbitro, salvo che le parti stesse non arrivino ad accordarsi per far designare il terzo arbitro da una delle persone da esse scelte. Gli arbitri nominati potranno, quando debbano essi designare l'arbitro, rimetterne la scelta ad un terzo.

Capacità per essere arbitro.

10. La capacità giuridica richiesta per essere arbitro è quella che, secondo il Diritto comune, occorre per esercitare la funzione di arbitro tra privati.

11. La capacità morale dovrà essere attribuita a preferenza alle persone che per la loro posizione indipendente e per le alte cognizioni giuridiche ispirino piena confidenza di decidere con rettitudine e imparzialità, e che non abbiano alcun interesse diretto o indiretto rispetto alla controversia insorta.

12. Le funzioni di arbitro possono essere attribuite ai Sovrani, ai giureconsulti ed ai pubblicisti, a condizione però che la persona designata, accettando, eserciti personalmente codeste funzioni e che non possa delegarle ad altri.

13. I corpi costituiti (*una Facoltà di Diritto o un Tribunale designato*) potranno essere scelti come arbitri.

Rifiuto di sottomettersi alla giurisdizione arbitrale.

14. La parte, la quale sostenga che sia il caso di giurisdizione arbitrale, e che dichiari di essere pronta a sottomettersi ad essa

difference which has arisen, must, in the absence of any agreement (*compromis*) or arrangement, notify this, in a diplomatic way, to the other party, and appoint one or two arbitrators, at the same time inviting the other party to appoint an equal number, when they will be in a position to proceed to the appointment of an Umpire, according to the preceding regulations.

15. If, however, the opposite party, to which this diplomatic notification is made, does not accept the proposal, it must, as a rule, return a diplomatic notification in which the reasons for its refusal are specified. The absence of such notification will be considered sufficient proof of refusal to appoint arbitrators in accordance with the intimation made to it by the other party.

Appeal to the Conference.

16. A refusal to go before an arbitration tribunal, constituted according to the preceding regulations, would justify an appeal to the Conference (provided for by Fiore, in a set of previous rules) at the instance of the party which considers itself aggrieved.

Such an appeal to the Conference may also be made by the opposite party, although refusing Arbitration, whether because it considers the subject of difference outside the limit of the arbitral clause, or for any particular circumstance of the case, as not being matter for reference, or because the refusal is based, generally, on Public Law.

17. An appeal to the Conference must also be made in the case where the parties may have undertaken by means of a formal Agreement (*compromis*) to submit to an arbitral tribunal, and as to the method of its constitution, if one of the parties does not appoint arbitrators according to the terms of the Agreement, or if the constitution of the tribunal cannot be completed because the appointed arbitrators cannot agree in the choice of an umpire, and if the parties cannot remove the difficulties in the way of proceeding with such choice.

per la decisione della controversia insorta, dovrà, in mancanza di compromesso o di accordo, notificare in via diplomatica ciò all'altra parte e nominare uno o due arbitri, invitando l'altra parte a nominare un numero eguale, onde procedere poi alla nomina del terzo arbitro, come nella regola precedente.

15. Qualora la parte avversa, alla quale sia stata fatta tale notificazione diplomatica, non accetti di sottomettersi alla giurisdizione arbitrale, dovrà in massima dichiararlo con nota diplomatica, nella quale i motivi del suo rifiuto siano formulati. Mancando tale nota, sarà ritenuta valida prova del suo rifiuto il non procedere essa alla nomina degli arbitri in seguito all'intimazione fatta dall'altra parte.

Appello alla Conferenza.

16. Il rifiuto di sottomettersi alla decisione del tribunale arbitrale, constatato come nella regola precedente, giustificherà appello alla Conferenza, ad istanza della parte che si ritenga lesa.

Tale appello alla Conferenza potrà aver luogo anche ad istanza della parte convenuta, qualora questa rifiuti la giurisdizione arbitrale, o perchè ritenga l'oggetto della controversia fuori dei limiti della clausola compromissoria, o perchè sostenga che l'oggetto della controversia stessa, per le particolari circostanze del caso, non possa essere materia di compromesso, o perchè in generale fondi sul Diritto comune il suo rifiuto a sottomettersi alla giurisdizione arbitrale.

17. Dovrà altresì ammettersi l'appello alla Conferenza, anche nel caso che le parti si siano accordate mediante il compromesso concluso di sottomettersi al tribunale arbitrale e circa il modo per costituirlo, se una delle parti non designi gli arbitri secondo fu convenuto col compromesso stesso, o quando la costituzione del tribunale arbitrale non possa essere effettuata a cagione del disaccordo degli arbitri designati circa la scelta del terzo arbitro; e che le parti non arrivino ad eliminare le difficoltà per procedere di questi alla scelta.

18. Whenever a dispute, because an arbitral tribunal has not been created, has to be referred to the Conference, the latter shall be competent to examine fully whether it is a case for arbitral reference, either because of an arbitral clause agreed upon by the parties themselves or on the general principles of Public Law. If, therefore, the Conference consider it a case for reference to an arbitral tribunal, it can itself appoint the necessary arbitrators.

19. The Conference may dispense with an arbitral jurisdiction for the decision of the dispute, and dispose of it itself, if it considers itself competent to do so, in accordance with the regulation determining its competency.

Procedure before the Tribunal.

20. It is incumbent on the parties, between whom the contention exists, to give precise details of all writings and signatures made by them in connection with the Agreement (*compromis*). This will be drawn up in the form of a treaty, and will be indispensable in every case of voluntary submission to Arbitration, even if it should follow from an arbitral clause previously stipulated.

In case of compulsory submission, the difference to be submitted to the adjudication of the arbiters shall be formulated by the Conference.

21. The Agreement must contain a clear and exact statement of the points in dispute, regarding which the parties appeal to the decision of the arbitrators.

Such points of discussion may refer to a question of particular law established between the parties, or to a question of fact, if the parties are agreed on the question of law, and expressly declare the same, and if the discussion concerning the application of such law relate to a question of fact.

22. The parties shall produce all the documents, deeds and memoranda which may give information to the tribunal, and

18. Ogniqualvolta che la controversia, par la mancata costituzione del tribunale arbitrale, sia deferita alla Conferenza, questa dovrà ritenersi competente ad esaminare in principio se sia o no il caso di giurisdizione arbitrale, o in virtù della clausola compromissoria fra le parti stesse concordata, o in virtù dei generali principii di Diritto comune. Qualora la Conferenza ritenga che sia il caso di sottoporre la decisione della controversia ad un tribunale arbitrale, portrà essa stessa designare gli arbitri mancanti.

19. La Conferenza potrà escludere la giurisdizione arbitrale e decidere la controversia, se sia il caso di ritenersi a ciò competente essa stessa a norma della reg. 1046.

Procedimento dinanzi al Tribunale arbitrale.

20. Incombe alle parti, fra le quali verte la controversia, il precisarne i punti mediante il compromesso da esse scritto e sottoscritto.

Tale atto serà fatto con le stesse forme di un trattato, e sarà necessario in ogni caso di giurisdizione arbitrale volontaria, anche quando essa abbia luogo, in virtù della clausola compromissoria, previamente stipulata.

In caso di giurisdizione arbitrale forzata, le controversie sottoposte al giudizio degli arbitri saranno formulate dalla Conferenza.

21. Il compromesso dovrà contenere la contestazione della controversia e precisare i punti, rispetto ai quali le parti debbano sottostare alla decisione degli arbitri.

Tali punti controversi possono concernere una questione di Diritto particolare stabilito far le parti stesse, o una questione di fatto, dato che le parti si trovino d'accordo sulla questione di Diritto e lo dichiarino espressamente, e che la controversia concerna l'applicazione di tale Diritto a questioni di fatto.

22. Incombe alle parti trasmettere tutti i documenti e gli atti e le memorie idonei ad illuminare il tribunale giudicante e

all documents and deeds which it may require for the elucidation of the case.

23. Delay on the part of either in producing the deeds and documents would justify a decision of the tribunal fixing a reasonable time for their production. If that period elapses, and the tribunal has not granted an extension of time, the inexcusable delay shall be considered as equivalent to a relinquishment, by the party, of the right to produce the documents necessary for its defence, and the tribunal may then give its award according to the information contained in the deeds placed at its disposal, and which are readily accessible.

24. The Tribunal has the right to call for any kind of proof it may consider necessary, and for all deeds and papers which may be useful and necessary for guiding it to a judicial decision.

The Nullity or Suspension of the Reference.

25. The Reference (*compromis*) shall be considered invalid, if any of the particulars necessary to render it valid as an international treaty, are lacking.

26. The Reference (*compromis*) will remain without effect and be considered invalid, if the parties between whom it was concluded should settle the dispute by means of an unexpected agreement, or an amicable arrangement, or in any other way.

27. Similarly, the Reference (*compromis*) would be considered invalid, if the conditions are absent under which an arbitral jurisdiction might be voluntarily instituted by the parties. The chief instances are the following:—

(*a*) When the contention applies to various points, and the parties come to an agreement, as regards one or other of these, without declaring formally that they wish to retain the Agreement to refer (*compromis*) in respect of those still in dispute;

(*b*) When the parties have agreed in appointing arbitrators and tutti gli atti e documenti che da esso siano richiesti per l'istruzione della causa.

23. Il ritardo di una delle parti nel trasmettere gli atti e documenti potrà giustificare la decisione del tribunale arbitrale che fissi un termine ragionevole per la trasmissione di essi. Elasso tale termine, e qualora il tribunale stesso non abbia accordata una proroga, il ritardo ingi stificato sarà reputato di per se stesso equivalente a rinuncia della parte a trasmettere gli atti in sostegno delle sue pretesse, ed il tribunale dovrà giudicare allo stato degli atti esistenti e presentati, e di quelli ch'esso medesimo d'ufficio potrà richiamare ed ottenere.

24. Il tribunale arbitrale portrà decretare ogni mezzo di prova e tutti gli atti istruttorii che reputi utili od opportuni per decidere con illuminato giudizio.

Estinzione o sospensione del compromesso.

25. Il compromesso dovrà essere reputato nullo, se manchi dei requisiti richiesti per la validità di un trattato internazionale e che trovansi contemplati nel tit. I del Lib. II.

26. Il compromesso potrà rimanere senza effetto e reputarsi estinto, se le parti, fra le quali fu concluso, arrivino a comporre la lite, mediante accordo sopravvenuto. o mediante una transazione, o altrimenti.

27. Dovrà del pari ritenersi estinto il compromesso, se venissero a mancare le condizioni sotto le quali la giurisdizione arbitrale fu dalle parti volontariamente istituita. Questo dovrebbe ammettersi principalmente :

a) nel caso che la controversia concernesse diversi punti, e che le parti arrívassero a mettersi d'accordo intorno all'uno o all'alto di essi, e che non dichiarassero formalmente di volere lasciar sussistere il compromesso a riguardo di quelli tuttora disputati;

b) quando essendosi accordate le parti circa la nomina di persone individualmente designate come arbitri, nel corso del giudizio one of these, in the course of the proceedings, should become incapable, or die, or resign.

(*c*) When either of those appointed shall procure a substitute to discharge the functions specially intrusted to him.

28. The Reference must be considered suspended if one of the parties refuse to accept the arbitrator appointed by the other, if no agreement has been reached respecting the choice of another arbitrator, or (if it be established that the case of refusal ought to be held as well-founded in law) until another qualified arbitrator has been appointed.

REFUSAL TO ACCEPT AN APPOINTED ARBITRATOR.

29. An arbitrator appointed may be validly objected to :

(*a*) If he does not possess the necessary qualification, according to Rule 10 ;

(*b*) If it can be shown that he has an interest in the case ;

(*c*) If, when a Sovereign is appointed, it can be shown that an identical question in law would have to be decided in another case affecting his own interests and those of another State ;

(*d*) If the Sovereign appointed arbitrator had previously given his good offices to adjust the dispute, or had acted as mediator ;

(*e*) If, owing to the changed condition of affairs, it can be shown that he is no longer in a position to give an award with that impartiality which was contemplated when the appointment was made.

30. If the party, whose arbitrator has been objected to, does not wish to appoint another arbitrator, such an objection would invalidate the reference, and that would necessitate adhering strictly to Rule 16. The parties can, however, by a Special Reference (*compromis*) refer to the decision of an arbitrator the

una di esse fosse divenuta incapace, o fosse morta, o avesse rinunciato:

c) quando la persona nominata avesse delegato ad altri l'esercizio delle funzioni di arbitro ad essa confidate.

28. Il compromesso dovrà ritenersi sospeso se una delle parti abbia ricusato l'arbitro designato dall'altra, fino a tanto che le parti non si siano accordate sulla scelta di un altro arbitro, o (qualora sia stato deciso che l'istanza di ricusa debba ritenersi ben fondata in Diritto) finchè non sia stato designato un arbitro capace.

Della ricusazione dell'arbitro designato.

29. L'arbitro designato potrà essere validamente ricusato:

a) se non abbia i requisiti di capacità a norma della reg. 10;

b) quando possa essere stabilito e provato ch'egli abbia interesse nella controversia;

c) quando, essendo designato un Sovrano, sia stabilito e provato che una questione identica in Diritto debba essere decisa in un'altra lite vertente nell'interesse di lui e di un altro Stato;

d) quando il Sovrano nominato come arbitro abbia prestato i suoi buoni uffici per comporre la contesa, o abbia fatto da mediatore;

e) quando, per le mutate condizioni di cose, possa essere stabilito e provato che esso non possa più pronunciare la sentenza con quella imparzialità sulla quale si faceva da prima principale assegnamento.

30. Qualora la parte, contro della quale l'arbitro fu ricusato, non voglia nominare un altro arbitro, tale rifiuto infirmerebbe il compromesso e converrà attenersi a quanto trovasi stabilito alla regola 16. Potranno però le parti stesse, con speciale compromesso, deferire ad un arbitrato di giudicare sull'incidente del

incident of the objection, but they cannot allow the constituted tribunal itself to judge the admissibility of the objection, neither can such faculty be considered as confided to them by the Instrument of Reference (*compromis*).

Judgment of the Tribunal.

31. An arbitral tribunal is declared to be definitively constituted as soon as the members are appointed, have accepted the appointment, have come together in the place and on the day appointed for their meeting, and each has been recognised as qualified to fulfil the duties of an arbitrator.

32. Whenever an arbitral tribunal is composed of several judges, they must be considered as invested with the power of exercising the functions entrusted to them, and of enjoying all the rights belonging to a judicial tribunal.

33. If the parties have not come to an agreement regarding the place which should form the seat of the tribunal, that choice shall be determined by the majority of the appointed arbitrators, and the place selected shall be changed at the will of the majority, if they should recognise any impediments to the convenient discharge of their functions existing in the place chosen for its seat.

34. The arbitral tribunal, when constituted, shall proceed to the appointment of one of its number as President; and those persons would be most eligible for the honour who, in the capacity of secretary, or some similar post, had acquitted themselves creditably in the exercise of their own functions. The President shall follow the rules of procedure adopted by the parties themselves, or those settled according to Public Law.

35. If the parties have not in the Agreement (*compromis*), or by a subsequent convention, fixed the procedure which has to be

rifiuto, ma non potrà ammettersi che il tribunale arbitrale costituito potesse giudicare esso medesimo dell'ammissibilità del rifiuto, nè che tale facoltà possa ritenersi compresa tra quelle attribuite ad esso col compromesso.

Giudízio del Tribunale arbitrale.

31. Il tribunale arbitrale si dichiarerà costituito definitivamente appena che i membri nominati avendo accettato, siano intervenuti alla riunione nel luogo e nel giorno designati per la sua convocazione, e ciascuno dei nominati sia stato riconosciuto capace di esercitare le funzioni di arbitro.

32. Il tribunale arbitrale ogni qual volta che sia composto di più giudici, deve essere reputato investito del potere di esercitare le funzioni ad esso attribuite, valendosi di tutti i diritti che spettano ad un tribunale giudicante.

33. Qualora le parti stesse non si siano accordate, a riguardo del luogo, che debba essere sede del tribunale arbitrale, la designazione di tale luogo sarà fatta a decisione della maggioranza degli arbitri nominati, e la sede stabilita potrà essere mutata, a giudizio pure della maggioranza, quando vi sia fondato impedimento, da questa riconosciuto, di adempiere convenientemente le funzioni nella località scelta come sede.

34. Il tribunale arbitrale costituito procederà alla nomina del Presidente scegliendolo nel proprio seno, e potrà aggregarsi le persone, che, in qualità di segretari o altrimenti, siano reputate da esso indispensabili per l'esercizio delle proprie funzioni. Esso seguirà pel regolamento di procedura quello che sia stato provveduto dalle parti stesse, o che trovisi stabilito secondo il Diritto comune.

35. Se le parti non abbiano nel compromesso stesso o con convenzione susseguente stabilito d'accordo la procedura, che debba essere seguita dal tribunale arbitrale, e che non vi sieno norme di

followed by the tribunal, it is fully at liberty to determine its own procedure.

36. The tribunal shall give its decision without great or unjustifiable delay, and with a complete knowledge of the case; suitable periods must be fixed for the presentation of documents; reasonable time must be granted to the parties to prepare, without precipitation, the defence of their rights; they shall be allowed to present case and counter-case; and nothing shall be neglected which may prove useful in securing an honest, serious, and clear decision.

37. The arbitral tribunal must be considered competent to interpret the Arbitration Agreement (*compromis*); to decide regarding the admissibility, or inadmissibility, of certain means of proof, and to determine all that is incidental to the main question, and which has arisen in the course of the trial.

38. It is the duty of the arbitral tribunal to pronounce its judgments according to the principles of Public Law, and in applying these it will have the power to interpret the regulations fixed, taking account of the State documents in which they are specified and determined, of the law established by the tribunals which have interpreted the same rules judging analogous cases, and of the opinion of publicists. It will also be equally competent to interpret the principles of any particular law established between the contending States.

39. The tribunal will estimate the proofs according to its own convictions and discretion, will decide as to the confirmation of facts according to its independent estimate of the value of the documents produced, will consider the particular circumstances of the case, and weigh everything carefully according to the principles of natural equity.

Award of the Tribunal.

40. The arbitral tribunal cannot decline to pronounce a defini-

Diritto comune, potrà il tribunale medesimo determinare liberamente le norme del procedimento.

36. Incombe al tribunale decidere la controversia senza grande ed ingiustificato ritardo e con perfetta cognizione di causa. E dovrà assegnare termini convenienti per la presentazione dei documenti: concedere alle parti un tempo ragionevole per preparare senza precipitazione la difesa dei loro diritti; ammetterle a presentare memorie e contromemorie; e non trascurare quanto possa riuscire utile per decidere con retto, serio ed illuminato giudizio.

37. Dovrà reputarsi di competenza del tribunale arbitrale l'interpretare il compromesso; il decidere circa l'ammissibilità o inammissibilità di certi mezzi di prova, e risolvere tutti gli incidenti, che possano concernere la questione principale e che siano sollevati nel corso del giudizio.

38. Incombe al tribunale arbitrale giudicare, secondo i principii del Diritto comune (*Confr. regole* 6, 7); e nell'applicarlo, potrà interpretare le regole fissate, tenendo conto dei documenti di Stato, nei quali il concetto di esse trovasi precisato e determinato; della giurisprudenza stabilita dai tribunali che abbiano interpretate le stesse regole giudicando casi analoghi; e dell'opinione dei pubblicisti. Esso sarà competente del pari ad interpretare i principii di Diritto particolare stabilito tra gli Stati contendenti.

39. Il tribunale valuterà le prove secondo le sue convinzioni ed il suo prudente arbitrio, e deciderà circa l'accertamento dei fatti, secondo il suo libero apprezzamento, circa la valutazione dei documenti prodotti, ed apprezzerà le particolari circostanze del caso, ponderandole accuratamente secondo i principii di equità naturale.

Norme per pronunziare la sentenza.

40. Il tribunale arbitrale non potrà rifiutarsi di pronunziare la

tive sentence on all points of the contention submitted for decision.

It cannot defer to an indefinite time, and beyond a reasonable limit, the pronunciation of the sentence, under pretext of not having been sufficiently enlightened either as to the questions of fact, or as to the juridical principles which they should apply.

41. If the parties have fixed the period within which the arbitrators shall give their award, such period shall date from the day on which the tribunal was definitely constituted in accordance with Rule 31.

They shall, however, consider themselves competent to decide whether they will be able to give their award within the fixed term, and if they cannot, they will fix the briefest period within which they can do so, and they will notify this in a provisional award to the parties interested; should such notification be accepted by them without comment, the period fixed in the Agreement (*compromis*) shall be considered legally extended according to the notification of the provisional award.

42. The tribunal may decide that, with the provisional award, an equitable proposal may be made to the parties with the design of promoting agreement, or of arriving at an amicable settlement. The refusal of such a proposal would not justify the suspension of its functions, but it will still be under obligation to settle the difference and to give a definite decision.

43. Every decision, whether provisional or definitive, shall be made by the majority of all the appointed arbitrators, and they must take part in voting, excepting in case of *force majeure*.

44. The excusable absence of one of the appointed arbitrators would authorise the tribunal to defer its decision, if the reason for his absence be only temporary. If, however, it is likely to be

sentenza definitiva su tutti i punti di controversia sottoposti alla sua decisione.

Esso non potrà ritardare a tempo indefinito e oltre un termine ragionevole la pronunziazione della sentenza col pretesto di non essere sufficientemente illuminato circa le questioni di fatto o circa i principii giuridici, che dovrebbe applicare.

41. Qualora le parti stesse avessero fissato il termine entro cui gli arbitri dovessero pronunciare la sentenza, tale termine non comincerebbe a decorrere, se non dal giorno in cui il tribunale dovesse ritenersi definitivamente costituito a norma della reg. 31.

Dovrà però ritenersi competente esso medesimo a decidere nel suo seno se possa pronunciare la sentenza nel termine fissato, e in caso di negativa fisserà il termine più breve entro cui potrà pronunciare la sua sentenza definitiva, e notificherà tale sua sentenza provvisionale alle parti interessate; e qualora fosse da esse accettata tale notificazione senza osservazioni, il termine fissato nel compromesso dovrà ritenersi legalmente protratto a norma di quanto sia stato stabilito con la sentenza provvisoria notificata.

42. Il tribunale arbitrale potrà decidere con sentenza provvisoria che sia fatta alle parti qualche proposta equa coll'intendimento di provocare fra di esse l'accordo o di arrivare ad una transazione. Il rifiuto di tali proposte non potrebbe giustificare la sospensione delle sue funzioni, esso sarà bensì sempre tenuto a risolvere la controversia e a decidere definitivamente la lite.

43. Ogni decisione sia essa provvisoria o definitiva, sarà presa a maggioranza di tutti gli arbitri nominati ed incombe a ciascuno di essi l'intervenire al momento della votazione, salvo il caso di forza maggiore.

44. L'assenza giustificata di uno degli arbitri nominati autorzzerà il tribunale a differire la sua decisione, se la causa che avesse cagionato l'assenza potesse venire a cessare. Qualora essa fosse

permanent, or of long duration, the tribunal must adhere to the original regulation respecting the choice of an arbitrator, by replacing the absent arbitrator, and providing anew for its regular constitution.

45. If, on the contrary, the absence of the arbitrator, at the moment of taking the vote, was due to a resolution adopted, or to an intrigue, the tribunal must decide, by a majority of those present, the suitable method to be taken in order to obviate the inconvenience, and to place itself in a position to fulfil its functions and to give its award.

46. If the methods adopted by the tribunal should prove ineffective, and the fact transpire that it was due to the connivance of an interested Government, for the purpose of placing an obstăcle in the way of pronouncing a definite award, such disloyal proceeding will be considered as in opposition to the principles of international law, and will justify an appeal to the Conference, as in the case of an arbitrary refusal to submit to arbitral jurisdiction.

47. It is incumbent on each of the arbitrators present at the moment of voting an award, to append his signature. Should, however, a dissenting arbitrator refuse to do so, the sentence will be valid, provided it be signed by the majority, and provided they sign a declaration to the effect that the arbitrator who dissented was present at the time of voting, and that he had refused to sign the decision arrived at by the majority.

48. The arbitral sentence must be given in writing, and must contain the reasons of fact and law and the definite provisions relating to the contested points, which formed the subject of the decision.

Validity of the Award.

49. The award of the arbitrators shall be regarded as final, and as a complete settlement of the dispute submitted for Arbitration.

permanente o duratura bisognerà attenersi alle regole innanzi stabilite per la scelta degli arbitri a fine di surrogare l'arbitro assente e provvedere alla regolare costituzione del tribunale.

45. Laddove l'assenza di un arbitro, nel momento in cui si dovasse pronunciare la sentenza, fosse l'effetto di un partito preso o di un intrigo, spetterà al tribunale di deliberare a maggioranza dei presenti circa i provvedimenti adatti ad ovviare all'inconveniente, onde porter essere in condizione di espletare le proprie funzioni pronunziando la sentenza.

46. Qualora i provvedimenti decretati dal tribunale riuscissero inefficaci, e vi fosse fondata presunzione di connivenza da parte del Governo interessato, col proposito di mettere cosi un ostacolo alla pronunziazione della sentenza definitiva, tale procedimento sleale sarà qualificato in opposizione ai principii del Diritto internazionale, e potrà motivare l'appello alla Conferenza, così come nel caso di arbitrario refiuto di sottostare alla giurisdizione arbitrale.

47. Incombe a ciascuno degli arbitri presenti al momento della votazione della sentenza, il sottoscriverla. Qualora però un arbitro dissenziente rifiutasse di far ciò, la sentenza sarà valida, purchè sottoscritta dalla maggioranza, e purchè questa medesima sottoscriva la dichiarazione che l'arbitro che dissentiva era presente al momento della votazione, e che aveva rifiutato di sottoscrivere la decisione presa a maggioranza.

48. La sentenza arbitrale deve essere redatta in iscritto e dovrà contenere i motivi in fatto e in diritto e le disposizioni definitive relative ai punti contestati, che abbiano formato oggetto della decisione.

Efficacia della sentenza.

49. La sentenza degli arbitri dovrà essere riguardata come definitiva e come soluzione compiuta della controversia sottoposta all'arbitrato.

It will be notified to both parties by the tribunal itself which has pronounced it, and its notification shall be considered legally made and completed, when an authentic copy thereof, containing the grounds and reasons of the decision, has been delivered to the representative of each of the parties and such delivery has been entered in the minutes.

50. The text of the award, together with all the documents and deeds relating to the case, shall be deposited in the archives of a neutral State, and publicity shall be given to the fact that this has been done, and also particulars of all documents, which will be enumerated in an annexed note.

51. The notification of the award places the contending parties under the obligation of recognising its judicial authority and of loyally carrying out all that the tribunal has decided, and that without any reserve or restriction.

52. If the award has imposed an obligation which weighs upon the finances, or if it otherwise requires legislative provisions before it can be executed, it shall nevertheless be valid in respect of the State involved, and its authority shall not be subordinated to the condition of approval or ratification on the part of the legislative powers of the said State.

53. The State which has formally refused to execute an arbitral award, or which, in effect, when requested by the other party, has not taken note of, or executed, its provisions, will be held answerable for such a proceeding, the non-observance of an award given by an arbitral tribunal being generally considered an arbitrary act, and in opposition to the principles of international law.

54. The proceeding of a State, which does not loyally execute the award of an arbitral tribunal, can be justified only in the single case of an appeal being made to the Conference, and of its recognising that, in some respect or other, the award might be considered null and void, or that through the intervention of some

Essa sarà notificata all'una ed all'altra parte a cura del tribunale stesso, che l'abbia proferita, e la sua notificazione sarà reputata legalmente fatta e compiuta, allorchè una copia autentica della medesima, contenente i motivi e le disposizioni, sia stata consegnata al rappresentante di ciascuna delle parti e di tale consegna sia stato redatto processo verbale.

50. Il testo della sentenza e tutti i documenti e gli atti del giudizio, saranno depositati negli archivi di Stato di un paese neutrale, e sarà data pubblicità a quanto concerna l'eseguito deposito della stessa e di tutti i documenti relativi che saranno enumerati in una nota annessa.

51. La notificazione della sentenza impone all'una ed all'altra delle parti contendenti di riconoscere nella decisione del tribunale l'autorità di giudicato e di osservare ed eseguire lealmente quanto mediante essa sia stato deciso, e senza alcuna riserva o restrizione.

52. Qualora la sentenza abbia imposto un onere, che graviti sulla finanza, o che altrimenti esiga provvedimenti legislativi onde adempirvi, essa sarà nondimeno efficace rispetto allo Stato gravato, e l'autorità sua come giudicato non potrà essere subordinata alla condizione della approvazione o della ratifica da parte del potere legislativo dello Stato stesso.

53. Lo Stato, il quale rifiutasse formalmente di eseguire la sentenza arbitrale, o che, di fatto, richiesto dall'altra parte non osservasse e non eseguisse quanto con la stessa fosse stato disposto, sarà tenuto a rispondere di tale suo procedimento, dovendo in massima presumersi l'inosservanza di una sentenza resa da un tribunale arbitrale un fatto arbitrario, e in opposizione coi principii del Diritto internazionale.

54. Il procedimento da parte di uno Stato, che non eseguisca lealmente la sentenza del tribunale arbitrale potrà essere giustificato nel solo caso che si facesse appello alla Conferenza e che questa riconosca la sentenza affetta da qualche vizio di nullità, o quando riconosca, che per le sopravvenute impreviste circostanze

unforeseen circumstances, it cannot be executed, or that its execution should be suspended either in part or altogether.

Grounds of the Nullity of an Arbitral Award.

55. An arbitral sentence will be considered invalid:—

(*a*) If the decision be not made by the voting, and in the presence of, all the appointed arbitrators;

(*b*) If the grounds of fact and of law are altogether absent;

(*c*) If its terms are contradictory;

(*d*) If it be not delivered in writing, and signed by all the arbitrators, or if the missing signature of one of them is not accompanied by a minute, recording the fact that the arbitrator who has not signed, was present at the voting, and took part in the decision.

56. An arbitral sentence may be disputed by the party which refuses to execute it, and may be annulled:—

(*a*) If the arbitrators have gone beyond the limits of the Reference (*compromis*), or has been nullified, or might be considered extinct;

(*b*) If it had been given by persons who had not the legal or moral qualification to be arbitrators, or had lost such qualification in the course of the trial, or by an arbitrator who could not legally act as substitute for another;

(*c*) When founded upon error, or obtained by fraud;

(*d*) When the forms of procedure stipulated in the Agreement (*compromis*) under penalty of nullity, or those established by Public Law, or those which must be considered indispensable, because required by the very nature of an arbitral judgment, have not been observed.

57. The question of taking action for annulling an arbitral sentence must be referred to the Conference, either at the

essa debba essere reputata ineseguibile, o che ne debba essere sospesa in tutto o in parte l'esecuzione.

Motivi di nullità di una sentenza arbitrale

55. La sentenza arbitrale sarà reputata nulla:

a) se la decisione non sia stata votata coll'intervento e la presenza di tutti gli arbitri nominati;

b) se manchi del tutto di motivi in fatto e in diritto;

c) se il dispositivo sia contraddittorio;

d) se non sia stata redatta in iscritto e sottoscritta da tutti gli arbitri, o se la mancata sottoscrizione di uno di essi non resulti da processo verbale, che constati l'intervento dell'arbitro che non sottoscrisse e la sua presenza al momento della decisione e della votazione.

56. La sentenza arbitrale potrà essere impugnata dalla parte che rifiuti di eseguirla e potrà essere annullata:

a) se gli arbitri avessero pronunciato fuori dei limiti del compromesso, ovvero sopra un compromesso nullo o che dovesse reputarsi estinto;

b) se fosse stata pronunciata da persona, che non avesse la capacità legale o morale per essere arbitro, o che avesse perduta tale capacità nel corso del giudizio, o da un arbitro che non potesse legalmente surrogare un altro assente;

c) quando fosse fondata sull'errore, o estorta con dolo;

d) quando le forme procedurali stipulate nel compromesso sotto pena di nullità, o quelle che fossero stabilite per Diritto comune, o quelle che secondo questo devono reputarsi indispensabili, perchè richieste dalla natura del giudizio arbitrale, non fossero state osservate.

57. Il giudizio intorno all'azione di annullamento di una sentenza arbitrale dovrà essere deferito alla Conferenza o sulla

instance of that party which began by calling the award in question, and based upon that reason its refusal to carry it into execution; or at the instance of the other party, which desires to obtain compulsory powers in order to make it execute what has been decided.

58. The Conference will judge the reasons adduced as the grounds of the nullity, and should it not recognise such reasons as valid, and therefore reject the appeal, it may itself adopt the coercive means by which the opposite party may be compelled to execute whatever was determined by the award.

59. The Conference may also declare the execution of the award suspended owing to a change of circumstances, as in the case of the suspension of a treaty.

60. The State which does not observe what the Conference has decided, in regard to the execution, nullity, or suspension, of an arbitral award, will subject itself to the procedure established by Rules 1054, 1055 (which refer to the procedure of the Conference).

istanza della parte stessa, che in via principale impugni la sentenza fondando su tale motivo il suo rifiuto di eseguirla, o sulla istanza dell'altra parte, che voglia ottenere il contringimento forzato, onde far eseguire quanto fu deciso.

58. La Conferenza giudicherà sui motivi dedotti a fondamento della nullità, e qualora essa non riconosca tali motivi esistenti e rigetti l'istanza di annullamento, potrà essa stessa decretare i mezzi coercitivi per costringere la parte opponente ad osservare e ad eseguire quanto con la sentenza sia stato disposto.

59. La Conferenza potrà inoltre dichiarare sospesa l'esecuzione della sentenza per le mutate sopravvenute circostanze così come per la sospensione di un trattato.

60. Lo Stato, che non osservasse quanto la Conferenza avesse deciso circa l'esecuzione, l'annullamento o la sospensione della sentenza arbitrale sará assoggettato al procedimento stabilito alle regole 1054, 1055.

ARBITRATION TRIBUNALS.

An Exposition.

By W. Evans Darby, LL.D.,

Secretary of the Peace Society.

1. Arbitration tribunals may be special or general, temporary or permanent, and (in the case of the last) restricted or open to all. In either case the mode of their creation is the same.

2. It is essential to Arbitration that contending States should formally agree to refer their difference to an independent tribunal, and should bind themselves to abide by its award.

3. It is also necessary that the persons, or the States, chosen to form the tribunal should formally accord their consent, and accept the obligation to proceed with the enquiry and to give their award.

4. Accordingly, the reference to Arbitration is made by a special agreement (*compromis*), which is signed on behalf of the contending parties; which expressly states the question or questions to be submitted, giving a summary of the points of fact or law involved, defining the limits of the Arbitration, and, in some instances, indicating the course of procedure; and which, except in cases of material error or flagrant injustice, implies their engagement to submit in good faith to the award.

5. This Agreement may result, either from a general Treaty, a special (*i.e.* an Arbitration) Treaty, an arbitral clause inserted in a Treaty, or a Protocol of an International Congress to which the concurring States may have been parties.

TRIBUNAUX D'ARBITRAGES.

UN EXPOSÉ DE

M. W. EVANS DARBY

Docteur en Droit, Secrétaire de la "Peace Society."

1. L'arbitrage international est spécial ou général, occasionnel ou permanent, et dans ce cas, ouvert ou clos. Dans tous les cas, l'arbitrage est institué par une convention.

2. Pour constituer l'arbitrage il est essentiel que les Etats qui ont un sujet de contestation entre eux s'accordent préalablement à en déférer la décision à un tribunal étranger, au jugement duquel ils s'engagent à se conformer.

3. Il est nécessaire, en outre, que les personnes ou les Etats, choisis pour former ce tribunal, donnent leur consentement à en faire partie, à procéder à l'instruction du litige et à rendre jugement.

4. Or, les parties en présence signent un compromis, c'est-à-dire une convention spéciale, précisant nettement la question ou les questions à débattre, exposant l'ensemble des points de fait ou de droit qui s'y rattachent, traçant les limites du rôle dévolu à l'arbitre, et dans quelques instances, déterminant la procédure qui sera observée au cours de l'arbitrage, et, sauf les cas d'erreur matérielle ou d'injustice flagrante, impliquant l'engagement de se soumettre de bonne foi à la décision qui pourra intervenir.

5. Ce compromis peut résulter, soit d'un traité général ou spécial (dit traité d'arbitrage), soit d'une clause (dite compromissoire) insérée dans un traité, ou dans un protocole de congrès international auquel les mêmes Etats aient adhéré.

6. The Agreement is valid when it has been ratified by the chiefs of the signatory States in the conditions and forms required by their respective laws and, if necessary, by the Treaties which limit their liberty in regard to other States.

7. It is usual, in appointing an Arbitration tribunal, to fix, in the agreement, a period, counting from the date of its installation, during which it shall examine and decide upon the questions submitted to it for adjudication. It is, also, usual to fix a period for the Treaty to remain in force, reckoning from the date when it shall come into operation, and to agree that unless either of the parties to the Treaty shall have given notice to the other of a wish for its termination, it shall continue in force for another similar period, and so on.

8. Special Arbitration tribunals (*ad hoc*) may consist of one or more judges, who may be Princes, Sovereign Governments, Corporations, or individuals of repute and recognised fitness: where more than one are chosen, an umpire (*sur-arbitre*) is generally appointed, by agreement, in order to secure a definite award.

9. A permanent tribunal may be formed by the nomination of a given number of members by each of the concurring States, as agreed upon between themselves. These may not necessarily be jurists by profession, but statesmen, diplomatists, men who have filled judicial offices, publicists, or other persons of high reputation and standing. Ultimately these may be drawn from a recognised Corps, College, or Council.

10. Such a tribunal may be formed by any group of States, even two only, for international affairs relating to themselves. In case of doubt an Agreement providing for a permanent tribunal shall be considered as unrestricted (see No. 1.), *i.e.* any nation may accede to it by a simple declaration of its will.

11. Where the course of procedure is not prescribed in the Agreement, it is understood that the tribunal will determine it for

6. Le compromis est valide lorsqu'il a été ratifié par les chefs des Etats signataires dans les conditions et dans les formes requises par leurs lois respectives, et, s'il est nécessaire, par les traités qui limitent leur liberté vis-à-vis d'autres Etats.

7. Il est d'usage, en constituant un tribunal d'arbitrage, qu'on fixe dans le compromis le délai, compté du jour où il sera déclaré installé, pendant lequel il examinera et décidera sur les questions soumises pour son adjudication. Il est aussi d'usage qu'on fixe la période pendant laquelle le traité restera en vigueur, à partir du jour où il en sera fait application, et qu'on s'accorde qu'il continuera pour une nouvelle période, si le traité n'est pas dénoncé par une des parties avant la date de l'échéance ; et ainsi de suite.

8. Un tribunal spécial *(ad hoc)* peut consister en un seul ou plusieurs juges, qui peuvent être des princes, des gouvernements souverains, des corporations, ou de simples particuliers de bonne réputation et position. Quand il y en a plusieurs choisis, on nomme, en général, un sur-arbitre, d'un commun accord, afin d'arriver à une sentence définie.

9. Un tribunal permanent peut être constitué par la nomination d'une ou plusieurs personnes par chaque Etat signataire, suivant les dispositions du compromis. Ces membres ne seront pas nécessairement juristes de vocation, mais aussi hommes d'Etat, diplomates, publicistes ou autres hommes, citoyens les plus considérés. Plus tard, on les choisira d'un corps reconnu, collège ou conseil.

10. La création du tribunal résulterait de la convention arrêtée entre deux ou plusieurs Etats de recourir à l'arbitrage pour tout différend surgissant entre eux. Dans le doute, une convention d'arbitrage permanent sera considérée comme ouverte ; c'est-à-dire que toute nation peut y accéder par une simple manifestation de sa volonté.

11. A défaut de stipulations spéciales, le tribunal établira lui-

itself; and in any case where doubts arise as to the scope of the reference, the terms of the Agreement must be interpreted in the widest sense.

12. The establishment of a permanent international tribunal of Arbitration presupposes the possibility of framing its constitution, jurisdiction, and procedure on a basis which will secure impartiality of enquiry and decision on every question submitted to it.

13. The Arbitration tribunal, when constituted, forms an independent body, having a distinct judicial authority; it is, therefore, not bound by the previous decrees of any other tribunal, on the questions submitted to its jurisdiction; and, although nominated by Governments, its members are in no sense to be regarded as the representatives, subjects or mouthpieces of Governments.

14. It should be treated as a diplomatic mission of the first rank, both as to the honours to be paid to its members, the immunities which they enjoy, and the protection afforded to them in the exercise of their functions.

15. The members of a permanent tribunal, in order to secure their absolute independence, should be appointed for life or for a sufficiently long period; they should be absolved from all political allegiance, while in office; they should be provided with adequate salaries and retiring pensions, and assured of a social rank sufficient to satisfy the requirements of their office.

16. At the commencement of each year the members of the tribunal should, by ballot, elect one of their number to act as President.

17. The tribunal should also appoint a Chief Secretary, who shall be the only recognised official medium of communication, and who should rank on a footing of equality with the principal Secretaries of State of all nations.

même sa procédure. Toutefois, dans le doute sur la portée du litige, l'interprétation la moins stricte doit prévaloir.

12. La création d'un tribunal international permanent d'arbitrage présuppose la possibilité d'établir sa constitution, sa juridiction et sa procédure en manière d'assurer l'impartialité d'investigation et de décision sur tous les points en litige.

13. Le tribunal arbitral, une fois constitué, est un corps indépendant, ayant une autorité judiciaire. Les arbitres ne sont pas liés par les arrêts précédents d'un autre tribunal quelconque, sur les questions qui leur sont proposées. Bien que nommés par les gouvernements, les membres du tribunal ne pourront pas être considérés comme leurs représentants ou leurs instruments.

14. Le tribunal doit être traité comme une mission diplomatique de premier rang, soit quant aux honneurs qui lui sont dûs, et aux immunités et la protection dont jouissent ses membres dans l'exercice de leurs fonctions.

15. Pour assurer l'indépendance absolue du tribunal on donnera aux fonctions de ses membres une durée suffisante ; on les dégagera de toute attache avec un Etat quelconque pendant qu'ils seront en office ; on leur assurera des salaires et des pensions libérales, et on leur donnera un rang qui satisfasse à tous les besoins de leur office.

16. La cour élit, au scrutin secret, dans son sein, un président, pour une durée d'une année.

17. La cour nomme aussi un chef-secrétaire qui, seul, pourra entretenir des relations avec des gouvernements, etc. Il sera mis sur le même rang que les principaux secrétaires d'Etat de toutes les nations.

18. If the place of meeting be not designated in the Agreement, it should be decided by a majority of the members of the tribunal, and should be situated on neutral territory.

19. At their first meetings, the members should take the necessary steps for the constitution of the tribunal by the election of the requisite officers and servants, and for the proper conduct of its business, according to the rules of procedure, which may be already established, or which it shall determine for itself.

20. The tribunal shall further keep a record of its proceedings and also a register, in which shall be entered the procedure followed, the demands of the claimants, and the awards and decisions rendered.

21. The proceedings of the tribunal must be conducted according to the recognised rules of judicial procedure, subject only to the special provisions made by the tribunal for its own guidance.

22. One of the first duties of the tribunal should be to frame a code of procedure providing for the mode in which disputes and differences between nations should be submitted to it, and especially such a procedure in regard to the particular case to be adjudicated upon, as shall secure the presentment and development of distinct and clear issues upon which its judgment is sought.

23. The rules of procedure approved by the tribunal cannot be modified or annulled except with the consent of all parties, if they were fixed in the Arbitration Agreement, or with the consent of the majority of the members if they were framed by the tribunal itself. The interpretation of these rules, or additions to them, may always be decided by a simple majority of votes.

24. The periods of time fixed by the tribunal may be prolonged

18. A défaut de stipulation spéciale, le tribunal choisira l'endroit où il doit siéger, par une majorité des voix

19. Les arbitres, dans leurs premières réunions, nomment les officiers et les facteurs nécessaires : ils décideront sur la direction des affaires du tribunal, selon la procédure déjà établie, ou qui sera établie par le tribunal.

20. Le tribunal tiendra parmi ses archives les procès-verbaux des séances et aussi un livre d'enregistrement dans lequel on inscrira la procédure suivie, les demandes des réclamants et les jugements et décisions rendus.

21. Le tribunal arbitral établit lui-même la procédure à suivre, en appliquant autant que possible les règles de la procédure ordinaire.

22. Le premier devoir du tribunal sera d'élaborer un code de procédure fixant la manière en laquelle les différends entre nations doivent lui être soumis et particulièrement telle procédure dans la contestation à juger, qui assurera la présentation et le développement de questions distinctes et claires sur lesquelles un jugement est désiré.

23. Les règles de procédure approuvées par le tribunal ne peuvent être modifiées ou abrogées, si ce n'est avec le consentement de toutes les parties, si elles étaient établies dans la convention d'arbitrage, ou avec le consentement de la majorité des arbitres, si elles étaient leur œuvre. Le tribunal pourra, toutefois, à la simple majorité des voix, interpréter ces règles ou les développer par d'autres.

24. Les délais établis par le tribunal pourront être prolongé

by it, provided that all the parties be admitted to profit by the extension in an equal degree.

25. Members of the tribunal may not be represented by substitutes; all vacancies shall be filled up as in the first appointment, provision being made in the Agreement for the appointment by the respective States, parties to the Agreement, of new members to fill the place of those who may cease to be members by retirement or death.

26. A submission to Arbitration is determined by the expiration of the period of time fixed by the Agreement, by the conclusion between the parties themselves of a direct arrangement, or, finally, by the delivery of the award, which should be given within the time fixed in the Agreement.

27. The intervention of a third party is not admissible, except with the consent of the parties in the case. But on the settlement of the issues, the tribunal should possess the power to permit the intervention of third parties on due and sufficient cause being shown that their interests are affected, or likely to be affected, by any decision the tribunal may arrive at, and on its decision on the main issue between the original parties to the dispute, the tribunal should be empowered to make such terms as regards such intervening parties as will safeguard their interests.

28. Cross claims may not be brought before the tribunal unless they have been submitted to it by the Agreement, or the parties concur in submitting them to its decision.

29. The tribunal may, before giving a formal award, and at any convenient point, make equitable propositions to the contending parties with a view to settlement, it being understood that such proposals have no judicial character.

30. The award must be in conformity with the principles of existing International Law, as established between, or accepted

par lui-même, à condition que toutes les parties soient admises à en profiter en mesure égale.

25. Les arbitres ne peuvent être substitués ; pour remplacer les arbitres, on doit observer les formes et les conditions adoptées pour leur nomination ; il sera pourvu dans le compromis que de nouveaux membres soient choisis par les Etats, parties au compromis, pour remplacer les arbitres empêchés de remplir leurs fonctions par suite de décès ou de résiliation.

26. L'arbitrage prend fin, soit à l'expiration du délai stipulé dans le compromis, soit par la conclusion entre les parties en cause d'un arrangement direct, soit enfin par le prononcé de la sentence, qui doit être rendue dans le délai fixé par le compromis.

27. L'intervention d'un tiers n'est admissible qu'avec le consentement des parties en cause. Mais dans ses exposés, le tribunal peut permettre l'intervention de tierces parties lorsqu'il est évident pour lui que leurs intérêts sont ou seront vraisemblablement mis en cause par le jugement qui sera rendu, et, dans la décision sur la partie essentielle du litige entre les litigants primitifs, il a le droit de faire des stipulations en vue de sauvegarder les intérêts des intervenants.

28. Les demandes reconventionnelles ne peuvent être portées devant le tribunal que si elles lui sont déférées par le compromis, ou que les parties sont d'accord pour les soumettre à sa décision.

29. Le tribunal arbitral peut, avant de rendre sa sentence, et lorsqu'il le croit utile, faire aux parties des propositions équitables dans le but d'arriver à une transaction ; mais il est bien entendu qu'il agit en dehors de ses fonctions proprement dites.

30. Les arbitres, pour prononcer leur sentence, doivent se conformer aux principes du droit international existant, tel qu'il

by, the contending parties; with general International Law, or, in other instances, with that National Law which appears applicable according to the precepts of International Law.

31. The award must be given by a majority of votes, unless it is expressly stipulated in the Agreement that unanimity is indispensable; whether this majority shall be relative or absolute is a point to be settled by the tribunal itself, the whole of which is bound by the majority.

32. The award should be made in the form of a written document, prepared in duplicate, and formally delivered to the Agents of the parties affected thereby.

33. The points submitted to Arbitration, once the decision has been formally given, cannot be reconsidered without a new Agreement.

34. The Award is obligatory and without appeal; but its execution does not lie within the functions of the tribunal, that being a matter for the contending parties alone.

35. The decision of the tribunal, however, has for the contending parties the effect of a regular transaction, and binds them for the same reasons and on the same conditions as Treaties. They are, therefore, honourably to execute it as they would a Treaty by which they themselves had settled their respective rights as the Arbitrators have done for them.

36. But its reconsideration by the same tribunal may be demanded if the judgment has been based upon any erroneous or false document, or is the result of an error arising in the course of the trial.

37. An arbitral decision may be disregarded in the following cases:—

1. When the tribunal has clearly exceeded the powers given to it by the instrument of submission.

est établi entre les parties par les traités ou la coutume ; le droit international général ; et aux points en litige d'une autre nature, le droit national qui paraît applicable d'après les préceptes du droit international.

31. Le jugement doit être rendu à la majorité des voix, à moins que, dans les conditions de l'arbitrage, on n'ait expressément déterminé que l'unanimité serait indispensable.

Le tribunal décidera si la majorité doit être relative ou absolue. La majorité lie le tribunal entier.

32. La décision sera rendue sous la forme de sentence écrite, en double exemplaire ; ceux-ci seront remis aux mandataires des parties.

33. On ne pourra pas admettre de demandes de correction ou de revision de la sentence sans une nouvelle convention.

34. La sentence est obligatoire et sans appel, mais les arbitres ne peuvent disposer d'aucun moyen pour contraindre les parties à s'y conformer. L'exécution de la sentence sera l'affaire des parties contestantes.

35. La décision des arbitres a pour les parties les effets d'une transaction régulière, et elle les oblige par les mêmes raisons et aux mêmes conditions que les traités ; elles sont tenues de l'exécuter comme elles feraient d'un traité par lequel elles régleraient leurs droits respectifs comme l'ont fait les arbitres.

36. Mais il est reconnu le droit d'en demander la revision devant le même tribunal, si on a jugé sur un document faux ou erroné, ou si la sentence a été l'effet d'une erreur quelconque dans le procès.

37. La sentence arbitrale est nulle dans les cas suivants :

1. Lorsque le tribunal a éprouvé un excès de pouvoir ;

2. When it is guilty of an open denial of justice.
3. When its award is proved to have been obtained by fraud or corruption.
4. And when the terms of the award are equivocal.
5. Some authorities add that the decision may also be disregarded if it is absolutely contrary to the rules of justice or International Law.

38. The cost of maintaining the tribunal shall be borne *pro ratâ* by the States concurring in its organisation. The cost of any particular reference to Arbitration shall be borne by the contending parties in equal shares; unless the award includes the payment of costs.

39. A permanent tribunal, besides hearing and deciding judicially matters in difference, should be empowered, at the instance of any two or more nations, to express an extra-judicial opinion on any question of law or interpretation of Treaties, with the object of preventing differences arising in the future.

40. It should also be ready, in view of conferences or congresses of Sovereigns and Statesmen, to suggest modifications and alterations with reference to International Law on points of difference which remain unsettled, and on which conflict of opinion may exist.

2. Lorsque la teneur de la sentence est absolument contraire aux règles de la justice ;
3. Lorsque la sentence a été obtenue par fraude ou corruption ;
4. Lorsque les termes de la sentence sont équivoques ;
5. Selon quelques autorités : lorsque la sentence est absolument contraire aux règles de justice ou de droit international.

38. Chacun des Etats contractants contribuera, dans des proportions à déterminer, aux frais du tribunal. Les frais de chaque procédure seront supportés par chacune des nations litigantes, par parts égales, à moins que le jugement ne comprenne le paiement des frais.

39. Outre le devoir de trancher par voie juridique les litiges qui lui sont soumis, le tribunal aura celui d'exprimer, sur la demande de deux ou plusieurs nations, son opinion sur des questions de droit ou sur l'interprétation de traités, en vue de prévenir des litiges dans l'avenir.

40. Il devra aussi se préparer à faire des propositions aux conférences ou congrès de souverains et d'hommes d'Etat, pour des modifications aux lois internationales sur des points qui n'ont pas encore été réglés, et sur lesquels les opinions diffèrent.

RULES RELATING TO A TREATY OF INTERNATIONAL ARBITRATION.

Prepared by the Special Committee of the International Law Association, appointed in London 10th October, 1893, and revised by the Conference at Brussels, 1st and 2nd October, 1895.

1. Unless it be intended that all possible differences between the nations, parties to the Treaty, are to be referred to Arbitration, the class of differences to be referred must be defined.

2. If the Agreement for Arbitration does not specify the number and names of the Arbitrators, the Tribunal of Arbitration shall be constituted according to rules prescribed by that Agreement or by another Convention.

3. If the Tribunal is to be specially constituted, the place ot meeting must be fixed. This should be outside the territories of the parties to the controversy.

4. If the Tribunal consists of more than two members, provision should be made for the decision of all questions by a majority of the Arbitrators; but the dissentient members should have the right of recording their dissent.

5. Each party should be required to appoint an agent to represent it in all matters connected with the Arbitration.

6. The Treaty should provide that if doubts arise as to whether a given subject of controversy be comprised among those agreed upon as subjects of Arbitration in it, and if one of the parties require the doubt to be settled by Arbitration, the other party must submit to such Arbitration, but may require that the judgment be limited to the admissibility of the demand for Arbitration.

7. Unless the Treaty otherwise provide, the procedure should be by case, counter-case, and printed argument, each delivered by both parties simultaneously at a fixed date, with final oral argument. The periods of time allowed for the delivery of cases, counter-cases, and printed arguments should be fixed by the Treaty, but the Tribunal should have the power of extending the time. The Tribunal itself should fix the time for hearing th oral argument.

RÈGLES POUR SERVIR À L'ÉLABORATION D'UN TRAITÉ D'ARBITRAGE INTERNATIONAL

Etablie par un Comité Spécial de l'Association de Droit International constitué à Londres le 10me *Octobre* 1893, *revisées par le Congrès de Bruxelles le* 1er *et* 2me *Octobre* 1895.

1. La nature des contestations qui seront soumises à l'arbitrage, devra être déterminée, à moins toutefois qu'il ne soit convenu entre les nations, parties au traité, que toute contestation, quelle qu'elle soit, surgissant entre elles, relèvera du tribunal arbitral.

2. A défaut de désignation, dans le compromis, du nombre et des noms des arbitres, le tribunal arbitral sera composé selon les prescriptions du compromis ou d'une autre convention.

3. Si un tribunal spécial doit être constitué, le lieu de sa réunion sera fixé en dehors du territoire des nations en cause.

4. Au cas où le tribunal comprendrait plus de deux membres, des dispositions spéciales devront être prises pour que la décision de toutes les questions soient tranchées à la majorité des arbitres. Mais la minorité aura le droit de faire consigner son dissentiment.

5. Chaque partie sera invitée à désigner un mandataire pour la représenter pour tout ce qui pourrait toucher à l'arbitrage.

6. Au cas où un doute s'élèverait sur le point de savoir si tel sujet donné de contestation est compris parmi ceux soumis à l'arbitrage, et où l'une des parties demanderait que ce doute fût tranché par arbitrage, le traité prévoira que l'autre partie devra accepter le dit arbitrage, sauf le droit pour elle de réclamer que le jugement à intervenir soit restreint à la recevabilité de cette demande d'arbitrage.

7. A moins de disposition contraire dans le traité, la procédure consistera en un exposé de la demande, une réponse et des mémoires imprimés produits par les deux parties, concuremment, à la date déterminée; elle se terminera par un débat oral. Le délai pour produire la demande, la réponse et les mémoires imprimés sera fixé par le traité, mais le tribunal aura le pouvoir de proroger le délai. Le tribunal lui-même fixera la date du débat oral.

8. Either party should be entitled to require production of any document in the possession or under the control of the other party, which in the opinion of the Tribunal is relevant to a question in dispute, and to the production of which there is, in its opinion, no sufficient objection.

9. Neither party should be entitled to put in evidence documents (hereinafter called "domestic documents") which, having existed, or purporting to have existed, before the difference arose, were in possession of or known by one party or its predecessors in title, and not communicated to the other party or its predecessors in title before the difference arose.

10. Solemn written statements made by a witness before a public officer should be admissible in evidence as proof of relevant facts, subject to the right hereinafter mentioned of cross-examining the witness. The value of such statements would be for the Tribunal to determine.

11. Either party should be entitled to require the other to produce, for oral examination before the Tribunal at the hearing, any witness making on behalf of that other party such a statement as is mentioned in Article 10, whether the witness be amenable to the jurisdiction of the other party or not. When a witness cannot be produced before the Tribunal, the Tribunal may commission the judicial authorities exercising jurisdiction over the place of the witness's domicile to hold the necessary cross-examination. If it is found impossible to procure the attendance of the witness for cross-examination, it shall be open to the Tribunal to reject his evidence.

12. Irrelevant evidence, domestic documents, and the statements of witnesses not produced for oral examination though required, may, on the application of the party against which they are adduced, be expunged by the Tribunal; and the Tribunal, on a like application, should be at liberty to direct the reprinting of any volume of case, counter-case, printed argument, or appendix, in which the same should appear or be discussed.

13. The decision should be embodied in a written award in duplicate, made and delivered to the agents within a specified time from the close of the hearing. Interlocutory judgments or orders need not be published, but shall be notified to the agents of the parties.

8. Chacune des parties en cause aura le droit d'exiger la production de tout document qui sera en sa possession ou à sa disposition, que le tribunal jugera pertinent à la cause e à la production duquel il ne trouvera pas d'objection suffisante.

9. Aucune des parties ne pourra apporter comme preuve des documents qualifiés ci-dessous "écrits privés," qui, ayant existé ou étant présumé avoir existé avant que le différend ne surgît auraient été en la possession ou à la connaissance d'une des parties ou de ses auteurs et qui n'auraient pas été communiqués à l'autre partie ou à ses auteurs avant que la contestation ne surgît.

10. Les dépositions écrites faites par un témoin devant un officier public pourront être admises comme preuve des faits pertinents, sauf le droit mentionné plus bas de faire contre-examiner le témoin. Le tribunal appréciera la valeur de ces dépositions.

11. Chaque partie aura le droit d'exiger que l'autre partie produise, pour être interrogé oralement devant le tribunal, tout témoin ayant fait en faveur de cette partie la déposition prévue à l'art. 10, que ce témoin soit ou non justiciable des cours et tribunaux de la dite partie. Si un témoin ne peut être produit devant le tribunal, celui-ci aura la faculté de charger l'authorité judiciaire ayant juridiction au lieu du domicile du témoin pour procéder au contre-interrogatoire. Au cas où il serait impossible d'amener le témoin pour être contre-examiné, le tribunal aura la faculté de repousser la déposition.

12. A la demande de la partie contre laquelle ils sont produits, le tribunal peut rejeter toute preuve non pertinente, tous écrits privés, ainsi que les dépositions de témoins qui n'auront pas été soumis à l'interrogatoire oral, quoique cette formalité ait été requise ; à la même requête, le tribunal aura la faculté de faire réimprimer tous exposés de demandes, réponses, mémoires imprimés ou annexes, dans lesquels ceux-ci seraient produits ou discutés.

13. La décision sera rendue sous la forme de sentence écrite, en double exemplaire ; ceux-ci seront remis aux mandataires des parties dans un délai déterminé qui courra à partir de la clôture des débats. Les jugements et ordonnances interlocutoires ne seront pas publiés ; mais ils seront notifiés aux mandataires des parties.

RULES RELATING TO A PERMANENT TRIBUNAL OF INTERNATIONAL ARBITRATION.

Prepared by the Special Committee of the International Law Association, appointed in Brussels, 2nd October, 1895, *and accepted by the Conference at Buffalo, U.S.A.*, 31*st August*, 1899.

1. A permanent High Court of International Arbitration shall be formed by any number of Independent States associating themselves together for the purpose.

2. This High Court shall undertake the settlement of International disputes by means of Arbitration, and the Contracting Parties shall bind themselves to submit to its decision all the disputes, whatever be their nature or cause, which may arise between them, when such cannot be adjusted in a friendly way by the ordinary course of diplomacy.

3. The Court shall be composed of a given equal number of Members, nominated by each State, and any State afterwards acceding to the Court shall thereupon nominate its quota of members.

4. The appointment of the Members of the Court shall be for life, or for a definite number of years. In the event of death, bodily or mental incapacity, or resignation of a Member, the State by which he was appointed shall fill up the vacancy within six months.

5. If a State for some grave cause desires to remove one of its Members, it shall notify his proposed removal, with the cause,

RÈGLEMENTS ET STATUTS RELATIFS À LA CRÉATION D'UN TRIBUNAL PERMANENT D'ARBITRAGE INTERNATIONAL.

Etablis par un Comité Spécial de l'Association de Droit International constitué à Bruxelles le 2 *Octobre* 1895, *acceptées par le Congrès de Buffalo, E.U.A., le* 31 *Août* 1899.

1. La Haute Cour permanente d'Arbitrage international sera établie par l'entente spéciale de deux ou de plusieurs Etats indépendants.

2. La Haute Cour se charge du règlement des différends internationaux par la voie d'arbitrage. Les parties contractantes s'engageront à soumettre à son jugement tous les litiges, qu'elles qu'en soient la nature et la cause qui viendraient à surgir entre elles, si l'on n'a pu les régler à l'amiable par des négociations diplomatiques ordinaires.

3. Tous les Etats nommeront le même nombre de membres (nombre à déterminer) devant siéger à la Haute Cour. Tout Etat qui entre plus tard dans l'Association nommera, dès son accession, son contingent de représentants.

4. Les membres de la Haute Cour seront nommés à vie ou pour une période à déterminer. Au cas où l'un des membres vient à mourir ou à se démettre de ses fonctions, ou se trouve par suite d'incapacité mentale ou physique dans l'impossibilité de siéger, l'Etat nominateur devra, dans les six mois qui suivront, pourvoir à son remplacement.

5. Si, pour un motif grave, un Etat voulait retirer le mandat de l'un de ses Représentants, le fait motivé sera porté à la connaissance de tous les autres Etats contractants. Et si dans le délai

to the other States, and the removal shall take effect, unless some other contracting State shall within one month protest against it.

6. In lieu of appointing permanent Members the contracting States may agree that their Members be appointed as occasion for their action arises. But in that case they shall be chosen from among the higher judicial officers of the appointing State.

7. Members shall not be represented by substitutes.

8. The Court, when its Members are appointed, shall organise itself by choosing a President and a Vice-president from among its Members, and shall appoint such officers and attendants as it may require.

9. The Court thus constituted shall have power to fix and vary its place of meeting, and the place of its permanent office (bureau). It shall make its own rules of procedure, and shall especially give its attention to the establishment and development of a system or code of International Law, which shall have a recognised authority. Its office shall have care of the archives, and the conduct of all administrative business.

10. It may also establish general rules for practice and procedure before the Commissions or Tribunals appointed by it, as hereinafter provided, for the hearing of any controversy submitted under the provision of these rules.

11. Controversies arising between any two or more of the contracting States shall be by those States referred to the Court by a Special Treaty, which shall clearly and definitely state the object and scope of the litigation, bind the parties to place at the disposal of the Court all means in their power for the elucidation of the case, and shall also contain a stipulation to the effect that all the parties to the Agreement shall abide by the rules and regulations of the Court, and loyally execute whatever Award it may give in regard to the said controversy. Any State, though not a Contracting State, can apply to the Court, under the conditions prescribed by the Court's rules of procedure.

d'un mois, à partir de la dite notification, aucune réclamation ou protestation ne parvient au Gouvernement nominateur, la révocation aura son plein effet.

6. Au lieu de membres permanents, les Etats contractants peuvent, par arrangement général, nommer des membres temporaires désignés au fur et à mesure des besoins. En ce cas, les Représentants seront choisis parmi les magistrats de l'ordre le plus élevé de l'Etat nominateur.

7. Les arbitres ne pourront se faire remplacer par des substituts.

8. Sitôt réunie, la Cour devra choisir dans son sein un Président et un Vice-Président, lesquels nommeront à leur tour tels fonctionnaires et employés qu'ils jugeront convenable.

9. La Cour, ainsi constituée, aura le droit de désigner et changer le lieu de ses délibérations et le siège de son bureau. La Cour établira elle-même sa procédure et donnera tous ses soins à l'élaboration d'un Code de Droit International. Ce Code jouira d'une autorité incontestée. Le Bureau aura charge des Archives de la Cour et gérera les affaires purement administratives.

10. Elle peut aussi établir des règlements de procédure pour toutes les Commissions et Tribunaux constitués par elle, ainsi qu'il le sera expliqué ci-après, pour l'arbitrage des différends à elle soumis en conformité des présentes dispositions.

11. Dès qu'il surgira un différend entre deux ou plusieurs des Etats contractants, ces Etats en déféreront le règlement à la Cour, en vertu d'une Convention spéciale (ou Compromis), laquelle spécifiera, clairement et distinctement, la cause et l'objet du différend. Par le Compromis les Etats s'engageront à placer devant la Cour tous les documents concernant l'affaire en question. Elle contiendra aussi l'engagement spécial d'accepter comme final l'arrêt de la Cour et d'en assurer l'exécution. Tout Etat, bien que non contractant, peut s'adresser à la Cour dans les conditions prescrites par les règlements de procédure de la Cour.

12. No question shall be revived by virtue of this Treaty, concerning which a definite Agreement shall already have been reached. In such cases Arbitration shall be resorted to only for the settlement of questions concerning the validity, interpretation, or enforcement of such Agreement.

13. When a controversy is to be adjudicated upon by the High Court, it shall be referred to a Special Commission or Delegation of the whole body, hereinafter styled the Arbitral Tribunal.

14. The Arbitral Tribunal is thus composed:—

(*a*) If the controversy is between two States only, each State chooses from among the Members of the High Court an equal number of arbitrators, one or more, as may be agreed upon by the Special Treaty.

(*b*) If three are parties to the controversy, and two have a common interest, the third State shall choose as many Arbitrators as the two other States together; and the same principle shall apply whenever there is an inequality in the number of States taking part on either side of the controversy.

(*c*) It shall be left to the Special Treaty (or Agreement) to determine whether a State shall or shall not choose its own Members of the High Court as its Arbitrators, or some of its Arbitrators.

(*d*) The other Members of the High Court shall then choose from among themselves, or otherwise, one additional Arbitrator.

(*e*) If, by reason of the fact that all the States are parties to the controversy there are no other Members of the High Court, one additional Arbitrator must be chosen from outside by the other Arbitrators, or he shall be chosen by virtue of some provision in the Special Treaty.

(*f*) The provisions of Article 5 shall be applied to the additional Arbitrator. He shall be Chairman *de jure* of the Tribunal.

15. When the Arbitrators are chosen, either one of the Con-

12. Le Compromis n'aura l'effet de réouvrir aucune affaire, qui aurait déjà été l'objet d'un arrangement préalable, si ce n'est pour soumettre à l'arbitrage la validité, l'interprétation, ou la mise en exécution du dit arrangement.

13. Tout différend dont la Cour sera saisie devra, être déféré à une Commission prise dans son sein et appelée le Tribunal Arbitral.

14. Ce Tribunal est ainsi composé :

(1°) Dans le cas d'un différend entre deux Etats, chacun choisira parmi les membres de la Haute Cour, un nombre égal de représentants, un ou plusieurs, selon ce qui aura été stipulé dans le Compromis.

(2°) Si le différend concerne trois Etats et que deux se trouvent avoir, dans la circonstance des intérêts identiques, le troisième Etat nommera autant de délégués à lui seul que les deux autres Etats réunis, et le même principe sera appliqué toutes les fois qu'il y aura inégalité dans le nombre des Etats formant les deux parties du différend.

(3°) Le Compromis spécifiera si chaque Etat pourra choisir ses délégués en totalité ou en partie parmi ses propres représentants près la Haute Cour.

(4°) Les représentants des divers Etats, non engagés dans l'affaire en question, désigneront un délégué additionnel pris parmi eux ou choisi en dehors de la Cour.

(5°) Dans le cas où le différend concernerait tous les Etats représentés à la Haute Cour, on pourvoirait à la nomination d'un délégué additionnel choisi en dehors de la Cour par les autres délégués ou bien choisi en vertu d'un arrangement spécial mentionné dans le Compromis.

(6°) Les dispositions de l'article 5 s'appliquent au délégué additionnel. Le délégué additionnel sera de droit président du Tribunal Arbitral.

15. Sitôt que la nomination des délégués est bien et dûment

tracting Parties may take the initiative in calling them together, while inviting the other party, or parties, to join them in taking the necessary steps. The express or tacit refusal to provide for the formation, or the first convocation, of the Arbitral Tribunal shall be considered tantamount to a withdrawal from the Treaty by the State which thus refuses; so that it shall no longer be able to profit thereby when it may choose to appeal to it.

16. If the Arbitral Tribunal is formed expressly for a particular dispute, its place of meeting will be arranged for in the Agreement, or decided by the Arbitrators themselves, and should be outside the territory of the parties to the controversy.

17. Its Members, at their first meetings, shall take the necessary steps for the constitution of the Arbitral Tribunal by the election of the officers and servants, and for the proper conduct of its business, according to the rules of procedure, which may be already established, or which it shall determine for itself.

18. Where the course of procedure is not prescribed in the Agreement, or by the Court (Rule 10) it is understood that the Arbitral Tribunal will determine it for itself.

19. The Arbitral Tribunal, when constituted, forms an independent body, having a distinct judicial authority; it is, therefore, not bound by the previous decrees of any other Tribunal, on the questions submitted to its jurisdiction; and although nominated by Governments, its Members are in no sense to be regarded as the representatives, subjects, or mouthpieces, of Governments.

20. It should be treated as a diplomatic mission of the first rank, both as to the honours to be paid to its Members, the immunities which they enjoy, and the protection afforded to them in the exercise of their functions.

faite, l'une des deux parties peut prendre l'initiative de leur convocation en invitant l'autre ou les autres parties à s'unir à elle à cet effet. Tout refus tacite ou exprimé de concourir à la formation, ou convocation, du Tribunal Arbitral, équivaut à la radiation de l'Etat qui refuse de la liste des Etats contractants; cet Etat sera dès lors exclus de toute participation aux avantages de la Haute Cour au cas où il lui plairait plus tard de faire appel à ses décisions.

16. Si le Tribunal Arbitral est convoqué à seule fin de régler un litige spécial, le Compromis désignera le lieu de réunion du Tribunal. Le choix du lieu de réunion peut être laissé à la décision des délégués. En tout cas les assises du Tribunal devront se tenir hors du territoire des parties.

17. Dès leur première réunion les membres du Tribunal auront soin de pourvoir à l'élection de son bureau, et à la solution des différentes questions en conformité des règlements de procédure déjà existants au moment de la convocation du Tribunal, ou bien de ceux qu'il jugerait opportuns dans la circonstance.

18. En tant que la procédure n'aura pas été déterminée, soit par le Compromis soit par la Haute Cour, le Tribunal déterminera lui-même son mode de sa procédure.

19. Dès le moment de sa constitution, le Tribunal forme un corps indépendant, d'une compétence judiciaire distincte; et dans les questions, soumises à sa juridiction, il n'est donc pas lié par les décisions d'aucun autre tribunal, et ses membres, bien que nommés par les Gouvernements, ne peuvent être considérés sous aucun rapport comme les représentants, sujets, ou avocats de leurs Gouvernements respectifs.

20. En ce qui concerne les honneurs, immunités, privilèges et protection à eux dûs, pendant l'exercice de leurs fonctions, les membres du Tribunal seront assimilés aux diplomates de premier ordre.

21. The Arbritral Tribunal has jurisdiction to decide on the regularity of its constitution, and on the validity and interpretation of the reference to itself.

22. In any case where doubts arise as to the scope of the reference, the terms of the Agreement must be interpreted in the widest sense.

23. The Agent appointed by each of the parties in the case shall watch over its interests or the interests of those under its jurisdiction, and undertake their defence; and shall present the case, counter-case, and printed argument and proofs.

24. Rules of procedure cannot be modified or annulled except with the consent of all parties, if they were fixed in the Arbitration Agreement, or with the consent of the majority of the Members if they were framed by the Court, or by the Arbitral Tribunal itself. The interpretation of these rules, or additions to them, may always be decided by a simple majority of votes.

25. Any periods of time fixed by the Arbitral Tribunal may be prolonged by it provided that all the parties be admitted to profit by the extension in an equal degree.

26. The Arbitral Tribunal cannot avail itself of the services of Experts, except with the approval of all parties, or by a unanimous vote of its Members.

27. A submission to Arbitration is determined by the expiration of the period of time fixed by the Agreement, by the conclusion between the parties themselves of a direct arrangement, or, finally, by the delivery of the Award, which should be given within the time fixed in the Agreement.

28. The intervention of a third party is not admissible, except with the consent of the parties in the case. But on the settlement

21. Le Tribunal Arbitral est juge compétent de la régularité de sa constitution, et de la validité et interprétation de son mandat.

22. Au cas où l'étendue de son mandat ne serait pas clairement et distinctement spécifiée, les articles du Compromis seront interprétés dans leur sens le plus large.

23. Le chargé d'affaires nommé par chacune des parties prendra soin des intérêts de la partie qui l'aura nommé, ou des clients de cette partie ; il se chargera de leur défense, établira le dossier de l'affaire, présentera leurs arguments, fournira les imprimés et autres documents s'y rapportant au Tribunal Arbitral.

24. Les Règlements de Procédure établis par le Compromis ne peuvent être modifiés ou annulés que par le consentement des toutes les parties, ou sans la majorité des voix des membres s'ils étaient établis par la Cour, ou par le Tribunal. Leur interprétation ou les additions désirables sont laissées à la majorité simple du Tribunal.

25. Le Tribunal Arbitral sera libre d'étendre toute période de temps préalablement fixée par lui, pourvu que l'extension soit à l'avantage commun et égal de toutes les parties.

26. Le Tribunal ne peut faire appel aux lumières et connaissances spéciales d'Experts, si ce n'est avec l'approbation de toutes les parties ou bien par un vote unanime de ses membres.

27. La soumission d'un différend à l'Arbitrage devient de nulle valeur quand la période de temps fixée par le Compromis est expirée, quand les parties se sont mises d'accord par un arrangement direct, ou par le fait même de la sentence arbitrale du Tribunal, sentence qui doit être rendue dans la limite de temps spécifiée dans le Compromis.

28. L'intervention d'un tiers n'est admissible que si toutes les parties consentent.

of the issues, the Arbitral Tribunal shall possess the power to permit the intervention of third parties on due and sufficient cause being shown that their interests are affected, or likely to be affected, by any decision the Tribunal may arrive ; at and on its decision on the main issue between the original parties to the dispute, the Tribunal shall be empowered to make such terms in regard to such intervening parties as will safeguard their interests.

29. Cross claims may not be brought before the Arbitral Tribunal unless they have been submitted to it by the Agreement, or the parties concur in submitting them to its decision.

30. The Award must be given by a majority of votes, unless it is expressly stipulated in the Agreement that unanimity is indispensable; whether this majority shall be relative or absolute is a point to be settled by the Arbitral Tribunal itself, the whole of which is bound by the majority.

31. Both the High Court and the Tribunals appointed from it shall keep an exact record, and shall preserve correct and dated minutes or notes, of all their proceedings.

32. The cost of maintaining the Court shall be borne equally by all the States concurring in its creation and maintenance. The cost of any particular reference to Arbitration shall be borne by the contending parties in equal shares (each, however, bearing the cost of preparing and presenting its own case, counter-case, and printed argument), unless the Award includes the payment of costs.

Cependant dans les cas où l'arrêt du Tribunal affecterait les intérêts d'un tiers, le Tribunal, après preuve faite par ce dernier de l'effet probable de la sentence arbitrale sur les dits intérêts, pourra admettre l'intervention. Dans ces cas, le Tribunal, en rendant sa sentence définitive entre les parties, pourra leur imposer les conditions qu'il jugera nécessaires pour sauvegarder les intérêts de ces tiers.

29. Aucune contre-réclamation ne sera admise devant le Tribunal Arbitral, à moins qu'elle n'ait été mentionnée dans le Compromis, ou bien que les parties en soient d'accord pour la soumettre aux décisions du Tribunal.

30. La sentence arbitrale doit être rendue à la majorité des voix, à moins que le Compromis ne demande expressément l'unanimité; la question de savoir si la majorité devra être absolue ou relative, est un point laissé à la discrétion du Tribunal lui-même, qui est, en tant que Corps, lié par le vote de la majorité.

31. La Haute Cour et les Tribunaux dresseront des procès-verbaux de toutes leurs réunions, délibérations, minutes ou comptes-rendus. Leurs actes et décisions seront dûment datés et conservés.

32. Les frais de la Haute Cour seront à la charge de tous les Etats contractants, chacun supportant une part égale. Les frais des cas soumis à l'arbitrage seront à la charge et par partie égale des Etats intéressés, à moins que la sentence arbitrale ne règle la question. Cependant, chaque Etat supportera les frais de préparation et de présentation de son dossier, de sa cause, de ses réclamations, documents imprimés et autres.

THE HAGUE PEACE CONFERENCE, 1899.

CONVENTION FOR THE PEACEFUL REGULATION OF INTERNATIONAL CONFLICTS.

As the Convention will have to remain open for signature until the 31st December, 1899, the Contracting Powers and their Plenipotentiaries will, until this date, append their signatures according to the following order, adopted by the Conference at its plenary sitting of the 28th July, 1899:—

His Majesty the Emperor of Germany, King of Prussia; His Majesty the Emperor of Austria, King of Bohemia, &c., and King Apostolic of Hungary; His Majesty the King of the Belgians; His Majesty the Emperor of China; His Majesty the King of Denmark; His Majesty the King of Spain, and, *in his name*, Her Majesty the Queen Regent of the Realm; the President of the United States of America; the President of the United States of Mexico; the President of the French Republic; Her Majesty the Queen of Great Britain and Ireland, Empress of India; His Majesty the King of the Hellenes; His Majesty the King of Italy; His Majesty the Emperor of Japan; His Royal Highness the Grand Duke of Luxembourg, Duke of Nassau; His Highness the Prince of Montenegro; Her Majesty the Queen of the Netherlands; His Imperial Majesty the Shah of Persia; His Majesty the King of Portugal and Algarves, &c.; His Majesty the King of Roumania; His Majesty the Emperor of all the Russias; His Majesty the King of Servia; His Majesty the King of Siam; His Majesty the King of Sweden and Norway; The Swiss Federal Council; His Majesty the Emperor of the Ottomans; and His Royal Highness the Prince of Bulgaria.

Animated by a strong desire to co-operate for the maintenance of general Peace;

LA CONFERENCE DE LA PAIX.

La Haye, 1899.

CONVENTION POUR LE RÈGLEMENT PACIFIQUE DES CONFLITS INTERNATIONAUX.

La Convention devant rester ouverte à la signature jusqu'au 31 décembre 1899, les Puissances Contractantes et Leurs Plénipotentiaires seront inscrits à cette date conformément à l'ordre suivant, adopté par la Conférence dans sa séance plénière du 28 juillet 1899 :

Sa Majesté l'Empereur d'Allemagne, Roi de Prusse; Sa Majesté l'Empereur d'Autriche, Roi de Bohême, etc., et Roi Apostolique de Hongrie ; Sa Majesté le Roi des Belges ; Sa Majesté l'Empereur de Chine ; Sa Majesté le Roi de Danemark ; Sa Majesté le Roi d'Espagne, et en Son Nom Sa Majesté la Reine-Régente du Royaume ; le Président des Etats-Unis d'Amérique ; le Président des Etats-Unis Mexicains : le Président de la Republique Française ; Sa Majesté la Reine du Royaume-Uni de la Grande-Bretagne et d'Irlande, Impératrice des Indes ; Sa Majesté le Roi des Hellènes ; Sa Majesté le Roi d'Italie ; Sa Majesté l'Empereur du Japon ; Son Altesse Royale le Grand-Duc de Luxembourg, Duc de Nassau ; Son Altesse le Prince de Monténégro ; Sa Majesté la Reine des Pays-Bas ; Sa Majesté Impériale le Schah de Perse ; Sa Majesté le Roi de Portugal et des Algarves, etc. ; Sa Majesté le Roi de Roumanie ; Sa Majesté l'Empereur de Toutes les Russies ; Sa Majesté le Roì de Serbie ; Sa Majesté le Roi de Siam ; Sa Majesté le Roi de Suède et de Norvège ; le Conseil Fédéral Suisse ; Sa Majesté l'Empereur des Ottomans et Son Altesse Royale le Prince de Bulgarie.

Animés de la ferme volonté de concourir au maintien de la paix générale ;

Resolved to assist with all their efforts the friendly settlement of international disputes;

Recognising the solidarity which unites the members of the Society of Civilised Nations;

Wishing to extend the empire of law and to strengthen the sentiment of international justice;

Convinced that the permanent institution of an Arbitral jurisdiction, accessible to all, in the midst of the independent Powers, may contribute effectively to this result;

Considering the advantages of a general and regular organisation of Arbitral procedure;

Deeming, with the August Initiator of the International Peace Conference, that it is of the utmost importance to embody in an international Agreement the principles of equity and of law on which repose the security of States and the welfare of peoples;

And desiring to conclude a Convention for this purpose, have appointed the following as their Plenipotentiaries, viz.: . . . .

. . . .

Who, after having produced their full credentials, which have been found in proper and due form, have agreed upon the following provisions:

SECTION I.—THE MAINTENANCE OF GENERAL PEACE.

ART. 1.—In order to prevent, as far as possible, the recourse to force in the relations between States, the Signatory Powers agree to employ all their efforts to bring about the pacific adjustment of international differences.

SECTION II.—GOOD OFFICES AND MEDIATION.

ART. 2.—In case of grave disagreement or conflict, before appealing to arms, the Signatory Powers agree that they will have recourse, so far as circumstances permit, to the good offices or Mediation of one or more friendly Powers.

ART. 3.—Independently of this recourse, the Signatory Powers

Résolus à favoriser de tous leurs efforts le règlement amiable des conflits internationaux ;

Reconnaissant la solidarité qui unit les membres de la société des nations civilisées ;

Voulant étendre l'empire du droit et fortifier le sentiment de la justice internationale ;

Convaincus que l'institution permanente d'un juridiction arbitrale, accessible à tous, au sein des Puissances indépendantes peut contribuer efficacement à ce résultat ;

Considérant les avantages d'une organisation générale et régulière de la procédure arbitrale ;

Estimant avec l'Auguste Initiateur de la Conférence Internationale de la Paix qu'il importe de consacrer dans un accord international les principes d'équité et de droit sur lesquels reposent la sécurité des Etats et le bien-être des peuples ;

Désirant conclure une Convention à cet effet ont nommé pour Leurs plénipotentiaires, savoir :

. . . .

Lesquels, après s'être communiqué leurs pleins pouvoirs, trouvés en bonne et due forme, sont convenues des dispositions suivantes :

TITRE I. — DU MAINTIEN DE LA PAIX GÉNÉRALE.

ARTICLE PREMIER. — En vue de prévenir autant que possible le recours à la force dans les rapports entre les Etats, les Puissances signataires conviennent d'employer tous leurs efforts pour assurer le règlement pacifique des différends internationaux.

TITRE II. — DES BONS OFFICES ET DE LA MÉDIATION.

ART. 2. — En cas de dissentiment grave ou de conflit, avant d'en appeler aux armes, les Puissances signataires conviennent d'avoir recours, en tant que les circonstances le permettront, aux bons offices ou à la médiation d'une ou de plusieurs Puissances amies.

ART. 3. — Indépendamment de ce recours, les Puissances signa-consider it useful that one or more Powers that are not concerned in the conflict should offer of their ov initiative, so far as the circumstances lend themselves to it, their good offices or their Mediation to the contending States.

The Powers not concerned in the conflict have the right o offering their good offices or their Mediation even during the course of hostilities.

The exercise of this right can never be considered by either of the disputing parties as an unfriendly act.

ART. 4.—The function of Mediator consists in reconciling the opposing claims, and in appeasing the resentments which may be caused between the contending States.

ART. 5.—The duties of a Mediator cease from the moment when it is announced, either by one of the disputing parties, or by the Mediator himself, that the means of conciliation proposed by him are not accepted.

ART. 6.—Good offices and Mediation, whether at the request of the parties in conflict, or on the initiative of Powers taking no part therein, have exclusively the character of advice, and are devoid of any obligatory force.

ART. 7.—The acceptance of Mediation cannot have the effect, in the absence of an Agreement to the contrary, of interrupting, retarding, or hindering mobilisation and other measures preparatory to war.

If it (Mediation) is undertaken after the opening of hostilities, it will not, in the absence of an Agreement to the contrary, interrupt current military operations.

ART. 8.—The Signatory Powers agree to recommend the application, in circumstances which permit of it, of special Mediation in the following form :—

In the case of a grave disagreement endangering Peace, the contending States shall each choose one Power to which they may entrust the mission of entering into direct communication with the Power chosen by the other side, for the purpose of preventing the rupture of pacific relations.

taires jugent utile qu'une ou plusieurs Puissances étrangères au conflit, offrent de leur propre initiative, en tant que les circonstances s'y prêtent, leurs bons offices ou leur médiation aux Etats en litige.

Le droit d'offrir les bons offices ou la médiation appartient aux Puissances étrangères au conflit, même pendant le cours des hostilités.

L'exercice de ce droit ne peut jamais être considéré par l'une ou l'autre des Parties en litige comme un acte peu amical.

ART. 4. — Le rôle du médiateur consiste à concilier les prétentions opposées et à apaiser les ressentiments qui peuvent s'être produits entre les Etats en conflit.

ART. 5. — Les fonctions du médiateur cessent du moment où il est constaté, soit par l'une des Parties en litige, soit par le médiateur lui-même, que les moyens de conciliation proposés par lui ne sont pas acceptés.

ART. 6. — Les bons offices et la médiation, soit sur le recours des Parties en conflit, soit sur l'initiative des Puissances étrangères au conflit ont exclusivement le caractère d'un conseil et n'ont jamais force obligatoire.

ART. 7. — L'acceptation de la médiation ne peut avoir pour effet, sauf convention contraire, d'interrompre, de retarder ou d'entraver la mobilisation et autres mesures préparatoires à la guerre.

Si elle intervient après l'ouverture des hostilités, elle n'interrompt pas, sauf convention contraire, les opérations militaires en cours.

ART. 8. — Les Puissances signataires sont d'accord pour recommander l'application, dans les circonstances qui le permettent, d'une médiation spéciale sous la forme suivante :

En cas de différend grave compromettant la Paix, les Etats en conflit choisissent respectivement une Puissance à laquelle ils confient la mission d'entrer en rapport direct avec la Puissance choisie d'autre part, à l'effet de prévenir la rupture des relations pacifiques.

During the continuance of their mandate, the duration of which, unless the contrary is stipulated, cannot exceed 30 days, the disputing States cease all direct negotiation in reference to the subject of the dispute, which is to be considered as referred exclusively to the mediating Powers. These must apply all their efforts to arranging the difference.

In case of the actual rupture of pacific relations, these Powers remain charged with the common mission of profiting by every opportunity of re-establishing Peace.

SECTION III.—INTERNATIONAL COMMISSIONS OF INQUIRY.

ART. 9.—In disputes of an international character, which involve neither their honour nor their essential interests, and which spring from a difference in their estimate of matters of fact, the Signatory Powers consider it useful that the Parties which have not been able to agree by diplomatic means, should institute, so far as circumstances will permit, an International Commission of Inquiry, entrusted with the duty of facilitating he settlement of these disputes by clearing up the questions of fact by means of an impartial and conscientious examination.

ART. 10.—International Commissions of Inquiry are constituted by Special Convention between the Parties in litigation. This Agreement of Inquiry shall specify the facts to be examined and the extent of the powers of the Commissioners.

It shall regulate the procedure of the Commission.

The inquiry proceeds by hearing the adverse parties.

The procedure and time allowed for the investigation, so far as they are not fixed by the Agreement of Inquiry, are determined by the Commission itself.

ART. 11.—International Commissions of Inquiry are to be formed, unless it is stipulated to the contrary, in the manner determined by Art. 32 of the present Convention.

ART. 12.—The disputing Powers undertake to furnish to the

Pendant la durée de ce mandat dont le terme, sauf stipulation contraire, ne peut excéder trente jours, les Etats en litige cessent tout rapport direct au sujet du conflit lequel est considéré comme déféré exclusivement aux Puissances médiatrices. Celles-ci doivent appliquer tous leurs efforts à régler le différend.

En cas de rupture effective des relations pacifiques, ces Puissances demeurent chargées de la mission commune de profiter de toute occasion pour rétablir la paix.

TITRE III. — DES COMMISSIONS INTERNATIONALES D'ENQUÊTE.

ART. 9. — Dans les litiges d'ordre international n'engageant ni l'honneur ni les intérêts essentiels et provenant d'une divergence d'appréciation sur des points de fait, les Puissances signataires jugent utile que les Parties, qui n'auraient pu se mettre d'accord par les voies diplomatiques, instituent, en tant que les circonstances le permettront, une Commission internationale d'enquête chargée de faciliter la solution de ces litiges en éclaircissant, par un examen impartial et consciencieux, les questions de fait.

ART. 10.—Les Commissions internationales d'enquête sont constituées par Convention spéciale entre les Parties en litige.

La Convention d'enquête précise les faits à examiner et l'étendue des pouvoirs des commissaires.

Elle règle la procédure.

L'enquête a lieu contradictoirement.

La forme et les délais à observer, en tant qu'ils ne sont pas fixés par la Convention d'enquête, sont déterminés par la Commission elle-même.

ART. 11. — Les Commissions internationales d'enquête sont formées, sauf stipulation contraire, de la manière déterminée par l'article 32 de la présente Convention.

ART. 12. — Les Puissances en litige s'engagent à fournir à la

International Commission of Inquiry, to the fullest extent that they shall consider possible, all the means and all the facilities necessary for the complete knowledge and exact appreciation of the facts in question.

ART. 13.—The International Commission of Inquiry shall present to the disputing Powers its report signed by all the members of the Commission.

ART. 14.—The report of the International Commission of Inquiry, being limited to the determination of matters of fact, has by no means the character of an Arbitral decision. It leaves the disputing Powers entire freedom as to the effect to be given to this determination.

SECTION IV.—OF INTERNATIONAL ARBITRATION.

I.—OF ARBITRAL JURISDICTION (*justice arbitrale*).

ART. 15.—International Arbitration has for its object the settlement of disputes between States by judges of their own choosing and on the basis of respect for Law.

ART. 16.—In questions of a judicial character, and especially in questions of the interpretation or application of International Treaties, Arbitration is recognised by the Signatory Powers as the most effective, and at the same time the most equitable, method of settling disputes which have not been determined by diplomacy.

ART. 17.—The Agreement to Arbitrate may be concluded for disputes already in existence, or for disputes about to arise (*contestations éventuelles*). It may deal with every sort of dispute or only with disputes of a specified category.

ART. 18.—The Arbitral Convention implies an engagement to submit in good faith to the Arbitral decision.

ART. 19.—Independently of general or special Treaties, which may already impose the obligation upon the Signatory Powers to have recourse to Arbitration, these Powers reserve to themselves

Commission internationale d'enquête, dans la plus large mesure qu'Elles jugeront possible, tous les moyens et toutes les facilités nécessaires pour la connaissance complète et l'appréciation exacte des faits en question.

ART. 13. — La Commission internationale d'enquête présente aux Puissances en litige son rapport signé par tous les membres de la Commission.

ART. 14. — Le rapport de la Commission internationale d'enquête, limité à la constatation des faits, n'a nullement le caractère d'une sentence arbitrale. Il laisse aux Puissances en litige une entière liberté pour la suite à donner à cette constatation.

TITRE IV. — DE L'ARBITRAGE INTERNATIONAL.

Chapitre I. — De la Justice arbitrale.

ART. 15. — L'arbitrage international a pour objet le règlement de litiges entre les Etats par des juges de leur choix, et sur la base du respect du droit.

ART. 16. — Dans les questions d'ordre juridique et en premier lieu dans les questions d'interprétation ou d'application des conventions internationales, l'arbitrage est reconnu par les Puissances signataires comme le moyen le plus efficace et en même temps le plus équitable de régler les litiges qui n'ont pas été résolus par les voies diplomatiques.

ART. 17. — La convention d'arbitrage est conclue pour des contestations déjà nées ou pour des contestations éventuelles.

Elle peut concerner tout litige ou seulement les litiges d'une catégorie déterminée.

ART. 18. — La convention d'arbitrage implique l'engagement de se soumettre de bonne foi à la sentence arbitrale.

ART. 19. — Indépendamment des traités généraux ou particuliers qui stipulent actuellement l'obligation du recours à l'arbitrage pour les Puissances signataires, ces Puissances se réservent the liberty to conclude, either before the ratification of the present Act, or afterwards, new Agreements, general or particular, with the object of extending compulsory Arbitration to all cases which they judge capable of being submitted to it.

II.—Of the Permanent Court of Arbitration.

Art. 20.—For the purpose of facilitating immediate recourse to Arbitration for international differences which have not been settled by diplomatic means, the Signatory Powers engage themselves to organise a permanent Court of Arbitration, accessible at all times and working, except there be a contrary stipulation of the Parties, in conformity with the rules of procedure inserted in the present Convention.

Art. 21.—The permanent Court has competence in all cases of Arbitration, unless the Parties agree to establish a special jurisdiction.

Art. 22.—An International Bureau established at The Hague is to act as the clerk's office (*greffe*) of the Court.

This Bureau is to be the intermediary for the communication relative to the meetings of the latter.

It will have care of the archives and the conduct of all the administrative business.

The Signatory Powers pledge themselves to communicate to the International Bureau of the Hague a faithful and certified copy of every Arbitral stipulation agreed upon between them, and of all judgments which affect them resulting from arbitral jurisdictions other than that of the Court.

They pledge themselves to communicate also to the Bureau the laws and regulations, and the documents eventually announcing the execution of the judgments pronounced by the Court.

Art. 23.—Each of the Signatory Powers shall designate, in the course of the three months following the ratification by it of the present Act, four persons, at the most, of recognised competence de conclure, soit avant la ratification du présent Acte, soit postérieurement, des accords nouveaux, généraux ou particuliers, en vue d'étendre l'arbitrage obligatoire à tous les cas qu'Elles jugeront possible de lui soumettre.

Chapitre II. — De la Cour permanente d'Arbitrage.

Art. 20.—Dans le but de faciliter le recours immédiat à l'arbitrage pour les différends internationaux qui n'ont pu être réglés par la voie diplomatique, les Puissances signataires s'engagent à organiser une Cour permanente d'arbitrage, accessible en tout temps et fonctionnant, sauf stipulation contraire des Parties, conformément aux Règles de procédure insérées dans la présente Convention.

Art. 21. — La Cour permanente sera compétente pour tous les cas d'arbitrage, à moins qu'il n'y ait entente entre les Parties pour l'établissement d'une juridiction spéciale d'arbitrage.

Art 22.—Uu Bureau international établi à la Haye, sert de greffe à la Cour.

Ce Bureau est l'intermédiaire des communications relatives aux réunions de celle-ci.

Il a garde des archives et la gestion de toutes les affaires administratives.

Les Puissances signataires s'engagent à communiquer au Bureau international de la Haye, une copie certifiée conforme de toute stipulation d'arbitrage intervenue entre elles et de toute sentence arbitrale les concernant et rendue par des juridictions spéciales.

Elles s'engagent à communiquer de même au Bureau, les lois, règlements et documents constatant·éventuellement l'exécution des sentences rendues par la Cour.

Art. 23.—Chaque Puissance signataire désignera, dans les trois mois qui suivront la ratification par elle du présent acte, quatre personnes au plus, d'une compétence reconnue dans les questions in questions of international law, enjoying the highest moral reputation, and willing to accept the duties of Arbitrators.

The persons thus nominated will be entered, with the title of Members of the Court, on a list which will be communicated by the Bureau to all the Signatory Powers.

Every modification of the list of Arbitrators shall be brought to the notice of the Signatory Powers by the Bureau.

Two or more Powers may agree to nominate one or more members in common.

The same person may be nominated by different Powers.

The members of the Court are appointed for a term of six years. Their appointment may be renewed.

In case of the decease, or the retirement of a member of the Court, the vacancy will be filled in accordance with the method established for nomination.

ART. 24.—When the Signatory Powers desire to apply to the permanent Court for the settlement of a difference which has arisen between them, the choice of Arbitrators to form a Tribunal qualified to deal with such difference, should be made from the general list of the members of the Court.

Failing the constitution of an Arbitral Tribunal by the direct agreement of the Parties, the procedure shall be as follows:—

Each Party names two Arbitrators, and these together choose an Umpire.

In case of an equality of votes, the choice of an Umpire is entrusted to a third Power, designated by the common agreement of the Parties.

If an agreement is not reached on this subject, each Party shall select a different Power, and the choice of the Umpire shall be made by the united action of the Powers thus selected.

The Tribunal being thus composed, the Parties shall notify to the Bureau their decision to make application to the Court, and the names of the Arbitrators.

The Arbitral Tribunal shall meet on the date fixed by the Parties.

de droit international, jouissant de la plus haute considération morale et disposées à accepter les fonctions d'arbitres.

Les personnes ainsi désignées seront inscrites, au titre de membres de la Cour, sur une liste qui sera notifiée à toutes les Puissances signataires par les soins du bureau.

Toute modification à la liste des arbitres est portée, par les soins du Bureau, à la connaissance des Puissances signataires.

Deux ou plusieurs Puissances peuvent s'entendre pour la désignation en commun d'un ou de plusieurs membres.

La même personne peut être désignée par des Puissances différentes.

Les membres de la Cour sont nommés pour un terme de six ans. Leur mandat peut être renouvelé.

En cas de décès ou de retraite d'un membre de la Cour il est pourvu à son remplacement selon le mode fixé pour sa nomination.

ART. 24.—Lorsque les Puissances signataires veulent s'adresser à la Cour permanente pour le règlement d'un différend survenu entre elles, le choix des arbitres appelés a former le Tribunal compétent pour statuer sur ce différend, doit être fait dans la liste générale des membres de la Cour.

A défaut de constitution du Tribunal arbitral par l'accord immédiat des Parties, il est procédé de la manière suivante :

Chaque Partie nomme deux arbitres et ceux-ci choisissent ensemble un sur-arbitre.

En cas de partage des voix, le choix du sur-arbitre est confié à une Puissance tierce, désignée de commun accord par les Parties.

Si l'accord ne s'établit pas à ce sujet, chaque Partie désigne une Puissance différente et le choix du sur-arbitre est fait de concert par les Puissances ainsi désignées.

Le Tribunal étant ainsi composé, les Parties notifient au Bureau leur décision de s'adresser à la Cour et les noms des arbitres.

Le Tribunal arbitral se réunit à la date fixée par les Parties.

The members of the Court shall enjoy diplomatic privileges and immunities, in the exercise of their functions, and outside their own Country.

ART. 25.—The Arbitral Tribunal shall usually sit at The Hague.

The place of its session can be changed by the Tribunal, except in case of *force majeure*, only with the consent of the Parties.

ART. 26.—The International Bureau at the Hague is authorised to place its offices and its staff at the disposal of the Signatory Powers for the performance of the duties of every special case of Arbitral jurisdiction.

The jurisdiction of the permanent Court may be extended, under the conditions prescribed by its Rules, to disputes existing between non-signatory Powers, or between Signatory Powers and those that are not signatory, if the Parties are agreed to have recourse to its jurisdiction.

ART. 27.—The Signatory Powers consider it a duty, in case a sharp conflict should threaten to break out between two or more of them, to remind these Powers that the permanent Court is open to them.

Consequently, they declare that the fact of reminding the Parties in conflict of the provisions of the present Convention and the advice given, in the higher interests of Peace, to apply to the permanent Court, can only be considered an exercise of Good Offices.

ART. 28.—A Permanent Administrative Council, composed of the diplomatic representatives of the Signatory Powers accredited to The Hague, and of the Minister for Foreign Affairs of the Netherlands, who shall discharge the functions of President, shall be constituted in that city as soon as possible after the ratification of the present Act by at least nine Powers.

Les membres de la Cour, dans l'exercice de leurs fonctions et en dehors de leur Pays, jouissent des privilèges et immunités diplomatiques.

ART. 25.—Le Tribunal arbitral siège d'ordinaire à La Haye.

Le siège ne peut, sauf le cas de force majeure, être changé par le Tribunal que de l'assentiment des Parties.

ART. 26.—Le Bureau international de La Haye est autorisé à mettre ses locaux et son organisation à la disposition des Puissances signataires pour le fonctionnement de toute juridiction spéciale d'arbitrage.

La juridiction de la Cour permanente peut être étendue dans les conditions prescrites par les Règlements, aux litiges existant entre des Puissances non signataires ou entre des Puissances signataires et des Puissances non signataires, si les Parties sont convenues de recourir à cette juridiction.

ART. 27.—Les Puissances signataires considèrent comme un devoir, dans le cas où un conflit aigu menacerait d'éclater entre deux ou plusieurs d'entre Elles, de rappeler à celles-ci que la Cour permanente leur est ouverte.

En conséquence, Elles déclarent que le fait de rappeler aux Parties en conflit les dispositions de la présente Convention, et le conseil donné, dans l'intérêt supérieur de la paix, de s'adresser à la Cour permanente ne peuvent être considérés que comme actes de Bons Offices.

ART. 28.—Un Conseil administratif permanent, composé des représentants diplomatiques des Puissances signataires accrédités à La Haye et du Ministre des Affaires Etrangères des Pays-Bas qui remplira les fonctions de Président, sera constitué dans cette ville le plus tôt possible après la ratification du présent Acte par neuf Puissances au moins.

This Council shall be charged with establishing and organising the International Bureau, which shall remain under its direction and under its control.

It shall notify the Powers of the constitution of the Court, and shall provide for its installation.

It shall determine its procedure, as well as all other necessary regulations.

It shall decide all administrative questions which may arise touching the official working of the Court.

It shall have absolute power as to the nomination, suspension, or dismissal of the functionaries and *employés* of the Bureau.

It shall fix their emoluments and salaries, and control the general expenditure.

The presence of five members, at meetings duly convoked, shall suffice to enable the Council to deliberate in valid form. Decisions are taken by a majority of votes.

The Council shall communicate without delay to the Signatory Powers the Rules adopted by it, and shall address to them each year a report on the labours of the Court, on the discharge of the administrative services, and on the expenditure.

ART. 29.—The expenses of the Bureau shall be borne by the Signatory Powers in the proportion established for the International Bureau of the Universal Postal Union.

III.—OF ARBITRAL PROCEDURE.

ART. 30.—With a view to promote the development of Arbitration the Signatory Powers have resolved on the following Rules, which shall apply to arbitral procedure so far as the Parties have not agreed on other rules.

ART. 31.—Powers which have recourse to Arbitration shall sign a special Agreement, or *compromis*, clearly defining the object of the dispute, as well as the extent of the powers of the Arbitrators. This Agreement implies an engagement by

Ce Conseil sera chargé d'établir et d'organiser le Bureau international, lequel demeurera sous sa direction et sous son contrôle.

Il notifiera aux Puissances la constitution de la Cour et pourvoira à l'installation de celle-ci.

Il arrêtera son règlement d'ordre ainsi que tous autres règlements nécessaires.

Il décidera toutes les questions administratives qui pourraient surgir touchant le fonctionnement de la Cour.

Il aura tout pouvoir quant à la nomination, la suspension ou la révocation des fonctionnaires et employés du Bureau.

Il fixera les traitements et salaires et contrôlera la dépense générale.

La présence de cinq membres dans les réunions dûment convoquées suffit pour permettre au Conseil de délibérer valablement. Les décisions sont prises à la majorité des voix.

Le Conseil communique sans délai aux Puissances signataires les règlements adoptés par lui. Il leur adresse chaque année un rapport sur les travaux de la Cour, sur le fonctionnement des services administratifs et sur les dépenses.

ART. 29.—Les frais du Bureau seront supportés par les Puissances signataires dans la proportion établie pour le Bureau international de l'Union postale universelle.

Chapitre III.

DE LA PROCÉDURE ARBITRALE.

ART. 30.—En vue de favoriser le développement de l'arbitrage, les Puissances signataires ont arrêté les règles suivantes qui seront applicables à la procédure arbitrale, en tant que les Parties ne sont pas convenues d'autres règles.

ART. 31.—Les Puissances qui recourent à l'arbitrage signent un acte spécial (compromis) dans lequel sont nettement déterminés l'objet du litige ainsi que l'étendue des pouvoirs des arbitres.

the Parties to submit themselves in good faith to the Arbitration decision.

ART. 32.—Arbitration functions may be conferred upon a single Arbitrator, or on several Arbitrators, named by the Parties at their discretion, or chosen by them from among the members of the permanent Court of Arbitration established by the present Act.

In default of the constitution of the Tribunal by the direct agreement of the Parties it shall be formed in the following manner:—

Each Party shall name two Arbitrators, and they shall choose together an umpire (*sur-arbitre*).

In case of an equality of votes, the choice of the Umpire shall be entrusted to a third Power, designated by the agreement of the Parties.

If an agreement is not come to on this subject, each Party shall designate a different Power, and the choice of the Umpire shall be made by agreement between the Powers thus designated.

ART. 33.—When a Sovereign, or the Head of a State is chosen as an Arbitrator, the Arbitration procedure shall be settled by him.

ART. 34.—The Umpire is by right President of the Tribunal.

When the Tribunal does not include an Umpire it shall itself appoint its President.

ART. 35.—In case of the decease or resignation or incapacity from any cause of one of the Arbitrators, the vacancy shall be filled in the way appointed for his nomination.

ART. 36.—The place where the Tribunal shall sit is to be designated by the Parties. In default of such designation, the Tribunal shall sit at the Hague.

The place of session thus fixed upon cannot be changed, except in case of *force majeure*, by the Tribunal without the consent of the Parties.

ART. 37.—The Parties have the right to name to the Tribunal

Cet acte implique l'engagement des Parties de se soumettre de bonne foi à la sentence arbitrale.

ART. 32.—Les fonctions arbitrales peuvent être conférées à un arbitre unique ou à plusieurs arbitres désignés par les Parties à leur gré, ou choisis par Elles parmi les membres de la Cour permanente d'arbitrage établie par le présent Acte.

A défaut de constitution du Tribunal par l'accord immédiat des Parties, il est procédé de la manière suivante :

Chaque Partie nomme deux arbitres et ceux-ci choisissent ensemble un sur-arbitre.

En cas de partage des voix, le choix du sur-arbitre est confié à une Puissance tierce, désignée de commun accord par les Parties.

Si l'accord ne s'établit pas à ce sujet, chaque Partie désigne une Puissance différente et le choix du sur-arbitre est fait de concert par les Puissances ainsi désignées.

ART. 33.—Lorsque un Souverain ou un Chef d'Etat est choisi pour arbitre la procédure arbitrale est réglée par Lui.

ART. 34.—Le sur-arbitre est de droit Président du Tribunal.

Lorsque le Tribunal ne comprend pas de sur-arbitre, il nomme lui-même son président.

ART. 35.—En cas de décès, de démission, ou d'empêchement, pour quelque cause que ce soit, de l'un des arbitres, il est pourvu à son remplacement selon le mode fixé pour sa nomination.

ART. 36.—Le siège du Tribunal est désigné par les Parties. A défaut de cette désignation le Tribunal siège à la Haye.

Le siège ainsi fixé ne peut, sauf le cas de force majeure, être changé par le Tribunal que de l'assentiment des Parties.

ART. 37.—Les Parties ont le droit de nommer auprès

delegates or special Agents, to act as intermediaries between them and the Tribunal.

They are, moreover, authorised to entrust the defence of their rights and interests before the Tribunal to Counsel or Advocates named by them for that purpose.

ART. 38.—The Tribunal decides upon the choice of languages of which it will make use, and which it shall authorise to be employed before it.

ART. 39.—The arbitral procedure comprises as a general rule two distinct phases: the Examination of evidence and the Hearing.

The Examination of evidence consists in the presentation made by the respective Agents to the members of the Tribunal and to the opposing Party, of all printed or written instruments and of all documents containing the matters pleaded in the case.

This communication shall take place in the form, and at the times fixed by the Tribunal by virtue of Article 49.

The Hearing shall consist in the oral discussion of the matters presented by the Parties before the Tribunal.

ART. 40.—Every document produced by one of the Parties must be communicated to the other Party.

ART. 41.—The oral hearing shall be under the direction of the President.

It shall be published only in accordance with a decision of the Tribunal made with the consent of the Parties.

It shall be recorded in minutes written out by secretaries appointed by the President. These minutes alone are to be regarded as authentic.

ART. 42.—The examination of evidence being closed, the Tribunal has the right to refuse to admit all new acts or documents which the Representatives of one of the Parties wish to submit to it without the consent of the other.

ART. 43.—The Tribunal, however, shall be free to take into

du Tribunal des délégués ou agents spéciaux, avec la mission de servir d'intermédiaires entre Elles et le Tribunal.

Elles sont en outre autorisées à charger de la défense de leurs droits et intérêts devant le Tribunal, des conseils ou avocats nommés par Elles à cet effet.

ART. 38.—Le Tribunal décide du choix des langues dont il fera usage et dont l'emploi sera autorisé devant lui.

ART. 39.—La procédure arbitrale comprend en règle générale deux phases distinctes : l'instruction et les débats.

L'instruction consiste dans la communication faite par les agents respectifs, aux membres du Tribunal et à la Partie adverse, de tous actes imprimés ou écrits et de tous documents contenant les moyens invoqués dans la cause. Cette communication aura lieu dans la forme et dans les délais déterminés par le Tribunal en vertu de l'article 49.

Les débats consistent dans le développement orale des moyens des Parties devant le Tribunal.

ART. 40.—Toute pièce produite par l'une des Parties doit être communiquée à l'autre Partie.

ART. 41.—Les débats sont dirigés par le Président.

Ils ne sont publiés qu'en vertu d'une décision du Tribunal, prise avec l'assentiment des Parties.

Ils sont consignés dans les procès-verbaux rédigés par des secrétaires que nomme le Président. Ces procès-verbaux ont seuls caractère authentique.

ART. 42.—L'instruction étant close, le Tribunal a le droit d'écarter du débat tous actes ou documents nouveaux qu'une des Parties voudrait lui soumettre sans le consentement de l'autre.

ART. 43.—Le Tribunal demeure libre de prendre en considéconsideration any new acts or documents to which the Agents or Counsel of the Parties shall call its attention.

In this case the Tribunal has the right to require the production of these acts or documents apart from the obligation of making them known to the opposite Party.

ART. 44.—The Tribunal may, moreover, require from the Agents of the Parties the production of all deeds, and demand all necessary explanations. In case of refusal the Tribunal may have the fact put on record.

ART. 45.—The Agents and Counsel of the Parties are authorised to present orally to the Tribunal all the pleas they consider useful for the defence of their cause.

ART. 46.—They have the right to raise objections or take exception. The decisions of the Tribunal upon these points shall be final and shall not give rise to any further discussion.

ART. 47.—The members of the Tribunal have the right to put questions to the Agents and Counsel of the Parties, and to demand from them explanations of doubtful points.

Neither questions put nor observations made by the members of the Tribunal in the course of the hearing shall be regarded as expressions of the opinion of the Tribunal in general, or of its members in particular.

ART. 48.—The Tribunal is authorised to settle its own competence, by interpreting the Agreement to arbitrate (*compromis*), as well as any other treaties which may be invoked in the matter, and also by applying the principles of International Law.

ART. 49.—The Tribunal has the right to make rules of procedure for the direction of the trial, to settle the forms and periods within which each Party must submit its motions, and to conduct all the formalities which shall regulate the taking of evidence.

ART. 50.—The Agents and Counsel of the Parties having

ration les actes ou documents nouveaux sur lesquels les agents ou conseils des Parties appelleraient son attention.

En ce cas, le Tribunal a le droit de requérir la production de ces actes ou documents, sauf l'obligation d'en donner connaissance à la Partie adverse.

ART. 44. — Le Tribunal peut, en outre, requérir des agents des Parties la production de tous actes et demander toutes explications nécessaires. En cas de refus, le Tribunal en prend acte.

ART. 45. — Les agents et les conseils des Parties sont autorisés à présenter oralement au Tribunal tous les moyens qu'ils jugent utiles à la défense de leur cause.

ART. 46. — Ils ont le droit de soulever des exceptions et incidents. Les décisions du Tribunal sur ces points sont définitives et ne peuvent donner lieu à aucune discussion ultérieure.

ART. 47. — Les membres du Tribunal ont le droit de poser des questions aux agents et aux conseils des Parties et de leur demander des éclaircissements sur des points douteux.

Ni les questions posées, ni les observations faites par les membres du Tribunal pendant le cours des débats ne peuvent être regardées comme l'expression des opinions du Tribunal en général ou de ses membres en particulier.

ART. 48. — Le Tribunal est autorisé à déterminer sa compétence en interprétant le compromis ainsi que les autres traités qui peuvent être invoqués dans la matière et en appliquant les principes du droit international.

ART. 49. — Le Tribunal a le droit de rendre des ordonnances de procédure pour la direction du procès, de déterminer les formes et délais dans lesquels chaque Partie devra prendre ses conclusions et de procéder à toutes les formalités que comporte l'administration des preuves.

ART. 50. — Les agents et les conseils des Parties ayant présenté presented all the explanations and evidence in support of their cause, the President of the Tribunal shall announce the hearing closed.

ART. 51.—The deliberations of the Tribunal shall take place with closed doors.

Every decision shall be taken by a majority of the members of the Tribunal.

The refusal of any member to take part in the vote shall be formally set forth in the minutes.

ART. 52.—The arbitral Judgment reached by a majority vote shall be accompanied by the reasons on which it is based. This shall be reduced to writing and signed by each member of the Tribunal.

Those of the members who are in a minority may, when signing, record their dissent.

ART. 53.—The arbitral Judgment shall be read out at a public session of the Tribunal, the Agents and Counsel of the Parties being present, or duly summoned.

ART. 54. — The arbitral Judgment, duly pronounced and notified to the Agents of the disputing parties, shall decide the question at issue finally and without appeal.

ART. 55.—The Parties may, however, in the Agreement to arbitrate, reserve to themselves the right to ask for a revision of the arbitral Judgment.

In this case, and in the absence of an Agreement to the contrary, the request should be addressed to the Tribunal which has given the Judgment. It can be based only on the discovery of new evidence, which would have been of such a nature as to exercise a decisive influence on the Judgment, and which, at the time the hearing was closed was unknown to the Tribunal itself and to the Party which has asked for the revision.

The revision can be granted only by a decision of the Tribunal expressly stating the existence of the new evidence tous les éclaircissements et preuves à l'appui de leur cause, le Président prononce la clôture des débats.

ART. 51. — Les délibérations du Tribunal ont lieu à huis clos.

Toute décision est prise à la majorité des membres du Tribunal.

Le refus d'un membre de prendre part au vote doit être constaté dans le procès-verbal.

ART. 52. — La sentence arbitrale, votée à la majorité des voix, est motivée. Elle est rédigée par écrit et signée par chacun des membres du Tribunal.

Ceux des membres qui sont restés en minorité peuvent constater, en signant, leur dissentiment.

ART. 53. — La sentence arbitrale est lue en séance publique du Tribunal, les agents et les conseils des Parties présents ou dûment appelés.

ART. 54. — La sentence arbitrale, dûment prononcée et notifiée aux agents des Parties en litige, décide définitivement et sans appel la contestation.

ART. 55.—Les Parties peuvent se réserver dans le compromis de demander la revision de la sentence arbitrale.

Dans ce cas et sauf convention contraire, la demande doit être adressée au Tribunal qui a rendu la sentence. Elle ne peut être motivée que par la découverte d'un fait nouveau qui eût été de nature à exercer une influence décisive sur la sentence et qui, lors de la clôture des débats, était inconnu du Tribunal lui-même et de la Partie qui a demandé la revision.

La procédure de revision ne peut être ouverte que par une décision du Tribunal constatant expressément l'existence du fait possessing the character set forth in the preceding paragraph, and declaring that the demand is admissible on that ground.

The Agreement (*compromis*) shall determine the period of time within which the request for revision must be made.

ART. 56.—The arbitral Judgment is obligatory only on the Parties who concluded the Agreement.

When it consists in the interpretation of a Convention to which other Powers than those in litigation have been parties, these shall notify to the other Powers the Agreement to arbitrate which they have made. Each of these other Powers has the right to intervene in the proceedings. If one or more of them shall avail themselves of this right, the interpretation embodied in the Judgment shall be equally binding on them also.

ART. 57.—Each Party shall bear its own expenses and an equal part of the expenses of the Tribunal.

GENERAL PROVISIONS.

ART. 58.—The present Convention shall be ratified with the briefest delay possible.

The ratifications shall be deposited at the Hague. There shall be drawn up a minute of the deposit of each ratification, of which a copy, certified correct, will be transmitted through diplomatic channels to all the Powers which have been represented at the International Peace Conference at the Hague.

ART. 59.—Non-signatory Powers, which have been represented at the International Peace Conference, may give their adhesion to the present Convention. For this purpose they will have to make known their adhesion to the contracting Powers by means of a written notification addressed to the Government of the Netherlands, and communicated by it to all the other contracting Powers.

nouveau, lui reconnaissant les caractères prévus par le paragraphe précédent et déclarant à ce titre la demande recevable.

Le compromis détermine le délai dans lequel la demande de revision doit être formée.

ART. 56.—La sentence arbitrale n'est obligatoire que pour les parties qui ont conclu le compromis.

Lorsqu'il s'agit de l'interprétation d'une convention, à laquelle ont participé d'autres Puissances que les Parties en litige, celles-ci notifient aux premières le compromis qu'elles ont conclu. Chacune de ces Puissances a le droit d'intervenir au procès. Si une ou plusieurs d'entre elles ont profité de cette faculté, l'interprétation contenue dans la sentence est également obligatoire à leur égard.

ART. 57.—Chaque Partie supporte ses propres frais et une part égale des frais du Tribunal.

DISPOSITIONS GÉNÉRALES.

ART. 58.—La présente Convention sera ratifiée dans le plus bref délai possible.

Les ratifications seront déposées à la Haye.

Il sera dressé du dépôt de chaque ratification un procès-verbal, dont une copie, certifiée conforme, sera remise par la voie diplomatique à toutes les Puissances, qui ont été représentées à la Conférence Internationale de la Paix de la Haye.

ART. 59.—Les Puissances non signataires qui ont été représentées à la Conférence Internationale de la Paix pourront adhérer à la présente Convention. Elles auront à cet effet à faire connaître leur adhésion aux Puissances Contractantes, au moyen d'une notification écrite, adressée au Gouvernement des Pays-Bas et communiquée par celui-ci à toutes les autres Puissances Contractantes.

ART. 60.—The conditions on which the Powers which have not been represented at the International Peace Conference, may give their adhesion to the present Convention will form the object of a later agreement between the Contracting Powers.

ART. 61.—If it should happen that one of the High Contracting Parties denounce the present Convention, this denunciation would only take effect one year after the notification made by writing to the Government of the Netherlands and communicated by it immediately to all the other contracting Powers.

This denunciation will take effect only with regard to the Power which has given notification of it.

In witness hereof, the Plenipotentiaries have signed the present Convention, and have thereto affixed their seals.

Done at the Hague, the 29th July, 1899, in a single original which shall remain deposited in the Archives of the Government of the Netherlands, and copies of which, certified correct, shall be sent through diplomatic channels to the Contracting Powers.

ART. 60.—Les conditions auxquelles les Puissances, qui n'ont pas été représentées à la Conférence Internationale de la Paix, pourront adhérer à la présente Convention, formeront l'objet d'une entente ultérieure entre les Puissances Contractantes.

ART. 61.—S'il arrivait qu'une des Hautes Parties Contractantes dénonçât la présente Convention, cette dénonciation ne produirait ses effets qu'un an après la notification faite par écrit au Gouvernement des Pays-Bas et communiquée immédiatement par celui-ci à toutes les autres Puissances Contractantes.

Cette dénonciation ne produira ses effets qu'à l'égard de la Puissance qui l'aura notifiée.

En foi de quoi, les Plénipotentiaires ont signé la présente Convention et l'ont revêtue de leurs cachets.

Fait à La Haye, le vingt-neuf juillet mil huit cent quatre vingt-dix-neuf, en un seul exemplaire qui restera déposé dans les archives du Gouvernement des Pays-Bas et dont des copies, certifiées conformes, seront remises par la voie diplomatique aux Puissances Contractantes.

HISTORY OF THE PEACE CONFERENCE AT THE HAGUE.

THE EMPEROR'S MESSAGE.

On the 24th August, 1898, Count Muravieff, Russian Minister for Foreign Affairs, by order of the Emperor, made the following communication to all the foreign representatives accredited to the Court of St. Petersburg :—

The maintenance of general Peace, and a possible reduction of the excessive armaments which weigh upon all nations, present themselves in the existing condition of the whole world as the ideal towards which the endeavours of all Governments should be directed.

The humanitarian and magnanimous intentions of his Majesty the Emperor, my august master, have been entirely won over to this object.

In the conviction that this lofty aim is in conformity with the most essential interests and the legitimate views of all the Powers, the Imperial Government thinks that the present moment would be very favourable for an inquiry, by means of international discussion, as the most effectual means of securing to all peoples the benefits of a real and durable Peace, and, before all, of putting an end to the progressive development of the present armaments.

In the course of the last twenty years the longings for a general appeasement have grown especially pronounced in the conscience of civilised nations. The preservation of Peace has been put forward as the object of international policy. It is in its name that the great States have concluded between themselves powerful alliances ; it is the better to guarantee Peace that they have developed their military forces in proportions hitherto unprecedented, and still continue to increase them without shrinking from any sacrifice,

All these efforts, nevertheless, have not yet been able to bring about the beneficent results of the desired pacification.

The financial charges, following an upward course, strike at and paralyse public prosperity at its very source. The intellectual and physical strength of the nations, their labour and capital, are, for the most part, diverted from their natural application, and unproductively consumed. Hundreds of millions are devoted to obtaining terrible engines of destruction, which, though to-day regarded as the last word of science, are destined to-morrow to lose all value in consequence of some fresh discovery in the same field. National culture, economic progress, and the production of wealth are checked, paralysed, or perverted in their development.

Moreover, in proportion as the armaments of each Power increase, do they less and less fulfil the objects which the Governments have set before themselves. Economic crises, due in great part to the system of *armements à outrance* and the continual danger which lies in this accumulation of war material, are transforming the armed Peace of our days into a crushing burden which the peoples have more and more difficulty in bearing.

It appears evident, then, that if this state of things continue it will inevitably lead to the very cataclysm which it is desired to avert, and the horrors of which make every thinking being shudder in anticipation.

To put an end to these continual armaments, and to seek the means of warding off the calamities which are threatening the whole world—such is the supreme duty which is to-day imposed upon all States.

Filled with this sentiment, his Majesty has been pleased to order me to propose to all the Governments which have accredited representatives at the Imperial Court, the meeting of a Conference which should occupy itself with this grave problem.

This Conference would be, by the help of God, a happy

presage for the century which is about to open. It would collect into one powerful focus the efforts of all the States which are sincerely seeking to make the great conception of universal Peace triumph over the elements of disturbance and discord. It would at the same time cement their agreement by a corporate consecration of the principles of equity and right on which rest the security of States and the welfare of peoples.

SAINT PETERSBURG, 12/24 *August*, 1898.

(Signed) COUNT MURAVIEFF.

The original ran as follows :—

D'ordre de l'Empereur, le comte Mouravieff a remis, le 24 août, à tous les représentants étrangers accrédités à St.-Pétersbourg la communication suivante :

Le maintien de la paix générale et une réduction possible des armements excessifs qui pèsent sur toutes les nations se présentent, dans la situation actuelle du monde entier, comme l'idéal auquel devraient tendre les efforts de tous les Gouvernements.

Les vues humanitaires et magnanimes de Sa Majesté l'Empereur, mon Auguste Maître, y sont entièrement acquises.

Dans la conviction que ce but élevé répond aux intérêts les plus essentiels et aux vœux légitimes de toutes les Puissances, le Gouvernement Impérial croit que le moment présent serait très favorable à la recherche, dans la voie d'une discussion internationale, des moyens les plus efficaces d'assurer à tous les peuples les bienfaits d'une paix réelle et durable, et de mettre avant tout un terme au développement progressif des armements actuels.

Au cours des vingt dernières années, les aspirations à un apaisement général se sont particulièrement affirmées dans la conscience des nations civilisées.

La conservation de la paix a été posée comme le but de la

politique internationale; c'est en son nom que les grands Etats ont conclu entre eux de puissantes alliances; c'est pour mieux garantir la paix qu'ils ont développé, dans des proportions inconnues jusqu'ici, leurs forces militaires, et qu'ils continuent encore à les accroître sans reculer devant aucun sacrifice.

Tous ces efforts pourtant n'ont pu aboutir encore aux résultats bienfaisants de la pacification souhaitée.

Les charges financières, suivant une marche ascendante, atteignent et paralysent la prospérité publique dans sa source; les forces intellectuelles et physiques des peuples, le travail et le capital, sont en majeure partie détournés de leur application naturelle et consumés improductivement. Des centaines de millions sont employés à acquérir des engins de destruction effroyables qui, considérés aujourd'hui comme le dernier mot de la science, sont destinés demain à perdre toute valeur à la suite de quelque nouvelle découverte dans ce domaine. La culture nationale, le progrès économique, la production des richesses se trouvent entravés, paralysés ou faussés dans leur développement.

Aussi, à mesure qu'ils s'accroissent les armements de chaque Puissance, répondent-ils de moins en moins au but que les Gouvernements s'étaient proposé. Les crises économiques, dues en grande partie au régime des armements à outrance, et au danger continuel qui gît dans cet amoncellement du matériel de guerre, transforment la paix armée de nos jours en fardeau écrasant, que les peuples ont de plus en plus de peine à porter. Il paraît évident dès lors, qui si cette situation se prolongeait, elle conduirait fatalement à ce cataclysme même qu'on tient à écarter, et dont les horreurs font frémir à l'avance toute pensée humaine.

Mettre un terme à ces armements incessants et rechercher le moyen de prévenir des calamités qui menacent le monde entier, tel est le devoir suprême qui s'impose aujourd'hui à tous les Etats.

Pénétré de ce sentiment, Sa Majesté l'Empereur a daigné m'ordonner de proposer à tous les Gouvernements, dont les Représentants sont accrédités près la Cour Impériale, la réunion d'une Conférence qui aurait à s'occuper de ce grave problème.

Cette Conférence serait, Dieu aidant, d'un heureux présage pour le siècle qui va s'ouvrir. Elle rassemblerait dans un puissant faisceau les efforts de tous les Etats qui cherchent sincèrement à faire triompher la grande conception de la paix universelle sur les éléments de trouble et de discorde. Elle cimenterait en même temps leurs accords par une consécration solidaire des principes d'équité et de droit sur lesquels reposent la sécurité des Etats et le bien-être des peuples.

(Signé) COMTE MOURAVIEFF.

SAINT-PÉTERSBOURG,

Le 12/24 *Août* 1898.

DEFINITION OF THE SCOPE OF THE CONGRESS.

This invitation having been accepted by a number of the Powers, it was followed by a second circular addressed on December 30th, 1898, by Count Muravieff, to the representatives of the Powers at St. Petersburg defining the scope of the proposed Conference, and indicating the topics to be discussed, as follows :—

When, in the month of August last, my August Master instructed me to propose to the Governments which have accredited representatives at St. Petersburg the holding of a Conference with the object of seeking the most effective means of securing to all peoples the blessings of real and lasting Peace, and before all, of putting a stop to the progressive development of the present armaments, there appeared to be nothing in the way of the realisation, at no distant date, of this humanitarian scheme.

The warm welcome given to the proceeding of the Imperial Government by nearly all the Powers, could not fail to strengthen this expectation. While highly appreciating the sympathetic terms in which the adhesions of most of the Powers were drafted, the Imperial Cabinet has also felt lively satisfaction at the testimonies of the very warm approval which have been addressed to it, and continue to be received, from all classes of society in various parts of the globe.

Notwithstanding the strong current of opinion which set in in favour of the ideas of general pacification, the political horizon has lately undergone a sensible change. Several Powers have undertaken fresh armaments, striving still further to increase their military forces, and in the presence of this uncertain situation it might be asked whether the Powers considered the present moment opportune for the international discussion of the ideas set forth in the circular of August (12th, old style) 24th, 1898.

Hoping, however, that the elements of disturbance agitating the political spheres will soon give place to a calmer disposition, of a nature to favour the success of the proposed Conference, the Imperial Government is of opinion that it would be possible to proceed forthwith to a preliminary exchange of views between the Powers, with the object—

(*a.*) Of seeking without delay means for putting a stop to the progressive increase of military and naval armaments—a question the solution of which becomes evidently more and more urgent in view of the fresh extension given to these armaments; and

(*b.*) Of preparing the way for a discussion of the questions relating to the possibility of preventing armed conflicts by the pacific means at the disposal of international diplomacy.

In the event of the Powers considering the present moment favourable for the meeting of a Conference on these bases, it would certainly be useful for the Cabinets to come to an understanding on the subject of the programme of their labours. The proposals to be submitted for international discussion at the Conference could in general terms be summarised as follows :—

1. An understanding not to increase for a fixed period the present effective of the armed military and naval forces, or the budgets pertaining to them ; a preliminary examination of the means by which a reduction might even be effected in future in the forces and budgets above mentioned.

2. To prohibit the use in the armies and fleets of any new kind of firearms whatever, and of new explosives, or any powders more powerful than those now in use either for rifles or cannon.

3. To restrict the use in military warfare of the formidable explosives already existing, and to prohibit the throwing of projectiles or explosives of any kind from balloons, or by any similar means.

4. To prohibit the use in naval warfare of submarine torpedo boats or plungers, or other similar engines of destruction; to give an understanding not to construct vessels with rams in the future.

5. To apply to naval warfare the stipulations of the Geneva Convention of 1864 on the basis of the articles added to the Convention of 1868.

6. To neutralise ships and boats employed in saving those overboard during or after an engagement.

7. To revise the declaration concerning the laws and customs of war elaborated in 1874 by the Conference of Brussels, which has remained unratified to the present day.

8. To accept in principle the employment of the good offices, of mediation and facultative Arbitration, in cases lending themselves thereto, with the object of preventing armed conflicts between nations; an understanding with respect to the mode of applying these good offices, and the establishment of a uniform practice in using them.

It is well understood that all questions concerning the political relations of States, and the order of things established by treaties, as generally all questions which do not directly fall within the programme adopted by the Cabinets, must be absolutely excluded from the deliberations of the Conference.

In requesting you, Monsieur, to be good enough to apply to your Government for instructions on the subject of my present communication, I beg you at the same time to inform it that, in the interest of the great cause which my August Master has so much at heart, his Imperial Majesty considers it advisable that the Conference should not sit in the capital of one of the Great Powers, where so many political interests are centred, which might perhaps impede the progress of a work in which all the countries of the universe are equally interested.

Accept, Monsieur, etc.,

(Signed) COUNT MURAVIEFF.

The following is the original text of this Circular :—

MONSIEUR L'ENVOYÉ.

Lorsqu'au mois d'août dernier mon Auguste Maître m'ordonnait de proposer aux Gouvernements, dont les Représentants se trouvent accrédités à Saint-Pétersbourg, la réunion d'une Conférence destinée à rechercher les moyens les plus efficaces d'assurer à tous les peuples les bienfaits d'une paix réelle et durable et de mettre avant tout un terme au développement progressif des armements actuels—rien ne semblait s'opposer à la réalisation plus au moins prochaine, de ce projet humanitaire.

L'accueil empressé fait à la démarche du Gouvernement Impérial par presque toutes les Puissances ne pouvaient que justifier cette attente. Appréciant hautement les termes sympathiques dans lesquels était conçue l'adhésion de la plupart des Gouvernements, le Cabinet Impérial a pu recueillir, en même temps avec une vive satisfaction, les témoignages du plus chaleureux assentiment qui lui étaient adressés et ne cessent de lui parvenir de la part de toutes les classes de la société de différents points du globe terrestre.

Malgré le grand courant d'opinion qui s'était produit en faveur des idées de pacification générale, l'horizon politique a sensiblement changé d'aspect en dernier lieu.

Plusieurs Puissances ont procédé à des armements nouveaux, s'efforçant d'accroître encore leurs forces militaires, et, en présence de cette situation incertaine, on pouvait être amené à se demander si les Puissances jugeaient le moment actuel opportun à la discussion internationale des idées émises dans la Circulaire du 12 24 août.

Espérant, toutefois, que les éléments de trouble qui agitent les sphères politiques feront bientôt place à des dispositions plus calmes et de nature à favoriser le succès de la Conférence projetée le Gouvernement Impérial est, pour sa part, d'avis qu'il serait possible de procéder dès à présent à un échange préalable d'idées entre les Puissances dans le but :

(*a*) de rechercher sans retard les moyens de mettre un terme à l'accroissement progressif des armements de terre et de mer—question dont la solution devient évidemment de plus en plus urgente en vue de l'extension nouvelle donnée à ces armements, et,

(*b*) de préparer les voies à une discussion des questions se rapportant à la possibilité de prévenir les conflits armés par les moyens pacifiques dont peut disposer la diplomatie internationale.

Dans le cas où les Puissances jugeraient le moment actuel favorable à la réunion d'une Conférence sur ces bases, il serait certainement utile d'établir entre les Cabinets une entente au sujet du programme de ses travaux.

Les thèmes à soumettre à une discussion internationale au sein de la Conférence pourraient, en traits généraux, se résumer comme suit :

1° Entente stipulant la non-augmentation pour un terme à fixer des effectifs actuels des forces armées de terre et de mer, ainsi que des budgets de guerre y afférents, étude préalable des voies dans lesquelles pourrait même se réaliser, dans l'avenir, une réduction des effectifs et des budgets ci-dessus mentionnés ;

2° Interdiction de la mise en usage, dans les armées et les flottes, de nouvelles armes à feu quelconques et de nouveaux explosifs, aussi bien que de poudres plus puissantes que celles adoptées actuellement, tant pour les fusils que pour les canons ;

3° Limitation de l'emploi, dans les guerres de campagne, des explosifs d'une puissance formidable déjà existants et prohibition du lancement de projectiles ou d'explosifs quelconques du haút des ballons ou par des moyens analogues ;

4° Défense d'employer dans les guerres navales des bateaux-torpilleurs sous-marins ou plongeurs, ou d'autres engins de destruction de la même nature; engagement de ne pas construire, à l'avenir, des navires de guerre à éperon ;

5° Adaptation aux guerres maritimes des stipulations de la Convention de Genève de 1864, sur la base des articles additionnels de 1868 ;

6° Neutralisation, au même titre, des navires ou chaloupes chargées du sauvetage des naufragés, pendant ou après les combats maritimes ;

7° Revision de la Déclaration concernant les avis et coutumes de la guerre, élaborée en 1874 par la Conférence de Bruxelles et restée non-ratifiée jusqu'à ce jour ;

8° Acceptation, en principe, de l'usage des bons offices, de la médiation et de l'arbitrage facultatif, pour des cas qui s'y prêtent, dans le but de prévenir des conflits armés entre les nations ; entente au sujet de leur mode d'application et établissement d'une pratique uniforme dans leur emploi.

Il est bien entendu que toutes les questions concernant les rapports politiques des Etats et l'ordre de choses établi par les traités, comme en général toutes les questions qui ne rentreront pas directement dans le programme, adopté par les Cabinets, devront être absolument exclues des délibérations de la Conférence.

En vous adressant, Monsieur l'Envoyé, la demande de bien vouloir prendre au sujet de ma présente communication les ordres de votre Gouvernement, je vous prie en même temps de porter à sa connaissance que dans l'intérêt de la grande cause, qui tient si particulièrement à cœur à mon Auguste Maître, Sa Majesté Impériale juge qu'il serait utile que la Conférence ne siége pas dans la capitale de l'une des grandes Puissances, où se concentrent tant d'intérêts politiques qui pourraient, peut-être, réagir sur la marche d'une œuvre à laquelle sont intéressés à un égal degré tous les pays de l'univers.

Veuillez recevoir, Monsieur l'Envoyé, l'assurance de ma considération la plus distinguée.

(Signé) COMTE MOURAVIEFF.

INVITATION TO THE HAGUE.

The next step in the development of the Emperor's proposal was the issue by the Foreign Minister of the Netherlands, after correspondence with the Court at St. Petersburg, of a circular addressed, on April 6th, 1899, to the diplomatic representatives of his country at the various Courts. After detailing the steps already taken, and noting that the Russian Government considered, for political reasons, that it was not desirable that the Conference should meet in either of the great capitals, he informed them that the Hague had been selected as its place of session, and instructed them to invite the Governments to which they were severally accredited, to take the necessary steps for their representation, and for the attendance of their delegates on May 18th following, at "the opening of the Conference, in which each Power, whatever may be the number of its Representatives, would have only one vote."

MEETING OF THE CONFERENCE.

The Conference held its first session in the "Huis ten Bosch" (House in the Wood), at the Hague, in the famous Orange Hall, on Thursday, May 18th, 1899. Twenty-six States were represented by rather more than a hundred Delegates. All the Delegates appointed, with their technical advisers, were present. The first sitting was of a merely formal character, and lasted only twenty-five minutes. M. de Beaufort, Foreign Minister of Holland, presided, and after welcoming the Delegates in a very felicitous speech, moved the despatch of a telegram of congratulation to the Tzar, and the appointment of M. de Staal as President of the Conference. Both resolutions were unanimously adopted. M. de Staal then assumed the presidential chair, made a suitable response, and proposed the sending of a message to Her Majesty the Queen of the Netherlands, which was warmly applauded by all present.

Appointment of Committees.

The following day, Friday, May 19th, the delegates met by invitation of the President, M. de Staal, in his apartments in the Vieux Doelen Hotel. It was agreed to appoint three Committees, to deal with the three groups of questions to be discussed, as follows:—

I.—Armaments.

(*a.*) The limitation of expenditure.
(*b.*) The prohibition of new firearms.
(*c.*) The limitation of the use of explosives.
(*d.*) The prohibition of the use of submarine boats.

II.—Laws of Warfare.

(*a.*) The application of the Geneva Convention to naval warfare.

(*b.*) The neutralisation of vessels engaged in saving the shipwrecked, during or after naval engagments.

(*c.*) The revision of the Declaration of Brussels of 1874, on the laws and customs of war.

III.—Mediation and Arbitration.

The Armaments Committee (43 members) was further divided into two sections; one military, with M. Beernaert, of Belgium as President, and Sir John Ardagh (Great Britain),

Captain Crozier (U.S.A.) and General Mounier (France) among the members; the other naval, with M. van Karnebeek (Holland) as President, and Sir John Fisher (Britain), Captain Mahan (U.S.A.) and Captain Siegel (Germany) among the members. The Laws of Warfare Committee (58 members) was also subdivided; M. Asser (Belgium) becoming President of the Geneva Convention Section, and Professor Martens (Russia) of the Brussels Conference Section. On both these Committees, most of the States were represented by their military and naval delegates. M. Bourgeois (France) was chosen President of the Mediation and Arbitration Committees (51 members) of which Sir Julian Pauncefote (Britain), Sir Henry Howard (Britain), Count Münster (Germany), Count Nigra (Italy), Dr. Andrew White (U.S.A.) and Mr. Seth Low (U.S.A.) were members.

Second Sitting.

Next day, Saturday, May 20th, there was a plenary sitting of the Conference, when Baron de Staal gave an important address, and communicated the replies of the Tzar and of Queen Wilhelmina. The sitting lasted thirty-five minutes, and the delegates separated for Whitsuntide, after which the work of the various Committees began.

The Arbitration Committee.

It is not proposed to follow the details of the work in these Committees. That of the third, the Arbitration Committee necessarily excites most interest. In its sitting of May 26th, M. de Staal brought forward the Russian project of Mediation and Arbitration. He was immediately followed by Sir Julian Pauncefote, who, on behalf of Great Britain, said that while gladly accepting the Russian Scheme as far as it went, he would have to propose that it be supplemented by the constitution of a Permanent International Tribunal. Mr. Holls on behalf of the American Delegates, announced that they were also preparing a scheme. A Committee was appointed to consider these projects, consisting of M. Descamps (President), Sir J. Pauncefote, Count Nigra and MM. Asser D'Estournelles, Holls, Lammasch, Martens, Odier, and Zorn. This Comité de Redaction, which met, for the first time, on May 29th, had to consider the following schemes :—

DOCUMENTS ÉMANÉS DE LA DÉLÉGATION RUSSE.

I.—ELÉMENTS POUR L'ÉLABORATION D'UN PROJET DE CONVENTION À CONCLURE ENTRE LES PUISSANCES PARTICIPANT À LA CONFÉRENCE DE LA HAYE.

BONS OFFICES ET MÉDIATION.

ARTICLE PREMIER.—A l'effet de prévenir, autant que possible le recours à la force dans les rapports internationaux, les Puissances signataires sont convenues d'employer tous leurs efforts pour amener, par des moyens pacifiques, la solution des conflits qui pourraient surgir entre Elles.

ART. 2.—En conséquence, les Puissances signataires ont décidé qu'en cas de dissentiment grave ou de conflit, avant d'en appeler aux armes, elles auront recours, en tant que les circonstances l'admettraient, aux bons offices ou à la médiation d'une ou de plusieurs Puissances amies.

ART. 3.—En cas de médiation, acceptée spontanément par des Etats se trouvant en conflit, le but du Gouvernement médiateur consiste dans la conciliation des prétentions opposées et dans l'apaisement des ressentiments qui peuvent s'être produits entre ces Etats.

ART. 4.—Le rôle du Gouvernement médiateur cesse du moment que la transaction proposée par lui ou les bases d'une entente amicale qu'il aurait sugérées ne seraient point acceptées par les Etats en conflit.

ART. 5.—Les Puissances jugent utile que, dans les cas de

dissentiment grave ou de conflit entre Etats civilisés concernant des questions d'intérêt politique—indépendamment du recours que pourraient avoir les Puissances en litige aux bons offices ou à la médiation des Puissances non impliquées dans le conflit—ces dernières offrent de leur propre initiative, en tant que les circonstances s'y prêteraient, aux Etats en litige leurs bons offices ou leur médiation, afin d'aplanir le différend survenu, en leur proposant une solution amiable qui, sans toucher aux intérêts des autres Etats, serait de nature à concilier au mieux les intérêts des Parties en litige.

ART. 6.—Il demeure bien entendu que la médiation et les bons offices, soit sur l'initiative des Parties en litige, soit sur celle des Puissances neutres, ont strictement le caractère de conseil amical, et nullement force obligatoire.

ARBITRAGE INTERNATIONAL.

ART. 7.—En ce qui regarde les cas de litige se rapportant à des questions de droit, et, en premier lieu, à celles qui concernent l'interprétation ou l'application des traités en vigueur,—l'arbitrage est reconnu par les Puissances signataires comme étant le moyen le plus efficace et en même temps le plus équitable pour le règlement à l'amiable de ces litiges.

ART. 8.—Les Puissances contractantes s'engagent par conséquent à recourir à l'arbitrage dans les cas se rapportant à des questions de l'ordre mentionné ci-dessus, en tant que celles-ci ne touchent ni aux intérêts vitaux, ni à l'honneur national des Parties en litige.

ART. 9.—Chaque Etat reste seul juge de la question de savoir si tel ou tel cas doit être soumis à l'arbitrage, excepté ceux énumérés dans l'article suivant et dans lesquels les Puissances signataires du présent Acte considèrent l'arbitrage comme obligatoire pour Elles.

ART. 10.—A partir de la ratification du présent Acte par toutes les Puissances signataires, l'arbitrage est obligatoire dans les cas suivants, en tant qu'ils ne touchent ni aux intérêts vitaux, ni à l'honneur national des Etats contractants.

I. En cas de différends ou de contestations se rapportant à des dommages pécuniaires éprouvés par un Etat, ou ses ressortissants, à la suite d'actions illicites ou de négligence d'un autre Etat ou des ressortissants de ce dernier.

II. En cas de dissentiments se rapportant à l'interprétation ou l'application des traités et conventions ci-dessous mentionnés :

1. Traités et conventions postales et télégraphiques, de chemins de fer ainsi qu'ayant trait à la protection de câbles télégraphiques sous-marins ; règlements concernant les moyens destinés à prévenir les collisions de navires en pleine mer ; conventions relatives à la navigation des fleuves internationaux et canaux interocéaniques.

2. Convention concernant la protection de la propriété littéraire et artistique, ainsi que la propriété industrielle (brevets d'invention, marques de fabrique ou de commerce et nom commercial) ; conventions monétaires et métriques ; conventions sanitaires, vétérinaires et contre le phylloxéra.

3. Conventions de succession, de cartel et d'assistance judiciaire mutuelle.

4. Conventions de démarcation, en tant qu'elles touchent aux questions purement techniques et non politiques.

ART. 11.—L'énumération des cas mentionnés dans l'article ci-dessus pourra être complétée par des accords subséquents entre les Puissances signataires du présent Acte.

En outre, chacune d'entre Elles pourra entrer en accord particulier avec une autre Puissance, afin de rendre l'arbitrage obligatoire pour les cas susdits avant la ratification générale, ainsi que pour étendre sa compétence à tous les cas qu'Elle jugera possible de lui soumettre.

ART. 12.—Pour tous les autres cas de conflits internationaux, non mentionnés dans les articles ci-dessus, l'arbitrage, tout en étant certainement très désirable et recommandé par le présent Acte, n'est cependant que purement facultatif, c'est-à-dire ne peut être appliqué que sur l'initiative spontanée de l'une des Parties en litige et avec le consentement exprès et de plein gré de l'autre ou des autres Parties.

ART. 13.—En vue de faciliter le recours à l'arbitrage et son application, les Puissances signataires ont consenti à préciser, d'un commun accord, pour les cas d'arbitrage international, les principes fondamentaux à observer pour l'établissement et les règles de procédure à suivre pendant l'instruction du litige, et le prononcé de la sentence arbitrale.

L'application de ces principes fondamentaux, ainsi que de la procédure arbitrale, indiquée dans l'appendice au présent article, pourrait être modifiée en vertu d'un accord spécial entre les Etats qui auraient recours à l'arbitrage.

COMMISSIONS INTERNATIONALES D'ENQUÊTE.

ART. 14.—Dans les cas où se produiraient entre les Etats signataires des divergences d'appréciation par rapport aux circonstances locales ayant donné lieu à un litige d'ordre international qui ne pourrait pas être résolu par les voies diplomatiques ordinaires, mais dans lequel ni l'honneur, ni les intérêts vitaux de ces Etats ne seraient engagés, les Gouvernements intéressés conviennent d'instituer une Commission internationale d'enquête, afin de constater les circonstances ayant donné matière au dissentiment et d'éclaircir sur les lieux par un examen impartial et consciencieux toutes les questions de fait.

ART. 15.—Ces Commissions internationales sont constituées comme suit : chaque Gouvernement intéressé nomme deux membres et les quatre membres réunis choisissent le cinquième membre, qui est en même temps le Président de la Commission. S'il y a partage de voix pour l'élection d'un Président, les deux Gouvernements intéressés s'adressent d'un commun accord, soit à un Gouvernement tiers, soit à une personne tierce qui nommera le Président de la Commission.

ART. 16.—Les Gouvernements entre lesquels s'est produit un

dissentiment grave ou un conflit dans les conditions indiquées plus haut, s'engagent à fournir à la Commission d'enquête tous les moyens et toutes les facilités nécessaires pour une étude approfondie et consciencieuse des faits qui y ont donné matière.

ART. 17.—La Commission d'enquête internationale, après avoir constaté les circonstances dans lesquelles le dissentiment ou le conflit s'est produit, présente aux Gouvernements intéressés son rapport signé par tous les membres de la Commission.

ART. 18.—La rapport de la Commission d'enquête n'a nullement le caractère d'une sentence arbitrale; il laisse aux Gouvernements en conflit entière faculté, soit de conclure un arrangement à l'amiable sur la base du rapport susmentionné, soit de recourir à l'arbitrage en concluant un accord *ad hoc*, soit enfin de recourir aux voies de fait admises dans les rapports mutuels entre les nations.

II.—PROJET DE CODE D'ARBITRAGE PROPOSÉ PAR LA DÉLÉGATION RUSSE.

ARTICLE PREMIER.—Les Puissances signataires ont approuvé les principes et règles ci-dessous pour la procédure d'arbitrage entre nations, sauf les modifications qui pourraient y être introduites dans chaque cas spécial d'un commun accord par les Gouvernements en litige.

ART. 2.—Les Etats intéressés, ayant accepté l'arbitrage, signent un acte spécial (compromis), dans lequel sont nettement précisées les questions soumises à la décision de l'arbitre, l'ensemble des faits et des points de droit qui s'y rattachent et, enfin, se trouve confirmé formellement l'engagement des deux Parties contractantes de se soumettre, de bonne foi et sans appel, à la sentence arbitrale qui sera prononcée.

ART. 3.—Les compromis ainsi conclus de plein gré par les Etats, peuvent établir l'arbitrage soit pour toutes contestations survenant entre eux, soit pour les contestations d'une catégorie déterminée.

ART. 4.—Les Gouvernements intéressés peuvent confier les fonctions d'arbitre au Souverain ou au Chef d'Etat d'une Puissance tierce avec l'assentiment de ce dernier. Ils peuvent également confier ces fonctions soit à une personne seule, choisie par eux, soit à un tribunal d'arbitrage constitué à cet effet

Dans le dernier cas et en vue de l'importance du litige, le Tribunal d'arbitrage pourrait être constitué de la manière suivante: chaque Partie contractante choisit deux arbitres et tous les arbitres réunis choisissent le sur-arbitre qui est *de jure* le président du Tribunal d'arbitrage.

En cas de partage des voix, les Gouvernements en litige s'adresseront d'un commun accord à un Gouvernement tiers ou à une personne tierce qui nommera le sur-arbitre.

ART. 5.—Si les Parties en litige n'arrivent pas à un accord sur le choix du Gouvernement tiers ou d'une personne tierce mentionnés dans l'article précédent, chacune de ces Parties nommera une Puissance non impliquée dans le conflit, afin que les Puissances ainsi choisies par les Parties en litige, désignent, d'un commun accord, un sur-arbitre.

ART. 6.—L'incapacité ou la récusation valable, fût-ce d'un seul des arbitres susindiqués, ainsi que le refus d'accepter l'office arbitral après l'acceptation ou la mort d'un arbitre choisi, infirme le compromis entier, sauf les cas où ces faits sonts prévus et réglés d'advance d'un commun accord des Parties contractantes.

ART. 7.—Le siège du Tribunal d'arbitrage est désigné, soit par les Etats contractants, soit par les membres du tribunal eux-mêmes. Le changement de ce siège du Tribunal n'est loisible qu'en vertu d'un nouvel accord entre les Gouvernements intéressés ou, en cas de force majeure, sur l'initiative du Tribunal même.

ART. 8.—Les Etats en litige ont le droit de nommer des délegués ou agents spéciaux, attachés au Tribunal d'arbitrage avec la charge de servir d'intermédiaires entre le Tribunal et les Gouvernements intéressés.

Outre ces agents, les susdits Gouvernements sont autorisés à charger de la défense de leurs droits et intérêts devant le Tribunal d'arbitrage des conseils ou avocats nommés à cet effet.

ART. 9.—Le Tribunal d'arbitrage décide dans quelles langues devront avoir lieu ses délibérations et les débats des parties.

ART. 10.—La procédure arbitrale doit généralement parcourir deux phases : préliminaire et définitive.

La première consiste dans la communication aux membres du Tribunal d'arbitrage, par les agents des Etats contractants, de tous les actes, documents et arguments imprimés ou écrits relatifs aux questions en litige.

La seconde—définitive ou orale — consiste dans les débats devant le Tribunal d'arbitrage.

ART. 11.—Après la clôture de la procédure préliminaire commencent les débats devant le Tribunal d'arbitrage qui son dirigés par le Président.

De toutes les délibérations sont tenus des procès-verbaux, rédigés par des secrétaires, nommés par le Président du Tribunal. Ces procès-verbaux seuls ont force légale.

ART. 12.—La procédure préliminaire étant close, le Tribuna d'arbitrage a le droit de refuser tous les nouveaux actes ou documents que les représentants des Parties voudraient lui soumettre.

ART. 13.—Toutefois, le Tribunal d'arbitrage reste souverainement libre de prendre en considération les nouveaux documents ou actes dont les délégués ou conseils des deux Gouvernements en litige ont profité dans leurs explications devant le Tribunal.

Ce dernier a le droit de requérir la représentation de ces actes ou documents et d'en donner connaissance à la Partie adverse.

ART. 14.—Le Tribunal d'arbitrage, outre cela, a le droit de requérir des agents des Parties la présentation de tous les actes ou explications dont il aura besoin.

ART. 15.—Les agents et conseils des Gouvernements en litige

sont autorisés à présenter au Tribunal d'arbitrage oralement toutes les explications ou preuves au profit de la cause à défendre.

ART. 16.—Ces mêmes agents et conseils ont également le droit de s'adresser au Tribunal avec des motions sur les matières à discuter.

Les décisions du Tribunal concernant ces motions sont définitives et ne peuvent donner lieu à aucune discussion.

ART. 17.—Les membres du Tribunal d'arbitrage ont le droit de poser aux agents ou conseils des Parties contractantes des questions ou de demander des éclaircissements sur des points douteux.

Ni les questions posées, ni les observations faites par les membres du Tribunal pendant le cours des délibérations ne sauraient être regardées comme énonciations des opinions du Tribunal en général, ou de ses membres en particulier.

ART. 18.—Le Tribunal d'arbitrage est seul autorisé à déterminer sa compétence par l'interprétation des clauses du compromis, et selon les principes du droit international ainsi que les stipulations des traités particuliers qui peuvent être invoqués dans la matière.

ART. 19.—Le Tribunal d'arbitrage a le droit de rendre des ordonnances de procédure sur la direction du procès, de déterminer les formes et délais dans lesquels chaque Partie devra présenter ses conclusions et de statuer sur l'interprétation des documents produits et communiqués aux deux Parties.

ART. 20.—Les agents et conseils des Gouvernements en litige ayant présenté tous les éclaircissements et preuves pour la défense de leurs causes, le Président du Tribunal d'arbitrage prononcera la clôture de la discussion.

ART. 21. — Les délibérations des membres du Tribunal d'arbitrage sur le fond du litige ont lieu à huis clos.

Toute décision définitive ou provisoire est prise à la majorité des membres présents.

Le refus d'un membre du Tribunal de prendre part au vote doit être constaté dans le procès-verbal.

ART. 22.—La sentence arbitrale, votée à la majorité des voix doit être rédigée par écrit et doit être signée par chacun des membres du Tribunal d'arbitrage.

Ceux des membres du Tribunal qui sont restés dans la minorité constatent, en signant, leur dissentiment.

ART. 23.—La sentence arbitrale est lue solennellement en séance publique du Tribunal et en présence des agents et conseils des Gouvernements en litige.

ART. 24.—La sentence arbitrale, dûment prononcée et notifiée aux agents des Gouvernements en litige, décide définitivement et sans appel la contestation entre les Parties et clôt toute la procédure arbitrale instituée par le compromis.

ART. 25.—Chaque Partie supportera ses propres frais et la moitié des frais du Tribunal d'arbitrage, sans préjudice de la décision du Tribunal touchant l'indemnité que l'une ou l'autre des Parties pourra être condamnée à payer.

ART. 26.—La sentence arbitrale est nulle en cas de compromis nul, ou d'excès de pouvoir ou de corruption prouvée d'un des arbitres.

La procédure indiquée ci-dessus concernant le Tribunal d'arbitrage s'applique également à partir du § 7 commençant par les mots : " Le siège du Tribunal d'arbitrage," dans le cas où l'arbitrage est confié à une personne seule au choix des Gouvernements intéressés.

Dans le cas où le Souverain ou le Chef d'Etat se réserverait de prononcer personnellement comme arbitre, la procédure à suivre serait fixée par le Souverain ou le Chef d'Etat lui-même.

III.—PROPOSITIONS RUSSES CONCERNANT LE TRIBUNAL D'ARBITRAGE.

a) ARTICLES QUI POURRAIENT REMPLACER L'ARTICLE I., 13.

ARTICLE PREMIER.—En vue de consolider, en tant que possible, la pratique de l'arbitrage international, les Puissances contractantes sont convenues d'instituer, pour la durée de . . . .

ans, un Tribunal d'arbitrage, auquel seraient soumis les cas d'arbitrage obligatoire énumérés dans l'article 10, à moins que les Puissances intéressées ne tombent d'accord sur l'établissement d'un Tribunal d'arbitrage spécial pour la solution du conflit survenu entre Elles.

Les Puissances en litige pourront également avoir recours au Tribunal ci-dessus indiqué dans tous les cas d'arbitrage facultatif, si un accord spécial à ce sujet s'établit entre Elles.

Il est bien entendu que toutes les Puissances, sans en excepter celles non contractantes ou celles qui auraient fait des réserves, pourront soumettre leurs différends à ce Tribunal en s'adressant au Bureau permanent prévu par l'article . . . . de l'appendice A.

ART. 2.—L'organisation du Tribunal d'arbitrage est indiquée dans l'appendice A au présent article.

L'organisation des tribunaux d'arbitrage institués par des accords spéciaux entre les Puissances en litige, ainsi que les règles de procédure à suivre pendant l'instruction du litige et le prononcé de la sentence arbitrale sont déterminées dans l'appendice B (Code d'arbitrage).

Les dispositions contenues dans ce dernier appendice pourront être modifiées en vertu d'un accord spécial entre les Etats qui auront recours à l'arbitrage.

b) ANNEXE AUX PROPOSITIONS RUSSES.

En cas d'acceptation des articles 1 et 2, il y aurait lieu :

1.—De rédiger l'appendice A mentionné dans l'article ;

2.—D'introduire dans le projet du Code d'arbitrage des modifications correspondantes.

c) APPENDICE A,
mentionné dans l'article additionel 2 des Propositions russes.

A défaut d'un compromis spécial, le Tribunal d'arbitrage prévu par l'article 13 sera constitué sur les bases suivantes :

§ 1.—Les Parties contractantes instituent un Tribunal permanent pour la solution des conflits internationaux qui lui seront déférés par les Puissances en litige, en vertu de l'article 13 de la présente Convention.

§ 2.—La Conférence désignera, pour le terme qui s'écoulera jusqu'à la réunion d'une nouvelle Conférence, cinq Puissances, afin que chacune d'elles, en cas de demande d'arbitrage, nomme un juge, soit du nombre de ses ressortissants, soit en dehors d'eux.

Les juges ainsi nommés constituent le Tribunal arbitral compétent pour le cas survenu.

§ 3.—Si parmi les Puissances en litige se trouvaient une ou plusieurs Puissances non représentées dans le Tribunal arbitral, en vertu de l'article précédent, chacune des deux Parties en litige aura le droit de s'y faire représenter par une personne de son choix en qualité de juge ayant les mêmes droits que les autres membres dudit Tribunal.

§ 4.—Le Tribunal choisit parmi ses membres son Président qui, en cas de partage de voix en nombre égal, aura la voix prépondérante.

§ 5.—Un Bureau permanent d'arbitrage sera institué par les cinq Puissances qui seront désignées en vertu du présent Acte pour constituer le Tribunal arbitral. Elles élaboreront le règlement de ce Bureau, en nommeront les employés, pourvoiront à leur remplacement le cas échéant et fixeront leurs émoluments. Ce Bureau, dont le siège sera à La Haye, comprendra un Secrétaire général, un Secrétaire adjoint, un Secrétaire-archiviste ainsi que le reste du personnel, lequel sera nommé par le Secrétaire général.

§ 6.—Les frais d'entretien de ce Bureau seront répartis entre les Etats dans la proportion établie pour le Bureau international postal.

§ 7.—Le Bureau rend annuellement compte de son activité aux cinq Puissances qui l'ont nommé et celles-ci communiquent le compte rendu aux autres Puissances.

§ 8.—Les Puissances entre lesquelles auraient surgi un litige s'adresseront au Bureau et lui fourniront les documents nécessaires. Le Bureau avisera les cinq Puissances ci-dessus mentionnées qui auront à constituer sans retard le Tribunal. Ce Tribunal se réunira d'ordinaire à La Haye; il pourra se réunir également dans une autre ville, si un accord s'établit à cet effet entre les Etats intéressés.

§ 9.—Pendant le fonctionnement du Tribunal, le Bureau lui servira de Secrétariat. Il suivra le Tribunal en cas de déplacement. Les archives de l'arbitrage international seront déposées au Bureau.

§ 10.—La procédure du Tribunal susdit sera régie par les prescriptions du Code d'arbitrage.

TRANSLATION OF THE RUSSIAN PROPOSALS.

I.—ELEMENTS FOR THE ELABORATION OF A CONVENTION TO BE CONCLUDED BY THE POWERS PARTICIPATING IN THE HAGUE CONFERENCE.

GOOD OFFICES AND MEDIATION.

ART. 1.—In order to prevent, as far as possible, recourse to force in international relations, the Signatory Powers are agreed to employ every effort to bring about by pacific means the solution of conflicts which may arise among them.

ART. 2.—In consequence the Signatory Powers are decided, in the event of serious disagreement or conflict, before appealing to arms, to have recourse, so far as circumstances will permit, to the good offices or mediation of one or more friendly Powers.

ART. 3.—In the event of mediation being spontaneously accepted by States in conflict, the aim of the mediatory Government consists in endeavouring to bring about a conciliation between the States.

ART. 4.—The *rôle* of the mediatory Government ceases from the moment when the compromise proposed by it, or the bases of a friendly agreement which it may have suggested, shall not have been accepted by the States in conflict.

ART. 5.—Should the Powers consider it advisable, in the event of a serious disagreement or conflict between civilised States regarding questions of political interest, the Powers not implicated in the conflict shall offer of their own initiative, so far as circumstances are favourable, their good offices or their mediation to the disputing States in order to remove the difference that has arisen by proposing an amicable solution which, without affecting the interests of other States, shall be of a conciliatory nature in the best interests of the parties in dispute.

ART. 6.—It remains well understood that mediation and the employment of good offices, either at the instance of the parties in dispute or of neutral Powers, shall bear strictly the character of friendly counsel and in no way of compulsory force.

INTERNATIONAL ARBITRATION.

ART. 7.—In so far as regards a dispute relating to questions of right, and primarily to those affecting the interpretation or application of treaties in force, Arbitration is recognised by the Signatory Powers as being the most efficacious and most equitable means of settling these disputes in a friendly manner.

ART. 8.—The Contracting Powers therefore undertake to have recourse to Arbitration in cases relating to questions of the above-mentioned order, so far as these affect neither the vital interests nor the national honour of the parties in dispute.

ART. 9.—Each State remains the sole judge of the question whether this or that case shall be submitted to Arbitration, excepting the cases enumerated in the following article, where the Signatory Powers consider Arbitration as compulsory.

ART. 10.—After the ratification of the present Act by all the Signatory Powers, Arbitration is obligatory in the following cases, so far as they affect neither the vital interests nor the national honour of the contracting States.

I. In the event of differences or disputes relating to pecuniary damages sustained by a State or its subjects, arising from illegal actions or negligence of another State or its subjects.

II. In the event of disagreements relating to the interpretation or application of treaties and conventions hereinafter mentioned:

1. Postal, telegraph, and railway treaties and conventions, and those relating to the protection of submarine cables; regulations as to the means of preventing the collision of ships at sea; conventions relating to the navigation of international rivers and inter-oceanic canals.

2. Conventions regarding the protection of literary and artistic property, industrial property, (patents, &c.), monetary and metrical conventions, sanitary conventions, &c.

3. Conventions relating to legal proceedings.

4. Conventions relating to purely technical and non-political questions of delimitation.

ART. 11.—The above list may be completed by subsequent arrangements among the Signatory Powers. Moreover, each Power shall be able to enter into a special arrangement with another Power for the purpose of rendering Arbitration obligatory in the above-mentioned cases before the general ratification, and also to extend the scope of Arbitration to all cases which it is considered possible to submit to it.

ART. 12.—In all other cases of international conflicts not mentioned in the above articles, Arbitration, while certainly being very desirable and recommended by the present Act, is nevertheless purely facultative—that is to say, it can only be applied on the spontaneous initiative of one of the parties in dispute and with the express consent of the other parties.

ART. 13.—With the view of facilitating recourse to Arbitration and its application, the Signatory Powers are agreed to formulate a common arrangement for the employment of International Arbitration and for the fundamental principles to be observed in the drawing up of the rules of procedure to be followed pending the inquiry into the dispute and the pronouncement of the decision of the Arbitrators. The application of these fundamental principles, as also of the Arbitration procedure indicated in the Appendix to the present article, may be modified by virtue of a special arrangement between States which may have recourse to Arbitration.

INTERNATIONAL COMMISSIONS OF INQUIRY.

ART. 14.—In cases in which divergences of views occur between the Signatory States in connection with local circumstances giving rise to litigation of an international character which cannot be settled by the ordinary diplomatic means, but in which neither the honour nor the vital interests of these States are engaged, the Governments interested agree to institute an International Commission of Inquiry in order to arrive at the causes of the disagreement and to clear up on the spot, by an impartial and conscientious examination, all questions of fact.

ART. 15.—These international Commissions shall be constituted as follows:—Each Government interested shall appoint two members, and the four members united shall choose a fifth member who shall at the same time be president of the Commission. If the votes shall be divided for the choice of a president the two Governments interested shall appeal either to another Government or to a third party, who shall appoint the president of the Commission.

ART. 16.—Governments between which a grave disagreement or conflict shall arise in the circumstances indicated above, shall engage to furnish the Commission of Inquiry with all means and facilities necessary for a thorough and conscientious study of the facts.

ART. 17.—The International Commission of Inquiry, after having acquainted itself with the circumstances out of which the disagreement or conflict arose, shall submit to the Governments interested a report signed by all the members of the Commission.

ART. 18.—The report of the Commission of Inquiry shall in no wise have the character of an arbitration judgment. It leaves the Governments in conflict at full liberty, either to conclude a friendly arrangement on the basis of the said report, or to have recourse to Arbitration by concluding an agreement *ad hoc*, or else by resorting to the active measures allowable in the mutual relations between nations.

II.—A DRAFT CODE OF ARBITRATION, PROPOSED BY THE RUSSIAN DELEGATION.

ART. 1.—The Signatory Powers have approved the principles and rules below mentioned for the procedure of Arbitration among nations, save for the modifications which may be introduced in each particular case by mutual agreement by the Governments in dispute.

ART. 2.—The States interested, having accepted Arbitration, shall sign a special Act (*compromis*), in which are clearly set forth the questions submitted to the decision of the Arbitrator, and the full facts and the considerations of law connected with them, and a formal undertaking shall be given by the contracting parties to submit, in good faith and without subsequent appeal, to the Arbitral award which shall be pronounced.

ART. 3.—The Arbitration Conventions thus concluded by the States concerned with their full consent may provide for Arbitration either for all disputes arising between them, or for disputes of a certain fixed category.

ART. 4.—The Governments interested may entrust the functions of Arbitrator to the Sovereign or chief of the State of a third Power, with the consent of this last. They may also entrust these functions either to a single person selected by them or to an Arbitration Tribunal appointed for the purpose. In the latter event, and in view of the importance of the dispute, the Arbitration Tribunal may be constituted in the following manner:—Each contracting party shall choose two Arbitrators. These Arbitrators having met, shall agree upon the umpire, who will be *de jure* the president of the Tribunal. In the event of a division of votes the disputing Governments will appeal by a common accord to a third Government or a third person, who will appoint the umpire.

ART. 5.—If the disputing parties do not agree on the choice of the third Government or third person, mentioned in the preceding article, each of these parties shall appoint a Power not implicated in the dispute, in order that the Power thus chosen by the disputing parties may appoint an umpire by common agreement.

ART. 6.—The incompetence or inadmissibility of one only of the above-mentioned Arbitrators, or his refusal to accept the office of Arbitrator, once his consent has been given, or the death of an Arbitrator, invalidates the entire Agreement (*compromis*), except in the case where these circumstances are foreseen and provided for by common agreement between the contracting parties.

ART. 7.—The Arbitration Tribunal shall meet at a place designated either by the Contracting States or by the members of the Tribunal. The meeting place can only be changed by a fresh agreement between the interested Governments, or, in case of *force majeure*, on the initiative of the Tribunal itself.

ART. 8.—Disputing States have the right to appoint delegates or special agents attached to the Tribunal of Arbitration, and empowered to act as intermediaries between the Tribunal and the Governments interested. Besides these agents the above-mentioned Governments are authorised to nominate councillors or advocates to defend their rights and interests before the Tribunal of Arbitration.

ART. 9.—The Tribunal of Arbitration shall decide in what language the deliberations and discussions of the parties shall be held.

ART. 10.—The procedure of Arbitration shall generally be divided into two parts—namely, preliminary and definitive, the first consisting in the communication to the members of the Tribunal by the agents of the Contracting States, of all the documents and arguments printed or written regarding the questions in dispute; and the second, definitive or oral, in discussions before the Tribunal of Arbitration.

ART. 11.—On the conclusion of the preliminary procedure the discussions before the Arbitration Tribunal will begin and will be directed by the President. Records of the whole proceedings will be made by secretaries appointed by the President of the Tribunal. These Records will alone have legal force.

ART. 12.—The preliminary procedure having been ended, the Arbitration Tribunal shall have the right to reject all new documents which the representatives of the parties may desire to submit to it.

ART. 13.—The Arbitration Tribunal, nevertheless, always remains absolutely free to take into consideration new documents or records of which the delegates or councillors of the Governments in dispute have taken advantage in their explanations before the Tribunal.

The latter has the right to demand the production of these documents, and to notify them to the opposing party.

ART. 14.—The Arbitration Tribunal has, besides, the right to call upon the agents of the Parties to submit all the documents or explanations which it requires.

ART. 15.—The agents and councillors of the Governments in dispute shall be authorised to lay before the Tribunal orally all the explanations and proofs in support of the cause they have to defend.

ART. 16.—The same agents and councillors also have the right to lay before the Tribunal motions on the subjects under discussion. The decisions of the Tribunal concerning these motions are definitive, and cannot give rise to any discussion.

ART. 17.—The members of the Arbitration Tribunal have the right to put questions to the agents or councillors of the Contracting Parties, or to ask for enlightenment on doubtful points. Neither questions submitted nor observations made by members of the Tribunal in the course of the deliberations shall be regarded as an expression of opinion by the Tribunal as a whole or by the individual members composing it.

ART. 18.—The Arbitration Tribunal is alone authorised to determine its competence by the interpretation of the clauses of the Agreement (*compromis*) and in accordance with the principles of international law, with due consideration for any special treaties which may be involved.

ART. 19.—The Arbitration Tribunal has the right to establish rules of procedure, and to determine the manner and periods of time in which each party is to present its documents, and to decide on the interpretation of the documents produced and communicated to the two Parties.

ART. 20.—On the agents and councillors of the litigant Governments having presented all the explanations and proofs in defence of their respective pleas, the President of the Arbitration Tribunal will close the debates.

ART. 21.—The deliberations of the members of the Tribunal on the ground of litigation are to be held with closed doors. Every decision, whether definitive or provisional, is taken by the majority of the members present. The refusal of a single member of the Tribunal to take part in the voting must be stated in the records.

ART. 22.—The Arbitral Award, arrived at by a majority of votes, must be drawn up in writing and signed by each of the members of the Arbitration Tribunal. Those members of the Tribunal who are in the minority shall, when signing, state their disagreement with the Award.

ART. 23.—The Award shall be solemnly read at a public sitting of the Tribunal and in the presence of the agents and councillors of the Governments in dispute.

ART. 24.—The Award, duly made and notified to the agents of the Governments in dispute, shall decide, definitively and without appeal, the dispute between the Parties, and close the arbitration proceedings instituted by the Agreement (*compromis*).

ART. 25.—Each Party to a dispute will defray its own expenses and half the expenses of the Arbitration Tribunal, without prejudice to the decision of the Tribunal regarding any indemnity which one or other of the Parties may be ordered to pay.

ART. 26.—The Arbitral Award is null and void in case of the Reference (*compromis*) being invalid, or if the Tribunal has exceeded its powers, or when corruption is proved on the part of one of the Arbitrators.

The above regulations regarding the Arbitration Tribunal, from Section 7, beginning with the words "The Arbitration Tribunal shall meet," apply equally to cases in which Arbitration is entrusted to a single individual chosen by the Governments interested. In a case in which the Sovereign or chief of a State gives his Award personally as Arbitrator, the procedure would be determined by the Sovereign or the chief of the State himself.

III.—RUSSIAN PROPOSALS CONCERNING AN ARBITRATION TRIBUNAL.

(*a*.) Articles which might replace Article I., 13.

1. With a view to consolidate, as far as possible, the practice of International Arbitration, the Contracting Powers have agreed to form, for a period of . . . . years, an Arbitration Tribunal, to which should be referred the cases of obligatory Arbitration enumerated in Article 10, unless the interested Powers agree on the establishment of a special Arbitration Tribunal for the solution of the dispute that has arisen between them.

The Powers in dispute may also have recourse to the Tribunal referred to above in all cases of optional Arbitration, if a special agreement on this subject be arrived at between them.

It is understood that all the Powers, without excepting the non-contracting Powers, or those which have made reservations, may submit their differences to this Tribunal by addressing the Permanent Bureau, provided for by Article . . . . of Appendix A.

2. The organisation of the Arbitration Tribunal is shown in Appendix A. of the present Article.

The organisation of the Arbitration Tribunals instituted by special agreements between the Powers in dispute, and also the rules of procedure to be followed during the examination of the case, and the delivery of the Arbitral Award, are determined in Appendix B (Code of Arbitration).

The arrangements contained in this latter Appendix may be modified by a special agreement between the States which have recourse to Arbitration.

(*b.*) ANNEX TO THE RUSSIAN PROPOSALS.

In case of the acceptance of Articles 1 and 2, it would be expedient:

1. To draw up Appendix A, mentioned in the Article.

2. To introduce corresponding modifications into the Draft of the Arbitration Code.

(*c.*) APPENDIX A.

Mentioned in Additional Article a) 2, of the Russian Proposals.

In default of a Special Convention (*compromis*), the Arbitration Tribunal provided for by Article 13 shall be constituted on the following bases:—

1. The Contracting Parties establish a Permanent Tribunal for the settlement of international disputes, which shall be referred to it by the contending Powers, by virtue of Article 13 of the present Convention.

2. The Conference shall designate, for the period which shall elapse before the meeting of a new Conference, five Powers, in order that each of them, in case of a request for Arbitration, may appoint a Judge, either from the number of their subjects, or outside that number.

The Judges thus appointed constitute the Arbitration Tribunal competent for the case that has arisen.

3. If amongst the Powers in dispute were one or more Powers not represented in the Arbitration Tribunal, in virtue of the preceding Article, each of the two Parties in dispute shall have the

right to have itself represented in it by a person of its choice as Judge, having the same rights as the other members of the said Tribunal.

4. The Tribunal shall from amongst its members choose its President, who, in case of an equal division of votes, shall have the casting vote.

5. A Permanent Bureau of Arbitration shall be appointed by the five Powers who shall be designated in virtue of the present Act to constitute the Arbitration Tribunal. They shall draw up the Regulations of this Bureau, appoint its employés, provide for replacing them when need arises, and fix their emoluments. This Bureau, which shall be located at the Hague, shall consist of a General Secretary, an Assistant Secretary, a Recorder, and an adequate staff, which shall be appointed by the General Secretary.

6. The expenses of maintenance of this Bureau shall be divided amongst the States in the proportion fixed for the International Postal Bureau.

7. The Bureau shall annually render an account of its work to the five Powers who have appointed it, and these shall communicate the Report to the other Powers.

8. The Powers between whom a dispute has arisen shall apply to the Bureau, and furnish to it the necessary documents. The Bureau shall advise the five Powers above mentioned, who shall without delay form the Tribunal. This Tribunal shall, as a rule, meet at the Hague; or it may meet in some other town, if an agreement to that effect be arrived at amongst the interested States.

9. During the time that the Tribunal is at work, the Bureau shall serve as its Secretariat. It shall follow the Tribunal in case of removal. The archives of the International Arbitration shall be deposited at the Bureau.

10. The procedure of the above Tribunal shall be governed by the rules of the Code of Arbitration.

THE BRITISH ARBITRATION PROPOSALS.

PERMANENT ARBITRATION TRIBUNAL.

I.—SIR JULIAN PAUNCEFOTE'S FIRST PROPOSAL:—

ART. 1.—With the view of facilitating an immediate recourse to Arbitration on the part of those States who may not succeed in settling their differences by diplomatic means, the Signatory Powers have undertaken to organise in the following manner a permanent Tribunal of Arbitration, accessible at all times, and governed by the code of Arbitration prescribed in this Convention, so far as it may be applicable, and in conformity with stipulations made in arrangements decided upon between the parties in litigation.

ART. 2.—To this effect a central office will be established permanently at X, where the archives of the Tribunal will be preserved, and which will be entrusted with the conduct of its official business. A permanent Secretary, an Archivist, and sufficient staff will be appointed who will reside on the spot. The office will be the intermediary for communications relative to the meeting of the Tribunal at the instance of the parties in litigation.

ART. 3.—Each Signatory Power will transmit to the others the names of two persons of its nationality, recognised in their country as jurists or publicists of merit, enjoying the highest reputation for integrity, disposed to accept the functions of Arbitrators, and possessing all the necessary qualities. Persons thus designated will be Members of the Tribunal, and will be inscribed as such in the central office. In case of the death or retirement of a Member of the Tribunal, provision will be made for his being replaced in the same manner as for his nomination.

ART. 4.—The Signatory Powers, desiring to apply to the Tribunal for the pacific settlement of differences which may arise amongst them, will notify this desire to the Secretary of the central office, which will then furnish them immediately with a list of the Members of the Tribunal. The Powers in question will thereupon select from this list the number of Arbitrators agreed upon in the arrangements. They will have, moreover, the power of adding Arbitrators other than those whose names are inscribed in the list. The Arbitrators thus chosen will form the Tribunal for the Arbitration, and will meet on the date fixed by the parties in litigation. The Tribunal will sit generally at X, but will have the power of sitting elsewhere, and of changing its place from time to time, according to circumstances, as may suit its convenience, or that of the parties in litigation.

ART. 5.—Any State, although not a Signatory Power, will be able to have recourse to the Tribunal under the conditions prescribed by the regulations.

ART. 6.—The Government X. . . .. is directed to install at X. . . . in the name of the Signatory Powers, as soon as possible after the ratification of this Convention, a permanent Council of Administration, composed of five Members and one Secretary. It will be the duty of the Council to establish and organise a central office, which will be under its direction and control. It will issue from time to time the necessary regulations for the proper working of the central office, and will also settle all questions which may arise concerning the working of the Tribunal, or which may be submitted to it by the central bureau. The Council will have absolute power as regards the nomination, the suspension, or the dismissal of all functionaries or employees. It will fix salaries and control general expenses. The Council will elect its president, who will have a preponderating voice. The presence of three Members will suffice to constitute a quorum, and decisions wlll be taken by a majority of votes. The fees of the Members of the Council will be fixed by agreement between the Signatory Powers.

ART. 7.—The Signatory Powers agree to contribute in equal shares the expenses of the Administrative Council and the central office. The expenses of each arbitration will be chargeable in equal parts to the States in litigation.

A Permanent Council.

II.—Sir Julian Pauncefote's New Proposal :—

To replace Article 6.

There shall be constituted at the Hague a Permanent Council, composed of the Representatives of the Signatory Powers residing in that city, and the Minister for Foreign Affairs of the Netherlands, as soon as possible after the ratification of the present Convention. This Council shall be commissioned to establish and organise a Central Bureau, which shall remain under its direction and control. It shall take steps to establish the Tribunal; it shall issue from time to time the regulations necessary for the proper conduct of the Central Bureau. Similarly it shall decide all questions which may arise relating to the working of the Tribunal, or refer them to the Signatory Powers. It shall have absolute power as to the appointment, suspension or dismission of the officers and employés of the Central Bureau. It shall fix their salaries and emoluments, and have control of the general expenditure. The presence of five members at a meeting duly summoned shall constitute a quorum, and the decisions shall be taken by a majority of votes.

[*Translation.*]

DOCUMENTS ÉMANÉS DE LA DÉLÉGATION ANGLAISE.

Tribunal Permanent D'Arbitrage.

a) *Proposition de* S. Exc. Sir Julian Pauncefote.

1.—Dans le but de faciliter le recours immédiat à l'arbitrage pour les Etats qui n'auraient pas réussi à régler leurs différends par la voie diplomatique, les Puissances signataires s'engagent à organiser de la manière suivante un "Tribunal permanent d'arbitrage" accessible en tous temps, et qui sera régi par le Code d'arbitrage prescrit dans cette Convention en tant qu'il serait applicable et conforme aux dispositions arrêtées dans le compromis entre les Parties litigantes.

2.—A cet effet, un Bureau central sera établi en permanence à (X), dans lequel les archives du Tribunal seront conservées, et qui sera chargé de la gestion de ses affaires officielles. Un Secrétaire permanent, un Archiviste et un personnel suffisant seront nommés, qui habiteront sur les lieux.

Le Bureau sera l'intermédiaire des communications relatives à la réunion du Tribunal à la requête des Parties litigantes.

3.—Chaque Puissance signataire transmettra aux autres les noms de deux personnes de sa nationalité reconnues dans leur pays comme juristes ou publicistes de mérite et jouissant de la plus haute considération quant à leur intégrité, qui seraient disposées à accepter les fonctions d'arbitre et posséderaient toutes les qualités requises. Les personnes ainsi désignées seront membres du Tribunal et seront inscrites comme tels au Bureau central.

En cas de décès ou de retraite d'un membre du Tribunal, il sera pourvu à son remplacement de la même manière que pour sa nomination.

4.—Les Puissances signataires désirant avoir recours au Tribunal pour le règlement pacifique des différends qui pourraient surgir entre Elles, notifieront ce désir au Secrétaire du Bureau central qui leur fournira sur-le-champ la liste des membres du Tribunal. Elles choisiront dans cette liste le nombre d'arbitres convenu dans le compromis.

Elles auront en outre la faculté de leur adjoindre des arbitres autres que ceux dont les noms seront inscrits dans la liste. Les arbitres ainsi choisis formeront le Tribunal pour cet arbitrage.

Ils se réuniront à la date fixée par les Parties en litige.

Le Tribunal siégera d'ordinaire à (X), mais il aura la faculté de siéger ailleurs et de changer son siège de temps en temps selon les circonstances et sa convenance ou celle des Parties en litige.

5.—Tout Etat, quoique n'étant pas une des Puissances signataires, pourra avoir recours au Tribunal dans les conditions prescrites par les Règlements.

6.—Le Gouvernement de (X) est chargé d'installer à (X), au nom des Puissances signataires le plus tôt possible après la ratification de cette Convention, un "Conseil d'administration" permanent qui sera composé de cinq membres et d'un Secrétaire. Ce conseil aura pour devoir d'établir et d'organiser le Bureau central qui sera sous sa direction et son contrôle.

Il émettra de temps en temps les Règlements nécessaires au bon fonctionnement du Bureau central. Il réglera de même toutes les questions qui pourraient surgir touchant le fonctionnement du Tribunal, ou qui lui seraient référées par le Bureau central. Il aura des pouvoirs absolus quant à la nomination, la suspension ou la démission de tous les fonctionnaires et employés, il fixera leurs salaires et il contrôlera la dépense générale. Le Conseil élira son Président, qui aura voix prépondérante. La présence de trois membres suffira pour constituer les séances, et les décisions seront prises à la majorité des voix. Les honoraires des membres du Conseil seront fixés par un accord entre les Puissances signataires.

7.—Les Puissances signataires s'engagent à supporter par parties égales les frais du Conseil d'administration et du Bureau central. Les frais se rattachant à chaque arbitrage incomberont aux Etats en litige en partie égale.

b) Proposition Nouvelle de Sir Julian Pauncefote concernant le Conseil Permanent.

Article 6 *nouveau.*

Un Conseil permanent composé des représentants des Puissances signataires résidant à La Haye et du Ministre des affaires étrangères des Pays-Bays sera constitué dans cette ville le plus tôt possible après la ratification de la présente Convention. Ce Conseil aura pour mission d'établir et d'organiser le Bureau central, lequel demeurera sous sa direction et sous son contrôle. Il procédera à l'installation du Tribunal; il émettra, de temps en temps, les règlements nécessaires au bon fonctionnement du Bureau central. De même, il réglera toutes les questions qui pourraient surgir touchant le fonctionnement du Tribunal, ou il en référera aux Puissances signataires. Il aura des pouvoirs absolus quant à la nomination, la suspension ou la révocation des fonctionnaires et employés du Bureau central. Il fixera leurs traitements et salaires, il contrôlera la dépense générale. La présence de cinq membres dans la réunion, dûment convoquée, suffira pour délibérer valablement et les décisions seront prises à la majorité des voix.

AMERICAN SCHEME.

I.—Special Mediation.

Proposal by Mr. Holls, *United States Delegate.*

The Signatory Powers are agreed to recommend the application, in circumstances which will allow of it, of a Special Mediation, under the following form:

In case of a grave disagreement menacing Peace, the States in dispute shall choose respectively a neutral Power, with the mission of entering into direct relations with the aim of preventing the rupture of peaceful relations.

For the space of twenty days, if no other period of time is stated, the question in dispute is considered as referred exclusively to those Powers. They must apply all their efforts to settle the difference and to re-establish as far as possible the *status quo ante.*

In case of a rupture of pacific relations, these Powers remain charged with the common mission of taking advantage of every opportunity of re-establishing Peace.

II.—Proposal for an International Tribunal.

Resolved —That in order to aid in the prevention of armed conflicts by pacific means, the representatives of the Sovereign Powers assembled together in this Conference be and they hereby are requested to propose to their respective Governments a series of negotiations for the adoption of a general Treaty, having for its object the following plan, with such modifications as may be essential to secure the adhesion of at least nine Sovereign Powers, four of whom at least shall have been signatories of the Declaration of Paris, the German Empire being for this purpose the successor of Prussia, and the Kingdom of Italy the successor of Sardinia :—

ART. 1.—The Tribunal shall be composed of persons nominated on account of their personal integrity and learning in international law by a majority of the members of the highest Court at the time existing in each of the adhering States, one from each Sovereign State participating in the Treaty, and shall hold office until their successors are nominated by the same body and duly appointed.

ART. 2.—The Tribunal shall meet for organisation at a time and place to be agreed upon by the several Governments, but not later than six months after the general Treaty shall be ratified by nine Powers as hereinbefore proposed, and shall organise itself by the appointment of a permanent clerk, and such other officers as may be found necessary, but without conferring any distinction upon its own members. The Tribunal shall be empowered to fix its place of session and to change the same from time to time as the interests of justice or the convenience of the litigants may seem to require, and to fix its own rules of procedure.

ART. 3.—The Tribunal shall be of a permanent character, and shall be always open for the filing of new cases, subject to its own rules of procedure, either by the contracting nations or by others that may choose to submit them, and all cases and counter-cases, with the testimony and arguments by which they are to be supported or answered, are to be in writing or in print. All cases, counter cases, evidence, arguments, or opinions, expressing judgment, are to be accessible after the award has been given to all who will pay the necessary charges of transcription.

ART. 4.—Any and all questions of disagreement between

Signatory Powers may, by mutual consent, be submitted by the nations concerned to this International Tribunal for decision, but every such submission shall be accompanied by an undertaking to accept the award.

ART. 5.—The bench of Judges for each particular case shall consist, as may be agreed upon by the litigating nations, either of the entire bench or of any smaller uneven number, not less than three to be chosen from the whole Court. In the event of a bench of three Judges only, no one of those shall be either a native subject or a citizen of the States whose interests are in litigation in the case.

ART. 6.—The general expenses of the Tribunal are to be equally divided, or upon some equitable basis, between the adherent Powers, but those arising from each particular case shall be provided for as may be directed by the Tribunal. The presentation of a case wherein one or both of the parties may be a non-adherent State shall be admitted only upon condition of a mutual agreement that the States so litigating shall pay respectively a sum to be fixed by the Tribunal for the expenses of the adjudication. The salaries of the Judges may be so adjusted as to be paid only when actually engaged in the duties of the Court. Where one or both of the parties are non-adherent States, they shall only be admitted on condition that the litigating States come to a common agreement to pay respectively such sum as the Tribunal shall fix to cover the expenses of the proceedings.

ART. 7.—Every litigant before the International Tribunal shall have a right to a rehearing of the case before the same Judges within three months after the notification of the decision, on alleging newly-discovered evidence or submitting questions of law not heard and decided at the former hearing.

ART. 8.—This Treaty shall become operative when nine Sovereign States such as are indicated in the resolution shall have ratified its provisions.

[*Translation.*]

DOCUMENTS ÉMANÉS DE LA DÉLÉGATION AMÉRICAINE.

I.—Médiation Spéciale.

Proposition de M. Holls, *délégué des Etats-Unis d'Amérique.*

Les Puissances signataires sont tombées d'accord de recommander l'application, dans les circonstances qui peuvent le permettre, d'une Médiation spéciale, sous la forme suivante :

En cas de différend grave menaçant la Paix, les Etats en litige choisissent respectivement une Puissance neutre, avec la mission d'entrer en rapport direct à l'effet de prévenir la rupture des relations pacifiques.

Pendant une durée de vingt jours, sauf stipulation d'un autre délai, la question en litige est considérée comme déférée exclusivement à ces Puissances. Elles doivent appliquer tous leurs efforts à régler le différend et à rétablir autant que possible le *statu quo ante.*

En cas de rupture effective des relations pacifiques, ces Puissances demeurent chargées de la mission commune de profiter de toute occasion pour rétablir la Paix.

II.—Projet de Tribunal International.

Il est décidé que, en vue d'aider à prévenir les conflits armés par des moyens pacifiques, les représentants des Puissances souveraines assemblés à cette Conférence sont invités par la présente résolution à proposer à leurs Gouvernements respectifs d'entrer en négociations aux fins de conclure un traité général qui aura pour objet le plan ci-dessous, avec telles modifications qui seraient indispensables pour assurer l'adhésion d'au moins neuf Puissances souveraines, desquelles huit au moins devront être des Puissances européennes ou américaines, et quatre au moins devront avoir été au nombre des signataires de la Convention de Paris, l'Empire d'Allemagne étant considéré comme succédant à la Prusse et le Royaume d'Italie à la Sardaigne.

(1) Le Tribunal sera composé de personnes se recommandant par leur haute intégrité et leur compétence dans le droit international, qui seront nommées par la majorité des membres de la plus haute Cour de justice existant dans chacun des Etats adhérents. Chaque Etat signataire du traité aura un représentant au Tribunal. Les membres de celui-ci siégeront jusqua'à ce que des successeurs leur aient été donnés en due forme par le même mode d'élection.

(2) Le Tribunal s'assemblera, en vue de s'organiser, à une époque et à un endroit dont conviendront les différents Gouvernements. Toutefois il ne faudra pas que ce soit plus de six mois après la ratification du traité général par les neuf Puissances mentionnées ci-dessus. Le Tribunal désignera un Greffier permanent et tels autres employés qui seront jugés nécessaires. Le Tribunal aura le pouvoir de désigner le lieu où il se réunira et pourra en changer de temps en temps, selon que les intérêts de la justice ou les convenances des litigants sembleront l'exiger. Il fixera les règles de la procédure qu'il suivra.

(3) Le Tribunal aura un caractère permanent et sera toujours prêt à accueillir, dans les limites de ses règles propres de procédure, les cas nouveaux et les cas contraires, soit que ces cas lui soient soumis par les Nations signataires, soit qu'ils le soient par toutes autres Nations qui désireraient recourir à lui ; tous les cas et cas contraires, ainsi que les témoignages et les arguments pour les appuyer ou les combattre, devront être écrits ou imprimés. Tous cas, cas contraires, dépositions, arguments et considérants de jugements devront, après que la sentence aura été prononcée, être à la disposition de tous ceux qui seraient disposés à payer les frais de leur transcription.

(4) Tout différend quel qu'il soit entre Puissances signataires peut, de commun accord, être soumis par les Nations intéressées au jugement de ce Tribunal international, mais, dans tous les cas où le Tribunal sera saisi, les intéressés devront s'engager, en s'adressant à lui, à accepter sa sentence.

(5) Dans chaque cas particulier, la Cour sera composée

d'après les Conventions intervenues entre les Nations litigantes, soit que le Tribunal tout entier siège, soit que les Nations litigantes désignent quelques-uns seulement de ses membres en nombre impair et non inférieur à trois. Dans le cas où la Cour ne comprendrait que trois juges, aucun d'eux ne pourra être originaire, sujet ou citoyen des Etats dont les intérêts sont en cause.

(6) Les frais généraux du Tribunal seront répartis également ou en proportion équitable entre les Puissances adhérentes, mais les frais occasionnés par chaque cas particulier seront à la charge de ceux que le Tribunal indiquera. Les traitements des juges pourront être fixés de telle façon qu'ils ne soient payables que lorsque lesdits juges rempliront effectivement leurs fonctions au Tribunal. Les cas dans lesquels l'une des parties ou toutes les deux seraient un Etat non-adhérent ne seront admis qu'à la condition que les Etats litigants prennent de commun accord l'engagement de payer respectivement telle somme que le Tribunal fixera pour couvrir les frais de la procédure.

(7) Tout litigant qui aura soumis un cas au Tribunal international aura droit à une seconde audition de sa cause devant les mêmes juges, endéans les trois mois après que la sentence aura été notifiée, s'il déclare pouvoir invoquer des témoignages nouveaux ou des questions de droit non soulevées et non tranchées la première fois.

(8) Le Traité proposé ici entrera en force quand neuf Etats souverains dans les conditions indiquées dans la résolution, auront ratifié ses stipulations.

DOCUMENT ÉMANÉ DE LA DÉLÉGATION ITALIENNE.

Dans le but de prévenir ou de faire cesser les conflits internationaux, la Conférence de la Paix, réunie à La Haye, a résolu de soumettre aux Gouvernements qui y sont représentés les articles suivants, destinés à être convertis en stipulations internationales.

Article Premier.—En cas d'imminence d'un conflit entre deux ou plusieurs Puissances, et après l'insuccès de tout tentative de conciliation au moyen de négociations indirectes, les Parties en litige sont obligées de recourir à l'arbitrage dans les cas indiqués par le présent Acte.

Art. 2.—Dans tous les autres cas, la médiation ou l'arbitrage sont recommandés par les Puissances signataires, mais demeurent facultatifs.

Art. 3.—Chacune des Puissances signataires du présent Acte, non impliquées dans le conflit, a, en tout cas, et même pendant les hostilités, le droit d'offrir aux Parties contendantes ses bons offices ou sa médiation, ou de leur proposer de recourir à la médiation d'une autre Puissance également neutre ou à l'arbitrage.

Cette offre ou cette proposition ne peut être considérée par l'une ou l'autre des Parties en litige comme un acte peu amical, même dans le cas où la médiation et l'arbitrage, n'étant pas obligatoires, seraient récusés.

Art. 4.—La demande ou l'offre de médiation a la priorité sur la proposition d'arbitrage.

Mais l'arbitrage peut ou doit être proposé selon les cas, non seulement lorsqu'il n'y a pas de demande ou offre de médiation, mais aussi lorsque la médiation aurait été récusée ou n'aurait pas abouti à la conciliation.

Art. 5.—La proposition de médiation ou d'arbitrage, tant qu'elle n'est pas formellement acceptée par toutes les Parties en litige, ne peut avoir pour effet, sauf convention contraire, d'interrompre, retarder ou entraver la mobilisation et autres mesures préparatoires, ainsi que les opérations militaires en cours.

Art. 6.—Le recours à la médiation ou à l'arbitrage conformément à l'article 1er est obligatoire :

1°. . . . .

2°. . . . .

[*Translation.*]

THE ITALIAN PROPOSALS.

With the object of preventing or putting a stop to international conflicts, the Peace Conference assembled at the Hague has resolved to submit to the Governments represented the following Articles, which are to be converted into international stipulations:

ART. 1.—In the event of the imminence of a conflict between two or more Powers, and after the failure of all attempts at conciliation by means of indirect negotiations, the contending Parties will be obliged to have recourse to mediation or Arbitration in the cases indicated by the present Act.

ART. 2.—In all other cases mediation or Arbitration will be recommended by the signatory Powers, but will remain optional.

ART. 3.—Each of the signatory Powers not involved in the conflict has, in all cases, even during hostilities, the right to offer to the contending Parties its good offices or its mediation, or to propose to them to have recourse to the mediation of another Power equally neutral, or to Arbitration. This offer or proposal cannot be considered by one or the other of the contending Parties as an unfriendly act, even in cases where mediation and Arbitration, not being obligatory, would be rejected.

ART. 4.—A demand for, or an offer of, mediation has priority over a proposal of Arbitration; but Arbitration may, or must be proposed, according to the circumstances of the case, not only when there is no demand for or offer of mediation, but also when mediation would have been rejected or would not have led to conciliation.

ART. 5.—A proposal of mediation or Arbitration, so long as it has not been formally accepted by all the contending Parties, cannot have the effect, unless there be a Convention to the contrary, of interrupting, delaying, or impeding mobilisation and other preparatory measures, or military operations in progress.

ART. 6.—Recourse to mediation or Arbitration in conformity with Article 1 is obligatory in case:—

1st, ...

2nd, ...

The Arbitration Committee met for the first time, to consider the proposals of the Drafting Committee, on June 5th; on July 7th the complete scheme drawn up by that Committee was presented for its consideration; the Committee adjourned till the 17th, in order that the scheme might be referred by the delegates to their respective Governments: and on July 25th the report of its labours was considered and adopted, and its deliberations brought to an end.

FINAL PROCEEDINGS OF THE CONFERENCE.

A plenary meeting of the Conference, which lasted only twenty minutes, was held on June 20th, when the Articles, elaborated by the second Committee, for the application of the principles of the Geneva Convention to naval warfare, were adopted; and a Committee was appointed to draw up the "Final Act," or complete statement of the decisions of the Conference. This Committee consisted of Count Nigra (president), MM. Seth Low, Asser, Martens, Renault, Descamps, and Baron Stengel, with M. Raffalovich as secretary. On July 5th the Conference met and adopted the rules of war, and the supplementary resolutions passed by the second section of the Second Committee. On July 21st the Conference held a plenary session, in order to discuss and adopt the resolutions of the First Committees, and on July 25th the Conference adopted the Arbitration project, with the last amendments, subject to the following declaration, in regard to Article 27, by the American delegates:—

"Nothing contained in this Convention shall be so construed as to require the United States of America to depart from its traditional policy of not entering upon, interfering with, or entangling itself in the political questions or internal administration of any foreign State. Nor shall anything contained in the said Convention be construed to require a relinquishment by the United States of America of its traditional attitude towards purely American questions."

THE "FINAL ACT."

The Final Protocol was then considered and adopted. The preamble to the Arbitration Convention states that the order in which the signatures should be appended to it was adopted by the Conference at its plenary session of the 28th July, 1899.

After detailing the names and qualifications of the delegates, this Final Act stated the results of the Conference in the following terms :—

In the series of meetings, in which the above-mentioned delegates have been throughout inspired by the desire to realise in the largest possible measure the generous views of its august initiator and the intentions of their Governments, the Conference has drawn up, for the signature of the plenipotentiaries, the text of the Conventions and Declarations hereafter enumerated and appended to the present Act.

I. A Convention for the pacific settlement of international conflicts.

The text of this is given herein.

II. A Convention concerning the laws and customs of war on land.

The Signatory Powers bind themselves to issue instructions to all their land forces in conformity with the Articles of this Convention.

III. A Convention for the adaptation to naval warfare of the principles of the Geneva Convention of 1864.

Appended to this Convention, as it appears in the Final Act, are three additional Articles in the form of a final disposition.

IV. Three declarations—

I. "The undersigned, as plenipotentiary delegates at the International Peace Conference, duly authorised by their Governments to this effect, inspired by the sentiments which found expression in the declaration of St. Petersburg of December 11th (November 29th, O.S.), 1868, and taking into consideration the final clause of that declaration, hereby declare that the contracting parties prohibit, for a period of five years, the throwing of projectiles or explosives from balloons or by other new analogous means.

II. "The undersigned, as plenipotentiary delegates, etc., hereby declare that the contracting parties prohibit the use of projectiles which have for the sole object the diffusion of asphyxiating or deleterious gases.

III. "The undersigned, as plenipotentiary delegates, etc., hereby declare that the contracting parties prohibit the use of bullets which expand or flatten easily in the human body, as, for instance, bullets with a hard case which case does not cover the whole of the enclosed mass, or contains incisions."

Obedient to the same inspiration, the Conference also unanimously adopted the following resolution :—

"The Conference considers that the limitation of military charges at the present time weighing upon the world is greatly to be desired for the increase of the material and moral welfare of humanity."

It also expressed the following opinions (*vœux*) dealing mainly with the suggestions in the Russian programme which it was found impossible to embody in definite Conventions :—

I. The Conference, taking into consideration the preliminary steps taken by the Swiss Federal Government for the revision of the Geneva Convention, expresses the wish that a special Conference be shortly convened for the purpose of revising this Convention.

II. The Conference expresses the opinion that the question of the rights and duties of neutrals should be inscribed on the programme of a Conference to be held at an early date.

III. The Conference expresses the opinion that questions relative to the type and the calibre of rifles and naval artillery, such as have been examined by it, should be the subject of study by the different Governments, with a view to arriving eventually at a uniform solution by means of a further Conference.

IV. The Conference is of opinion that the Governments, taking into account the proposals made in the Conference, should make a study of the possibility of an agreement concerning the limitation of armed forces on land and sea, and of naval budgets.

V. The Conference is of opinion that the proposal tending to declare the inviolability of private property in war at sea should be remitted to the consideration of a future Conference.

VI. The Conference is of opinion that the proposal regulating the question of the bombardment of ports, towns, and villages by a naval force should be remitted to the consideration of a future Conference.

The following is the text of the additional protocol appended to the Final Act, and fixing December 31st, 1899, as the latest date by which the Governments represented at the Conference are to give in their adhesion.

Additional Protocol to the Final Act.

Considering that a certain number of the Governments represented at the Peace Conference have not yet found themselves able to sign the Conventions and declarations, the text of which has been fixed by the Conference, the undersigned, as plenipotentiary delegates, at the moment of proceeding to sign the Final Act, have agreed as follows:—The Conventions and declarations, the text of which is annexed to the Final Act, can be signed by the Governments represented at the Conference, either at once or at a future date, but at the latest by December 31st, 1899. After

December 31st, 1899, adhesion to the Conventions can be made in conformity with the final dispositions of the aforesaid Conventions. Adhesion to the declarations can be made by means of a notification addressed to the Government of the Netherlands and communicated by it to all the Governments who have signed the declaration.

This "Final Act" was signed by the delegates of all the Powers on the morning of the 29th July, 1899.

THE FINAL SITTING.

The last session took place in the afternoon of the same day, July 29th, and lasted about half-an-hour. The President delivered his closing address, in which he expressed the thanks of the Conference to the Queen of the Netherlands and the Dutch Government, to the Chairmen and reporters of the various Committees and sub-Committees, and other officers, and also in appropriate terms his appreciation of the work of the Conference. A letter, dated May 29th, was read, from the Pope to the Queen of the Netherlands, giving assurance of his "warm sympathy" with the Conference. Count von Münster expressed the thanks of the Conference to M. de Staal and M. van Karnebeek; and Baron D'Estournelles made a final speech, in which he anticipated "future meetings of the Parliament of Man."

It was also announced that sixteen States had already signed the Arbitration Convention (including France, Russia, and the United States—Great Britain signed a few days later), fifteen the other two Conventions, seventeen the first declaration (projectiles from balloons), sixteen the second (asphyxiating shells), and fifteen the third (expanding bullets).

M. de Staal closed the Conference by tapping on his desk with his hammer, and uttering the words "Messieurs, la séance est levée."

RESULTS OF THE PEACE CONFERENCE AT THE HAGUE.

The success of the Conference cannot yet be fully gauged; but that it was successful beyond all anticipation does not admit of question. It was in fact the opening of a new era for mankind. The adoption of the Arbitration Scheme was in itself an epoch-making event. But that was not its only, though it may be considered its main, result.

If that crowning success had not been achieved, and the Conference were to be judged alone by what may be termed its minor, or auxiliary, work, it would still have proved itself fruitful and useful, and worthy the effort of the Russian Emperor.

The meeting of this diplomatic body marks a stage, and is a distinct step forward, in the historical development of the world. It is mainly significant because of its place in history, and for what it renders possible and, according to human probability, certain, rather than for what it actually accomplished. The *Edinburgh Review* very truly observes that "justice is not done to the labours of the Peace Conference, their significance is not understood until we recognise that they continue a process of development which has long been going on, and that they are one of the many steps taken of late towards extending, systematising, and organising Arbitrations in disputes between nations," and so of preparing and originating the new and better order of International Society.

It may be true, as was affirmed, that after the Hague gathering every nation will go on exactly as it did before it, making just what provision it thinks needful for war, aggressive or defensive. But the world will not be in the same condition as if the Hague Conference had never met.

For the nations have, with a surprising accord, resolved to make use, for the common benefit, of all the experience obtained by several of them in the series of efforts previously made toward the settlement of disputes by pacific methods. And the agreement to which their expert representatives have come for the establishment of a permanent machinery, to be always available for that object, puts the whole of civilised mankind, in a very real sense, on a level of potential advantage with those who have led the way in this great forward movement of humanity. No one supposes that war is abolished. But the Hague Conference has at least succeeded in interposing new obstacles in the way of its commencement, and in "extending, systematising, and organising" the influences for making peace.

It thus "marks," as Ambassador White said of it, "the first stage of the abolition of the scourge of war." It justifies the statement of M. Bourgeois in his great speech in the Conference itself. "There are certain persons," said he, "ignorant of the power of the idea, who pretend that what the Conference has done is very little." He, however, avowed his conviction that it was only when the Conference was dissolved, and they were able to contemplate its work from a distance, they would understand the immense value of the progress which had been achieved.

THE IMPERIAL RESCRIPT.

The publication of the remarkable document in which the Emperor issued his invitation, was alone an event of immense significance.

1.—It begins by recognising an imperative ideal of Government, and declaring that it consists in the maintenance of general Peace and the reduction of armaments.

2.—It makes not only a distinct admission but a formal confession of the absolute failure of the policy adopted by Europe for at least a century, upon which the fabric of modern society is built, viz., that which is expressed in the maxim so loudly acclaimed, and still so confidently asserted, *Si vis pacem, para bellum.*

3.—It contains a scathing and startling impeachment of the military system, and an accurate description of its terrible results and its threatening dangers, which has not been contradicted by any one, because the facts do not admit of question.

4.—It has had the effect of reopening discussion, in all quarters, on the first principles of national armament and defence. The justification of conditions, which have gradually grown up under the pressure of practical requirements, is called in question; and the instinct of nations, whether for self-protection or aggrandisement, which is a larger factor in history than abstract reason, is summoned to render an account of its promptings before the bar of inexorable logic.

5.—The response evoked was remarkable, and carried with it evidence of a genuine public dissatisfaction, in all parts of Europe, with the heavy, futile, unending burdens of the Armed Peace, and of immense relief and satisfaction at the proposal to deal with the oppressive evil, and to seek the benefits of a real and durable Peace.

6.—The terms of the Imperial Rescript have been unreservedly endorsed by popular opinion. The reasons given for the invitation were sound and strong; the peoples of the world have discussed them and have unanimously accepted them; and they, too, have reached the conclusion that war is not only barbarous, but that the burdens of preparation for it are deterrents of civilisation, injurious both to the State and to the individual, and a standing menace to the very existence of society. Such an admission by the united judgment and voice of the civilised world cannot leave matters as they were. To make it is the first condition of reform and the first step towards better things.

7.—It gives the highest official and authoritative sanction to the dreams and schemes, the efforts and contentions of the Peacemakers—those who, prior to its issue, were considered as mere visionaries and faddists, but whose labours and teachings have been proved to be the soberest wisdom and the truest patriotism.

8.—Taken altogether, the Emperor's Rescript has issued in

what amounts to an actual change of front—to a reconsideration, if not an actual reversal, of the mistaken policy of the civilised world, which has resulted in so much mischief. That has long been advocated as the necessary first step.

And lastly,

9.—The Emperor, by launching his indictment against the rising and overflowing tide of military expenditure, and making his audacious but earnest and true-hearted appeal, emancipated Europe, so to say, from a sort of intoxication which was preventing it from stopping in the mad outlay on armaments. It is noteworthy that since the Conference was mooted there has been less talk of increased outlay on improved armaments, fewer outbursts of military bravado and gratuitous provocation. The second Muravieff note, which explicitly stipulated that the Conference should not discuss any territorial changes, showed, moreover, that the problems would have to be discussed in a pacific and conciliatory spirit, excluding all hankerings for a settlement of pre-existing international difficulties. And, if there was no conviction how to reach a solution of the question of Peace or war, there was a feeling that any Power would incur suspicion or odium if, on the plea of reviving or strengthening pacific tendencies, it attempted to leave behind it the germ of a conflict to arise out of latent dissensions. This peaceful feeling pervading the assembled nations has been the first great benefit resulting from the Conference, and this alone would be enough to render it an important event in the annals of the time.

THE PEACE CONFERENCE.

1.—The Conference itself is an historical fact of such vast importance that only the future can declare its full significance. The assembly represented twenty-six Governments, whose dominions and dependencies comprise nine-tenths of the planet, whose populations, according to careful computation, consist of 1,400 millions out of the total 1,600 millions of its inhabitants.

It was an assembly—no longer Amphictyonic but world-wide—including nearly all the civilised Governments of the globe met to seek by international discussion the solution of questions affecting their common relations and mutual interests. Two months were spent in the friendly discussion of difficult and even dangerous topics, and at length, without dissension and even with practical unanimity, important decisions were arrived at, which have been given forth for the further education of the nations, or embodied in Treaties for their united action.

2.—The Conference was a fact altogether unique in history. It was a new thing in the earth. For the first and only time have the nations of the world come together to promote international Peace. It has thus been proved that they can meet together in peaceful conference and discuss matters of common interest, notwithstanding their essential and natural differences. Russia, for instance, may be a despotism, but it meets other countries in a common Parliament. The value of the Conference is not confined to its splendid achievements. It will exercise a great moral influence as a witness to the essential solidarity of civilisation. It is a beginning which must have important consequences.

3.—The Conference has been especially declared to be, and accepted as, the first of a series, and, therefore, the beginning of a new political order. It used every means in its power to make this idea accepted, and so to propagate itself. Whatever defects therefore may have attended its discussions and decisions, there will be ample opportunity for remedying them in the future. It is a precedent in history, that will surely be followed. This may be confidently expected as one of the fruits of the meeting at the Hague.

4.—The meeting of the Peace Conference has furnished a new illustration of the power of public opinion. The evidence of the force and influence of public sentiment was clear to any one who was at the Hague during the week or ten days that preceded the assembling of the Conference on the 18th of May. The atmosphere of the Hague was at first most unpromising. The Roman Catholics were angered because, in deference to Italy, the Pope was not invited. The Dutch of the capital were annoyed, and therefore distrustful, because President Kruger was left out, the Transvaal being considered a vassal State. The Members of the Conference were diplomats who had been trained to believe that the natural relations of States are distrust, suspicion, rivalry, and enmity, and that the main dependence of domestic prosperity is armed preparation against the encroachments of other States. As it was thought certain that the Powers would not consent to Disarmament, it seemed to be agreed that the Conference itself would be a failure. But before it actually met, a change came over the spirit of those diplomats residing at the Hague who were to be its members. The people at home had been heard from so unmistakably, that the men of politics and diplomacy were first silenced, and then transformed into active agents for the accomplishment, to use the words of one of them, of "some little thing."

Even after the change in the sentiment of the Conference began to be observable, it was thought the plans of Arbitration were impossible. But the people at home thought otherwise, and their opinions and moods found expression not only in newspapers, but in letters and petitions.

The principal outcomes of the Conference make it possibly one of the greatest of human agents that have ever existed for the advancement of civilisation. But its main importance is that it expresses the will of the people who, in our modern times, have the last word. Their ideal is Peace, and the Conference discovered this and obeyed it. In view of this, it matters little whether the Tsar's hope was a dream or the cunning devices of disingenuous statesmen. The Conference was not controlled by the Tsar, or Muravieff, or the Kaiser, but by the people, and especially by the people of the United States, Great Britain, France, and Germany, before whose concentrated purpose even rulers must bow.

5.—The value of the Conference is exhibited less in the details of its transactions than in the spirit which animated its proceedings. "Looking back over the whole period of the Conference," said Mr. Holls, "its most beautiful feature on the whole was the admirable spirit manifested by practically all the delegates." This spirit must have its reflex action upon the nations represented. It is impossible that these prolonged Conferences, carried on between men of such importance, should not leave a trace behind to impel them to a common effort to prevent bloodshed. It is impossible that the spirit of deliberations carried on in their name should not react upon those represented, and, therefore, that the breath of humanity which has blown through these deliberations, should not leave its mark on all brows—impossible that it should disappear altogether without leaving its trace on all minds. To have promoted the sense of goodwill and mutual confidence among the diplomatists of the world is thus a great step towards the maintenance of general and permanent Peace. And as regards the work of the Conference, the substantial Conventions and Resolutions are not so much calculated to impress the Conscience of Humanity as the Expressions of opinion which are embodied in the Final Act.

THE WORK OF THE CONFERENCE.

The Conference met to shake off the yoke of militarism from the nations, to humanise war, and to diminish the chances of war. The mere fact of its meeting was a recognition of the truth that justice and righteousness are ideas transcending the divisions between States; and throughout its deliberations it sought, with greater or less success, to graft this principle on the stock of present-day politics. No international gathering has ever attempted half so much, for absolute and complete success would have meant the foundation of a new political world. The Conference has not made a new world; but, where the aims are so vast and so revolutionary as those proposed, it is bare justice to estimate its work rather by what it has done than by what it has not, and with our eyes fixed on the future, not turned back on the past.

The formal results of the work of the Conference are contained in a series of Conventions, Declarations, and Resolutions, which constitute the Final Act, and it is a source of great satisfaction that in agreeing to all these there was a majority of the nations represented, and that in most there was absolute unanimity.

The Imperial Rescript, and the more detailed Circular which followed it, made mention of a series of topics which naturally grouped themselves under three main heads—ARMAMENTS—LAWS AND USAGES OF WARFARE—MEDIATION AND ARBITRATION. The performances of the Conference are not, it is true, of equal value in each of these sections. But it is noteworthy and satisfactory that in no section have its deliberations proved entirely barren, even at the moment, and that the results in each would alone justify its meeting, and be sufficient reward for its labours.

THE ARREST OF ARMAMENTS.

On the question of armaments, agreement between the Powers was, as had been anticipated, plainly out of the question; the difficulties were insurmountable, and national distrust too deep. Recognising this fact, there was absolute agreement among the members of the Conference, and they have given to the world, and to succeeding Conferences, some important Resolutions, which were adopted without a dissentient voice.

The Conference declares, for instance, that the limitation of military burdens is greatly to be desired for the increase of the material and moral well-being of humanity; and it resolves that the Governments, taking into consideration the proposals made at the Conference, should study the possibility of an agreement concerning the limitation of military and naval forces and of war budgets. This indeed is a sufficiently strong endorsement of the Tsar's Rescript, and an ample justification for his appeal.

It must not, however, be assumed too readily that the Conference has failed to provide the means of escape for the nations in connection with the checking of armaments. It has referred the question back to the respective Governments; but it has not given it up as insoluble. It has, in effect, passed a Resolution that the question of military and naval armaments should be made a department of foreign affairs in each country; and this will effect a serious and salutary change in the character of the debates on the Estimates, and admit of the raising of questions and pleas which could not have been raised, in the British House of Commons for instance, before the meeting of the Peace Conference. They will be quite regular in the future; and the debates ought in consequence to gain in definiteness, point and efficiency.

The Reform of the law of Maritime Capture is yet another means of combating the growth of naval expenditure indicated at the Conference. It was indeed decided, largely out of deference to England, that the question lay outside the scope of the present Conference, but it is something that the reform has been recommended for discussion at a future Conference. It rests with the advocates of the reform to see that this recommendation does not become a dead letter.

Indirectly the end may prove to have been attained, though directly it was not. To declare a reduction of armaments desirable for the raising of the material and moral well-being of mankind, as the Conference has done, is to sharpen wits, not to acquiesce in dull failure. Such a declaration is a condemnation of the system which will render it impossible to continue it on the same scale as heretofore. On this question, however, legislation was impracticable. That was anticipated from the outset. But by referring the problem to the Governments for further study, the Conference declared its belief that it was capable of solution. The causes of the present terror — the distrust, rivalry and mutual suspicion which have accumulated armaments—operate too strongly to admit of their removal by direct agreement. The indirect method of removal, by the substitution of new means of settling difficulties and by rendering their adoption easy and their results certain, which will gradually supersede them, will be far more effective. This is how the arrest of armaments will be eventually secured. Formulas and Treaties for their limitation are impossible; provide the substitute, and gradually, as the new juridical order develops and is established, the older system will die a natural and necessary death. It will doubtless be found that, even as regards the limitation and lessening of armaments, the delegates at the Conference builded better than they knew. Sir Julian Pauncefote declared his belief that the decision of the Conference will make it difficult to continue arming on the same scale as before.

Other Declarations about Armaments.

Three Declarations follow, forbidding the throwing of projectiles from balloons, the use of those only intended to diffuse asphyxiating gases, and the employment of expansive bullets. Something has thus been done in the way of mitigating the horrors of war in future, but the regulations, however admirable, appear somewhat inconsistent. It seems inconsistent to object to the Dum-dum bullet while allowing the dynamite gun or death-dealing lyddite shell; to prohibit the dropping of explosives from balloons, but to raise no objection to the blowing-up of an iron-clad by a torpedo. War is at the best a horrible thing, and these Resolutions will do little directly to mitigate its cruelties. And yet, indirectly, much. The declaration that, in the estimation of the Conference, such a mode of destroying besieged cities, filled with defenceless women and children, would not be in accordance with the civilised methods of war, and that the "great and beautiful civilising mission" of a Christian nation should not be advanced by instruments which the rest of the world condemns, cannot fail to have effects that will be incalculable. It is an appeal to the moral sense, whose operation may be safely left to time; it is a judgment, which will surely extend itself to the whole procedure of war as essentially opposed to civilisation. Since the world is governed by ideas, it does not require much imagination to perceive how beneficent the work of the Conference may prove in this direction. Nations which refuse to regard the public opinion and the moral sense of the world, put themselves in the wrong and come to be regarded as the common enemies of mankind. The effect of the judgment of the Conference in regard to expansive bullets is even now apparent.

The Laws of War.

As regards the second group of topics proposed to the Conference, the result of its labours was the production of two detailed Conventions. By one of these, the rules of the Geneva Convention of August 22nd, 1864, relating to the succour of the sick and wounded during an engagement or a campaign, have been extended to warfare at sea. By the other, which consists of sixty articles, divided into four sections, dealing with the status of belligerents, the treatment of prisoners of war, hostilities, armistice, and the like, has been secured the acceptance of a complete code of military law, a task which many international lawyers, in the light of the Brussels Conference of 1874, have declared to be a sheer impossibility. Concerning these, which belong to the minor work of the Conference, the semi-official *Norddeutsche Allgemeine Zeitung* gives its verdict thus :—" Any one examining the full results of the Conference as a whole must admit that the very extension of the Geneva Convention, to naval warfare, and the detailed definition of the laws and usages of war, constitute in themselves a weighty advance of civilisation, which secures to the Conference an honourable place in history. . . . The decisions of the Hague Conference for restricting and humanising war are a valuable legacy of the expiring to the coming century, a legacy which will bring lasting glory to the noble originator of the Conference idea, the Emperor Nicholas."

The Chief Work of the Conference.

But the great work of the Conference was the Convention for

the Pacific Settlement of International Conflicts, which lays the foundations broad and deep for an international system of judicature.

The starting point of this new International Charter is the formal declaration by all the Powers that henceforth they will use all their efforts to prevent war and to maintain Peace. The Instrument then proceeds to define the methods by which they will attempt to attain this end :—

1.—They agree, when two of them quarrel, to appeal for the good offices and mediation of the other Powers.

2.—They agree that if the disputants forget this obligation, any of the Powers not concerned in the dispute shall themselves take the initiative, and tender their good offices and mediation.

3.—They agree to recommend that, when Powers are on the point of going to war, they should each place their case, for a period not exceeding thirty days, in the hands of a friendly neutral Power, which would thus become a special mediator for preventing war, or for bringing it to a close if it should break out.

4.—They deem it useful when Powers cannot settle a dispute diplomatically, and when they are not willing to accept Arbitration, that International Commissions of Investigation should be appointed to clear up difficulties by an impartial examination of the facts.

5.—They have provided for the establishment of a Permanent Court of Arbitration :

1. When nine Powers have ratified the Convention, the representatives of the Signatory Powers at the Hague meet under the Dutch Minister of Foreign Affairs, as a permanent Administrative Council to establish and direct a permanent Bureau on which the Court rests.
2. In the course of three months after ratification, each Power nominates competent Arbitrators (not more than four each) whose names, inscribed on a list of Arbitral Judges, form the Court.

3. Any two disputing Powers, who decide to appeal to the Court, select two Arbitrators each from the list of members of the Court ; the four so nominated then select an Umpire, and the Tribunal, thus constituted, hears the case.

6.—They have devised and agreed upon a complete code of Arbitration procedure.

7.—In order to make the Arbitration provisions as binding as possible, the Powers declare it to be a duty, whenever any dispute reaches an acute stage, to call the attention of the disputants to the provisions of the present Convention and invite them to apply to the Court.

8.—The Powers reserve to themselves the right, even before ratification, to conclude separate Treaties with each other, making a recourse to Arbitration obligatory in all cases they please.

9.—They also provide for the adhesion of non-signatory or non-represented Powers to the present Convention.

Remarks Thereon.

"The main point of the whole thing," says Mr. Seth Low, "is that Arbitration has been made easy; it was only possible before. There is a great deal of public opinion in the air in favour of Arbitration, and so there is of electricity, and that electricity is useless until there is a motor. The Peace Conference has furnished the standing parts of the machinery, which will admit of the practical working of Arbitration; it has furnished the motor."

"In the history of International Law," says Mr. Holls, "the Conference undoubtedly marks an important epoch. Several new principles have been introduced by the common consent of all the nations there assembled, notably those of Special Mediation, the useful auxiliary of International Commissions of Enquiry, and the Code of Procedure which distinctly resembles English and American equity practice more than anything else.

The great merit of the Arbitration Scheme, urges the *Leeds Mercury*, is that it is the first recognition by Europe—indeed by the world—of the truth that each State has a vital interest in preventing warfare between other States, quite independently of any particular relations. The signatories to the Hague legislation make themselves directly responsible for using every effort to prevent war; and they do so for no other purpose than to declare that war, as such, is an outrage on the common instincts of the civilised world, and with no reference to particular quarrels out of which they might or might not derive some advantage.

This means a great step forward. It is true that there are symptoms of danger all round to the great ideal of national development on the lines of an ordered freedom, and that all the smaller nations, from Ireland downwards, have a hard struggle for their own independence. But it is none the less important to secure the common consciousness of a common standard of civilisation, for the general allegiance to such a standard will prove a breakwater against the hundred forces which threaten the Peace of Europe and the Freedom of the weaker States.

The weakness of the Arbitration Scheme, urges Mr. Stead, is that it does not make Arbitration obligatory. We are also told that a Court which cannot enforce its decisions is quite powerless to prevent war, and thus useless. But such reasoning leaves out of court human nature, the power of public opinion, and the facts of actual experience. The existence of a permanent and responsible Arbitration Court will be a constant invitation to argument and discussion; and soon the popular pressure upon Governments not to fight until they have at least tried what can be done by Arbitration will be irresistible.

Within recent years a greater willingness has been shown generally to resort to Arbitration in the case of disputes which threaten to break the Peace. The formation of a properly-constituted Tribunal gives this idea definite shape. No Power will be compelled to submit a dispute to the Court, but there will be a moral coercion which will have great weight with intending combatants.

There is nothing compulsory in the provisions of the Pacific Convention, but its moral effects will be incalculable. It opens a way of escape for nations that desire to avoid war; and one of the facts brought out very clearly by recent events is that all nations have this desire. It will, in the future, be harder to begin a war; it will be easier to keep the peace.

Though the enlistment of soldiers, the invention of murderous weapons, and the perfecting of war organisation will not stop, and perhaps will not be slackened, the work of the Conference has interposed new difficulties in the way of making war. The means for carrying on war will remain as plentiful as before, but steps have been taken for putting off the occasion when these means may be used. There will be a longer pause before fighting begins between civilised nations; the facts will be more fully investigated; the combatants will have an opportunity of considering their position and the consequences of an appeal to the sword; tempers will have time to cool; an appeal on the part of the onlookers will be acknowledged as a necessary duty, and second thoughts suggested by friendly mediators may be the means of averting a conflict.

The Conference has not succeeded in making war impossible, but it *has* succeeded in focussing the humanitarian sentiments of the age, and as Mr. Arthur Mee, writing in the *Morning Herald*, has well said, "there will be no more rushing heedlessly on to war."

"War there may be, but it will be war after calm reflection, war after the people have counted the cost, war after the soldier has realised its horrors. In the gravest crisis, there will be a pause at the Hague between the passions of the people and the rattle of the sword. It is a wonderful thing that the Governments of the world have set up a Universal Parliament of Peace. It is not quite, perhaps, the Brotherhood of man, but that great consummation seems nearer since the delegates left the Hague."

Though not the recognition of that brotherhood, it has been rightly argued, by Mr. Stead and others, that it is the first direct, definite step towards the Federation of mankind. It is more. It is, within certain well defined limits, and for a distinct object, the highest and most important of any, an actual Federation, by formal instrument, of nine-tenths of the human race. It is the first step that counts; and this one, arising as it does out of the natural trend and development of things, must lead to others.

A Philosophical Estimate.

This is finely and forcibly reasoned by Mr. Raymond L. Bridgman, who argues in the *New England Magazine* that if the Conference at the Hague had failed to accomplish any direct purpose whatever, it would nevertheless have been a success, because the inspiration of the Conference, both in regard to the giving of the invitation by the Tzar of Russia and its acceptance on the part of the participating nations, was a progressive step in the self-consciousness of mankind to a higher realm of truth, to a better idea of humanity, to a closer bond of sympathy and to a more imperative form of duty. This self-consciousness, too, is on a higher plane to-day than it was before the Conference at the Hague was held.

1.—In consequence of that Conference, the practice of settling national disputes by reason rather than by force has been greatly promoted. The participating nations have come to a more definite conception of the rights of nations, whether great or small, in their people and territory, and they have tried to recognise those rights, regardless of the degree of military force by which they are defended, and to formulate practicable ways of maintaining them by reason rather than by arms. That is, in the minds of the nations to-day there is a clearer perception than ever before that might must be subordinated to right, that though a nation may be technically sovereign, as a man is technically free, yet upon both nation and man there rests the imperative of doing right.

2.—The results of the Hague Conference are one more step toward the attainment of the Constitution of the Republic of Nations—the republic in which all mankind shall be members;

in other words, of the Federation of the World. This constitution is inherent in the laws which control the development of humanity.

3.—The Conference at the Hague opens the door to further action by the participating nations; and their action will involve an increase in the number of participants, until, in the rapid extension of the new International system, and in the conquest of all outlying parts of the world by quick communication, no community of men shall be excluded.

4.—Nations being sovereign only in respect to other nations, and not in respect to the body of Law above them, and all nations being subject to one and the same body of supreme law, it follows that the peace, progress, and unity, of mankind will be greatly hastened if there be specific statement of this law and formal submission to it on the part of the so-called sovereign nations. International Law is the beginning of this statement and submission. It testifies not only to the common recognition by civilized nations of the supreme law which is equally over them all, but also to the growth of the new force, which makes for the elevation of the man and of the nation, viz.—the power of public opinion. It necessitates, first of all, on the part of nations good faith. That is, nations must be absolutely honest with each other. The only power to enforce a principle of international law is public opinion, plus the moral sense in each nation itself, apart from its recognition of moral worth in others. Thus far there is a body of international law without other than this moral sanction. It is growing constantly, it is being elaborated with increasing nicety. It is being more largely recognised as the judgment and conscience of mankind, which no nation can persistently defy and maintain its standing in the family of nations.

5.—What the nations have already done, or are contemplating, is a mere beginning of the expression of the political constitution of the body politic of mankind. The nations are just beginning to get together. Reason now stands at the door, demanding, on the basis of its inherent rightness, that it be given the throne of authority which is now held by force—that Arbitration should be substituted for the sword.

6.—When the present stage of progress shall have been completed, there will follow a development in prosperity such as would occur in a community whose people had been devoting much of their strength to mutual destruction, but should suddenly make peace and work with equal energy for mutual benefit.

7.—But this new development of mankind necessitates a means of apprehending and of expressing the principles in the political constitution of mankind : that is, there must be a Court, a Congress, of Nations.

8.—The self-consciousness of mankind has already recognised honesty, mercy, and worth. It stands almost ready to recognise reason as higher than brute force.

9.—A higher force is operating in history. It is comparatively modern. It is gaining in strength rapidly. It is already recognised by the foremost nations. More than this, it is inevitable in the nature of things that the higher force will win. Either man is wholly brute, or that in him which is higher than brute will dominate the brute. The common consciousness of man affirms that it is higher than the brute.

10.—It is possible that the united will of mankind, in our lifetime may rise to the height of its own nature, and lift the development of the nations from the domain of material force into the bright realm of reason and sympathetic helpfulness.

11.—Obstacles to the unification of the nations are less mountainous than formerly, and are steadily diminishing.

12.—The ages in human history before the participation of mankind in the Congress of nations are necessarily the imperfect ages in political relations. Mankind has not found its true unity. Its parts are often mutually hostile ; there is no realisation of a combined whole, and no enthusiasm in race spirit. Hints of this unity, however, point the way to it; and the local pride and national patriotism of the present, illustrate feebly the tremendous enthusiasm of mankind which will fill the earth when local communities shall have been absorbed into nations (a process which is visibly reaching completion) and when national boundaries shall have faded into insignificance in the all-embracing unity of the body politic of mankind. Then will the entire human race first realise its race-consciousness, and then will the real history of mankind begin.

The Peace Conference in the Light of History.

This account of the development of humanity, with its optimistic outlook towards the future, corresponds with the actual facts of history. It has been truly pointed out by an American newspaper, the *Philadelphia Record*, that in order to appreciate the labours of the Conference at their true value, it is necessary to recognise the fact that this development is very gradual, and therefore, that the decline of warfare and the growth of the Peace sentiment have been, and probably will continue to be slow—discouragingly slow perhaps—to men of extremely sanguine temperament. Those, it says, who confine their attention to their own time and their immediate surroundings may be inclined to the pessimistic conclusion that human nature will be in the future very much the same as it has been in the past, and that war is an incurable evil. If, however, the conditions of life during past ages be examined and comparisons made, a steady development of human sympathy and the gradual sapping of the military spirit will be discernible.

At a comparatively recent time in the history of mankind, a battle was regarded by men of our own race as a religious rite, wherein the priests of warring clans sacrificed the foemen in honour of their tribal gods. The student may read how our Teutonic ancestors hacked off the arms of their captives and cast the severed members into the blazing fires of their altars. Wherever they marched their route was marked by wanton massacre, in which neither age nor sex was spared. Occasionally the monotony of putting a whole nation to the sword was relieved by a variation in cruelty, as when the Franks, during the invasion of Gaul, rolled their waggons over 200 maidens and cast their mangled bodies to the dogs.

When conditions had become more settled, tribal raids gave place to the vendetta and to private war, and the average man could not enjoy even a precarious lease of life unless he became a liegeman to a strong lord in his vicinity. The development of the power of the kings in turn curbed the warlike spirit of the feudatory barons, and led to the establishment of the king's peace, and the enactment of laws to compel the kinsmen of one slain in a quarrel to accept a fine in compensation, and to desist from private vengeance. But it was long indeed before the established Courts of Justice took the place of the ordeal and the judicial combat, and the present order of society was evolved out of the old condition of chaos and misrule.

In the course of the Middle Ages the manners of men by slow degrees became milder; a city might be sacked and its inhabitants slaughtered for having too stubbornly resisted a siege, but the practice was no longer universal. Enough of ferocity remained, however, and the undertaking of the Church to establish the "Truce of God" was considered quite as chimerical as would be a proposal for universal disarmament in our own times. Nevertheless the "Truce of God" was established. The Church at first secured the exemption of her holidays from bloodshed; then Sundays were made equally free, and, finally, an oath was enacted from every male communicant upon obtaining the age of twelve that fighting should cease on Wednesday evening of each week and not be resumed until Monday morning. Although not universally adopted, the "Truce of God" brought peace to vast regions which had theretofore been the scene of endless rapine and murder.

It would be possible to trace the amelioration of social life through successive stages up to the present time, each stage showing a distinct advance in humanity and a decline in brutality. The most successful nations, from a material point of view, are no longer those which are the most incessant fighters, but those which have developed to the highest degree the arts of peace and the pursuits of commerce. The essentially martial Turks, for instance, occupy a low place in the family of nations, while the commercial Englishmen are far in the van. In the light of past history the achievements of the Peace Conference must be regarded as marking a new epoch. Peace-makers may be obliged to look to a still distant future for the final consummation of their hopes; but it cannot be denied that the establishment by universal consent of a permanent International Court to which all nations may appeal for a judgment of their differences must mark a point of departure quite as significant as was the proclamation in a more brutal age of the "Truce of God."

Its Place in History.

But the working of this higher law of human development, and the place of the Peace Conference as an illustration of it, may be determined with even greater precision. Four stages have been noted by students of history, not distinct in time, but, like the stages of geologic development, overlapping, blending, shading off into each other. In the first and lowest, every man has to protect himself, the injured party depends for redress entirely upon his own resources, and there are no restraints on the exercise of the foulest passions; in the second stage the customs of the community, and the laws promulgated by its rulers, impose limitations upon the right of private vengeance and the practice of private war, at first the restrictions are few and rudimentary, but in time they grow into an elaborate code. The third stage is reached when, side by side with the old method, there exists, in full operation, an alternative method of justice before impartial tribunals, who decide each case on its merits as administrators of a passionless law; and the fourth stage is marked by the universal establishment of the judicial system and the entire abolition of the old brute method of private warfare. This is the history of Christendom. Public, or international warfare, has obeyed the same law, and followed the same course of development. The third stage had already been reached, and now the Conference furnishes the first step of the fourth. Indeed, its labours belong to, and illustrate, all four stages. The legislation affecting uncivilised and inhuman means and methods of warfare refer to the first, the brute stage; the Conventions regulating the practice of war between so-called civilised nations belong to the second, the semi-barbarous stage; but the Arbitration Scheme, while it assumes, and is based upon, the practice of Arbitration in the third stage, really initiates the fourth, in which the permanent institution of Arbitration, as an international system of settlement, will entirely supersede that of the sword, which has become intolerable, and was therefore faithfully and fearlessly exposed and condemned in the Tzar's Rescript.

By no Means a Finality.

This transitional character of the Conference was fully apprehended by it, and is faithfully represented in its proceedings. It was, consciously and avowedly, initial and preparatory; the inauguration of a new régime, the first of a series belonging to the new age. In no sense can the Conference be said to close any page of history; and on no single question does it profess to utter a final word, or even to admit final failure. It is emphatically a beginning. And so, as says the *Leeds Mercury*, there is another sense in which the work of the Conference has yet to be completed. A Conference can only legislate: it is for others to act in the spirit of that legislation. Even the crowning work of the Conference—the Arbitration Project and the International Court established under it — a work which carries with it possibilities of greater benefit to the human race, than any diplomatic document ever drafted, will fail to realise its destiny unless the friends of Peace are unwearied in their efforts. It is all important that the work just begun should not be allowed to rest for a moment. And it has further to be remembered that the whole fabric of Peace rests on international righteousness.

The institution of a Permanent International Court of Arbitration will not render the work of resisting wrong by the ordinary means unnecessary. On the contrary it will make it all the more necessary; for the Court, however high the principles or intentions of its founders, must be largely affected by the existing condition of political morality. In the Permanent Court the friends of Peace have a most potent ally, but not a champion to do their work.

Meanwhile a great impetus has been given to the Peace movement by the recent Conference. It is true that not all was accomplished that was at first designed, and that was strongly and almost universally hoped. But there has been a distinct admission of the rightness and practicability of our aims, an admission that we are on right lines; the way has been made easy for future progress; the actual work of the Conference is beyond anything hitherto attained, and in itself of inestimable practical value, and it may be confidently expected that future Peace conferences will follow that of the Hague. Quite apart from the Conventions that were or were not signed, and the Resolutions adopted, the success of the Conference must be sought in the sentiment aroused in favour of Peace, the friendly relations established between the Powers, the better understanding that prevails as to what each wants, the proved practicability of holding such Conferences, which was declared to be impracticable, and the familiarity gained with diplomatic gatherings having disarmament and the establishment of general Peace as their end and aim.

INSTANCES OF INTERNATIONAL ARBITRATION SINCE THE PACIFICATION OF 1815.

The *Herald of Peace and International Arbitration* (London) some years ago published a number of instances wherein Arbitration, or Mediation, has been successfully tried during the present century. The Hon. David Dudley Field, of New York, subsequently made some further additions to the list, which has been revised from time to time. We have now further revised this list, and collected other cases still more recent, bringing the category up to date.

Since the general pacification of 1815 there have been nearly two hundred instances of Arbitration (or involving the application of the principle) for the settlement of international disputes, some of them involving grave questions of International Law. This list, therefore, is a most conclusive proof of the practicability of Arbitration, as a chief means for the settlement of international disputes. It includes the following :—

1. Arbitration between **GREAT BRITAIN** and the **UNITED STATES**, relating to certain Islands in Passamaquoddy Bay, and Grand Menan, in the Bay of Fundy. By Article 4 of the Treaty of Ghent, 24th December, 1814, it was referred to two Commissioners, Messrs. Thomas Barclay and John Holmes, one appointed by each Government, who held their first meeting at St. Andrews, New Brunswick, September 23rd, 1816, and at their last in New York, November 24th, 1817, rendered a final award, which divided the ownership, with preponderance against the United States.

2. **GREAT BRITAIN** and the **UNITED STATES.** By Article 5 of the Treaty of Ghent a similar Arbitration Commission, consisting of Mr. Thomas Barclay and Mr. C. P. Van Ness, was appointed to determine the North Eastern Boundary of the United States from the source of the River St. Croix to the River St. Lawrence. This Commission held its first meeting September 23rd, 1816, and its last in New York, April 13th, 1822, when, failing to agree, the Commissioners made separate reports to their respective Governments, and the matter was again referred to Arbitration by a Convention concluded September 29th, 1827 (which see, No. 14)

3. **GREAT BRITAIN** and the **UNITED STATES**, to determine the Northern Boundary of the United States along the middle of the Great Lakes, &c., to the water communication between Lakes Huron and Superior. By Article 6 of the Treaty of Ghent, 1814, this was referred to a similar Commission, consisting of Messrs. John Ogilvy and Peter B. Porter, which, on June 18th, 1822, reached a satisfactory agreement. By Article 7 of the Treaty of Ghent the further determination of the line of boundary to the Lake of the Woods was also referred to this Commission, but on this point they were unable to agree, and it was finally determined by the Treaty of August 9th, 1842, generally known as the Webster-Ashburton Treaty.

4. **FRANCE** and the **ALLIED POWERS**, in 1815. By the Treaty of Paris of November 20th, 1815, *Arbitration Commissions* were appointed for the final decision of cases in the liquidation of sums due by France in foreign countries, as already determined by the Treaty of May 30th, 1814. The contracting parties agreed to appoint Commissions of Liquidation for the examination of claims, and Commissions of Arbitration to decide on cases on which the former Commission should fail to agree. The British Commissioners were: for the former, Messrs. C. A. Mackenzie and G. L. Newnham ; and the latter, Messrs. Geo. Hammond and D. R. Morier.

5. **FRANCE** and the **NETHERLANDS**, in 1815. Objection of the Government of the Netherlands against France relative to the payment of the interest of its debt for the half-year, March—September, 1813. By the Paris Treaty of November 20th, 1815, the question was submitted for Arbitration to a Commission of Seven, two named by each Power, and three others chosen amongst neutral Powers. The Commission was required to meet in Paris, February 1st, 1816. Its work was completed and the Arbitral decision given, 16th October, 1816, in favour of France.

6. **GREAT BRITAIN** and **FRANCE** in 1815. Disputes respecting inheritance of the Duchy of Bouillon, between Philippe D'Auvergne, a vice-Admiral in the British Navy, and Prince de Rohan, actual Duke of Bouillon. By final Act of the Congress of Vienna, 9th June, 1815, it was referred to five Arbitrators, who gave their award 1st July, 1816, in favour of Prince de Rohan. This was the second instance of Arbitration in regard to the inheritance of the Duchy—the former having occurred in the Seventeenth Century, when it was referred to Arbitrators by Article 28 of the Treaty of Nimeguen, February 23rd, 1678.

7. **CANTONS** of **TESSIN** and **URI**, in 1815. Question of payment "every year to the Canton of Uri of a moiety of the produce of the tolls in the Levantine Valley." By Article 6 of the Declaration of March 20th, 1815, embodied in Article 81 of the final Act of the Congress of Vienna, it was referred to "a Commission appointed by the Diet." A decision was rendered August 15th, 1816.

8. The **UNITED STATES** and **GREAT BRITAIN**, in 1818. Obligation to restore slaves in the possession of the British at the time of the ratification of the Treaty of Ghent, and other matters, as set forth in the first Article of that Treaty (December 24th, 1814). The question of the true construction of that Article was referred to the Emperor of Russia by Treaty of October 20th, 1818. His decision was given April 22nd, 1822, in favour of America, and was at once accepted. (See also No. 12.)

9. The **UNITED STATES** and **SPAIN**, in 1818. Mutual claims arising out of excesses committed during the war, prior to 1802, by subjects of both nations. These were, by a Convention dated 11th August, 1802, referred to a Mixed Commission, composed of five Members, appointed two by each Government and the fifth by common consent. The Convention was not ratified until 21st December, 1818, proclaimed at Washington December 22nd. Meanwhile fresh claims had arisen of a similar kind. This Treaty was annulled by the Treaty of Florida, concluded February 22nd, 1819, by Article 9 of which the parties renounced their respective claims, and Florida was ceded to the United States.

10. The **UNITED STATES** and **SPAIN**, in 1819. By Article 11 of the Treaty of Florida (February 22nd 1819), the United States, exonerating Spain from all demands for the American claims that had been renounced, undertook "to make satisfaction for the same" [*i.e.* to their own subjects], "to an amount not exceeding five millions of dollars," and for this purpose to appoint a Commission of three citizens of the United States, which should, within three years from its first meeting, "receive, examine, and decide upon the amount and validity of all the claims included within the descriptions above mentioned." The Article further provided that "the Spanish Government shall furnish all such documents and elucidations as may be in their possession, for the adjustment of the said claims according to the principles of justice, the laws of nations, and the stipulations of the treaty between the two parties of 27th October 1795. In March, 1821, President Monroe appointed as Commisioners Messrs. H. L. White, of Tennessee, W. King, of Maine, and L. W. Tazewell, of Virginia, with Tobias Watkins as Secretary, and Joseph Forrest, as clerk. The Board met and adopted Rules of Procedure June 14th, 1821; and on June 8th, 1824, the day of their final meeting, made the report of their awards.

11. The **UNITED STATES** and **SPAIN**, in 1819; East and West Florida Claims. The ninth Article of the Treaty of Florida, closes with the following stipulations: "And the high contracting parties, respectively, renounce all claim to indemnities for any of the recent events or transactions of their respective

commanders and officers in the Floridas. The United States will cause satisfaction to be made for the injuries, if any, which, by process of law, shall be established to have been suffered by the Spanish officers, and individual Spanish inhabitants, by the late operations of the American army in Florida."

By an Act of March 3rd, 1823, Congress authorised and directed the Judges of the Superior Courts at St. Augustine and Pensacola to form a Tribunal to carry the foregoing stipulations into effect, and by it the claims were adjusted; the proceedings which involved many important points, and much diplomatic correspondence between the two Governments, continuing until 1884, papers on the subject being presented to the Senate by President Arthur on April 18th of that year.

12. The **UNITED STATES** and **GREAT BRITAIN**, in 1822. The amount to be paid by Great Britain under the award of the Emperor of Russia (No. 8) was, by a Convention concluded under the Emperor's mediation, July 12th, 1822, referred to a Mixed Commission, consisting of one "Commissioner" and one "Arbitrator," who should "meet and hold their sittings as a Board in the City of Washington." The Commissioner on the part of the United States was Langdon Cheves, the arbitrator, Henry Sewell, and on the part of Great Britain George Jackson and John McTavish, who met on August 25th, 1823, succeeded by September 11th, 1824, in reaching an agreement, and held their last session March 26th, 1827, their functions having been terminated by the Convention of London, ratified November 13th, 1826, under which Great Britain paid 1,204,960 dollars in full settlement of all the claims.

13. **GREAT BRITAIN** and **SPAIN**, in 1823. Redress demanded for injuries to British property during the Napoleonic wars. After the British forces had been ordered to make reprisals on Spanish property, on March 12th, 1823, a Convention was concluded at Madrid, which provided for a Mixed Commission, consisting of two members from each nation, to sit in London. Any difference on which they were equally divided, was to be referred to the Spanish Envoy in London, and a law officer of the crown, and if they could not agree, to an umpire determined by lot. "Great and almost insuperable difficulties presented themselves in respect to carrying this Convention into effect," but on October 28th, 1828, a Convention was signed by which Spain agreed to make good the sum of £900,000 in specie in full settlement of the English claims registered by the Mixed Commision, and Great Britain agreed to make good the sum of £200,000 for the Spanish claims, similarly registered.

14. The **UNITED STATES** and **GREAT BRITAIN**, in 1827. Dispute about the North-Eastern boundary of the United States. Referred to Arbitration by Treaty of September 29th, 1827. The King of the Netherlands was chosen Arbitrator in 1829. His award, which was given January 10th, 1831, was not accepted by the United States, as being beyond competency, and the matter was afterwards settled by a compromise, in the Treaty of October 9th, 1842 already referred to (see No. 3), as the Webster-Ashburton Treaty.

15. **GREAT BRITAIN** and **BRAZIL**, in 1829. Difference relative to capture of British ships in 1826-7. By a Convention, signed at Rio de Janeiro, 5th May, 1829, it was referred to a Mixed Commission of four members, with the stipulation that "if the majority do not agree it shall be further referred to the Brazilian Secretary of State and the British Minister at Rio de Janeiro."

16. The **UNITED STATES** and **DENMARK**, in 1830. Question of mutual indemnities and claims, which had their origin in the Napoleonic wars. Denmark renounced her claims and agreed to pay 650,000 dollars. The question of the full amount of claims left was referred by Treaty signed at Copenhagen, March 28th, 1830, and ratified at Washington 5th June, 1830, to a Board of Commissioners composed of three American citizens, to be named by the President of the United States, with the advice and consent of the Senate, who "shall adjudge and distribute the sums mentioned in Arts. 1 and 2" of the Treaty. The Commissioners were George Winchester, Wm. J. Duane and Jesse Hoyt, and their Secretary, Robert Fulton. The last meeting of the Board was held on the 28th March, 1833, when its work was done.

17. **GREAT BRITAIN** and **BUENOS AYRES** (now Argentine Republic), in 1830. Claim for indemnification for illegal acts and violences committed by Privateers in late war with Brazil. By treaty signed at Buenos Ayres 19th July, 1830, it was referred to a Mixed Commission (consisting of Michael Bruce and Manuel Morens), which met in London, and liquidated the claims, amounting to £21,030 15s. 5d.

18. **UNITED STATES** and **FRANCE**, in **1831**. Claims and counter-claims, arising out of belligerent depredations at sea during the Napoleonic wars, some of them dating prior to 1800. By a Convention signed July 4th, 1831, they were referred to a Commission which by an Act of Congress of July 13th, 1832, consisted of three Commissioners, Messrs. G. W. Campbell, of Tennessee, John K. Kane, of Pennsylvania, and R. M. Saunders of North Carolina who were appointed by the President. The labours of the Commission proved to be very onerous, and its existence was twice prolonged, first for a year, and then till the 1st January, 1836,. A diplomatic rupture occured in consequence of the award. January 1836, but this was healed through the mediation of Great Britain, and the award was accepted. The aggregate of the awards was $9,362,193 (£1,872,438), the last instalment of which was duly paid by France in 1836.

19. **THE UNITED STATES** and **NAPLES**, in 1833. By a Convention signed October 14th, 1832, the King of the two Sicilies agreed to pay to the United States 2,115,000 Neapolitan ducats, in settlement of claims arising out of depredations on American vessels during the Napoleonic wars; and by an Act of Congress, March 2nd, 1833, provision was made for the appointment by the President, by and with the consent of the Senate, of a Board of three Commissioners "to receive and examine all claims under the Convention of October 14th, 1832, which were provided for by the said Convention according to the provisions of the same, and the principles of justice, equity, and the law of nations." It was further provided that the Board should have a Secretary, versed in the French and Italian languages, and a clerk. Messrs. Wyllys Silliman, John R. Livingston, Jun. and Joseph S. Cabot were appointed Commissioners, Thomas Swann, Jun., Secretary, and John W. Overton, clerk. The Commission having disposed of all the claims, made its final report March 17th, 1835.

20. **BELGIUM** and **HOLLAND**, in 1834. Referred to the Plenipotentiaries of Great Britain, France, Russia, and Austria, who met in London in 1834, and effected a satisfactory arrangement, by which European peace and the independence of Belgium and Holland were secured. A Permanent Treaty between the two Countries was signed at London, April 19th, 1839.

21. The **UNITED STATES** and **SPAIN**, in 1834. New claims against Spain arising after the comprehensive settlement by the Treaty of 1819, in consequence of the war between Spain and her American colonies. The following modes of settlement were proposed to Spain: either by a Convention for the establishment of a Mixed Commission, to meet at Washington, to decide upon the mutual claims, and to strike the balance, or by a Convention stipulating for the payment of a gross sum. The latter was accepted, and on these terms a Convention was signed, February 17th, 1834, by which the contracting parties renounced, released, and cancelled all claims which either might have upon the other, of whatever denomination or origin they might be, from the 22nd, February, 1819 (the date of the Florida Convention), till the date of settlement; and by Art. 1 of the Convention the United States undertook to adjudicate on the distribution of the sum agreed upon. On June 29th, 1836, the President and Senate appointed Louis D. Henry, of North Carolina, as Commissioner, J. J. Mumford, of New York as Secretary, and C. Van Ness as clerk; they met as a Board on July 30th, 1836; the business was disposed of, and the Commissioner made his final report, January 31st, 1838.

22. **FRANCE** and **MEXICO**, in 1839. Mutual claims, arising out of the recent war between the two countries, terminated by the Treaty of Vera Cruz, March 9th, 1839, which provided for Arbitration. Referred to the English Sovereign, Queen Victoria, who gave her award on August 1st, 1844, to the effect that the claims on both sides were invalid, the acts of both countries being justified by the state of hostilities between them.

23. The **UNITED STATES** and **MEXICO**, in 1839. Claims by citizens of the United States against the Government of Mexico. Referred under Treaty of April 11th, 1839, to four Commissioners, two from each country, and, failing their agreement, to the King of Prussia, who appointed Baron Roenne, his Minister at Washington, as Arbitrator. Under his presidency, the Commission met at Washington, and adjudicated on some of the claims, which were decided in favour of the United States.

The remaining claims were referred in 1843 to another Commission by a Convention signed at Mexico, January 13th. The American Senate ratified this Convention, with an amendment which was never accepted by Mexico, and war resulted in 1846, at the close of which, by the Treaty of Guadaloupe Hidalgo, February 2nd, 1848, payment of the money was provided for, and the affair settled. This is the only case of Arbitration which has been followed by war. But this war was succeeded by an Arbitration Treaty, which is the first of the kind recorded between independent nations. The 21st Article of this Treaty of Guadaloupe Hidalgo contained an Agreement to arbitrate future difficulties between the two countries, and to this general obligation, says Prof. Moore, "all subsequent arbitral arrangements between the two countries may, in a measure, be referable."

24. **GREAT BRITAIN** and **PORTUGAL**, in 1840. Claims of British subjects for services in the army and navy of Portugal during the late war. A Mixed Commission was appointed, November 6th, 1840, to sit in London, consisting of two Commissioners, co-equal in power, "their decisions to be final when they were agreed in opinion," and an Umpire, if necessary, "who shall be the Minister of some third Power, resident in London." Awards amounting to £162,500 were made 26th August, 1842, which sum was being paid by Portugal 28th March, 1844.

25. The **UNITED STATES** and **PERU**, in 1841. Peruvian indemnity, settled by a Convention signed at Lima, March 17th, 1841, "on account of seizure, damage or destruction of property at sea, or in the ports and territories of Peru, by order of the Peruvian Government or under its authority." By the first Article of this Convention it was provided that the indemnity should be distributed "in the manner and according to the rules that shall be prescribed by the Government of the United States." By an Act of Congress, August 8th, 1846, the Attorney-General, Mr. John Mason, was directed "to adjudicate the claims in accordance with the principles of justice, equity and the law of nations, and the stipulations of the Convention." The completion of the task passed into the hands of his successor, Mr. Nathan Clifford, who on 7th August, 1847, reported the awards to the Secretary of State, as required by the Act of Appointment.

26. **FRANCE** and **GREAT BRITAIN**, in 1842. Portendic claims, *i.e.*, claims for injuries sustained by British merchants, in consequence of the absence of any notification of the blockade of the Portendic coast of Morocco by France. The whole of the claims were, by an Agreement done in duplicate at Paris, the 14th day of November, 1842, referred to the King of Prussia, who gave his award November 30th, 1843, in favour of Great Britain. By a Mixed Commission, appointed in 1844, to fix the amount of the indemnity, &c., France was adjudged to pay 42,000 francs, which sum was voted by the French Chamber in its legislative session of 1845.

27. **SARDINIA** and **AUSTRIA**, in 1845. Dispute respecting the interpretation of Article 2 of the Convention of 1751, which regulated the Sardinian Salt Trade. Referred to the Emperor Nicholas of Russia, as Arbitrator. He proposed to accept the rôle of Mediator, and in that capacity gave a judgment which was accepted, and so settled the matter.

28. **GREAT BRITAIN** and the **UNITED STATES**, in 1846. The San Juan Water Boundary. It had been decided that the line of boundary from the point on the 49th parallel of latitude up to which it had been already ascertained, should be continued westward along the said parallel "to the middle of the channel which separates the continent from Vancouver's Island, and thence

southerly through the middle of the said channel and of Fuca Straits, to the Pacific Ocean." The dispute arose respecting this latter portion of the boundary. By a Treaty of Washington concluded on the 15th of June, 1846, and ratified in the Senate by a vote of forty-one to fourteen, it was referred to a Joint Commission, the members of which, Archibald Campbell and Lieut. John G. Parke for the United States, and Captains James C. Prevost and Henry Richards, R.N., for Great Britain, were appointed early in 1857. The Commissioners held six formal meetings, the last of which was on December 3rd, 1857, when they finally disagreed. Nothing more was done until 1871, when by Articles 34-37 of the Treaty of Washington, the question was referred to the Emperor of Germany. (See No. 72.)

29. The **UNITED STATES** and **BRAZIL**, in 1849. By a Convention concluded at Rio de Janeiro, January 27th, 1849, a settlement was effected of the long-pending claims of citizens of the United States against the Government of Brazil. The Convention provided for the distribution of this indemnity among the claimants by the Government of the United States. It was recommended that the Tribunal appointed for this purpose should sit at Rio de Janeiro, and in this some of the claimants concurred. The Act of Congress, approved March 29th, 1850 made provision for the appointment of a Commissioner to sit in Washington, and of a clerk to assist him. On July 1st, 1850, George P. Fisher, of Delaware, was appointed Commissioner, and Mr. Philip N. Searle, of New York, Clerk. Thirty-eight claims were adjudicated upon, and 59 awards given, a report being rendered and attested, June 30th, 1852.

30. **GREAT BRITAIN** and **GREECE**, in 1850. Claims against Greece. By means of the good offices of the French Government it was agreed to submit these to Arbitration. Convention signed at Athens, July 18th, 1850; ratified December 9th, 1850, referring to a Mixed Commission:—Messrs. Patrick F. C. Johnstone (appointed by Great Britain) and G. T. O'Neill (by Greece), and M. Leon Béclard, Convener and Umpire (appointed by France). All claims were settled otherwise but that of M. Pacifico, who claimed £21,295 and was awarded £150.

31. **FRANCE** and **SPAIN**, in 1851. Question of indemnities arising from seizures by the fleets of both countries going back to the years, 1823-24, and especially relating to the Spanish ships, the "Veloce Mariana" and the "Vittoria" and the French frigate, "La Vigie." By the convention of Madrid, February 15th, 1851, the King of the Netherlands was chosen Arbitrator. His award was given April 30th, 1852, partly in favour of both, but the indemnity under the award was not settled before the convention of February 16th, 1862, by which the two Governments made themselves responsible for payment.

32. The **UNITED STATES** and **PORTUGAL**, in 1851. Nonfulfilment of neutral duty in permitting the destruction of the American ship, "General Armstrong," by a British fleet in the port of Fayal, in the Azores, belonging to Portugal, in September, 1814. Referred by a Treaty of the 26th February, 1851, to the Emperor of the French, who by his award, given November 30th, 1852, declared that the privateer was the aggressor, and that the Portuguese Government was not responsible for what had taken place. This instance of Arbitration is important as averting a serious conflict, which threatened between the two countries; and because the award entailed a curious legal process between the United States Government and the owners of the privateer for whom it was acting.

33. **CANADA** and **NEW BRUNSWICK**, in 1851. An Inter-provincial Arbitration. A Boundary Question between these two States had been referred to two Commissioners, Captains Pipon and Henderson, to report on a line which would satisfy "the strict legal claims of both provinces." Their report was accepted by the Executive Council of New Brunswick, but not of Canada. The British Government suggested Arbitration. This suggestion was accepted, and it was agreed that the Arbitration should be held in London. Dr. Travers Twiss, and Thomas Falconer, Esq., were appointed Arbitrators; they chose Judge

Stephen Lushington, of the Admiralty Court, as Umpire. On the 17th of April, 1851, they made an award (Mr Falconer dissenting) which was duly carried into effect.

34. The **UNITED STATES** and **GREAT BRITAIN**, in 1853. Various claims, including that for value of slaves who captured the ship "Creole" and sailed to a British port, where they were liberated. The claims numbered 115. They were, by a Convention signed February 8th, 1853, referred to a Mixed Commission, consisting of Messrs. Nathaniel G. Upham (U.S.A.), and Edmund Hornby (Eng.), with Mr. Joshua Bates, of London, as umpire. "No case of Arbitration," said a writer in the *North American Review* "has ever been more successful than this. Damages were awarded in some thirty claims, and many important decisions were pronounced by this Commission." Of the 40 American claims, 12 were allowed, with damages amounting to £68,131; and of the 75 British, 19, with damages £57,252.

35. **GREAT BRITAIN** and the **UNITED STATES**, in 1854. Reserved fisheries question, arising out of Article 1 of the Convention between the two countries, signed at London the 20th October, 1818. By a Treaty signed June 5th, 1854, the dispute was referred to a Mixed Commission—one from each side, the two thus appointed to select an Umpire—which was organised in 1855. Its labours were suspended in October, 1856, and the Commission did not meet again until July 17th, 1857, when the Hon. John Hamilton Gray, of New Brunswick, was chosen by lot as Umpire. His awards were made on the 17th April, 1858. They were not final however, and changes followed in the Membership of the Commission, which terminated its labours in 1866, when "all the delimitation had been completed except on a small section of the southern coast of Newfoundland and a section of the coast of Virginia."

36. **GREAT BRITAIN** and **PORTUGAL**, in 1855. Claim against Portuguese Government by Mr. and Mrs. Croft, arising out of a denial by the Portuguese administrative authorities of a patent of registration in reference to the payment of a marriage portion from the Barcellinhos family, the rights to which had been accorded to them by judicial decisions. The Senate of Hamburg was chosen Arbitrator. Award given February 7th, 1856, in favour of the Portuguese Government.

37. The **UNITED STATES** and **NEW GRANADA**, in 1857. Question of claims arising out of rights acquired by the United States on the Isthmus of Panama under Treaty with New Granada, of 1846, and especially for damages caused by a riot at Panama, 15th April, 1856. Referred, under Convention concluded September 10th, 1857 (but ratified and proclaimed at Washington, November 8th, 1860), to a Mixed Commission, composed of two Commissioners, Messrs. Elias W. Leavenworth (U.S.A.), and José Marcelino Hurtado (N.G.), and an umpire, Mr. N. G. Upham, of New Hampshire, who adjudicated on part of the claims only, With regard to the others the Commissioners were unable to agree, and on the 9th March, 1862, the Commission adjourned *sine die*. The unsettled claims formed the subject of a new Adjudication, New Granada paying 345,307 dollars. (See No. 55)

38. **HOLLAND** and **VENEZUELA**, in 1857. The question of sovereignty over the Island of Aves in the province of Barcelona, Venezuela, which is rich in guano. Submitted by a Convention of the 5th August, 1857, to the Arbitration of the Queen of Spain. Her award, which was given in June, 1865, declared the island the property of the Venezuelan Republic, but imposed the payment of an indemnity to Holland for the loss of the fishery rights of her subjects.

39. **GREAT BRITAIN** and **BRAZIL**, in 1858. Settlement of outstanding private claims. By a Convention signed at Rio de Janeiro, June 2nd, 1858, and ratified at London, September 9th, these were referred to a Mixed Commission of two members, with Umpire to be chosen by lot if necessary. They held their first Meeting on the 10th March, 1859.

40. The **UNITED STATES** and **CHINA**, in 1858. Distribution of the

Chinese indemnity (settled by a Convention, signed at Shanghai, November 8th, 1858), for the destruction of American property, when the foreign factories at Canton were burned, and the foreigners were compelled to flee the city on the night of December 14th, 1856. A Tribunal of two Commissioners, Mr. Charles W. Bradley, U. S. Consul at Ningpo, and Mr. Oliver E. Roberts, late Vice Consul at Hong Kong, was appointed by the President. By the Convention it was agreed that in the adjudication of claims, the Chinese Government should be represented by an officer appointed to act for it. They concluded their labours, January 13th, 1860. The whole amount awarded being $489,788. A surplus remained after the payment of all claims; the return of the money was proposed, but the Chinese Government declined to accept it.

41. The **UNITED STATES** and **CHILI**, in 1858. Claim of compensation for silver bars and coin, taken by the Chilian admiral, Lord Cochrane, from a brig, the "Macedonian," belonging to an American citizen, and sold by him for 70,400 piastres. The dispute must have ended in war. By a treaty concluded November 10th, 1858, it was referred to the King of the Belgians, whose award, given May 15th, 1863, sustained the American claims, and condemned Chili to refund three-fifths of the sum appropriated, together with interest. Chili paid $42,000.

42. **GREAT BRITAIN** and the **ARGENTINE REPUBLIC**, in 1858. Claims by British subjects for losses sustained during the disorders of the Civil War in the Republic. These, by a Convention of the 21st August, 1858, were referred for settlement to a Tribunal consisting of Commissioners appointed by the Argentine Government and the Minister Plenipotentiary of her Britannic Majesty or his representative, and the amounts to be settled by them were recognised as a National Debt by the Argentine Government.

43. The **UNITED STATES** and **PARAGUAY**, in 1859. Claims against Paraguay by the "United States and Paraguay Navigation Company." After a naval demonstration by the United States, the question was referred by formal Convention, signed February 4th, 1859, to a Commission of two members, one chosen by each country, with provision for choosing an umpire. The American Commissioner, appointed by President Buchanan, as the result of an Act of Congress, May 16th, 1860, was Mr. Cave Johnson; the Commissioner on the part of Paraguay was Don José Berges. The last session of the Commission was held on the 13th August, 1860, when the Commissioners filed an unanimous Award which was adverse to the claims of the Company. Notwithstanding this, "on the ground that the Convention admitted liability, and that the Commissioners, by going into the merits of the case, had exceeded their competency, the United States repudiated the award, and has since endeavoured to settle the claim by negotiation." (Prof. J. Bassett Moore.)

44. **GREAT BRITAIN** and **HONDURAS**, in 1859. British Claims against the Republic of Honduras, as to the possession of lands by settlers. By the Convention of February 28th, 1859, signed at Comayagua, these were referred to a Mixed Commission, consisting of Mr. James Macdonald, and Mr. Leon Alvarado, with Mr. E. O. Crosby, Minister of the United States to Guatemala, as Umpire. The Claims were declared to be void; the Report of the Umpire bore date November 21st, 1862.

45. The **UNITED STATES** and **COSTA RICA**, in 1860. Pecuniary claims of citizens of the United States, arising from injuries "through the action of the authorities of Costa Rica." Referred to a Mixed Commission, Benj. F. Rexford (U.S.A.), and D. Luis Molina (Costa Rica), by treaty concluded at San José, July 2nd, 1860, ratified at Washington November 9th, 1861, the Umpire to be chosen by the other two members, or by the Belgian Minister to the U.S A. The umpire chosen was Chevalier Joseph Bertinatti, the Italian Minister at Washington, who awarded $25,704, December 31, 1862, to the claimants.

46. **GREAT BRITAIN** and **PORTUGAL**, in 1861. Claims of Messrs. Yuille, Shortridge & Co., British subjects, against Portuguese Government for losses incurred through breach of treaty. Referred to the Senate of Hamburg as Arbitrator. The Award, which was given in 1861, has not been published by the British Government, or, apparently, by the Portuguese.

47. The **UNITED STATES** and **ECUADOR**, in 1862. Mutual Claims. By a treaty signed at Guayaquil, November 25th, 1862, ratified at Quito July 27th, 1864, and proclaimed September 8th, 1864, these were referred to a Mixed Commission of two, consisting of a citizen of each State, who, with an umpire or Arbitrator, should undertake "the mutual adjustment of claims." The Commissioners were Messrs. Frederick Hassaurek (U.S.A.), and J. J. Flores (Ecuador), afterwards F. U. Tamariz, and the Umpire Dr. A. Destruge. The Commission expired by limitation August 17th, 1865, all the business before it having been disposed of. The Award, dated August 18th, 1865, fixed $94,799 as the amount to be paid by Ecuador.

48. The **UNITED STATES** and **PERU**, in 1862. Alleged illegal capture and confiscation of American ships, "Lizzie Thompson" and "Georgiana," which was referred to the King of the Belgians by an agreement, signed at Lima, December 20th, 1862. The King of the Belgians, perceiving after an examination of what had been published on the controversy, that the Arbitration would be "of a very delicate nature by reason of the special circumstances," declined to act, and in view of the declaration of the Arbitrator, and especially of the reasons which he gave for it, the Government of the United States decided to accept his adverse opinion, and to treat the claims as finally disposed of.

49. **GREAT BRITAIN** and **BRAZIL**, in 1863. Imprisonment of three British naval officers from the ship "La Forte" at Rio de Janeiro on June 7th, 1862. Referred to the King of the Belgians, Leopold I., who decided, June 18th, 1863, that "in the mode in which the laws of Brazil had been applied towards the English officers, there was neither premeditation of offence, nor offence to the British navy."

50. The **UNITED STATES** and **PERU**, in 1863. Various claims, by citzens of each country against the Government of the other, were, by a Convention signed at Lima, January 12th, ratified April 18th, and proclaimed May 19th, 1863, referred to a Mixed Commission of four members (two chosen by each) and an Umpire. The Commissioners chosen were Messrs. E. George Squier and James S. Mackie (U.S.A.), and F. B. Alvarez and S. Tarara (Peru), and the Umpire Gen. Pedro A. Herran, a citizen of Colombia, then in Lima. The awards were in favour of the United States by a preponderance of 63,500 Peruvian Soles.

51. The **UNITED STATES** and **GREAT BRITAIN**, in 1863. By a treaty concluded July 1st, 1863. Hudson's Bay and Puget's Sound Agricultural Companies' claims; these were referred to two arbitrators, Hon. John Rose, of Canada, and ex-Judge Alexander Johnson, of New York, and an Umpire chosen by them, who awarded 450,000 dollars to the Hudson's Bay Company, and 200,000 dollars to the Puget's Sound Company. Their award was given September 10th, 1869, the Umpire, Mr. Benj. R. Curtis, refusing to sign.

52. **GREAT BRITAIN** and **PERU**, in 1864. The Senate of Hamburg arbitrated on claims for compensation, on account of the alleged false imprisonment and banishment from Peru of a British subject, Captain Thomas Melville White, who had been arrested at Callao (March 23rd, 1861), kept in prison at Lima (until January 9th, 1862), and expelled the country. An indemnity of £4,500 sterling was claimed on his behalf by the British Government. The award, which was given on April 12th, 1864, decided that the claim was based upon a partial and exaggerated statement, and was entirely inadmissible, inasmuch as the procedure adopted by the Peruvian law-courts had been quite regular and according to the laws of the country. The parties, however, had to pay their own costs, those of the Commission to be equally divided between them.

53. **GREAT BRITAIN** and **ARGENTINE REPUBLIC**, in 1864. Losses arising out of a decree issued by the Argentine Government on February 13th, 1845, prohibiting vessels from Monte Video from entering Argentine ports. Decided by a protocol of the 15th July, 1864, to submit the matter to Arbitration, and by a further protocol of January 18th, 1865, it was submitted to Jose Joaquin Perez, the President of Chili, who gave his award August 1st, 1870, in favour of the Argentine Republic.

54. **VICEROY OF EGYPT** and the **SUEZ CANAL COMPANY**, in 1864. Various disputes connected with the Suez Canal undertaking. Referred, at the request of the Viceroy, to the Emperor, Napoleon III., by whom it was decided against the Viceroy. The award was given July 6th, 1864, and was followed by a Firman of March 19th, 1868, determining afresh the concession to the Canal Company on the newly prescribed bases.

55. The **UNITED STATES** and **COLOMBIA**, in 1864. Claims against the latter, as representing the late Republic of New Granada, arising out of treaty rights on the Isthmus of Panama. These were the claims not determined by the former Commission (No. 37). Referred by a treaty concluded February 10th, 1864, and ratified 19th August, 1865, to a Mixed Commission consisting of two members, appointed by each country, and an Umpire. Sir Frederick Bruce was chosen umpire. "Questions that would have been causes of war were thus settled quietly and equitably." The date of the last award was May 18th, 1866. The Awards given in favour of the United States, including those of the former Commission, under the Treaty of September 10th, 1857, amounted to $345,307.

56. The **UNITED STATES** and **SALVADOR**, in 1864. Claim of Mr. Henry Savage, a citizen of the United States, for losses through sale of gunpowder. An agreement was made with the Government of Salvador to submit the claim to Arbitration in Guatemala, and signed in triplicate, May 4th, 1864. The referees, Messrs. M. J. Dardon, A. Andreu, and Fermin Armas, on February 21st, 1865, "finally adjudicated" the Claim "in favour of Mr. Savage."

57. **FRANCE** and **VENEZUELA**, in 1864. By a Convention between these Powers in 1864, provision was made for the decision, by a Mixed Commission, of the "claims of French subjects for expropriations, damages, and injuries of the nature of those for which, according to the law of nations, the Government of the Republic [of Venezuela] is responsible."

58. The **UNITED STATES** and **VENEZUELA**, in 1866. Claims by citizens of the United States, against the Government of Venezuela. Many of these were of long standing and large in amount, and some of them involved important principles of International Law. Referred to a Mixed Commission, Messrs. David M. Talmage and Gen. A. Guzman Blanco, after protracted and difficult negotiations, by treaty, April 25th, 1866, ratified at Caracas April 17th, 1867, where the Commission met August 30th, 1867. Its last session was held August 3rd, 1868, all the claims submitted to it having been disposed of. Awards were given in favour of the United States amounting to a total of $1,253,310. But the proceedings were impeached for alleged fraud on the part of the Tribunal, and see further, No. 119.

59. **GREAT BRITAIN** and **MEXICO**, in 1866. By a Convention signed June 26th, 1866, and ratified November 19th of the same year, it was agreed to refer to a Mixed Commission the claims of British Subjects against Mexico. (*British and Foreign State Papers, lvi.* 7.)

60. **FRANCE** and **PRUSSIA**, in 1867. Question of surrender of LUXEMBURG to France, which was resisted by Germany. Submitted to a Conference of the Great Powers, which met in London, May 7th-11th, 1867, under the presidency of Lord Stanley. The Arbitrators agreed upon a treaty, guaranteeing the neutrality of the province, the retirement of the Prussian garrison, and the dismantling of the Fortress of Luxemburg.

61. **GREAT BRITAIN** and **SPAIN**, in 1868. The "Mermaid" difficulty. Claim for compensation for the loss of the schooner "Mermaid," of Dartmouth, loaded with coals for Ancona, which, in passing the forts of Ceuta on the 16th October, 1864, was fired at and sunk. By an Agreement between Great Britain and Spain, signed at Madrid March 4th, 1868, the claim was referred to a Mixed Commission, consisting of four Commissioners, two to be named by each Government from persons belonging to the Diplomatic and Naval Services, with an Umpire to be named at their first meeting, and in case of disagreement as to the person to be chosen by lot out of two named by them. The Decision was given within three

months from the first meeting of the Commissioners, but the result has not been announced. It was in connection with this difficulty that the late Earl Derby in Parliament said, "UNHAPPILY THERE IS NO INTERNATIONAL TRIBUNAL to which cases of this kind can be referred, and THERE IS NO INTERNATIONAL LAW by which parties can be required thus to refer cases of this kind. *If such a tribunal existed, it would be a great benefit to the civilised world.*"

62. The **UNITED STATES** and **MEXICO**, in 1868. Various claims and counterclaims which had arisen since the Peace of Guadaloupe Hidalgo, in 1848. By a Convention, dated July 4th, 1868, these were referred to a Mixed Commission, consisting of two Commissioners, an American and a Mexican, W. H. Wadsworth, and F. G. Palacio, together with an Umpire, Mr. Francis Lieber, who died October 2nd, 1872, This Commission was appointed for a term of three and a-half years, but in 1871 by a new Convention, concluded April 19th, it was prolonged to January 31st, 1873. In the interval a new Convention, dated November 27th, 1872, prolonged for two years the action of the treaty of 1868; but inasmuch as this Convention was not ratified by the Mexican Congress before January 31st, 1873, it was mutually agreed to modify its terms, so as not merely to prolong but to renew the Convention of 1868. Accordingly the revised treaty of 27th November, 1872, was ratified by both Congresses—by the U.S. Congress on the 8th March, and the Mexican on the 29th April, 1873. This Treaty revived the old Commission, which had ceased to act, and new Commissioners were appointed, Sir Edward Thornton, the British Minister at Washington, being chosen Umpire, the Commissioners now being Mr. M. M. de Zamacona (Mexico), and Mr. W. H. Wadsworth, who served as Commissioner for the U.S.A from the first meeting to the last. On April 16th, 1874, the Umpire, Sir Edward Thornton, gave his award on the claims made by Mexico, in favour of the United States. Thereupon the United States' Commissioner abandoned all claims on the part of his countrymen against Mexico. After this award objection was raised, on the ground of false evidence and fraud, and the functions of the Commission were extended by a new Convention concluded November 20th, 1874, and those of the Umpire still farther until November 20th, 1876, by a Convention proclaimed June 29th, 1876. The Umpire gave his award that any attempt to re-open the subject was inadmissible—"That it was impossible to go back upon accomplished facts and an executed sentence." The Umpire closed his labours November 20th, 1876. Some doubt remained, however, in regard to two of the principal awards in favour of the United States, and says Prof. Moore in 1891, "Pending efforts to secure a competent investigation of this charge, the United States has suspended the distribution of the money paid by Mexico upon them."

63. **GREAT BRITAIN** and **VENEZUELA**, in 1868. Claims of British subjects against Venezuelan Government, of which there were 79. By Convention signed at Caracas, 21st September, 1868, these were referred to two Commissioners, Dr. Juan de Dios Mendez and Geo. Fagan, British Chargé d'Affaires, who were to choose an Umpire by lot, if necessary. Their Report was given at Caracas, November 15th, 1869. Total amount awarded, 312,587 dols.

64. The **UNITED STATES** and **PERU**, in 1868. Mutual claims presented to either Government *since* the sittings of the Mixed Commission, which met in Lima in 1863 (see No. 50), and other claims specified. These were now by a new Convention, concluded at Lima, December 4th, 1868, ratified June 4th, 1869, and proclaimed July 6th, 1869, submitted to an Arbitral Commission of two members and an Umpire, the latter to be chosen by agreement or lot. This Commission sat in 1869 and made awards on a number of claims. The Commissioners were Mr. Michel Vidal and L. B. Cisneros, and, later, Dr. Manuel Pino. By a singular coincidence two Umpires were appointed, Mr. F. A. Elmore and Mr. T. Valenzuella. The Commission finally adjourned, and its Report of Awards was dated February 26th, 1870, all the business before it having been disposed of.

65. **TURKEY** and **GREECE**, in 1869. Cretan insurrection. Conference of Great Powers, at the instance of Prussia, was called at Paris, January and February, 1869. Though not an Arbitration in the technical meaning of the word, yet, as involving the principle, it deserves to be reckoned among instances of successful Arbitration. The proposals of the Conference were accepted by Greece.

66. **GREAT BRITAIN** and **PORTUGAL**, in 1869. Rival claims to sovereignty over the island of Bulama, one of the Bisagos Islands at the mouth of the Rio Grande River, Senegambia, on the West Coast of Africa, and to a certain portion of territory opposite to that island on the mainland. Referred under protocol of January 13th, 1869, to General Ulysses S. Grant, the President of the United States, whose award, given April 21st, 1870, was in favour of Portugal.

67. The **UNITED STATES** and **BRAZIL**, in 1870. Claim against Brazil, for the loss of the whale-ship "Canada" and her cargo, by the illegal interference of the Brazilian officials. Submitted for Arbitration under a protocol of March 14th, 1870, to the British Minister at Washington, Sir Edward Thornton, whose award, July 11th, 1870, was favourable to the United States. Amount awarded $100,740.

68. **UNITED STATES** and **SPAIN**, in 1870. Seizure of the steamer "Colonel Lloyd Aspinwall," by the Spanish authorities, in 1870. Submitted for Arbitration to a Mixed Commission, consisting of Mr. Juan M. Caballos and Mr. John P. Williams, who selected Mr. Johannes Rösing as Umpire. His decision, which awarded $19,702 in gold, was made November 15th, of the same year.

69. The **UNITED STATES** and **SPAIN**, in 1871. Claims which had arisen out of the last insurrection in Cuba, in 1868, on account of the alleged wrongs and injuries committed by the Spanish authorities in that island. Submitted by diplomatic Agreement, concluded at the United States Legation, Madrid, February 12th, 1871, to a Mixed Commission composed of two Arbitrators, an American and a Spaniard, and an Umpire, a citizen of a third Power, which met at Washington, May 31st, 1871. This Commission adopted a special rule of procedure, and its labours were prolonged for several years. But it underwent a number of changes and viscissitudes owing to the death of its members, from which cause it had as many as four Umpires. By a Protocol signed at Washington, May 6th, 1882, its labours were extended to January 1st, 1883, but were actually concluded December 27th, 1882, the last decision of the Umpire bearing date February 22nd, 1883. By an Agreement of June 2nd, 1883, concluded between the Acting Secretary of State and the Spanish Minister, provision was made for the winding-up of the Commission and the disposition of its records.

70. The **UNITED STATES** and **GREAT BRITAIN**, in 1871, on the "Alabama" claims. By the Treaty of Washington, May 8th, 1871, the dispute was referred to a High Commission, consisting of five members, nominated by America, Great Britain, Italy, Switzerland, and Brazil, viz., Mr. Chas. Francis Adams, Sir Alex. Cockburn, Count Ed. Sclopis, Mr. Jacob Staempfli and Viscount d'Itajuba. This Commission met December 5th, 1871, at Geneva, and on September 14th, 1872, gave its decision, which awarded 15,500,000 dollars (£3,100,000) to the United States. *This is one of the most important instances of Arbitration, and forms a distinct historical landmark.*

71. The **UNITED STATES** and **GREAT BRITAIN**, in 1871. Sundry claims by the subjects of both countries, arising out of the Civil War. Referred by the Treaty of Washington (Arts. 12-18), to a MIXED COMMISSION of three members, respectively appointed by Great Britain, the United States, and Spain, which sat until September 25th, 1873, when it adjudged the United States to pay £386,000 to Great Britain.

72. The **UNITED STATES** and **GREAT BRITAIN**, in 1871. Revival of the SAN JUAN dispute. A question of boundary, which involved the exact interpretations of the 1st Article of the Treaty of Washington of June 15th, 1846. The Commission appointed by that Treaty were unable to agree, and the subject had involved long diplomatic correspondence, dating back prior to 1803. It was now referred by the same Treaty (*i.e.* of Washington, 1871, Arts. 34-42), to the Emperor of Germany, whose award, given at Berlin, October 21st, 1872, sustained the American claim. (See No. 28.)

73. The **UNITED STATES** and **GREAT BRITAIN**, in 1871. About Nova Scotia Fishery Rights. By the Treaty of Washington, Arts. 18-25, May

8th, 1871, referred to three Commissioners, Sir Alexander Galt, Mr. Ensign H. Kellogg, and Mr. Maurice Delfosse, who met at Halifax, June 15th, 1877, and on the 23rd of the following November, awarded 5,500,000 dollars (£1,100,000) to Great Britain, the American Commissioner dissenting and withdrawing from the Arbitration. The award, however, was accepted, the amount voted by Congress, and on the 21st November, 1878, Mr. Welsh, under instructions from the President of the United States, delivered to the British Government a draft for the amount of the Award.

74. The **TRANSVAAL REPUBLIC** and **OTHERS**, in 1871. Question as to the ownership of a small district between the Modder and Vaal rivers (where the town of Kimberley now stands) in which diamonds had been discovered. The Governor of Natal was recognised as Arbitrator by the Griquas, the Batlapin, and the President of the Transvaal Republic. The claims of the last-named State were disposed of by his decision. He awarded the tract in dispute to the Griqua Claimant, Waterboer, including in his award the part claimed by the Orange Free State, which had refused Arbitration. The Free State, whose case had not been stated, much less argued before the Arbitrator, protested, and was after a time able to appeal to a judgment delivered by a British Court, which found that Waterboer had never enjoyed any right to the territory. Meanwhile, before the Award, Waterboer had offered his territory to the British, and the country was forthwith erected into a Crown Colony. The British Government, therefore, without either admitting or denying the Free State title, declared that a district in which it was difficult to keep order amid a turbulent and shifting population ought to be under the control of a strong Power, and offered the Free State a sum of £90,000 in settlement of whatever claim it might possess. The acceptance by the Free State, in 1876, of this sum closed the controversy.

75. **JAPAN** and **PERU**, in 1872. Seizure of the Peruvian barque, "Maria Luz," engaged in the Coolie trade, in the Japanese port of Kanagawa, and the liberation as slaves of those on board. The dispute was getting embittered when it was referred, by a Protocol drawn up by common consent at Tokei, 15th and 25th June, 1873, to Alexander II., the Emperor of Russia, whose decision, given at Ems on May 17th, 1875, was in favour of Japan.

76. **GREAT BRITAIN** and the **UNITED STATES**, in 1872. Boundary from the N.W. angle of the Lake of the Woods to the Rocky Mountains, on the 49th parallel of latitude. Referred, under the treaty of 1846, to a Joint-Commission, of which the American member, Mr. Archibald Campbell, was appointed under an Act of Congress, March 19th, 1872, the English Commissioner being Major D. R. Cameron ; by which the delimitation was duly effected. The labours of the Commission were concluded in 1876.

77. **GREAT BRITAIN** and **PORTUGAL**, in 1872. A dispute, which had lasted since 1823, about various territories and islands situated on Delagoa Bay. Referred, by a Protocol signed at Lisbon, 25th September, 1872, to M. Thiers, the President of the French Republic. His successor, Marshal MacMahon, by his award, on July 24th, 1875, decided that the Portuguese title was established to all the territories in question. The decision was a serious blow to British hopes, and has become increasingly serious with the further development of the country. Yet it was mitigated by a provision, contained in the Agreement for Arbitration, that the Power against whom the decision might go, should have thereafter, from the successful Power, a right of pre-emption as against any other State desiring to purchase the territory.

78. **GREAT BRITAIN** and **COLOMBIA**, in 1872. Pecuniary claims of British Firm of Merchants (Cotesworth & Powell, of London), against Colombia. Referred to a Mixed Commission, Dr. Schumacher, German Resident, and Dr. Ancizar, on December 14th, 1872. A new Commission, owing to removal and death, was appointed, consisting of Mr. Scruggs, the Minister of the United States at Bogota, and Ex-President General Salgar. The case involved important principles. The Arbitrators agreed in an award of 50,000 dollars ; the Commis-

sion closed its labours on the 5th November, 1875, and its decision and Award was published in the *Diario Oficial* of Bogota, December 18th and 21st, 1875, and was signed by both Commissioners.

79. **GREAT BRITAIN** and **BRAZIL**, in 1873. Claim advanced by the Earl of Dundonald against the Brazilian Government, for services which his father, Admiral Lord Cochrane, had rendered to Brazil during her War of Independence. Referred to the United States and Italian Ministers at Rio de Janeiro, Mr. James R. Partridge and Baron Cavalchini. On October 6th, 1873, they awarded the Earl of Dundonald £38,675.

80. **GREAT BRITAIN** and **FRANCE**, in 1873. Questions concerning duties levied in France on British Mineral Oils. By a Convention signed July 23rd, 1873, it was referred to a Joint Commission (Messrs. C. M. Kennedy and J. Ozenne), with power to name an Umpire, whose award, without reference to the Umpire, was given in Paris, January 5th, 1874, and adjudged to British claimants 314,393 francs.

81. **ITALY** and **SWITZERLAND**, in 1873. A Disputed boundary between the Swiss Canton of Ticino and Italy, which involved the ownership of the Alp of Cravairola. Referred December 31st, 1873, to a Mixed Commission with the Hon. Geo. P. Marsh, the United States Minister at Rome, as Umpire, who, on September 23rd, 1874, decided in favour of Italy.

82. **CHINA** and **JAPAN**, in 1874. Murder of Japanese citizens by Chinese, in the Island of Formosa. The two Governments were on the point of appealing to arms, when the Cabinets of London and Washington induced them to have recourse to Arbitration, and the dispute was referred to Sir Thomas F. Wade, the British Minister at Pekin, who, in 1876, awarded an indemnity of 500,000 taels to be paid by China, as reparation for the outrage.

83. **PERSIA** and **AFGHANISTAN** (SEISTAN BOUNDARY), in 1874. This was a dispute respecting the boundaries of the Persian and Afghan territories, on the N.W. frontier of India, which had for years been the source of constant bickerings between the Shah and the Amir. The treaty of March 4th, 1857, between Great Britain and Persia, provided that: "In case of differences arising between the Government of Persia and the countries of Herat and Afghanistan, the Persian Government engages to refer them for adjustment to the friendly offices of the British Government, and not to take up arms unless these friendly offices fail of effect." This question was so referred, and two British officers were appointed Arbitrators on behalf of the British Government, viz., General Goldsmid and General Pollock, by whom, at the beginning of the year 1870, was brought to a successful conclusion, "one of the most important boundary questions which our Government has had to decide."

84. **UNITED STATES** and **COLOMBIA**, in 1874. Claims for damages against Colombia for the capture of the American steamer "Montijo," in April, 1871, in Colombian waters, by insurgents in the State of Panama. Referred to a Mixed Commission, consisting of Mr. Bendix Koppel and Mr. Mariano Tanco, appointed under a Diplomatic Agreement of August 17th, 1874. Mr. Robert Bunch, the English Minister at Bogota, was chosen Umpire, by whom, July 25th, 1875, the sum of 33,401 dollars was awarded to the United States, and paid, Mr. Scruggs, the Minister Resident of the United States at Bogota, being "congratulated by his Government on the results of the Arbitration."

85. **PERU** and **CHILI**, in 1874. Disputed accounts in connection with the fleets of both Powers, which were in alliance during the war with with Spain of 1855. By a Protocol, signed at Lima, March 2nd, 1874, the controversy was referred to Mr. C. A. Logan, U.S. Minister at Valparaiso, whose award, given April 7th, 1875, adjudged to Chili a sum of 1,130,000 dollars, less 654,000 paid by Peru.

86. **ARGENTINE REPUBLIC** and **PARAGUAY**, in 1876. The El Chaco Boundary dispute. Referred, by treaty of February 3rd, 1876, to the President of the United States. The decision of President Hayes was given November 12th, 1878, in favour of Paraguay.

87. **GREATER BRITAIN: CANADA** and **ONTARIO.** In 1878. Messrs. Robt. A. Harrison, Edward Thornton, and F. Kincks having been appointed by the Governments of the above States "to determine the northerly and westerly boundary of the Province of Ontario, they completed their work and gave their Award at Ottawa, in the province of Ontario, August 3rd, 1878, duly signed by the three Arbitrators.

88. **GREAT BRITAIN** and **LIBERIA**, in 1878. In 1879, an effort, which began several years previously, for the Arbitration of a boundary dispute between Great Britain and Liberia came to an unsuccessful end. As early as 1871 the United States was asked to appoint an Arbitrator in the matter. In 1878 Commodore Schufeldt was named. He arrived at Sierra Leone January 19th, 1879. The investigation began, but the Commissioners were unable to reach an agreement as to the submission of the matter to the Arbitrator, and Commodore Schufeldt, after a lengthened detention in the neighbourhood of Sierra Leone, was compelled to depart, leaving his mission unfulfilled.

89. **GREAT BRITAIN** and **NICARAGUA**, in 1879. As to sovereignty over the Mosquito Indians, the question in dispute between them being the interpretation of certain Articles of the Treaty of Managua, signed on the 28th January, 1860. Referred to the Emperor of Austria, who appointed Herr Ungar, an Ex-Minister, and two Presidents of the Court of Cassation (Herr Schmerling and Herr Mailath) to act as Assessors. The Emperor's Award was given at Vienna, July 2nd, 1881, in favour of Great Britain.

90. **FRANCE** and **NICARAGUA**, in 1879. Alleged illegal seizure, in the Port of Corinto, November 23rd, 1874, of a French ship ("The Phare") laden with arms presumed to be for the use of the revolutionary party in Nicaragua. Referred, by an agreement dated October 15th, 1879, to the French Court of Cassation (Appeal), which had been selected by Nicaragua, and which, on July 19th, 1880, adjudged that State to pay 42,000 francs with interest.

91. The **UNITED STATES** and **FRANCE**, in 1880. Claims of compensation for injuries sustained by subjects of both Powers during the Mexican war of 1863, the American Civil war and the Franco-German war of 1870. By a Treaty concluded January 15th, and ratified June 23rd, 1880, these claims were referred to three Commissioners. one each appointed by the two Governments, viz., Mr. Asa O. Aldis and M. L. de Geofroy, who was succeeded, May 24th, 1883, by M. A. A. Lefaivre, and the third, the Baron de Arinos, by the Emperor of Brazil. The labours of this Commission (which sat in Washington from November 5th, 1880, to March 31st, 1884), not being terminated within the prescribed limit of two years, an extension of time (to April 1st, 1884), was granted by successive Conventions of July 19th, 1882, and February 8th, 1883, and its labours were continued until the claims were adjusted. Its final Award was given, and its labours closed, March 31st, 1884. Awards against the United States by a preponderance of $612,000.

92. **TURKEY** and **GREECE**, in 1880. Question of territory. Settled by Arbitration of the Great Powers, under Article 24 of the Treaty of Berlin, July 13th, 1878. This was a case of Compulsory Arbitration, the Powers, by an identic note of June 11th, 1880, informing the Sultan that they had decided that their representatives at Berlin should meet in Conference there, on the 16th June, in order to determine by a majority of votes upon the best boundary line to adopt. The Award of the Conference was signed at Berlin July 1st, 1880, and the decision of the Powers was given effect to in a treaty between Turkey and Greece, executed June 14th, 1881, under which the territory detached from Turkey, consisting of Thessaly and a part of Epirus, was ceded to Greece.

93. **CHILI** and **COLOMBIA**, in 1880. Dispute relative to the transportation of arms for Peru across the Isthmus of Panama. Referred by Convention, October, 1880, to the Arbitration of the President of the United States.—(*Panama Star and Herald*, October 16th, 1880.)

94. **COLOMBIA** and **COSTA RICA**, in 1880. Question of Boundary, as alluded to in various Treaties. By a Convention, signed at San José, December

25th, 1880, and ratified at Panama, December 9th, 1891, it was referred to the King of the Belgians, or, failing him, to the King of Spain or the President of the Argentine Republic. The Convention has this clause: "It is hereby agreed, and formally stipulated, that the question of limits, &c., shall never be decided by other means than those of Arbitration, as civilisation and humanity require." The King of the Belgians declined to act; an additional treaty on the subject was concluded at Paris January 20th, 1886, and the office of Arbitrator was accepted by the Queen Regent of Spain on behalf of His Majesty Alfonso XIII. The Arbitration lapsed, however, owing to a dispute between the contracting parties as to the time within which their cases were to be presented. Negotiations have since been undertaken for a new Treaty of Arbitration, but no definite result seems to have been reached.

95. **CHILI** and the **ARGENTINE REPUBLIC**, in 1881. A long-standing dispute about the Straits of Magellan and their land boundaries. It was agreed to refer this to Arbitration in 1878, in accordance with the provisions of the Treaty of 1856. It was so referred to the United States Ministers in those countries, Messrs. Thomas O. Osborn and Thomas A. Osborn, by Treaty of 23rd July, 1881, and their labours were concluded in September of that year. The boundaries were settled; the Straits of Magellan were made for ever neutral, their navigation was declared free to all nations: and fortifications or military establishments on their banks forbidden; and experts to complete the details were appointed by a Convention; but this Treaty proved not to be final. (See Nos. 164 and 189.)

96. **HOLLAND** and **ST. DOMINGO**, in 1881. Alleged illegal capture and confiscation of a Dutch ship, "Havana Packet," in August, 1877. By an Agreement signed at the Hague March 26th, 1881, it was referred to M. Grévy, the President of the French Republic, who condemned the Dominican Government, March 16th, 1883, to pay an indemnity of 140,000 francs.

97. **GREAT BRITAIN** and the **TRANSVAAL**, in 1881. Mutual claims for losses sustained in the recent hostilities. By Articles 6 to 9 of the Convention of April 5th, 1881, these were referred to a Commission consisting of the Hon. George Hudson, the Hon. Jacobus Petrus de Wet, and the Hon. John Gilbert Kotze; the decision of the said Commissioners, or of a majority of them to be final; and the proportionate share of the remuneration respectively, and of the expenses of the Commissioners and the Deputies, to be paid by the two Governments, according to the amount awarded against them.

98. **GREAT BRITAIN** and the **TRANSVAAL**, in 1881. Boundaries defined by the 1st Article of the Convention of the 5th April, 1881. By Article 19 of this Convention, it was agreed that the Royal Commission should forthwith appoint a person to mark off the boundary line in question, and to make arrangements between the owners of farms, on the one hand, and the authorities of the Barolong tribe on the other, in regard to the water supply.

99. **GREAT BRITAIN** and the **TRANSVAAL**, in 1881. Settlement of the native tribes of the Transvaal State. Articles 21-23 of the Convention of April 5th, 1881, provided that immediately after the taking effect of the Convention, a Native Location Commission will be constituted, consisting of the President, or in his absence the Vice-president of the State, or some one deputed by him, the Resident, or some one deputed by him, and a third person to be agreed upon by both, and such Commission will be a standing body for reserving and defining the boundaries of the locations allotted to the native tribes of the State.

100. **COLÒMBIA** and **VENEZUELA**, in 1882. A very delicate question of boundaries, which had been unsettled for fifty years. Referred to the King of Spain as Arbitrator, by a treaty signed at Caracas, September 14th, 1881, ratified June 9th, 1882, and proclaimed July 6th, 1882. King Alphonso XII. accepted the duties, and began studying the question, but died before giving his award. The question then arose whether the mandate given to him extended to his successor. This was settled by the ministers of the two countries in the affirmative, and, by a protocol signed in Paris on 5th February, 1886, their

decision was confirmed, and the Queen Regent Christina, who undertook the Arbitration on behalf of King Alphonso XIII., gave her award in May, 1891, very favourable to Colombia.

101. **MEXICO** and **GUATEMALA**, in 1882. Question of boundary. Referred by a Treaty of 27th September, 1882, to Commissioners, whose term of labour was extended by a protocol of 8th June, 1885, and prorogued by a Convention signed at Mexico, October 16th, 1886 (ratified, June 4th, 1887), for two years, ending 31st October. 1888.

102. **FRANCE** and **CHILI**, in 1882. Damages incurred by French subjects in the war between Chili, Peru, and Bolivia, called the Pacific war, through the operations of the Chilian forces. Referred, by Convention of November 2nd, 1882, to a Mixed Commission, consisting of three members, one to be nominated by the Emperor of Brazil, who appointed his Excellency F. Lopez Netto, Brazilian Minister to the United States, for all three Commissions (this and two following). On 20th May, 1885, the Emperor of Brazil appointed Lafayette R. Pereira instead of L. Netto, who adopted a point of view diametrically opposite to that of his predecessor, which, says Calvo, "was regrettable from the standpoint of the authority of Arbitration." This Commission began its work, but did not complete its functions, the question being settled by a Special Treaty between the two Governments, November 26th, 1887, the latter settling the claims by payment of a sum of 300,000 piastres.

103. **ITALY** and **CHILI**, in 1882. Similar claims by Italian subjects against the Government of Chili. Referred to a similar Mixed Commission of three, appointed by Italy, Chili, and Brazil, by Convention signed December 7th, 1882, ratified April 30th, 1883. The work of the Commission required two extensions of time, and ultimately, by a Protocol concluded January 11th, 1888, all claims then undecided by the Tribunal, to the number of 261, were settled by the Chilian Government paying 29,000 (piastres) Chilian silver dollars.

104. **GREAT BRITAIN** and **CHILI**, in 1883. Similar claims. Referred to a similar Mixed Commission, on January 4th, 1883. This Commission, constituted March 1st, 1884, installed anew, June 26th, 1886, and, by a Convention of August 16th, 1886, extended for six months longer, examined the different cases submitted to it, and allowed Great Britain 140,000 piastres. Awards, 1884-1887. Several claims were left unadjudicated upon, and by a protocol signed September 29th, 1897, a further sum of 100,000 dollars was paid in settlement of these. This Convention was one of several, all of which were substantially identical in terms. Under all of them the appointment of the third Commissioner was confided to the Emperor of Brazil, who designated Senhor Lopez Netto. He discharged the duties of President of the various Tribunals in 1884, but an Award rendered by his vote in November of that year gave rise to a discussion in the Press. In February, 1885, he returned to Brazil on the ground of ill-health, and the Emperor appointed as his successor Senhor Lafayette R. Pereira. (See No. 102.)

105. **EGYPT** and **FOREIGN POWERS**, in 1883. By a decree of January 13th, 1883, the Khédive instituted an International Commission to adjust claims growing out of the insurrectionary movements which had taken place in Egypt since June 10th, 1882.

106. The **UNITED STATES** and **CHINA**, in 1884. The Ashmore Fishery Claim. Referred early in 1884, to the Consuls of Great Britain and the Netherlands, as Arbitrators. They gave their Award on the 24th May, 1882, and adjudged Dr. Ashmore an amount of 4,600 dollars, to be paid within two months from the date of award.

107. **GERMANY** and **CHILI**, in 1884. Similar claims to above (see No. 104). Referred to a similar Commission by Convention of August 23rd, 1884. The Commission gave no award, since the claims were directly settled by a Convention of August 31st, 1886, and a protocol of April 22nd, 1887.

108. **BELGIUM** and **CHILI**, in 1884. Three similar claims of Belgian subjects. Referred to the Italo-Chilian Commission (No. 103) by a Convention of August 30th, 1884.

109. **AUSTRIA** and **CHILI**, in 1885. Similar claims. Referred to the German-Chilian Commission (No. 107) by a Convention of July 11th, 1885. The Commission was to meet at Santiago, and its sittings were to be secret, owing to the state of agitation in the country.

110. **SWITZERLAND** and **CHILI**, in 1886. Similar claims. Referred to the German-Chilian Commission (No. 107) by a Convention signed at Santiago, January 19th, and ratified by Switzerland, July 10th, 1886, and by Chili, October 7th, 1886.

111. The **UNITED STATES** and **HAYTI**, in 1884. Claims against Hayti on behalf of two American citizens, Captain Pelletier and Mr. Lazare, arising out of a charge of piracy against Captain Pelletier and the opening of a Bank by Lazare, and involving questions of administrative and judicial procedure. By a protocol signed May 24th, 1884, these claims were referred to Hon. Wm. Strong, formerly Judge of the Supreme Court, whose awards, dated June 13th, 1885, were adverse to Hayti. The United States, however, for what it deems valid reasons, has thus far declined to require their fulfilment; and according to a report of Mr. Olney, transmitted to the Senate 28th February, 1896, Hayti had not then paid the amount awarded.

112. **GREAT BRITAIN** and **GERMANY**, in 1884. Claims of British subjects as to the possession of certain islets and guano deposits, situated on the German Protectorate of Angra Pequêna, and neighbouring coast of South-west Africa. Referred to two Commissioners, Messrs. Bieber and Shippard, who early in 1885 failed to agree, whereupon Messrs. R. Kraul and Chas. S. Scott were appointed Commissioners. Their awards were given at Berlin, July 15th, and formally accepted by Great Britain, October 23rd, and by Germany, November 13th, 1886.

113. **GREAT BRITAIN** and **SOUTH AFRICAN REPUBLIC**, in 1884. South Western boundary of South African Republic. By Article 2 of the Treaty of London, February 27th, 1884, the question was referred to a Joint Commission, consisting of Captain Claude R. Conder, R.E., and Tielman Nieuwoudt de Villiers, Esq., with a Referee appointed by the President of the Orange Free State, Judge Meluis de Villiers. The Referee's award was given at Kunana, August 5th, 1885.

114. **GREAT BRITAIN** and **RUSSIA**, in 1885. Afghan Boundary. Referred by a protocol, signed at London, September 10th, 1885, to a Joint Commission, "to make an investigation on the spot jointly, for a more exact definition of the boundary line between the Russian possessions and Afghanistan," on which Great Britain was represented by Sir J. West Ridgway, the Russian Commissioner being Colonel Kuhlberg. The work was completed August 21st, 1886.

115. The **UNITED STATES** and **SPAIN**, in 1885. The seizure and detention of an American ship, the "Masonic" at Manilla, for alleged smuggling, January, 1879. By an Agreement of February 28th, 1885, the case was referred to Baron Blanc, the Italian Minister at Madrid. Award of 51,600 dols. to the United States, for Captain Blanchard, was given June 27, 1885—2,600 dols. more than was claimed.

116. **GREAT BRITAIN** and **GERMANY**, in 1885. Land claims of German subjects in Fiji. Referred to two Commissioners, (Dr. R. Krauel and Mr. R. S. Wright), one German and one English, who were instructed March 3rd, and gave their award on April 15th. Original claim £140,000; award to Germany, £10,620. The German Ambassador wrote on May 18th to the British Government that he was authorised to accept the award, and to give his receipt. The money was duly paid.

117. **UNITED STATES** and **HAYTI**, in 1885. Claims of citizens of the United States for damages sustained during a riot at Port au Prince 22nd and 23rd September, 1883. Referred for adjustment, on March 7th, 1885, to a Mixed Commission of two Americans and two Haytians, which completed its labours on the 28th of the following month. The Commissioners were Charles Weyman and Edward Cutts (afterwards Dr. J. B. Terres), on the part of the United States,

and B. Lallemand and C. A. Preston (afterwards Ségu Gentil), on the part of Hayti. On the 22nd and 24th of April, 1885, the Commissioners agreed on all the claims but two which were referred to the Governments. The total amount awarded was 5,700 dollars.

118. **GERMANY** and **SPAIN**, in 1885. The sovereignty of the Caroline Islands. Referred to the Pope, who, on October 22nd, 1885, made in favour of Spain a proposition, which was accepted by both Governments and was embodied in a protocol, December 17th, 1885, by which Spain was declared sovereign, and Germany was accorded freedom of navigation, commerce and fisheries.

119. **UNITED STATES** and **VENEZUELA,** in 1885. Re-submission to Arbitration of the claims against the latter country adjudicated upon in 1866 (see No. 58). Concerning this, Prof. J. Bassett Moore, of Columbia Coll., N.Y. observes: "Only once have members of our Arbitral Boards been charged with fraud. But the conduct of the Claims Commission at Caracas, under the convention of April 25th, 1866, was so seriously impeached that the United States and Venezuela, by a treaty concluded at Washington December 5th, 1885, agreed to have the claims re-heard by a new Commission. This Commission, composed of an American, a Venezuelan, and a third Commissioner chosen by the other two who was also an American, sat at Washington from September 3rd, 1889, to September 2nd, 1890. Its proceedings were characterised by a conscientious and impartial discharge of duty." The Commission adjourned September 2nd, 1890 Its report bears date September 10th, 1890.

120. **ARGENTINE REPUBLIC** and **BRAZIL,** in 1886. Question of the survey of certain rivers connected with the Misiones boundary. By an agreement signed at Buenos Ayres, 28th September, 1885, and ratified at Rio Janeiro, March 4th, 1886, it was referred to a Joint Commission of three, named by each Government, with three assistants, and the territories were neutralised till the accomplishment of its task. The Joint Commission entered upon its labours in 1887, and concluded them in 1890. (See also No. 130.)

121. **NICARAGUA** and **COSTA RICA,** in 1886. The validity of a Treaty of April 15th, 1858, delineating the frontiers, and of the right of the latter Republic to navigation on the River San Juan. Referred, under treaty signed at Guatemala, December 24th, 1886, ratified at Managua, June 1st, 1887, to President Cleveland, of the United States, as sole Arbitrator, who, after appointing Mr. Geo. L. Rives, Assitant Secretary of State, to examine the arguments and evidence, and receiving his report, gave his award, March 22nd, 1888, in favour of the validity of the Treaty of Limits of 1858, and settling the various points at issue under it. In 1898 a second award, dealing with new difficulties which arose as to the line thus determined, was rendered by Mr. E. P. Alexander, the Arbitrator appointed by President Cleveland; this was in favour of Costa Rica. This decision determines the boundary line in the lower part of the course of the San Juan River. (See also No. 167.)

122. **ITALY** and **COLOMBIA,** in 1886. A dispute relating to the nationality and claims for injury of an alleged Italian subject, who had been before the Colombian Courts as a partisan in the disturbances in Colombia in 1884 and 1885, but had found asylum on board an Italian ship. Referred to the Spanish Government as Arbitrator by protocol, signed at Paris May 24th, 1886. The award, in favour of Italy, declaring that Signor Cerruti, and the Italians who had given him asylum, had not infringed the laws of neutrality, and that he was entitled both to the restoration of his property and to damages from illegal procedures, was given January 26th, 1888. The Colombian Government accepted the results of the Award, and a Mixed Commission was organised at Bogota in accordance with the Third Article of the Protocol, for the purpose of determining the amount of the indemnities due to Cerruti. His claims, however, were not presented to the Commission, which dissolved because there was no business before it. (See No. 152.)

123. **BAKWENA** and **BAMANGWATO,** in 1887. Arbitration by the Administrator of British Bechuanaland, represented by Captain Goold Adams,

one of his officers, between these two African nations about rights to certain wells, at a place called Lopepe, on the road to the north from Molepolole to the Bamangwato. The award, to the effect that the wells should be equally divided, was joyfully accepted by both.

124. **GREAT BRITAIN** and **SPAIN**, in 1887. A marine collision between a Spanish man-of-war, "Don Jorge Juan" and a British merchant vessel, "Mary Mark," near Belize, July 9th, 1884. In April, 1887, Spain consented to Arbitration, and it ultimately was referred to a Mixed Commission, on which the Marquis Maffei, the Italian Minister at Madrid, was appointed Umpire. The award was given December 5th, 1887, by the two Arbitrators without appealing to the Umpire, and a small sum given to the owners of the British ship.

125. **UNITED STATES** and **HAYTI**, in 1888. Claim of C. A. Van Bokkelen, a citizen of the United States, for alleged arbitrary imprisonment and denial of rights. Under a protocol, signed May 22nd, 1888, Mr. Alex. Porter Moore, of the city of Washington, was appointed Arbitrator. His award, given December 4th, 1888, was averse to Hayti, and allowed the claimant suitable damages.

126. **PERU** and **ECUADOR**, in 1888. Question of ownership of a vast extent of territory east of Rio Bamba, watered by the rivers Tambez and Maragnon. Referred, by treaty signed at Quito, August 1st, 1887, and ratified April 14th, 1888, to the King of Spain, on whose behalf the Queen Regent, after long historical and geographical researches had been made, gave her decision.

127. **UNITED STATES** and **MOROCCO**, in 1888. Arrest of American consular *protégé* by the Moorish authorities at Fez. Indemnity demanded by American Government. Agreement between Mr. Lewis, the American Consul at Tangier, and the delegates of the Sultan, Muley Hassan, to refer to an Arbitral Commission, Mr. Lewis to name an umpire if necessary. Decision not ascertained.

128. **HOLLAND** and **FRANCE**, in 1888, in regard to boundaries between Cayenne and Surinam, *i.e.*, French Guiana and Dutch Guiana. The matter assumed importance, because of the discovery of gold fields in the disputed territory. Referred, on November 29th, 1888, to the decision of an Arbitrator. The Czar of Russia was chosen by common consent, but declined on the ground that the terms of the reference were too narrow. By a new convention, signed on April 28th, 1890, the scope of the reference was enlarged, and the Czar accepted the office of Arbitrator, after having received a formal assurance from the two Governments that his decision would be accepted as final. He appointed a Commission to examine the subject in controversy; and his award was given on May 25th, 1891, in favour of Holland, but without prejudice to rights of French settlers in the disputed territory.

129. **DENMARK** and the **UNITED STATES**, in 1888. Claim of Carlos Butterfield & Co., an American firm, against the Danish Government, in reference to the seizure of two American ships, the "Ben-Franklin" and the "Catherine-Augusta," at St. Thomas, in the West Indies, in the years 1854-5. By a convention signed December 6th, 1888, the case was submitted to the Arbitration of Sir Edmund Monson, the British Ambassador at Athens, whose award was given in favour of Denmark, January 22nd, 1890. The claim was rejected.

130. **BRAZIL** and **ARGENTINE REPUBLIC**, in 1889. Question of the Misiones Boundary, which had been a subject of contention for more than a century. Referred to President Harrison, by a treaty of September 7th, 1889, and settled by President Cleveland, who consented to act, June, 1893, in favour of Brazil. His decision, which was given February 5th, 1895, was delivered to the representatives of the contending parties, was the occasion of great rejoicing at Rio de Janeiro, while it was heartily accepted by Argentina, telegrams of congratulation being exchanged between the two countries. (See also No. 120.)

131. **GREAT BRITAIN, GERMANY** and **UNITED STATES**, in 1889. Conflict on the Island of Samoa, arising out of their respective rights. A Conference of the Plenipotentiaries of the three Governments was held at Berlin, by the final act of which, signed at Berlin June 14th, 1889, and ratified April 12th,

1890, it was decided to refer to the King of Sweden the appointment of the Chief Justice of Samoa, and, also, in order to adjust and settle all claims of aliens to titles of land, to appoint a Commission consisting of three members elected by each Government, together with an assistant, styled Natives' Advocate, who should be appointed by the Chief Executive of Samoa with the approval of the Chief Justice of Samoa. (See also No. 191.)

132. **GREAT BRITAIN** and **GERMANY,** in 1889. Dispute between the British East African Company and the German Company of Witu, in regard to rights as to the farming of customs. and the administration of the Island of Lamu, East Coast of Africa. Referred to Baron Lambermont, Belgian Minister of State. Award given August 17th, 1889, in favour of Great Britain, accepted by both Governments, and published with their consent.

133. **GREAT BRITAIN, UNITED STATES** and **PORTUGAL,** in 1890. Seizure of the DELAGOA BAY RAILWAY, which was constructed under a concession granted to an American citizen, by Portuguese Government, and annulment of its charter. By identic notes addressed to the President of Switzerland on August 13th, 1890, that country was asked to appoint three eminent Swiss Jurists as Arbitrators. M. Joseph Blaesi, M. Andreas Heusler, and M. Charles Soldau, were appointed by President Ruchonnet, September 15th, 1890. A Protocol to govern and regulate the submission was signed 13th June, 1891, and the Commissioners held their first meeting at Brunnen, August 3rd, 1891, when they drew up rules of procedure, and made other arrangements for the conduct of the Arbitration. The proceedings have been very slow. All the pleadings had been filed by the parties interested, and all the proofs laid before the Tribunal prior to March 31st, 1896; on that day an expert was appointed, and the number was increased to three on May 13th, 1896. The experts have returned from Africa and are said to have made their report, but the award of the Tribunal has not yet been given; December, 1899.

134. **GREAT BRITAIN** and **FRANCE,** in 1890. In reference to the French sphere of influence up to a line from Say, on the Niger to Barruwa, on Lake Tchad. By an Agreement, signed August 5th, 1890, it was referred to a Joint Commission, consisting of two Commissioners from each country, whose award was signed at Paris on June 26th, 1891; and a further decision on the point left undecided by them, as to the line of demarcation, was signed July 12th, 1893, and ratified by both countries.

135. **ITALY** and **PERSIA,** in 1890. Claim of M. G. Consonno, an Italian subject, against the Persian Customs for confiscation of goods. By a protocol signed at Teheran the 5th June, 1890, it was referred to Sir Wm. White, the British Ambassador at Constantinople, as Arbitrator. His award, given at Therapia 12th June, 1891, was to the effect that the goods be retained by the Persian Government, that it pay to the owner, M. Consonno, seventy-eight thousand francs, and that the two Governments pay the expenses between them.

136. **GREAT BRITAIN** and **HAYTI,** in 1890. Claims of British subjects against Hayti for supplies, loans, damages and injuries, and services. By a protocol concluded in 1890, it was agreed to submit these claims to a Mixed Commission, consisting of a British subject, a Haytian citizen, and an Umpire to sit at Port au Prince. The Commission thus provided for was in session at that City in 1892 (July), but the result has not been ascertained.

137. **FRANCE** and **HAYTI,** in 1890. Similar claims against the Haytian Government on the part of French subjects. Under a protocol similar in terms these were adjusted by a Mixed Commission at Port au Prince. This Commission also was in session in July, 1892.

138. **PERSIA** and **AFGHANISTAN,** in 1891. A long-standing dispute which at one time threatened to prove serious, between Persia and Afghanistan, in reference to the frontiers of the two countries in the Hashtadan District. It had been referred to the Viceroy of India, who entrusted the adjustment of all the details to General Maclean, British Consul-General at Meshed, in January, 1891. Both the Shah and the Ameer ratified the decision of the British Referee, which was given in the Viceroy's name.

139. **GREAT BRITAIN** and **FRANCE**, in 1891. Dispute as to the Newfoundland Lobster Fisheries. Referred, on March 11th, 1891, to an Arbitration Commission of seven, two representatives of each Government, and three specialists. These latter were: M. de Martens, Professor of law at the University of St. Petersburg; M. Rivier, formerly Member of the Supreme Court of Brussels, and President of the Institute of International Law; and M. Gram, Swiss Consul-General in Norway. The Colonists and the Government of Newfoundland, however, strenuously objected both to the former *modus vivendi* and to Arbitration. France too, declined to proceed with the Arbitration. Consequently nothing came of the agreement, and the difficulty has been allowed to continue. It has recently entered another acute stage and calls for immediate action, but is still unsettled; December, 1899.

140. **ITALY** and **PORTUGAL**, in 1891. Claims of an Italian subject, M. A. Lavarello against the Government of Portugal for damages alleged to have been caused by the Authorities of Cape Verde. By an Arbitration agreement made at the Hague, September 1st, 1891, this was referred to a jurisconsult appointed by the Government of the Netherlands. Mr. Jean Heemskerk was appointed Arbitrator, and on 12th March, 1893, gave his award that the claim was not well founded except in part, for which the sum of 12,347 lire, with compound interest from the 1st September, 1891, the date of the Submission, was adjudged to the heirs and assigns of the late Signor M. A. Lavarello.

141. **UNITED STATES** and **VENEZUELA**, in 1892. Claim originating in certain transactions in Venezuela in 1871 and 1872, concerning the seizure on the Orinoco, detention, and employment for war purposes in the Venezuelan Civil War, of certain steamships belonging to an American Company (the Venezuela Steam Transportation Company of New York), and the imprisonment of their crews, American citizens. After a diplomatic correspondence of twenty years, it was, by a Convention signed at Caracas on January 19th, 1892, referred to a Mixed Commission, consisting of three Commissioners, one from each, and a third belonging to neither, which was to give its decision within three months. The Commissioners were Mr. Noah L. Jeffries, Señor José Andrade, and the Umpire Señor Don Matiãs Romero, Mexican Minister at Washington, who resigned and was succeeded by Mr. A. Grip, Minister of Norway and Sweden. An award was made March 26th, 1895, in favour of the United States, from which Señor Andrade dissented, and published a solemn protest against it. The amount awarded was $141,500, with interest.

142. Between **GREAT BRITAIN** and the **UNITED STATES**, in 1892, as to the Behring Sea Seal Fisheries. Referred by treaty, concluded February 29th, 1892, to a Commission of seven, consisting of Baron de Courcel, representing France (President of the Court); Lord Hannen and Sir John Thompson, Great Britain; Judge John T. Harlan and Mr. J. T. Morgan, United States; the Marquis Visconti Venosta, Italy; and Herr Gregers Gram, representing Sweden and Norway. The Court sat in Paris, and on August 15th, 1893, gave a divided award mainly in favour of Great Britain:—Against the United States claim of pelagic ownership; in favour of the United States admission of the necessity for regulation of pelagic sealing and of their proposals for doing so.

143. **FRANCE** and **VENEZUELA**, in 1892. Responsibility of the Venezuelan Government in a private lawsuit—that of a French contractor, M. A. Fabiani. The verdicts of the Venezuelan Law Courts were given in his favour, but the Government placed obstacles in the way of his obtaining their awards. Referred, February 24th, 1891 to the President of the Swiss Confederation, who was authorised, by the Federal Council, to accept the commission, November 1st, 1892. The award of the Federal Council, which was given on December 30th, 1896, by President Adrien Lachenal, recognises the justice of the claim and fixes the indemnity which the Venezuelan Government had to pay M. Fabiani at 4,346,656 francs instead of 46,000,000 as demanded. This Arbitration required the solution of numerous points involving questions of both public and private International Law and Civil Law; and the Award, which adduces ample explanations, valuable for the guidance of Arbitrators, will probably be classed as a document of the highest international value.

144. **COLOMBIA** and **VENEZUELA**, in 1892. Boundary Dispute. Referred to the King of Spain, on the initiative of General Guzman Blanco, by a Treaty dated 6th July, 1882. The death of His Majesty raised the question of the competency of his successor. This was settled by a protocol signed at Paris in the year 1887, which declared that the death of the King did not affect the jurisdiction ; and ultimately the Queen Regent, Christina, by an Award given on behalf of the young King, March 16th, 1891, fixed the line of demarcation favourable to Colombia. Venezuela, however, was not satisfied with this decision, and the matter was not finally closed until 1894, when, in an Agreement dated April 4th, 1894, the two Governments embodied their views as to the several points relating to the frontiers as defined in the arbitral sentence.

145. **UNITED STATES** and **CHILI**, in 1892. Various claims, amounting to 385, of subjects of both countries, dating back to 1849 and 1850. By agreement of August 7th, 1892, these were referred to a Mixed Commission, consisting of two Arbitrators, Mr. John Goode (U.S A.), and Mr. Domingo Gana, the Chilian Minister at Washington, and an Umpire, Dr. Alfred de Claparède, Swiss Minister at Washington, who was appointed by the Swiss Federal Council in the latter capacity. The Commission met at Washington, under the presidency of the Umpire, and dealt with claims amounting to £3,877,000, allowing only £48,000 against Chili, sixteen claims involving a total of £1,800,000 not having been dealt with. It held its last session April 9th, 1894, and a comprehensive report of its proceedings was presented to Mr. Gresham, Secretary of State, on April 30th, 1894.

146. **GREAT BRITAIN** and **FRANCE**, in 1892. Delimitation of frontier between French Guinea and Sierra Leone. A Convention signed at Paris, June 28th, 1882, but laid before Parliament in 1892, arranging for settlement of the territorial limits, referred these to a technical Commission of two, to be appointed by each country, who should determine them by enquiry on the spot.

147. **GREAT BRITAIN, RUSSIA** and **AFGHANISTAN**, in 1893. Vexed questions regarding the use by Afghans and Russians respectively of the waters of the River Kushk, on the N.W. frontier of Afghanistan. Referred to an Anglo-Russian Joint Commission. Colonel Yate, who had been British representative at Penjdeh, was selected to represent Great Britain, and the Commission was directed to settle these questions on the spot, which was done.

148. **GREAT BRITAIN** and **FRANCE**, in 1893. Greffühle Concessions. The Arbitration was to ascertain the amount (if any) of damages to M. Greffühle, a French subject, by reason of the English protectorate over Zanzibar, M. Greffühle having a contract from the Sultan, extending over a term of years, for the exclusive mintage of coin for the use of the Sultanate. The Arbitrator appointed was Mr. R. B. Martin, M.P., without power of appeal, and his award was given, July 19th, 1893, in favour of M. Greffühle.

149. **UNITED STATES** and **ECUADOR**, in 1893. Alleged illegal arrest of an American citizen, Mr. Julio Romano Santos, of Bahia, on a charge of complicity in a revolutionary movement. After various negotiations, the matter was, by Agreement of February 28th, 1893, submitted to Arbitration, the British Minister at Quito, Mr. Mallet, being requested to act as Arbitrator, or that he or his successor should name an Arbitrator. Mr. Jones, who succeeded him, nominated Mr. Alfred St. John, British Consul at Callao, to act as Arbitrator. Before he had completed his examination of the evidence submitted to him, the parties agreed upon an award of 40,000 dollars to M. Santos. Mr. St. John agreed to put this arrangement on record, and stated in his award, 22nd September, 1896, that the parties having solicited sentence in favour of the claimant, he decided that Ecuador should pay 40,000 dollars to the United States Government.

150. **CHILI, FRANCE** and **PERU**, in 1893. Claims of Peruvian Bondholders relative to a sum of money lodged in the Bank of England, and derived from the sale of Peruvian Guano, which had been exploited by Chili. By an Agreement, dated 23rd July, 1892, between France and Chili, it was decided between the Governments of France and Chili to refer the matter to the Arbitra-

tion of the President of the Swiss Federal Tribunal or to that body in its entirety. The Peruvian Government, however, disputed their competency to settle it without its consent. In June, 1893, the three contending parties addressed to Switzerland a formal request for Arbitration which was acceded to on the 24th March, 1894. The Arbitral Court was then composed of three members of the Federal Tribunal of Justice, viz., Dr. Hafner, President, and Judges Broye and Morel, who were to decide the procedure to be adopted, and all questions which should arise. (Still pending, December, 1899.)

151. **GREAT BRITAIN** and **CHILI**, in 1893. Claims of British subjects arising out of the Chilian Civil War of 1891. These were referred by a Convention, concluded September 26th, 1893, and ratified at Santiago, April 24th, 1894, to a Mixed Commission, to consist of a member appointed by each Government, and a third appointed by both jointly, but belonging to neither, and in case of their disagreement, by the King of the Belgians. Her Britannic Majesty appointed Mr. Lewis Joel, who was succeeded in December, 1894, by Mr. Alfred St. John, British Consul at Callao; the President of Chili appointed Señor Luis Aldunate, and the King of the Belgians named Mr. Camille Janssen. The Mixed Commission held their first meeting, elected Mr. Janssen President, and adopted rules of procedure, October 24th, 1894, but began the work of adjudication 28th August, 1895. There were 130 claims, amounting to £259,431. These were variously dealt with. Sums amounting to £17,852 were awarded, and a lump sum was ultimately paid by the Chilian Government for all claims outstanding at the last session of the Commission, March 6th, 1896.

152. **ITALY** and **COLOMBIA**, in 1894. The Cerruti Claim. This interesting case has involved considerable difficulty. The dispute arose thus: In 1885 a civil war broke out in Colombia, and from the beginning of the rebellion Messrs. Cerruti & Co., a commercial firm established in one of the departments of Colombia were, or were supposed to be, in open revolt against the Government. The local authorities for that reason confiscated Cerruti's property, and Signor Cerruti being an Italian subject took refuge on an Italian ship. The question of his nationality was submitted to Spain and settled, as narrated, in No. 122. By a Convention concluded the 18th August, 1894, after diplomatic correspondence continuing for some years, the question of the Cerruti claims was referred to President Cleveland as Arbitrator, and he awarded £60,000 to Cerruti. This was accepted by Colombia, who paid the indemnity. The Arbitrator, however, ordered also payment of the claims of all the creditors of Signor Cerruti. This was resisted, and a rupture involving considerable strain between the two countries existed, until the matter was settled by the submission of Colombia and the further payment of £300,000 (1,500,000 dollars).

153. **COLOMBIA**, **ECUADOR**, and **PERU**, in 1894. By a Convention, signed at Lima, by the Plenipotentiaries of these countries, December 15th, 1894, it was agreed to submit to the King of Spain, as Arbitrator, the question of ownership of a portion of the Amazonic territories of Mainas, Quijos and Canelos, claimed by each of those nations. The Queen Regent, early in 1896, herself, by unanimous request, accepted the office. (Result not known.)

154. **NORWAY** and **SWEDEN** and **CHILI**, in 1895. Claims of subjects of Sweden and Norway against Chili arising out of the Chilian Civil War of 1891. By a Convention signed July 6th, 1895, between Chili and Sweden and Norway, it was agreed to refer these to the Anglo-Chilian Tribunal (see No. 151). Two such claims were submitted, the Tribunal gave judgment on one of them, and declared itself incompetent to recognise the other. The records of the various claims (British and Scandinavian) and the awards of the Commission were edited by Mr. Martinez, and printed by the Chilian Government.

155. **GREAT BRITAIN** and **PORTUGAL**, in 1895. Differences with regard to the frontiers of Manicaland. By treaty, signed at Lisbon, June 11th, 1891, which defined the spheres of influence of both countries, it was agreed that the limits should be decided by an Anglo-Portuguese Commission, with Umpire if necessary. In the month of June, 1892, the Commissioners of the two

Governments endeavoured to trace the boundary line according to the stipulations of the Treaty, but a difference having arisen between them, the settlement was referred to their Governments. By a Convention signed in London on the 7th January, 1895, the question was submitted to the Italian Government, by whom Count Vigliani, a distinguished lawyer, who was Minister of Justice and President of the Court of Appeal, was appointed Arbitrator. His award was given at Florence on 30th January, 1897, and is a very long and valuable document. The decision, which delimitated the frontier, was partly in favour of each. The Commissioners for the delimitation necessary on the spot were subsequently appointed and arrived at a final agreement, the line of demarcation fixed by the Arbitrator being slightly modified, as the result of mutual concessions.

156. **RUSSIA** and **AFGHANISTAN**, in 1895. Delimitation of the Pamir Boundary. By an agreement entered into between Great Britain and Russia in March, 1895, it was referred to an Anglo-Russian Joint Commission on which Colonel Girard represented Great Britain. Its work was completed satisfactorily in 1895, and, according to Col. Girard's testimony, with the utmost cordiality between the representatives of the two Governments.

157. **GREAT BRITAIN** and **NICARAGUA**, in 1895. Alleged personal injuries to British subjects, including Mr. Hatch, Vice-Consul at Bluefields, and others in the Mosquito Reserve, at the time of a war between Nicaragua and Honduras in December, 1893, and, as stated in the Convention, "owing to the action of the Nicaraguan authorities in the course of the year 1894." The British claimed an indemnity of £15,000, and the cancelling unconditionally of the decrees of exile. Nicaragua submitted to the British ultimatum so far as to pay the indemnity; the rest of the ultimatum was, by a Convention signed at London, November 1st, 1895, referred to a Mixed Commission, the third member of which it was agreed should be a jurist, not a citizen of any American State, to be selected by agreement between Great Britain and Nicaragua, or, failing such agreement, by the President of the Swiss Confederation. The claim also included the seizure of the schooner "Anglia" by Nicaraguans. (Result not known.)

158. **PERU** and **BOLIVIA**, in 1895. Claim of Bolivian Government, arising out of the presence of some soldiers on board one of the Lake Titicaca steamers in the late Peruvian civil war, 1890, and the escape of other Peruvian soldiers to Bolivian territory after a battle. Monsignor Macchi, Apostolic Delegate to Peru, and the French, Italian and Colombian Ministers at Lima, secured, through their interference, an agreement to a reference to Arbitration. By a protocol signed at Lima, August 26th, 1895, it was agreed to refer to the Arbitration of some South American Government the question whether Peru should salute the Bolivian flag as part of the reparation for her acts, and on September 7th, 1895, a further protocol to that effect was signed at Lima, designating Brazil as Arbitrator, or, in case of refusal, Colombia. (Result unknown.)

159. **HAYTI** and **SAN DOMINGO**, in 1895. Delimitation of frontier. Referred to Pope Leo XIII. as Arbitrator, by autograph letters from Presidents of both countries, Gen. Hippolyte and Gen. Heureaux, to whose request His Holiness acceded. Commissioners were sent to Rome to present their respective claims, and received at the Vatican. A despatch, dated January 24th, 1897, announced that the Pope had declined to act in view of the claims formulated by the Haytians, but subsequent reports still speak of the matter as under reference to His Holiness, others that he declines to proceed because of the form of the reference.

160. **GREAT BRITAIN** and **HOLLAND**, in 1895. Question of indemnity for the ship "Costa Rica Packet," which was seized by the Dutch authorities at Ternate, in the East Indian Archipelago, November, 1891, on a technical charge of piracy, and arrest and detention of the captain, Mr. Carpenter. According to the terms of the Convention, signed at the Hague, May 16th, 1895, referring the question to an Arbitrator, the Emperor of Russia, in September, 1895, by request of the two Governments, named M. de Martens, Councillor of State at St.

Petersburg, as Arbitrator. His decision, dated 13th February, but announced March 1st, 1897, awarded £8,550, with interest, from November 2nd, 1891, to be paid by the Dutch Government, together with a further sum of £250 as costs.

161. **FRANCE** and **CHILI**, in 1895. By a Convention of October 13th, 1895, expressed in substantially the same terms as the Anglo-Chilian Convention of September 26th, 1893, (see No. 151), it was agreed that the claim of French citizens against Chili, growing out of the Civil War in the latter country of 1891, and the subsequent events, should be referred to a Mixed Commission. But by an Agreement signed at Santiago, February 2nd, 1896, the two Governments settled the claims directly, and so dispensed with the Arbitration. The sum total of the claims was upwards of 1,000,000 francs. The French Government adopted in discharge of them the sum of £5,000, or about 125,000 francs.

162. **GERMANY** and **HAYTI**, in 1895. Claims of German subjects against Hayti arising on or after August 5th, 1888. These were adjusted in the same mode as the similar Claims of British subjects and French citizens referred to in Nos. 136 and 137; that is, they were referred to a Mixed Commission which sat at Port au Prince.

163. **GREAT BRITAIN** and the **UNITED STATES**, in 1896. Amount of damages due to Canadian Dealers, resulting from the award of the Behring Sea Arbitration Court, in Paris, August 15th, 1893. By a convention signed February 8th, 1896, and ratified by the Senate in Executive Session, April 15th, 1896 (ratifications exchanged in London, June 3rd, 1896) a Mixed Commission was appointed, two members by the respective countries, with an umpire, if necessary, to be appointed jointly, or, in the case of non-agreement, by the Swiss President. The United States Government, by this Treaty, fully discharges its obligations under the Paris Award. Mr. Justice King, of the Canadian Supreme Court, was appointed by Great Britain, and Mr. Justice Putnam, of Maine, by the United States. The sittings of the Commission were held at Victoria, B. C., and on February 1st, 1897, their conclusion was celebrated by a farewell dinner; the written argument for Great Britain to be sent in by March 31st, and that for the United States by May 10th, 1897. A unanimous decision was given in December of the same year awarding a sum of 473,151 dollars to Great Britain, which was handed to Sir Julian Pauncefote on June 16th by Judge Day, and paid to the Marine Department, Ottawa, August 2nd, 1898.

164. **ARGENTINE REPUBLIC** and **CHILI**, in 1896. Frontier difficulties. For many years there has existed a difference in regard to these common boundaries. In 1881 this was referred to Arbitration (see No. 95), and a Treaty was the result. This, however, proved not to be final, and recently the question became complicated by fresh difficulties, arising out of the interpretation of the treaty in relation to the San Francisco boundary. After some delay, Argentina expressed its willingness to accept Arbitration on the point as desired by Chili, and it was agreed, April 17th, 1896, to refer to a Commission, Queen Victoria being requested to act as final Arbitrator if necessary, to which request Her Majesty acceded. The difficulties continued in a more or less acute condition until September 13th, 1898, when the two Governments simultaneously notified the British Government that the Arbitration might commence and that they were prepared to submit the boundary dispute to the Arbitration of Her Majesty without any reservation whatsoever. The British Tribunal appointed by Her Majesty consists of Lord Macnaghten (President), Major-General Sir John C. Ardagh, and Col. Sir Thomas H. Holdich, and held its first meeting, March 27th, at the Foreign Office, London. Pending. (See also No. 189.)

165. **GREAT BRITAIN** and **COLOMBIA**, in 1896. Dispute between a British firm, Messrs. Punchard, McTaggart, Lowther & Co., and a Provincial Government in Colombia, respecting construction of a railway between the river Magdalene and the town of Medellin. Referred, 12th August, 1896, to a Court of three Arbitrators, which the Swiss Federal Council commissioned February 2nd, 1897, at the request of the two Governments, the Court consisting of Dr.

Schmid, Dr. Weber, Jurists, and M. Weissenbach, Ex-Director of the Swiss Railways. The Arbitrators held their first meeting at Lausanne on the 8th February, 1897. On October 25th, 1899, their Award was given in favour of Great Britain, the Colombian claim being dismissed and the British firm awarded upward of 1,000,000 francs.

166. **GREAT BRITAIN** and **BRAZIL**, in 1896. Annexation of Islet of Trinidad by British Government in January, 1895. After great excitement in Brazil and diplomatic correspondence between the two Governments, the "good offices" of Portugal were accepted, and, when reasons for her decision had been submitted to the British, the island was, on September 1st, 1896, surrendered to Brazil.

167. **COSTA RICA** and **NICARAGUA**, in 1896. Boundary questions arising out of a previous Arbitration (see No. 121) and the disagreement of the Commissioners appointed as its result. By a Convention, signed at San José, through the mediation of the Government of Salvador, after war had been actually declared by Nicaragua, these were referred to a Mixed Commission with an Umpire appointed by the President of the United States. Gen. E. P. Alexander was appointed, and he gave his Award September 30th, 1897.

168. **GREAT BRITAIN** and **FRANCE**, in 1896. The Niger Boundary in West Africa. By an Agreement signed January 15th, 1896, a Joint Commission was appointed "to define the boundary between French and English territory in the regions west of the Lower Niger." As the result of their labours the Niger Convention was signed at the Quai d'Orsay, on June 14th, 1898, by the Members of the Joint Commission. This Commission had been for some time sitting in Paris, and had succeeded in removing all strain and danger of conflict between the two countries. A protocol approving the Treaty was also signed by Sir E. Monson, the British Ambassador, and M. Hanotaux, the French Minister for Foreign Affairs. Provision was made for the ratification of this Convention in six months, but on December 8th, 1898, a further protocol was signed at Paris, extending the period of ratification for another six months, dating from December 14th, 1898. The ratifications were exchanged June 13th, 1899.

169. **ITALY** and **BRAZIL**, in 1896. Claims of Italian Subjects against the Government of Brazil. By a protocol of February 12th, 1896, the President of the United States was named Arbitrator. The protocol, however, required the sanction of the Brazilian Congress and the approval of the Italian Government, and so far as is known, the matter is not yet disposed of (Dec. 1899).

170. **ITALY** and **BRAZIL**, in 1896. By another protocol of the same day (February 12th, 1896) it was agreed that the claims of Italian Subjects for requisition of animals, merchandise, and valuables, in the States of Rio Grande do Sul and Santa Catarina, should be referred te a Mixed Commission.

171. **GREAT BRITAIN** and **VENEZUELA**, in 1897. A long-standing dispute respecting territory which had become valuable through the discovery of gold. On behalf of Venezuela the United States demanded Arbitration. It also appointed independently a Commission to examine the question. By a Convention between Great Britain and the United States, signed at Washington, November 12th, 1896, an Arbitral Tribunal was agreed upon to determine the boundary line between British Guiana and Venezuela, consisting of four members to be appointed by the two Governments, and a fifth to be appointed by the other four, or, failing agreement, by the King of Sweden. To this agreement Venezuela acceded, but claimed the right of representation on the Tribunal. The Treaty of Reference was signed February 2nd, 1897, at Washington, Lord Herschell and Mr. Justice Richard Henn Collins, of the English Supreme Court of Judicature, being appointed on behalf of Great Britain, and Chief Justice Fuller and Mr. Justice Brewer, of the United States Supreme Court, on behalf of Venezuela. A preliminary sitting of the Commission was held in Paris, January 25th, 1899. Lord Herschell, the President, having died suddenly and unexpectedly in March, 1899, Lord Russell of Killowen, the Lord Chief Justice of England, was appointed

as his successor. The Tribunal sat in Paris in the months of June, July, August, and September, 1899, the question was fully argued before it, and its award was given on the 3rd October, and accepted as satisfactory by all parties.

172. **GREAT BRITAIN** and the **UNITED STATES**, in 1897. The boundary between Alaska and the British possessions. By a Convention signed Jan. 30th, 1897, by Mr. Olney and Sir Julian Pauncefote, the question was referred to a Joint Commission of four members, which were to hold their sittings in London and Washington. It was, however, included in the matters to be discussed by the Anglo-American Commission, appointed in June, 1898 (see No. 187). After long discussion, and with much difficulty, the Commissioners succeeded in reaching an Agreement to which all could subscribe, and were looking forward to a settlement of the boundary question and of conflicting mining interests generally in Alaska, when an Act passed by the British Columbia Legislature interfered The two Governments, however, reached an Agreement of the nature of a *modu vivendi*, roughly defining, by certain landmarks, the boundary from the Klondike section to British Columbia: a further Agreement of a similar kind was reached in October, 1899, but the adjudication is still pending.

173. **UNITED STATES** and **MEXICO**, in 1897. Claims for indemnity by two American citizens, Charles Oberlander and Barbara M. Messenger. for alleged hardships and outrages suffered by them while on the Mexican frontier. Referred to Arbitration under an old-standing agreement between the two countries. A Special Convention signed at Washington on the 2nd March, 1897, submitted the dispute to Señor D. Vicente G. Quesada, Minister of the Argentine Republic, at Madrid, with plenary powers as Arbitrator, who was to give his decision within six months from the date of the submission of the necessary evidence; provided for reasonable compensation to the Arbitrator and other common expenses of the Arbitration, to be paid in equal moieties by the two Governments; and for any award made to be final and conclusive. Any indemnity awarded, if in favour of the claimants or either of them, and of the contention of the United States, was to be paid by the Mexican Government within two years from the date of award.

174. **FRANCE** and **BRAZIL**, in 1897. The "Amapa" question, relating to a boundary dispute in French Guiana, involving more territory than the Venezuela dispute with Great Britain (see No. 170). By a Convention signed between M. Pichon, the French Minister at Rio de Janeiro and the Brazilian Minister for Foreign Affairs, announced by M. Hanotaux at a Cabinet Council in Paris, April 15th, 1897, it was agreed to submit this dispute to Arbitration. The Treaty was approved by the Chamber of Deputies at Rio Janeiro on November 26th, 1897; ratifications were exchanged, August 6th, 1898; and in September the text of this Convention, designating the Swiss Confederation as Arbitrator, was presented by both the French and Brazilian Ministers to its President, thus fairly placing the case in the hands of the Arbitrator. (Pending.)

175. **GREAT BRITAIN** and **GERMANY** in 1897. A claim by German merchants, the Messrs. Denhardt Brothers, in South Eastern Africa. Submitted to a Court of Arbitration at Zanzibar. Announced by Baron Richthofen, Director of the Colonial Department, in the Reichstag, Berlin, April, 1897.

176. **BOLIVIA** and **PERU** in 1897. A dispute about territory. Referred to the Arbitration of the Queen of Spain, May 12th, 1897. Result not known.

177. **COSTA RICA** and **COLOMBIA**, in 1897. A dispute relative to the delimitation of their common frontier. By a Treaty concluded at Bogota, 4th November, 1896, it was decided to refer the matter to the Arbitration of the President of the French Republic. President Faure signified his acceptance of the office of Arbitrator on June 17th, 1897. A Commission, consisting of Messrs. Roustan (Ambassador at Madrid), Delavand, Fouques-Duparc (Secretaries of Embassy), and Gabriel Marcel, was appointed by the President to examine all documents relative to the litigation, and held its first meeting October 2nd, 1897, at the Quai D'Orsay. (Pending.)

178. **FRANCE** and **GERMANY**, in 1897. A boundary dispute in reference to a portion of the "Hinterland" of Togo, on the Gold Coast, West Africa. Referred to a Joint Arbitration Commission, which began its sittings in Paris during the last week in May, 1897. The dispute proved easy of settlement, inasmuch as each party was able to produce documentary evidence, and on July 11th, 1897, it was announced that the Commission had concluded its labours, and an arrangement satisfactory to both contending parties had been reached.

179. **JAPAN** and **HAWAII**, in 1897. A dispute regarding Japanese immigration in the Sandwich Islands. Referred to three Arbitrators, two appointed by the disputants and the third by these two. Results not known, annexation by America probably interfering.

180. **LIPPE-DETMOLD** (a German Arbitration), in 1897. A claim to the regency, and therefore to the succession of the princely throne of Lippe-Detmold, arising out of the incurable illness of Prince Alexander, who succeeded his brother Waldemar on his death, in 1895. Through the mediation of the German Chancellor, the dispute was submitted to the Arbitration of the King of Saxony, whose decision, published in July, 1897, was in favour of Count Ernst of Lippe Biesterfeld.

181. **GREAT BRITAIN** and **BELGIUM**, in 1897. Arrest, detention and expulsion of a British subject, Mr. Ben Tillett, from Antwerp, in 1896. Referred to M. Arthur Desjardins, President of the French Court of Appeal (August, 1897), whose award, given January, 1899, was in favour of Belgium.

182. **UNITED STATES** and **HAYTI**, in 1897. Claim of an American citizen, Bernard Campbell, for 100,000 dollars. This claim grew out of injuries which he received from being beaten by men whom he alleged to be Haytian soldiers. The United States accepted the proposal of Hayti to arbitrate in December, 1897.

183. **TURKEY** and **GREECE**, in 1897. Adjudication follows, if it does not precede, and so prevent, war. By Article 1 of the Treaty of Peace between Turkey and Greece, a Delimitation Commission, consisting of delegates of the two parties interested, together with military delegates of the Ambassadors of the mediating Powers, was appointed to delimitate on the spot the new frontier line between Turkey and Greece. This Arbitration Commission began its work within fifteen days after the signing of the Treaty on September 18th, 1897.

Article 9 of the same Treaty provided that in the event of disagreements in the course of negotiations between the two countries, the contested points should be submitted by either party to the Arbitration of the Representatives of the Great Powers at Constantinople, whose decisions should be compulsory for both Governments. It was specially provided that such Arbitration might be exercised either by the Representatives themselves collectively, or by persons specially chosen by the parties interested, either directly or through the intermediary of special delegates, and that in the event of the votes being equally divided, the Arbitrators should choose an additional Arbitrator.

184. **UNITED STATES** and **SIAM**, in 1897. Attack by soldiers upon Mr. E. V. Kellett, the United States Vice-Consul in Siam, on the evening of November 19th, 1896. After some diplomatic correspondence, at length it was proposed that the Mixed Commission appointed to investigate should be constituted as a board of Arbitration, and to this the Siamese Government acceded. On September 20th, 1897, the Arbitrators, Messrs. John Barrett and Pierre Orto, rendered their award in favour of the United States.

185. **UNITED STATES** and **SIAM**, in 1897. Claim of Dr. M. A. Cheek, an American citizen, against the Government of Siam, for illegal seizure and sale of property in 1889. After voluminous correspondence, by an Agreement dated the 6th of July, 1897, it was referred to the Arbitration of Sir Nicholas J. Hannen, Governor of the Straits Settlements, who gave his award March 21st, 1898, in favour of the United States Government, and adjudged to the claimant 200,000 dollars in gold.

186. **GREAT BRITAIN** and **RUSSIA**, in 1898. Indemnity claimed by Great Britain for the alleged illegal seizure of Canadian Vessels in the sealing grounds of the Behring Sea within Russian jurisdiction. Submitted to M. Alphonse

Rivier, Professor of International Law in Brussels University as Arbitrator. By his death, in Brussels on the 21st July, 1898, the proceedings were interrupted; but M. H. Matzen, Professor at the University of Copenhagen, and President of the Danish Senate, has been appointed Arbitrator in his stead. (Pending.)

187. **GREAT BRITAIN** and **FRANCE**, in 1898. By Article 5 of the Niger Convention June 14th, 1898, provision is made for two fresh Commissions: the one to be appointed, within a year from its ratification, for the purpose of delimitating on the spot the frontiers west of the Niger, and the other within a period of two years from the same date to delimitate the frontiers east of that river. Subsequent difficulties having arisen in connection with territories in the neighbourhood of the Nile in Eastern Africa, a further Agreement was concluded in March, 1899, after considerable negotiations, dealing with these as a supplement of the Niger Convention. The arrangements provide for another Mixed Commission, which will complete the delimitation on the spot.

188. **GREAT BRITAIN** and the **UNITED STATES**, in 1898. An agreement between the United States and Canada was reached in May, 1898, and subsequently submitted to Great Britain for approval, for the creation of an Arbitral Joint Commission, to consider all subjects of controversy between the United States and Canada, and to frame a treaty between the Imperial Government and the former for the complete adjustment of these differences The High Joint Commission was composed of ten members—five from each side—viz., Lord Herschell, Sir Wilfrid Laurier, Sir Richard J. Cartwright Sir Louis H. Davies and John Charlton, Esq., M.P., on the one side; and Senator Gray, Mr. Kasson, Mr. Nelson Dingley, Jun., Mr. Fairbanks and ex-Secretary Foster on the other. The first meeting was held at Quebec, August 23rd, 1898, and Lord Herschell was appointed President. It was decided to discuss the following subjects in the order named, viz.: Behring Sea sealing; the fisheries on the Atlantic and Pacific coasts; the determination of the Alaska boundary (see No. 172); to arrange for the transit of bonded merchandise; alien labour laws; mining rights; the readjustment of customs duties; to revise the agreement regarding the presence of warships on the great lakes; the better defining of the frontier; extradition; wrecking and salvage rights. After remaining in session at Quebec for some three weeks the Commission adjourned to Washington, where its sittings were resumed and terminated by a brilliant banquet, December 20th. The work of the Commission was somewhat interrupted by the death of Mr. Dingley and the illness of Mr. Foster. After nearly eight months' deliberation, the Joint High Commission adjourned in February, 1899, without reaching any definite decision, to meet again on the 2nd August in Quebec. Since its adjournment it has sustained a further loss by the sudden and unexpected death of its President, Lord Herschell, in March, 1899. The Commission has not again met.

189. **CHILI** and **PERU**, in 1898. At the close of the war between Chili and Peru in 1884, the provinces of Tarapaca and Tacna were ceded by the latter to her victorious rival, on the understanding that at the end of ten years the future of Tacna should be determined by a *plebiscite* of its inhabitants. Owing to troubles in Peru, the decision has been deferred, but it has been finally agreed to submit the matter to the arbitration of the Queen of Spain, who will decide on the form the *plebiscite* shall take.

190. **ARGENTINE REPUBLIC, CHILI** and **BOLIVIA**, in 1898. A dispute respecting the delimitation of the Puña de Atacama, ceded by Bolivia to Argentina but claimed by Chili, which was not included in the Arbitration Protocol to be submitted to Queen Victoria (see No. 164) was by a protocol, signed by the representatives of the two Republics, November 12th, 1898, referred to a Conference of five members, named by each of the Governments, to meet forthwith in Buenos Ayres for a term of eight days only. Failing an agreement at the last sitting the matter was referred to the decision of an Arbitral Tribunal consisting of three persons, a delegate appointed by each Government and the United States Minister-Plenipotentiary to Buenos Ayres, the Hon. Mr. Buchanan. The labours of this demarcation commission were completed and the results announced by the Argentine Government through its various Ministers, March 25th, 1899.

191. **GREAT BRITAIN** and **BRAZIL**, in 1899. Guiana boundary question. The British proposal to submit this question to Arbitration was accepted by the Brazilian Government, March 8th, 1899, and Senor Joaquim Nabuco, who was formerly Secretary to the Brazilian Legation in London, was appointed Commissioner to negotiate the Arbitration Treaty with Great Britain and prepare the case.

192. **GREAT BRITAIN, GERMANY** and the **UNITED STATES**, in 1899. The Samoan difficulty. By the Arbitral Award of June 14th, 1889, the fourteen islands of Samoa were declared an independent and neutral territory, and arrangements were made (see No. 131) for its administration. These hitherto worked successfully, but during the present year, 1899, complications arose in connection with the succession to the throne, and civil war resulted. The three interested powers appointed a Joint Commission to consider the questions arising between themselves out of the alleged infraction of the Berlin Treaty of 1889. This "Samoan Joint High Commission" consisted of Mr. C. N. E. Eliot, C.B., of the Diplomatic Service, for Great Britain, Mr. Bartlett Tripp, formerly Minister to Austria, for the United States, and Baron Von Sternberg, First Secretary of the Embassy at Washington, for Germany, who were to proceed at once to the islands and begin their work without delay. The Commissioners sailed from San Francisco in the U.S. Cruiser "Badger," April 26th. They completed their work; held their last meeting at Apia; and left on the 18th August. An agreement for the partition of the Samoan Islands was signed at Washington, December 2nd, 1899.

193. **GREAT BRITAIN** and **RUSSIA**, in 1899. Claim of Messrs. Jardine, Matheson & Co., to property held by them in the Russian Concession at Hankow. It has been arranged between M. de Giers, the Russian Minister, and Mr. Bax Ironside, the British Chargé d'Affaires, to submit the question to an Arbitration Court, which, says the *Novoye Vremya*, will have to examine from a strictly legal standpoint the documents produced by the firm, the formalities observed, etc.

194. The **UNITED STATES** and **RUSSIA**, in 1899. Claims of American citizens resulting from the seizure of whalers by Russia in the Behring Sea, within seven miles of the Asiatic coast. A final protocol has been drawn up, and the final formalities are being concluded for submitting these to Arbitration, but the procedure is still in its initial stages.

195. **GREAT BRITAIN, GERMANY** and the **UNITED STATES**, in 1899. Question of compensation for losses sustained at Samoa by subjects of the three Powers during the recent disturbances. By an Agreement between the three Powers, signed in Washington on November 7th, 1899, these were referred to a Court of Arbitration, so far as the losses had arisen from unjustifiable military action on the part of officers of one or other of the signatory Powers. (See also Nos. 131 and 192.)

ANGLO-AMERICAN ARBITRATION TREATY, Signed at Washington, January 11th, 1897, and carried in the Senate on Wednesday, May 5th, by a majority of seventeen, forty-three voted for and twenty-six against. As, however, a majority of two-thirds was necessary to render the vote valid, the ratification of the Treaty was defeated.

ITALY and the **ARGENTINE REPUBLIC. GENERAL TREATY of ARBITRATION.** Provides that all disputes between the two countries shall be referred to an Arbitration Court, and though the Tribunal is not permanent, the provisions for its creation, as needed, are. Signed at Rome, July 23rd, 1898.

THE HAGUE CONVENTION. Adopted in a plenary sitting of the Peace Conference on July 29th, 1899, and signed immediately by the representatives of sixteen of the signatory Powers, to take effect as soon as nine at least agree.

WERTHEIMER, LEA & CO., PRINTERS, LONDON.

CORRIGENDA ET ADDENDA.

Page 502, line 2, *for* "in May" *read* "March 16th."

line 3, *add* "Venezuela . . . . sentence." lines 8 to 11, page 508.

Page 504, line 34, *for* "Mr." *read* "Hon."

line 35, *for* "assitant" *read* "assistant."

line 38, *for* "1898" *read* "1897."

Page 508, No. 144 same as No. 100, therefore *delete* lines 1 to 8 (to "Colombia"), and transfer remainder (lines 8 to 11) to end of No. 100, page 502.

Page 512, line 13, *after* "San José" *add* "April 8th, 1896."

Page 504, *after* No. 122 *add*:

122A. **HONDURAS** and **SALVADOR**, in 1886. Question of the boundary-line between the two Republics. By a Convention signed at Tegucigalpa, September 28th, 1886, ratified at San Salvador, July 27th, 1888, this was referred to four Commissioners—two land surveyors and two lawyers—appointed by the two Governments, and by them determined "within three months from the date of ratification."

Page 506, *after* No. 132, *add*:

132A. **BOLIVIA** and **PARAGUAY**, in 1889. Antagonistic boundary claims, concerning which a treaty (Tamayo-Aceval) had been definitively concluded, February 17th, 1887. This treaty, which recognised the rights of Bolivia, was not ratified, and this led to complications. "The differences, which had existed for some time, were happily adjusted by the intervention of the Argentine Republic, which accepted the part of Arbitrator."

Printed in Dunstable, United Kingdom

91220132R00298